D1526803

Stress, Trauma, and Children's
Memory Development

Stress, Trauma, and Children's Memory Development

Neurobiological,
Cognitive, Clinical,
and Legal Perspectives

EDITED BY

MARK L. HOWE,

GAIL S. GOODMAN,

AND DANTE CICCHETTI

OXFORD

UNIVERSITY PRESS

2008

OXFORD
UNIVERSITY PRESS

Oxford University Press, Inc., publishes works that further
Oxford University's objective of excellence
in research, scholarship, and education.

Oxford   New York
Auckland   Cape Town   Dar es Salaam   Hong Kong   Karachi
Kuala Lumpur   Madrid   Melbourne   Mexico City   Nairobi
New Delhi   Shanghai   Taipei   Toronto

With offices in
Argentina   Austria   Brazil   Chile   Czech Republic   France   Greece
Guatemala   Hungary   Italy   Japan   Poland   Portugal   Singapore
South Korea   Switzerland   Thailand   Turkey   Ukraine   Vietnam

Copyright © 2008 by Mark L. Howe, Gail S. Goodman, and Dante Cicchetti

Published by Oxford University Press, Inc.
198 Madison Avenue, New York, New York 10016

www.oup.com

Oxford is a registered trademark of Oxford University Press

Library of Congress Cataloging-in-Publication Data
Stress, trauma, and children's memory development : neurobiological, cognitive, clinical,
and legal perspectives / edited by Mark L. Howe, Gail S. Goodman, and Dante Cicchetti.
    p. ; cm.
Includes bibliographical references and index.
ISBN 978-0-19-530845-7
1. Memory disorders in children—Etiology. 2. Post-traumatic stress disorder in
children—Complications. 3. Psychic trauma in children—Complications.
4. Abused children—Mental health. 5. Memory in children.
I. Howe, Mark L. II. Goodman, Gail S. III. Cicchetti, Dante.
[DNLM: 1. Stress Disorders, Post-Traumatic. 2. Child Abuse.
3. Child. 4. Memory. 5. Repression.
WM 170 S9155 2008]
RJ506.M36S87 2008

618.92'8521—dc22   2007036868

9 8 7 6 5 4 3 2 1

Printed in the United States of America
on acid-free paper

Contents

Part III.   Clinical and Legal Perspectives

Contributors

Jennifer K. Ackil, Department of Psychology, Gustavus Adolphus College

Else-Marie Augusti, Department of Psychology, University of California, Davis

Patricia J. Bauer, Department of Psychology, Emory University

Alisa Miller Beyer, Department of Psychology, University of Kansas

Stephanie D. Block, Department of Psychology, University of California, Davis

Charles J. Brainerd, Cornell University

J. Douglas Bremner, Department of Psychiatry and Behavioral Sciences, Department of Radiology, Emory University School of Medicine

Deirdre Brown, Department of Psychology, Lancaster University

Sarah L. Bunnell, Department of Psychology, University of Kansas

Melissa M. Burch, School of Cognitive Science, Hampshire College

Dante Cicchetti, Institute of Child Development and Department of Psychiatry, University of Minnesota

Michelle Culver, Department of Psychology, University of California, Davis

Jennifer S. Curtis, Department of Psychology, University of Kansas

W. John Curtis, Mt. Hope Family Center, University of Rochester

Elizabeth L. Davis, Department of Psychology and Social Behavior, University of California, Irvine

Gail S. Goodman, Department of Psychology, University of California, Davis

Andrea F. Greenhoot, Department of Psychology, University of Kansas

LaTonya S. Harris, Department of Psychology, University of California, Davis

Mark L. Howe, Department of Psychology, Lancaster University

Michael E. Lamb, Department of Social and Developmental Psychology, Cambridge University

Linda J. Levine, Department of Psychology and Social Behavior, University of California, Irvine

Carryl P. Navalta, Developmental Biopsychiatry Research Program, McLean Hospital, Harvard Medical School

Christin M. Ogle, Department of Psychology, University of California, Davis

Yael Orbach, National Institute of Child Health and Human Development

Margaret-Ellen Pipe, Department of Psychology, Brooklyn College, City University of New York

Jodi A. Quas, Department of Psychology and Social Behavior, University of California, Irvine

Valerie F. Reyna, Cornell University

Martin H. Teicher, Developmental Biopsychiatry Research Program, McLean Hospital, Harvard Medical School

Susan Timmer, Department of Psychology, University of California, Davis

Akemi Tomoda, Developmental Biopsychiatry Research Program, McLean Hospital, Harvard Medical School

Sheree L. Toth, Mt. Hope Family Center, University of Rochester

Anthony Urquiza, Department of Psychology, University of California, Davis

Kristin Valentino, Mt. Hope Family Center, University of Rochester

Dana L. Van Abbema, Department of Psychology, St. Mary's College of Maryland

Prologue

Turning Science into Practice

MARK L. HOWE, GAIL S. GOODMAN,
AND DANTE CICCHETTI

Memory for emotional events captivates writers, scholars, citizens, and scientists. From theories, historic and recent, concerning the unconscious preservation of traumatic memories to those suggesting that traumatic experiences are well preserved in our conscious mind, theorists have tried to unravel the mysteries of emotion and memory. Across the centuries, the most popular belief has been that records of our experiences, particularly emotional and traumatic ones, are preserved with reasonable accuracy in our memory system. Even as recently as the early twentieth century, writers were suggesting that every experience, even the very earliest, "leaves its mark.... Nothing of good or evil is ever lost" (Thorndike, 1905, pp. 330–331). Further, it is thought that the earlier these experiences occur in childhood, the more formative they are, and the more likely they are to remain in memory, exerting their influence throughout our lives regardless of whether we can bring these experiences to consciousness (see Howe & Courage, 2004). Such ideas were pivotal in Freudian theory as well as in many other conceptions of social, emotional, and personality development (e.g., Ainsworth & Bowlby, 1991). Adverse early experience is thought to be at the root of later aberrant adult outcomes regardless of whether these experiences can be remembered (for reviews of these ideas, see Howe, in press; Kagan, 1996).

Recently, we have seen a steep rise in scientific research concerning the role of stress and trauma in memories for childhood experiences. Psychological science is now, more than ever, grappling with questions about whether traumatic childhood experiences are remembered differently than nontraumatic experiences. Does the fact that one has experienced trauma during childhood affect subsequent memory processing? Can children who have been maltreated remember and report those experiences accurately? Indeed, we are concerned not just with memory for traumatic and stressful events themselves but also with the long-term effects of these experiences on the course of "normal" memory development.

Few questions in developmental psychology have received as much international attention as have those concerning the impact of childhood trauma on memory. Until recently, the lack of scientific research to constrain theory has fueled controversy about such questions as "Does childhood trauma lead to deficits in memory, including a greater propensity for errors of commission (e.g., 'false memory') or errors of omission (e.g., 'lost memory')?" and "Are the neurohormonal changes that are linked to childhood trauma and stress associated with changes in children's basic memory processing abilities?" Scientists have also struggled with how to conceptualize and measure distress and other negative emotions—for instance, in terms of discrete emotions (fear, anger, sadness), physiological responsivity (e.g., through cortisol production; functional magnetic resonance imaging), or observer ratings.

To begin to answer these and other questions, the authors of the chapters in this book have focused on neurobiological, cognitive, clinical, and legal areas as they relate specifically to stress, trauma, and memory development. These areas were selected in order to (a) focus attention on the impact of stress and trauma on memory development by showcasing the most recent and innovative work and theories, (b) highlight the consequences of early traumatic experiences for subsequent memory performance, and (c) capture relations of early trauma to other measures of cognitive and clinical functioning in childhood, as well as to the longevity of trauma memories formed early in life.

In approaching these questions, we sought a translational approach, one in which science and practice converge. First, we wanted to provide a framework in which basic research on memory development can be expanded into the study of childhood trauma and maltreatment (for an overview, see Howe, Cicchetti, & Toth, 2006). Here, authors were asked to examine links between "normal" patterns of memory development and those observed when children had experienced stress and trauma. Second, we wanted to know what science tells us about the cognitive and neurophysiological underpinnings of memory development, trauma, and stress, to inform practice in the clinical and forensic realms. Of course, these latter areas, in turn, provide many of the questions to which basic science needs to attend to fully understand the complexities of stress, trauma, and memory development.

Neurobiological Perspectives

In the first part, "Neurobiological Perspectives," the authors present state-of-the-art research on the consequences for memory and memory development of the neurobiological changes that accompany childhood stress, trauma, and maltreatment. Specifically, in the first chapter, Bremner examines the interaction between brain development, trauma onset, memory, and the neurobiological consequences of trauma. He proposes a model of how stress-induced changes in brain systems involved in stress and memory mediate changes in traumatic memories in patients with childhood abuse–related mental disorders. The second chapter in this section is by Navalta, Tomoda, and Teicher. These authors take on the challenge of reviewing what is known about the clinical neuroscience of child abuse and providing new findings on the neuroanatomical effects of child abuse and how they are related to changes in memory processes. They conclude that there exists a growing body of evidence suggesting that memory deficits do exist for individuals with abuse histories and that these deficiencies are related to neuroanatomical anomalies. Our third chapter in this section, by Cicchetti and Curtis, uses event-related potentials (ERPs) to study memory functioning in infants and children in normal populations and in children who have experienced maltreatment. The authors suggest how future research using ERPs and memory in samples of maltreated and nonmaltreated infants and children can inform the design and implementation of randomized prevention and intervention trials with children who have experienced maltreatment. Together, the three chapters in this part provide the reader with an up-to-date picture of the neurobiological consequences of stress and trauma and their impact on the development of children's memory. As well, these chapters alert us to the many complexities of studying changes in neurobiological functioning as a consequence of stress, particularly in populations in which many of the relevant neural structures and systems are still developing. Despite these complexities, there is an emerging consensus concerning the changes that occur due to stress and maltreatment on memory-related neurobiological systems.

Cognitive Perspectives

In the second part, "Cognitive Perspectives," the authors examine memory for traumatic experiences and whether those experiences result in fundamental changes in children's memory development. In Chapter 4, Greenhoot, Bunnell, Curtis, and Beyer examine autobiographical memory for family violence using longitudinal data. These authors examine what is known about changes in autobiographical memory development and memory functioning that may be brought about by chronic exposure to stressful events such as abuse. Following this review, Greenhoot and colleagues present findings from their own research on these issues, integrating findings from their longitudinal study of children exposed to various forms of domestic violence and using these data to disentangle competing explanations concerning the mechanisms underlying these memory dysfunctions.

Chapter 5, by Ogle, Block, Harris, Culver, Augusti, Timmer, Urquiza, and Goodman, examines the claim that childhood trauma leads to a specific type of autobiographical memory functioning, namely "overgeneral memory." The authors provide a comprehensive review of scientific theory and research on autobiographical memory development, memory for trauma-related and nontrauma-related information in traumatized individuals, and autobiographical memory in nontraumatized and traumatized adolescents and adults. Finally, they present preliminary findings from an ongoing study that examines autobiographical memory development in documented child sexual abuse victims versus matched comparisons with participants who have no known history of child sexual abuse. Contrary to the overgeneral memory hypothesis, the authors conclude that individuals with child maltreatment histories, especially those with post-traumatic stress disorder (PTSD), may overfocus on trauma in their lives and in their pasts, and this focus may make their autobiographical memories particularly accurate, especially for trauma-related information.

Chapter 6, by Bauer, Burch, Van Abbema, and Ackil, examines children's memory for a naturally occurring disaster (a tornado). Specifically, these authors tackle the deeply rooted assumption that highly stressful and traumatic events are remembered differently relative to events that are more affectively neutral or positive. The authors evaluate this assumption using data from a study of children's reports of the experience of a tornado that devastated the town of St. Peter, Minnesota, in March of 1998. The evaluation is multidimensional, including analyses of the amount children remembered, the type of information remembered, and the extent to which their reports were affected by their conversational partners, namely their mothers. The authors conclude that although there are some differences between children's reports of traumatic and non-traumatic events (e.g., conversations about the tornado were longer and had greater breadth than those about the nontraumatic events), there are some very important similarities (e.g., the level of detail provided about the traumatic and nontraumatic events did not differ).

Chapter 7, by Davis, Quas, and Levine, looks at the role of discrete emotions and children's memory for stressful experiences. The argument here is that if we are to understand children's memory for stressful events, we need to look beyond "distress" as a unitary construct and begin to evaluate children's understanding or appraisals of stressful events as well as children's discrete emotional experiences and emotion regulation techniques. The argument continues that with development, children appraise situations and regulate their emotions in increasingly complex ways. Younger children, with similar but simpler appraisal processes than adults and limited emotion regulation strategies, are likely to have a more narrow focus.

Together these chapters provide an up-to-date exegesis of the study of children's memory for traumatic experiences and the consequences of stress, trauma, and maltreatment on subsequent memory development. Although in many circumstances traumatic experiences are remembered better than nontraumatic experiences, the two kinds of memories exhibit many similarities, including, but not limited to, susceptibility to interference, suggestion, forgetting, and false recollection. These chapters also alert us to the need to refocus some of our research efforts by focusing on the impact of events on the children who experience them, including the types of appraisals children make about these events as well as whether there are emotional sequelae associated with these experiences. Like those in the first part, these chapters remind us that a truly comprehensive understanding of stress, trauma, and memory development requires a multifaceted approach to research, one that benefits from interdisciplinary collaborations.

Clinical and Legal Perspectives

In our third and final part, "Clinical and Legal Perspectives," science is beautifully translated into practice in three unique chapters: one on forensic interviewing; one on the law and false memory; and our final chapter, on translating findings on memory development, stress, and maltreatment into good clinical technique. Chapter 8, by Brown, Lamb, Pipe, and Orbach, examines the problem of how best to question children in a forensic context. In this extensive review, the authors discuss how the quantity and quality of information elicited in forensic interviews with children reflects the behavior and capacities of both the child witness and the adult interviewers. They outline how even quite young children are capable of providing reliable testimony about abusive experiences when questioned appropriately. At the same time, because children need help retrieving, structuring, and reporting their experiences, there is a clear need to provide that support without degrading the quality of children's accounts. Guidelines for doing so are elaborated on in this chapter.

Chapter 9, by Brainerd and Reyna, provides an exhaustive review of children's spontaneous false memories and what these errors mean for the law. Research on developmental patterns in spontaneous false recollections (e.g., increases with age) is reviewed and the findings are linked to cases of child sexual abuse and the ensuing legal complications. The authors conclude by suggesting ways in which we might avoid eliciting false recollections, especially in cases where abuse has occurred.

In Chapter 10, Toth and Valentino use the literature on trauma and memory, particularly child maltreatment and memory, as the foundation for examining the clinical and social-policy implications of this research for children who have been victimized by abuse and neglect. Based on this review, the authors note that more research is still needed before the efficacy of trauma–specific versus more symptom-focused interventions for children who have been maltreated can be properly evaluated. That is, although for adults attention to trauma has been shown to increase the effectiveness of the intervention, there is considerably less research favoring this approach with maltreated children. Future investigations will require careful attention to the age at which the trauma occurred, the time between the trauma and the provision of treatment, and the developmental period during which the intervention is initiated.

Together, these chapters provide a state-of-the-art snapshot of how the findings from neuroscience and the cognitive and developmental sciences of stress, trauma, and children's memory development can be effectively translated into legal, clinical, and social policy. Documents containing specific prescriptions for investigating child maltreatment, questioning child witnesses, and treating children who have been maltreated continue to be drafted and continue to be informed by science. Thanks to a translational focus, science has been put into practice and practice has informed science about some of the problems still in need of rigorous inquiry.

Conclusion

So, what have we learned about the two very broad questions posed at the beginning of this prologue? First, can children remember traumatic experiences? The answer is yes, especially if they occur after the period known as infantile amnesia (Howe, in press) and care is taken with the manner in which children attempt to recollect this information (including the manner in which others pose questions). However, memories for these experiences are not immune to processes that affect nontraumatic memories, namely suggestion, false memories, interference, and normal forgetting.

Second, can stress, trauma, and maltreatment affect the course of normal memory development? The growing consensus is yes. In particular, evidence from the neurobiological chapters suggests this might be so, as do the chapters in the cognitive and clinical and legal sections. Although far from over, the story that is emerging is one in which maltreated children may be more hypersensitive to emotional stimuli, possibly due in part to heightened amygdala reactivity following high-intensity trauma exposure. These effects can have far-reaching consequences for memory functioning, including how information is encoded, stored, and consolidated, and even how it is retrieved (also see LaBar, 2007).

Although children who have been maltreated may not have less specific autobiographical memories than children who have not been maltreated, maltreated children may nevertheless experience greater memory errors.

However, as the chapters in this book attest, such memory errors are by no means commonplace or typical of much of maltreated children's remembering. Indeed, when seen, these effects depend jointly on individual difference factors such as neuroendocrine regulation, trauma symptoms, and dissociative experiences (also see Cicchetti, Rogosch, Howe, & Toth, 2007; Eisen, Goodman, Qin, Davis, & Crayton, 2007; Howe, Toth, & Cicchetti, 2006).

Overall, then, stress, trauma, and maltreatment can affect memory development as well as memory for the traumatic experience(s). The interactions are often complex and depend on a whole host of factors, all of which have been documented in the chapters here. The diversity of topics, viewpoints, and approaches presented in this book underline the intricacy of the problem we are dealing with when studying the effects of stress and trauma on children's memory development and then trying to translate these findings into practice. We hope the readers appreciate this complexity as well as the scientific and practical advances made by the writers of these superb chapters.

References

Ainsworth, M. S., & Bowlby, J. (1991). An ethological approach to personality development. *American Psychologist, 46,* 333–341.

Cicchetti, D., Rogosch, F. A., Howe, M. L., & Toth, S. L. (2007). *The effects of maltreatment on neuroendocrine regulation and memory performance.* Manuscript in preparation.

Eisen, M. L., Goodman, G. S., Qin, J., Davis, S., & Crayton, J. (2007). Maltreated children's memory: Accuracy, suggestibility, and psychopathology. *Developmental Psychology, 43,* 1275–1294.

Howe, M. L. (in press). The nature of infantile amnesia. In J. H. Byrne (Ed.-in-Chief) & R. Menzel (Vol. Ed.), *Learning theory and behavior. Learning and memory: A comprehensive reference* London, UK: Elsevier.

Howe, M. L., Cicchetti, D., & Toth, S. L. (2006). Children's basic memory processes, stress, and maltreatment. *Development and Psychopathology, 18,* 759–769.

Howe, M. L., & Courage, M. L. (2004). Demystifying the beginnings of memory. *Developmental Review, 24,* 1–5.

Howe, M. L., Toth, S. L., & Cicchetti, D. (2006). Memory and developmental psychopathology. In D. Cicchetti & D. J. Cohen (Eds.), *Developmental Psychopathology* (2nd ed.): *Vol. 2. Developmental Neuroscience* (pp. 629–655). New York: Wiley.

Kagan, J. (1996). Three pleasing ideas. *American Psychologist, 51,* 901–908.

LaBar, K. S. (2007). Emotional memory mechanisms in the human brain. *Current Directions in Psychological Science, 16,* 173–177.

Thorndike, E. L. (1905). *The elements of psychology.* New York: Seiler.

Part I
Neurobiological Perspectives

1

The Neurobiology of Trauma
and Memory in Children

J. DOUGLAS BREMNER

Goals of the Chapter

This chapter will outline the relation between stress and memory in children. The chapter will highlight the interactions among brain development, epoch of trauma onset, memory, and neurobiological consequences of trauma. This chapter will propose a model for how stress-induced changes in brain regions and systems involved in stress and memory mediate alterations in traumatic memories in patients with childhood abuse–related mental disorders. The chapter will also comment on the relevance of the model to current controversies about delayed recall of childhood abuse.

Childhood Trauma

Childhood trauma is an important public health problem in America affecting as many as one out of five children (MacMillan et al., 1997; McCauley et al., 1997). Childhood trauma can lead to post-traumatic stress disorder (PTSD), which affects about 8% of Americans at some time in their lives (Kessler, Sonnega, Bromet, Hughes, & Nelson, 1995), as well as depression (Franklin & Zimmerman, 2001; Prigerson, Maciejewski, &

Rosenheck, 2001), substance abuse (Bremner, Southwick, Darnell, & Charney, 1996d; Kessler et al., 1995), dissociation (Putnam, Guroff, Silberman, Barban, & Post, 1986), personality disorders (Battle et al., 2004; Yen et al., 2002), and health problems (Dube, Felitti, Dong, Giles, & Anda, 2003). For many abuse victims, PTSD can be a lifelong problem (Kendall-Tackett, 2005; Saigh & Bremner, 1999). This chapter reviews the relation between trauma and memory in children in the context of the neurobiology of trauma, brain development, and memory. The thesis of this chapter is that alterations in brain regions and neurochemical systems involved in memory and the stress response in patients with abuse-related PTSD lead to alterations in memory function.

Normal Development of Cognition and the Brain

Cognition and the brain undergo changes across the lifespan from early childhood to late life (Bremner, 2005a). Understanding these normal developmental changes is critical for determining the difference between normal development and pathology, as well as how they interact.

Normal memory formation involves encoding, consolidation, and retrieval. Encoding refers to the laying down of the memory trace, consolidation is the process by which the memory goes from short-term to long-term storage, and retrieval is the process by which long-term memories are retrieved from storage (Schacter, 1996). Memories can be divided into explicit (also known as declarative), or available for conscious recall, and implicit (also known as procedural). Explicit memory includes recall of facts or lists, while implicit memory includes memory that is not accessed by conscious recall, such as procedural memories like riding a bike, as well as conditioned responses.

Children do not develop the capacity for long-term autobiographical memory until 2 to 3 years of age (Bruce et al., 2005; Eacott & Crawley, 1998; Howe & Courage, 1993, 1997; Usher & Neisser, 1993). This coincides with the development of the ability to place events in the context of the who, what, and where of the self. Children do have memories before the age of 2, as measured by a variety of laboratory tasks, although explicit memories are not retrieved before this time period in later life (Eacott & Crawley, 1998).

Although the bulk of brain development occurs in utero, the brain continues to develop after birth (Giedd, Shaw, Wallace, Gogtay, &

Lenroot, 2006). In the first 5 years of life there is an overall expansion of brain volume related to development of both gray matter and white matter structures; however, from 7 to 17 years of age there is a progressive increase in white matter (felt to be related to ongoing myelination) and decrease in gray matter (felt to be related to neuronal pruning), while overall brain size stays the same (Casey, Giedd, & Thomas, 2000; Durston et al., 2001; Giedd et al., 1999b; Paus et al., 1999). Gray matter areas that undergo the greatest increases throughout the 7-to-17-years period of development include frontal cortex and parietal cortex (Rapoport et al., 1999; Sowell et al., 1999). Basal ganglia decrease in size, while corpus callosum (Giedd, Blumenthal, & Jeffries, 1999a; Thompson et al., 2000), hippocampus, and amygdala (Giedd, Castellanos, Rajapakse, Vaituzis, & Rapoport, 1997; Giedd et al., 1996b; Pfefferbaum et al., 1994) increase in size during early childhood, although there may be developmental-sex-laterality effects for some of these structures (Giedd et al., 1996a).

Stress and Memory

Stress at the time of memory encoding, consolidation, and retrieval can influence memory function. After President Kennedy's assassination, many people were able to remember where they were and what they were doing at the time (more than they could remember, say, what they ate for breakfast on that same date). This phenomenon came to be called "flashbulb memories" and became a subject of investigation (Brown & Kulik, 1977).

In the aftermath of the assassination attempt on President Reagan, stronger emotional reactions to hearing the news were associated with greater consistency of recall of the details of personal circumstances at the time of hearing the news from 1 to 7 months after the event (Pillemer, 1984). Some studies of the January 28, 1986, *Challenger* space shuttle explosion (Bohannon, 1988; Bohannon & Symons, 1992)—but not others (Neisser & Harsch, 1992)—showed a relation between emotional upset at the time the news was received and ability to recall personal circumstances several months after the explosion. Furthermore, a relation has been found between high emotionality and surprise and vividness of memories related to personal events (as opposed to national events) (Rubin & Kozin, 1984).

Experimental paradigms have also been used to assess the effects of stress on memory. Subjects exposed to a shocking film in which a young boy is shot in the face had impaired recall of details that preceded the violent act in the film (Loftus & Burns, 1982) and of words associated with the face (Christianson & Nilsson, 1984) relative to subjects who viewed a neutral film. In another study, subjects who viewed traumatic slides in which someone had been injured had better recall of central details and worse recall of peripheral details in comparison to those who viewed neutral slides (Christianson & Loftus, 1987, 1991). Subjects shown pictures of a crime scene focused on a gun or a knife to the exclusion of other details such as the faces in the picture, even after controlling for eye fixation on the central details of the scene (Christianson, Loftus, Hoffman, & Loftus, 1991). These studies showed that stress and emotion can enhance some aspects of memories and diminish others.

Stress and Memory in Children

Studies have also examined the effects of stress on memory in children. Three- to 4-year-old children interviewed after Hurricane Andrew were assessed for memory of the storm (Bahrick, Parker, Fivush, & Levitt, 1998). The authors found an inverted U curve, with best memory at intermediate levels of storm damage and a decrease in memory at the highest levels of storm damage.

Studies of healthy children 4 to 6 years of age who went to the doctor and had blood draws, injections, and genital and anal exams showed that children have reliable memories of the events and are resistant to suggestion (Goodman, Hirschman, Hepps, & Rudy, 1991; Saywitz, Goodman, Nicholas, & Moan, 1991). With decreases in age children became more susceptible to suggestion and had a decrease in reliability; they were also more susceptible to suggestion when interviewed by an adult than by a child, suggesting an eagerness to please authority (Ceci & Bruck, 1993; Ceci, Ross, & Toglia, 1987). Children have been shown to be resistant to abuse-related suggestions, such as "He took your clothes off, didn't he?"(Goodman & Aman, 1990; Rudy & Goodman, 1991). Reliability about genital exams was actually higher than for other parts of the physical exam (Saywitz et al., 1991). Children did not report the genital exam unless asked directly (Ceci et al., 1987). Children age 3 to 13 asked about a voiding cystourethrogram fluoroscopy they received at 2 to 6 years of age were less likely to recall information if the procedure had been stressful, and were less likely to recall information the younger they were at the time of the procedure (Quas et al., 1999). In another study children ages 3 to 18 with leukemia who underwent a painful lumbar puncture were assessed 1 week after the procedure (Chen, Zeltzer, Craske, & Katz, 2000). Children of all ages showed a high accuracy of recall, and accuracy increased with age.

Children with a history of abuse have also been shown to be accurate in remembering details of doctor's genital and anal exams. In a study of 189 3- to 17-year-olds, all children showed >70% accuracy in recalling details of the exam (Eisen, Qin, Goodman, & Davis, 2002). There were no differences in accuracy of recall between abused and nonabused children, and there was no relation with dissociative tendencies or other measures of psychopathology. Older age was the only factor that predicted accuracy of recall.

In summary, the empirical literature suggests that children can have accurate recall of stressful events. These studies, however, have primarily been conducted in normal children. We cannot assume that studies in normal children can be generalized to all children, including abused children. The few studies that were conducted on abused children did not specifically look at those with PTSD or other stress-related mental disorders. Since, as reviewed below, memory and stress responsive systems are altered in patients with stress-related mental disorders, extrapolation of findings from healthy subjects to abuse victims with mental disorders, which is the group of primary interest in the debate about delayed recall of childhood abuse, has limitations.

Long-Term Recall of Childhood Abuse

The relation between trauma and memory in children has been fraught with controversy (Bremner, 1999; Freyd & DePrince, 2001; Howe, Cicchetti, & Toth, 2006; Howe, Cicchetti, Toth, & Cerrito, 2004; Howe, Toth, & Cicchetti, 2006; Kihlstrom, 1995; Schacter, Coyle, Fischbach, Mesulam, & Sullivan, 1995; Williams & Banyard, 1999). At issue is whether delayed recall of childhood abuse can exist, whether these memories are implanted by therapists, and whether lost memories of abuse are related to altered memory function in abused individuals or are due to ordinary forgetting. We first review research studies related to memory and forgetting abuse, then the experimental literature on memory distortion and the controversy that has ensued in the literature on delayed recall of abuse, and finally findings from the neurobiology of trauma that are proposed as models for memory distortion in abused patients with mental disorders.

Several studies have shown varying degrees of lack of recall of childhood abuse events in later life. Williams studied 129 women with documented histories of sexual victimization in childhood (Williams, 1994). Thirty-eight percent reported no memory of the abuse. Factors associated with lack of recall included younger age and molestation by someone the women knew.

Widom and Morris (Widom & Morris, 1997) studied 1,196 victims of abuse or neglect 20 years after their initial assessments in childhood. Only 63% of individuals with documented sexual abuse in childhood reported this abuse in adulthood. Only 16% of men (compared to 64% of women) with documented sexual abuse reported childhood sexual abuse as adults. The authors concluded that there was "substantial under-reporting of childhood sexual abuse" that could be related to loss of memory, denial, or embarrassment about reporting abuse details. They also concluded that cultural or other social factors might explain why fewer men than women reported sexual abuse.

Alexander and colleagues (Alexander et al., 2005) studied 103 children involved in legal cases related to childhood abuse 10 to 16 years later. The authors found a 72% accuracy of remembering abuse. However, this was only in 94 of the subjects. Of the original 103, 3 said that they had never been abused even though they originally divulged abuse, and 2 said that the charges were false. Severity of PTSD was correlated with accuracy, and individuals who rated the abuse as their most traumatic life event had accurate memories of abuse regardless of PTSD severity. The authors concluded that memories of abuse were in general accurate.

Goodman et al. (2003) studied 175 individuals with documented childhood sexual abuse from age 4 to 17 at 13 years after the reported abuse. Of the subjects, 81% reported the documented abuse. Older age at the time when the abuse ended, maternal support, and more severe abuse were associated with a higher likelihood of disclosure.

Memory Distortion

Several studies in normal subjects have shown that memory is suscep-tible to distortions and deletions. For instance, in one study, subjects viewed a film of an automobile accident. When researchers used the verb "smashed" as opposed to the verb "hit" in relation to the film, subjects gave higher estimates of the speed of the automobiles, and more subjects incorrectly endorsed the statement that broken glass was associated with the accident (Loftus & Palmer, 1974). When subjects were shown a series of slides that told a story involving a stop sign followed by a narrative that misleadingly described a yield sign, they were more likely to falsely recall that the slides included a yield sign than subjects not given the misleading information (Loftus, Miller, & Burns, 1978). In another example known as the "Deese/Roediger-McDermott paradigm," after its originators, words that are highly associated with a "critical lure," when presented in a list, will be associated with a "false" recall of the absent "lure." So, for example, if a subject is presented with the words thread, pin, eye, etc., the subject may include the "critical lure" needle, even though it was not part of the original list (Roediger & McDermott, 1995).

Memory can also be distorted to fit with subjects' expectations. Children told a story about the Six Million Dollar Man being unable to carry a can of paint, when tested 3 weeks later, were more likely to change their recall to fit with their pretesting knowledge (Ceci, Caves, & Howe, 1981).

In another study, the parents of college students provided surveys of their children's childhood events, and the students were asked to recall the events in a series of interviews. In addition to the true events, students were asked to recall the details of a fictitious episode, such as knocking over a punch bowl at a wedding (Hyman, Husband, & Billings, 1995). By the third interview, 25% of students falsely recalled the punch bowl; in addition, they tended to elaborate more on their own true events with each interview. Based on a series of studies, Oakes and Hyman (2001) outlined factors involved in the creation of false childhood memories. First, the event must be plausible, or something the individual thinks could have happened. The subject must then create an image with a narrative. Finally, the individual forgets the source of the image and narrative and incorrectly attributes it to the self.

Pezdek and colleagues (Pezdek, Finger, & Hodge, 1997) used a similar paradigm involving both plausible (lost in the mall as a child) and implausible (received a painful rectal enema as a child) stories. Consistent with the model of Oates and Hyman, only the "lost in the mall" anecdote was falsely recalled. No subjects falsely recalled the painful enema event.

These studies highlight the fact that amnesia for the source of the information plays a critical role in many of these experimental paradigms of "false memory." For instance, studies have shown that if subjects are cued to pay attention to the source of the information they receive, the false-recall effect associated with misleading information is lost (Lindsay, 1990; Lindsay & Johnson, 1989).

A clinically relevant question is whether memories can be forgotten and still be potentially accessible at a later time, or whether these memories no longer exist as memory traces in the brain. Adherents to the latter view hold that delayed recall of abuse memories are secondary to "implanting" of abuse memories by overzealous therapists (Loftus et al., 1978). They claim that authentic memories can be "overwritten" by memories that are implanted or introduced through suggestion or other means. One study addressed the question of whether memories could be overwritten. Subjects who saw slides that included a hammer were then given the misleading information that a screwdriver had been among the slides. The subjects were then forced to recall whether they had seen a hammer or a screwdriver. Subjects did not falsely recall the screwdriver more than expected by chance (McCloskey & Zaragoza, 1985). The authors concluded that if the misleading information could overwrite the original memory, then the subjects would have falsely recalled the screwdriver more often. The authors concluded that there was not evidence that memories could be "overwritten."

The past two decades of research on false memory have generated as much heat as light on this topic, with the evolution of two different languages to describe the topic. In response to the original study by Williams (Williams, 1994), Loftus, Garry, and Feldman (1994) argued that a loss of memory about abuse is related to normal forgetting. They dichotomized normal "forgetting" and "repression," and argued that there is no evidence for repression.

The choice of language, however, can often shape the conception of an issue. Loftus and colleagues chose to frame the debate about false memories of abuse by using a term derived from psychoanalysis that refers to memories that are banished from consciousness because of the existence of a painful conflict. For a variety of reasons, psychoanalysis has been resistant to empirically based research; in fact, only very recently has a published, controlled trial of psychoanalysis been performed (Milrod et al., 2007). The concept of repression is a difficult one to test empirically, which has contributed to the heated rhetoric surrounding this issue.

For instance, Pezdek and Lam (2007) reviewed the last decade of research on memory for abuse and concluded that only 13% of the articles claiming to study false memory actually used the word as originally intended (De Prince and colleagues similarly found that 70% did not use true false memory paradigms; De Prince, Allard, Oh, & Freyd, 2004). Pezdek and Lam found that most studies used the Deese/Roediger-McDermott paradigm (false recall of a critical lure after being read a list of words highly associated to the critical lure) (Roediger & McDermott, 1995) or the introduction of misinformation. As the authors pointed out, however, the Deese/Roediger-McDermott paradigm is not a true false memory paradigm—that is, the implanting of previously nonexistent information. Pezdek and Lam concluded that false memories and flawed memories should not be conflated, and that the term *false memory* should not be indiscriminately applied to experimental studies on memory, since the public generally extrapolated the findings to abused patients.

Predictably, following publication of this article, the rhetoric erupted once again. Wade and colleagues (2007) disputed the need to apply a narrow definition of false memory to experimental paradigms in the literature. Pezdek later wrote that the main effect of the article was "[to] obfuscate rather than clarify the discussion of false memory" (Pezdek, 2007). These articles show that we are no closer to consensus regarding the topic of false memory than we were a decade ago.

Memory in Patients with Abuse-Related PTSD

Empirical studies do show, however, that patients with early abuse and the diagnosis of PTSD or other stress-related mental disorders have a variety of memory problems (Buckley, Blanchard, & Neill, 2000; Elzinga & Bremner, 2002). Adults with early childhood abuse (Bremner et al., 1995) were found to have deficits in verbal declarative memory function based on neuropsychological testing (Wechsler Memory Scale and Selective Reminding Test); similar findings were found in traumatized children (Moradi, Doost, Taghavi, Yule, & Dalgleish, 1999). One study in adult women with a history of childhood sexual abuse–related PTSD (Bremner, Vermetten, Nafzal, & Vythilingam, 2004) showed that verbal declarative memories are specifically associated with PTSD and are not a nonspecific effect of trauma exposure. Another study of women with early childhood sexual abuse in which some, but not all, of the patients had PTSD showed no difference between abused and nonabused women (Stein, Hanna, Vaerum, & Koverola, 1999). Children with PTSD related to mixed causes had deficits in verbal IQ compared to controls (Saigh, Yasik, Oberfield, Halamandaris, & Bremner, 2006). Another study in Lebanese youth with war-related PTSD showed deficits in scholastic performance compared to traumatized non-PTSD and nontraumatized youth (Saigh, Mroweh, & Bremner, 1997). Other types of memory disturbances studies in PTSD include gaps in memory for everyday events (dissociative amnesia) (Bremner, Steinberg, Southwick, Johnson, & Charney, 1993) and an attentional bias for trauma-related material (Moradi, Taghavi, Neshat-Doost, Yule, & Dalgleish, 2000). These studies suggest that traumas such as early abuse with associated PTSD result in deficits in verbal declarative memory.

In the 1994 comment by Loftus and colleagues on the report of Williams about 38% forgetting childhood abuse, the authors, after dismissing "repression," took on "amnesia," which they described as "trying to puff up [forgetting] with a scientific name to make it appear exotic... an example of psychological 'spin-doctoring,' the merging of science and politics."

However, spin doctors were not responsible for the description of the diagnosis of dissociative amnesia, which is an official disorder of the *Diagnostic and Statistical Manual of Mental Disorders*. This is the most common dissociative presentation of patients with PTSD, involving patients who have gaps in memory that are not due to normal forgetting and which can go from minutes to hours to days (Bremner et al., 1993). These symptoms of dissociative amnesia can include a lack of memory for episodes of childhood abuse. Some have argued that dissociative amnesia cannot be empirically verified; however, the same argument could be made for hallucinations in schizophrenics. The gold standard for psychiatric diagnosis continues to be self-reporting of symptoms.

Two studies have specifically looked at false memory paradigms in women with a history of childhood sexual abuse. Clancy, Schacter, McNally, and Pitman (2000) found that women with a history of delayed recall of childhood sexual abuse had an increase in false recall of the critical lure in the Deese/Roediger-McDermott paradigm. Bremner, Shobe, & Kihlstrom (2000) found that women with early childhood sexual abuse–related PTSD had higher rates of false recall on the Deese/Roediger-McDermott paradigm compared to abused non-PTSD women, nonabused non-PTSD women, and normal men. Given the range of memory problems in PTSD patients, one interpretation of these findings is that there is a tendency to "fill in" facts when concrete declarative memory fails, as seen in patients with, for instance, hepatic encephalopathy, who will confabulate when presented with a false start to an autobiographical story.

Neurobiology of PTSD: Relevance to Memory Recall of Abuse

PTSD is associated with long-term changes in the function and structure of brain regions and neurochemical systems involved in the stress response (Bremner, 2002; Bremner, 2005b; Pitman, 2001; Vermetten & Bremner, 2002a, 2002b) (Fig. 1.1). Brain regions that are felt to play an important role in PTSD include hippocampus, amygdala, and medial prefrontal cortex. Cortisol and norepinephrine are two neurochemical systems that are critical in the stress response (Fig. 1.1). The neurobiology of PTSD is reviewed below as a background to the development of a model by which

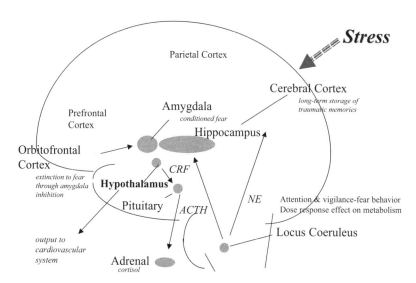

FIGURE 1.1. Functional neuroanatomy of traumatic stress. Lasting effects of trauma on the brain, showing long-term dysregulation of norepinephrine and cortisol systems and vulnerable areas of hippocampus, amygdala, and medial prefrontal cortex that are affected by trauma. ACTH: adrenocorticotropic hormone; CRF: corticotropin-releasing factor; NE: norepinephrine.

early abuse affects circuits and systems involved in memory, potentially leading to alterations in memory of early abuse.

The corticotropin-releasing factor (CRF)/hypothalamic-pituitary-adrenal (HPA) axis system plays an important role in the stress response. CRF is released from the hypothalamus, with stimulation of adreno-corticotropin hormone (ACTH) release from the pituitary, resulting in glucocorticoid (cortisol in humans) release from the adrenal, which in turn has a negative feedback effect on the axis at the level of the pituitary as well as central brain sites including hypothalamus and hippocampus. Cortisol has a number of effects that facilitate survival. In addition to its role in triggering the HPA axis, CRF acts centrally to mediate fear-related behaviors (Arborelius, Owens, Plotsky, & Nemeroff, 1999) and triggers other neurochemical responses to stress such as the noradrenergic system via the brainstem locus coeruleus (Melia & Duman, 1991). Stress also results in activation of the noradrenergic system, centered in the locus coeruleus. Noradrenergic neurons release a transmitter throughout the brain that is associated with an increase in alerting and vigilance behaviors, critical for coping with acute threat (Abercrombie & Jacobs, 1987; Bremner, Krystal, Southwick, & Charney, 1996b, 1996c).

There is increasing interest in the relation between trauma and memory (Elzinga & Bremner, 2002). Patients with trauma-related disorders such as PTSD demonstrate a wide range of deficits in memory. Brain areas, including hippocampus, amygdala, and medial prefrontal cortex, may mediate these alterations in memory (Bremner, 2003a) (Fig. 1.2). The hippocampus, a brain area involved in verbal declarative memory, is very sensitive to the effects of stress. Stress in animals was associated with damage to neurons in the CA3 region of the hippocampus (which may be mediated by hypercortisolemia, decreased brain-derived neurotrophic factor, and/or elevated glutamate levels) and inhibition of neurogenesis (Gould, Tanapat, McEwen, Flugge, & Fuchs, 1998; Magarinos, McEwen, Flugge, & Fluchs, 1996; McEwen et al., 1992; Nibuya, Morinobu, & Duman, 1995; Sapolsky, 1996; Sapolsky, Uno, Rebert, & Finch, 1990). High levels of glucocorticoids seen with stress were also associated with deficits in new learning (Diamond, Fleshner, Ingersoll, & Rose, 1996; Luine, Villages, Martinex, & McEwen, 1994). However, whether physiological levels of cortisol are actually toxic to the hippocampus continues to be debated (de Kloet, Oitzl, & Joels, 1999).

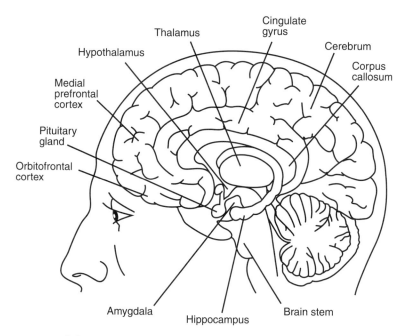

FIGURE 1.2. Brain areas involved in memory and the stress response. Brain areas that mediate memory, including the hippocampus, amygdala, and anterior cingulate, have been shown in brain imaging studies to be altered in patients with early-abuse-related PTSD. *Source:* Bremner, J. D. *Does Stress Damage the Brain?* Fig. 2.2, p. 44.

Antidepressant treatments were shown to block the effects of stress and/or promote neurogenesis (Czeh et al., 2001; Lucassen, Fuchs, & Czeh, 2004; Malberg, Eisch, Nestler, & Duman, 2000; Nibuya et al., 1995; Santarelli et al., 2003a). It has also been found that phenytoin blocks the effects of stress on the hippocampus, probably through modulation of excitatory amino acid–induced neurotoxicity (Watanabe, Gould, Cameron, Daniels, & McEwen, 1992). Other agents, including tianeptine, dihydroepiandosterone (DHEA), and fluoxetine, have similar effects (Czeh et al., 2001; D'Sa & Duman, 2002; Duman, 2004; Duman, Heninger, & Nestler, 1997; Duman, Malberg, & Nakagawa, 2001; Garcia, 2002; Lucassen et al., 2004; Malberg et al., 2000; McEwen & Chattarji, 2004). There is new evidence that neurogenesis is necessary for the behavioral effects of antidepressants (Santarelli et al., 2003b; Watanabe, Gould, Daniels, Cameron, & McEwen, 1992), although this continues to be a source of debate (Duman, 2004; Henn & Vollmayr, 2004).

The hippocampus demonstrates an unusual capacity for neuronal plasticity and regeneration. In addition to findings noted above related to the negative effects of stress on neurogenesis, it has recently been demonstrated that changes in the environment—for example, social enrichment or learning—can modulate neurogenesis in the dentate gyrus of the hippocampus and slow the normal age-related decline in neurogenesis (Gould, Beylin, Tanapat, Reeves, & Shors, 1999; Kempermann, Kuhn, & Gage, 1998). Rat pups that were handled frequently within the first few weeks of life (i.e., were picked up and then returned to their mother) had increased Type II glucocorticoid receptor binding that persisted throughout life, with increased feedback sensitivity to glucocorticoids and reduced glucocorticoid-mediated hippocampal damage in later life (Meaney, Aitken, van Berkel, Bhatnager, & Sapolsky, 1988). These effects appear to be due to a type of "stress inoculation" from the mothers' repeated licking of the handled pups (Liu, Diorio, Day, Francis, & Meaney, 2000). Considered together, these findings suggest that early in the postnatal period there is a naturally occurring brain plasticity in key neural systems that may "program" an organism's biological response to stressful stimuli. These findings may have implications for victims of childhood abuse.

The few studies of the effects of early stress on neurobiology conducted in clinical populations of traumatized children have generally been consistent with findings from animal studies (Cicchetti & Rogosch, 2001; Cicchetti & Walker, 2001; Gunnar & Vazquez, 2006; Hart, Gunnar, & Cicchetti, 1996). Research in traumatized children has been complicated by issues related to psychiatric diagnosis and assessment of trauma (Cicchetti & Walker, 2001). Some studies have not specifically examined psychiatric diagnosis, while others have focused on children with trauma and depression, and others on children with trauma and PTSD. Sexually abused girls (in which effects of specific psychiatric diagnoses was not examined) had normal baseline cortisol and blunted ACTH response to CRF (De Bellis et al., 1994), while women with childhood abuse–related PTSD had hypercortisolemia (Lemieux & Coe, 1995). Another study of traumatized children in which the diagnosis of PTSD was established showed increased levels of cortisol measured in 24-hour urine samples (De Bellis et al., 1999a). Emotionally neglected children from a Romanian orphanage had elevated cortisol levels over a diurnal period compared to controls (Gunnar, Morison, Chisolm, & Schuder, 2001). Maltreated school-aged children with clinical-level internalizing problems had elevated cortisol compared to controls (Cicchetti & Rogosch, 2001). Depressed preschool children showed increased cortisol response to separation stress (Luby et al., 2003). Adult women with a history of childhood abuse showed increased suppression of cortisol with low-dose (0.5 mg) dexamethasone (Stein, Yehuda, Koverola, & Hanna, 1997). Women with PTSD related to early childhood sexual abuse showed decreased baseline cortisol based on 24-hour diurnal assessments of plasma cortisol, increased cortisol pulsatility (Bremner, Vermetten, & Kelley, in press), and exaggerated cortisol response to stressors (traumatic stressors [Elzinga, Schmahl, Vermetten, van Dyck, & Bremner, in press] more than neutral cognitive stressors) (Bremner et al., 2002). We also found that patients with PTSD had less of an inhibition of memory function with synthetic cortisol (dexamethasone) than normal subjects (Bremner, Vythilingam, Vermetten, Newcomer, & Charney, 2005b). In a study of ACTH response to CRF challenge in children with depression with and without a history of childhood abuse, children with depression and abuse had an increased ACTH response to CRF challenge compared to children with depression without abuse. These children were in a chaotic environment at the time of the study, indicating that the ongoing stressors may have played a role in the potentiation of the ACTH response to CRF (Kaufman et al., 1997). Adult women with depression and a history of early childhood abuse had an increased cortisol response to a stressful cognitive challenge relative to controls (Heim et al., 2000) and a blunted ACTH response to CRF challenge (Heim, Newport, Bonsall, Miller, & Nemeroff, 2001). These studies suggest that early abuse is associated with long-term changes in the HPA axis.

Studies have also shown changes in the brain in patients with a history of early stress and PTSD as well as other mental disorders. A 12% reduction in left hippocampal volume in 17 patients with childhood abuse–related PTSD compared to 17 case-matched controls was found that was significant after controlling for confounding factors (Bremner et al., 1997) (Fig. 1.3) (also see color insert). In a recent meta-analysis, we pooled data from all of the relevant published studies and found smaller hippocampal volume for both the left and the right sides, equally in adult men and women with chronic PTSD (Kitayama, Vaccarino, Kutner, Weiss, & Bremner, 2005).

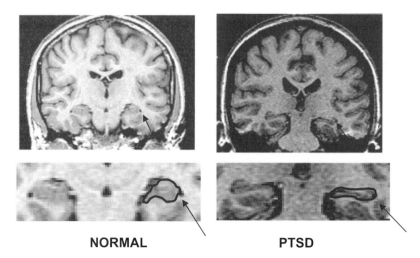

NORMAL   **PTSD**

FIGURE 1.3. Hippocampal volume reduction in PTSD on magnetic resonance imaging (MRI). There is smaller hippocampal volume in this patient with PTSD (right) compared to a control (left). *Source*: Bremner, J. D. Brain Imaging Handbook. Fig. 6.3, p. 101.

We hypothesize that stress-induced hippocampal dysfunction may mediate many of the symptoms of abuse-related PTSD that are related to memory dysregulation, including both explicit memory deficits as well as fragmentation of memory in abuse survivors.

We have also found smaller hippocampal volume in patients with other abuse-related mental disorders. Both women with early abuse and dissociative identity disorder (DID) (Vermetten, Schmahl, Lindner, Loewenstein, & Bremner, 2006) and women with early abuse and borderline personality disorder (BPD) (Schmahl, Vermetten, Elzinga, & Bremner, 2003b) had smaller hippocampal volume than controls.

In addition to the hippocampus, other brain structures, including the amygdala and prefrontal cortex, have been implicated in a neural circuitry of stress. The amygdala is involved in memory for the emotional valence of events and plays a critical role in the acquisition of fear responses. The medial prefrontal cortex includes the anterior cingulate gyrus (Brodmann's area 32) and subcallosal gyrus (area 25), as well as orbitofrontal cortex. Lesion studies demonstrated that the medial prefrontal cortex modulates emotional responsiveness through inhibition of amygdala function (Morgan & LeDoux, 1995). Conditioned fear responses are extinguished following repeated exposure to the conditioned stimulus in the absence of the unconditioned (aversive, e.g., electric shock) stimulus. This inhibition appears to be mediated by medial prefrontal cortical inhibition of amygdala responsiveness (Quirk, Garcia, & Gonzalez-Lima, 2006).

Animal studies also show that early stress is associated with a decrease in the branching of neurons in the medial prefrontal cortex (Radley et al., 2004). Women with PTSD related to childhood sexual abuse had smaller anterior cingulate volumes based on MRI measurements (Kitayama et al., 2005).

Based on findings related to the effects of antidepressants on neurogenesis, we assessed the effects of the selective serotonin reuptake inhibitor (SSRI) paroxetine on outcomes related to function of the hippocampus. We studied 28 patients with PTSD and treated them for up to a year with variable doses of paroxetine. Twenty-three patients completed the course of treatment, and MRI post-treatment was obtained in 20 patients. Neuropsychological testing was used to assess hippocampal-based declarative memory function and MRI was used to assess hippocampal volume before and after treatment. Treatment resulted in significant improvements in verbal declarative memory and a 4.6% increase in mean hippocampal volume. These findings suggested that long-term treatment with paroxetine is associated with improvement of verbal declarative memory deficits and an increase in hippocampal volume in PTSD (Vermetten, Vythilingam, Southwick, Charney, & Bremner, 2003).

Functional neuroimaging studies have been performed to map out the neural circuitry of PTSD related to early abuse (Bremner, 2003b; Bremner, 2005b; Bremner & Vermetten, 2001). These studies are consistent with dysfunction in a network of related brain areas including amygdala, medial prefrontal cortex, and hippocampus. We measured brain blood flow with positron emission tomography (PET) and $[^{15}O]H_2O$ during exposure to personalized scripts of childhood sexual abuse. Twenty-two women with a history of childhood sexual abuse underwent injection of $H_2[^{15}O]$ followed by PET imaging of the brain while listening to neutral and traumatic (personalized childhood sexual abuse events) scripts. Brain blood flow during exposure to traumatic versus neutral scripts was compared between sexually abused women with and without PTSD. Memories of childhood sexual abuse were associated with greater increases in blood flow in portions of anterior prefrontal cortex (superior and middle frontal gyri-Areas 6 and 9), posterior cingulate (Area 31), and motor cortex in sexually abused women with PTSD compared to sexually abused women without PTSD. Abuse memories were associated with alterations in blood flow in medial prefrontal cortex, with decreased blood flow in subcallosal gyrus–Area 25, and a failure of activation in anterior cingulate–Area 32. There was also decreased blood flow in right hippocampus, fusiform/inferior temporal gyrus, supramarginal gyrus, and visual association cortex in PTSD relative to non–PTSD women (Bremner et al., 1999a). This study replicated findings of decreased function in medial prefrontal cortex and increased function in posterior cingulate in subjects with combat-related PTSD during exposure to combat-related slides and sounds (Bremner et al., 1999b).

In another study by Shin et al. (1999), 8 women with childhood sexual abuse and PTSD were compared to 8 women with abuse without PTSD using PET during exposure to script-driven imagery of childhood abuse. The authors found increases in orbitofrontal cortex and anterior temporal pole in both groups of subjects, with greater increases in these areas in the PTSD group. PTSD patients showed a relative failure of anterior cingulate/medial prefrontal cortex activation compared to controls. The PTSD patients (but not controls) showed decreased blood flow in anteromedial portions of prefrontal cortex and left inferior frontal gyrus.

These studies have relied on specific traumatic cues to activate personalized traumatic memories and PTSD symptoms in patients with PTSD. Another method to probe neural circuits in PTSD is to assess neural correlates of retrieval of emotionally valenced declarative memory. In this type of paradigm, instead of using a traditional declarative memory task, such as retrieval of word pairs like "gold-west," which has been the standard of memory research for several decades, words with emotional valence, such as "stench-fear," are utilized (Bremner et al., 2001). We used PET in the examination of neural correlates of retrieval of emotionally valenced declarative memory in 10 women with a history of childhood sexual abuse and the diagnosis of PTSD and 11 women without abuse or PTSD. We hypothesized that retrieval of emotionally valenced words would result in an altered pattern of brain activation in patients with PTSD similar to that seen in prior studies of exposure to cues of personalized traumatic memories. PTSD patients during retrieval of emotionally valenced word pairs showed greater decreases in blood flow in an extensive area that included orbitofrontal cortex, anterior cingulate, and medial prefrontal cortex (Brodmann's Areas 25, 32, 9), left hippocampus, and fusiform gyrus/inferior temporal gyrus, with increased activation in posterior cingulate, left inferior parietal cortex, left middle frontal gyrus, and visual association and motor cortex (Fig. 1.4) (also see color insert). There were no differences in patterns of brain activation during retrieval of neutral word pairs between patients and controls.

Another study examined neural correlates of the Stroop task in sexually abused women with PTSD. The Stroop task involves color–naming semantically incongruent words (e.g., the word "green" is printed in the color red, and subjects are asked to name the color of the word). The Stroop task has consistently been found to be associated with activation of the anterior cingulate in normal subjects, an effect attributed to the divided attention or inhibition of responses involved in the task. Emotional Stroop tasks (e.g., where a trauma-specific word like "rape" is printed in a certain color, and the subject is asked to name the color) in abused women with PTSD have also been shown to be associated with a delay in color naming(Foa, Feske, Murdock, Kozak, & McCarthy, 1991). Women with early childhood sexual abuse–related PTSD ($n = 12$) and women with abuse but without PTSD ($n = 9$) underwent PET measurement of

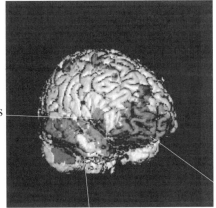

Left hippocampus

Medial prefrontal & orbitofrontal cortex

Fusiform, inferior temporal gyrus

FIGURE 1.4. Decreased medial prefrontal function with exposure to emotionally valenced words like "rape-mutilate." There was a decrease in medial prefrontal and hippocampal blood flow with exposure to trauma-related words in women with a history of early-childhood-abuse-related PTSD compared to controls. *Source:* Bremner et al., 2004.

cerebral blood flow during exposure to control, color Stroop, and emotional Stroop conditions. Women with abuse with PTSD (but not abused non-PTSD women) had a relative decrease in anterior cingulate blood flow during exposure to the emotional (but not color) classic Stroop task. During the color Stroop there were also relatively greater increases in blood flow in non-PTSD compared with PTSD women in right visual association cortex, cuneus, and right inferior parietal lobule. These findings were consistent with dysfunction of the anterior cingulate/medial prefrontal cortex in women with early abuse–related PTSD (Bremner et al., 2003a).

We compared hippocampal function and structure in 33 women with and without early childhood sexual abuse and PTSD. Women with abuse with and without PTSD were studied during encoding of a verbal memory paragraph compared to a control task in conjunction with measurement of brain blood flow with PET. There were significantly greater increases in blood flow during verbal memory encoding in the hippocampus in non-PTSD abused women relative to PTSD women. PTSD women also had smaller left hippocampal volume on MRI volumetrics compared to abused women without PTSD and non-abused, non-PTSD women. Differences in hippocampal activation were statistically significant after covarying for left hippocampal volume, suggesting that failure of activation was not secondary to smaller hippocampal volume in patients with PTSD (Bremner et al., 2003b).

We have extended functional imaging studies to patients with abuse-related mental disorders other than PTSD. In a study of women with early trauma and BPD, exposure to scripts of an abandonment situation were associated with decreased medial prefrontal and hippocampal blood flow (Schmahl et al., 2003a). Decreased medial prefrontal/anterior cingulate was seen in BPD women with early abuse during exposure to a script of their early trauma (Schmahl, Vermetten, Elzinga, & Bremner, 2004).

Although some studies have demonstrated increased amygdala function in PTSD, the experience to date suggests that increased amygdala involvement is not necessarily seen in all of the study paradigms applied to PTSD. It is more likely that specific tasks are required to show increased amygdala function in PTSD. For instance, we found increased amygdala activation during acquisition of fear in a classical fear conditioning paradigm in women with early childhood sexual abuse–related PTSD (Bremner et al., 2005a) (Fig. 1.5) (also see color insert).

Orbitofrontal Cortex

Superior Temporal Gyrus

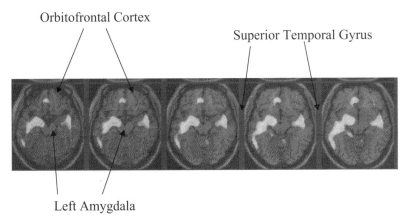

Left Amygdala

FIGURE 1.5. Increased amygdala function during acquisition of conditioned fear responses in women with early childhood abuse and PTSD. Lighter areas represent bilateral amygdala activation. There was greater amygdala activation with acquisition of fear responses (pairing of conditioned stimulus and unconditioned stimulus) in women with PTSD compared to controls; z > 3.09, p < 0.001. *Source:* Bremner et al., 2005.

Fewer brain–imaging studies have been performed in children with PTSD. Several studies have shown alterations in electroencephalogram (EEG) measures of brain activity in children with a variety of traumas who were not selected for diagnosis compared to healthy children. About half of the children in these studies had a psychiatric diagnosis. Abnormalities were located in the anterior frontal cortex and temporal lobe and were localized to the left hemisphere (Ito et al., 1993; Schiffer, Teicher, & Papanicolaou, 1995). Two studies have found reductions in brain volume in children with trauma and PTSD symptoms (Carrion et al., 2001; De Bellis et al., 1999b). One group did not find reductions in hippocampal volume either at baseline or over a longitudinal period (De Bellis, Hall, Boring, Frustaci, & Moritz, 2001; De Bellis et al., 1999b) while another group found an 8.5% reduction in hippocampal volume that was not significant after controlling for smaller brain volumes in the PTSD group (Carrion et al., 2001). One study used single–voxel proton magnetic resonance spectroscopy (proton MRS) to measure relative concentration of N–acetylaspartate and creatinine (a marker of neuronal viability) in the anterior cingulate of 11 children with maltreatment–related PTSD and 11 controls. The authors found a reduction in the ratio of N–acetylaspartate to creatinine in PTSD patients relative to controls (De Bellis, Keshavan,

Spencer, & Hall, 2000). Studies have also found smaller size of the corpus callosum in children with abuse and PTSD relative to controls (De Bellis et al., 1999b), as well as larger volume of the superior temporal gyrus (De Bellis et al., 2002). In a study of abused children in whom diagnosis was not specified, there was an increase in T2 relaxation time in the cerebellar vermis, suggesting dysfunction in this brain region (Anderson, Teicher, Polcari, & Renshaw, 2002).

In summary, adults with early-abuse-related mental disorders show evidence of decreased medial prefrontal and hippocampal function and structure, as well as increased amygdala function. Although changes in medial prefrontal and corpus callosum structure were found in children with PTSD, changes in hippocampal volume were not. This is explainable by findings in animals showing that early stress does not manifest as changes in hippocampal structure until adulthood (Brunson, Eghbal-Ahmadi, Bender, Chen, & Baram, 2001; Brunson et al., 2005).

These findings have implications for understanding alterations in memories of abuse in patients with abuse-related PTSD (Bremner, 1999; Bremner, 2001; Bremner, Krystal, Charney, & Southwick, 1996a). This hippocampus plays a role in the integration of the individual elements of memory in the context of space and time (Zola-Morgan & Squire, 1990). Dysfunction of the hippocampus in patients with abuse-related PTSD may lead to an inability to effectively retrieve memories of early abuse.

Dissociation is defined as a breakdown in memory, consciousness, and the sense of self. Dissociation at the time of trauma is often seen in trauma victims, and three studies have now found a correlation between smaller hippocampal volume and dissociative symptom severity (Bremner et al., 2003b; Stein, Koverola, Hanna, Torchia, & McClarty, 1997; Vermetten et al., 2006). We have hypothesized that dissociation at the time of trauma represents a behavioral correlate of stress-induced hippocampal damage (Bremner et al., 1996a). If so, hippocampally mediated dissociative amnesia may represent a mechanism of altered recall of early abuse.

Neurohormonal Modulation of Memory

Hormones released during stress, including catecholamines and cortisol, modulate the encoding and retrieval of memory (McGaugh, 2000).

Administration of epinephrine (which is released from the adrenal) affects memory retention with an inverted U-shaped curve. Memory improves up to a point and decreases with high doses (Gold & van Buskirk, 1975; Liang, Juler, & McGaugh, 1986). Lower doses of norepinephrine injected into the amygdala promote memory for an inhibitory-avoidance task, while higher doses inhibit memory (Liang, McGaugh, & Yao, 1990). In humans, noradrenergic beta-blocker medications blocked the formation of emotional memories (Cahill, Prins, Weber, & McGaugh, 1994), while enhanced norepinephrine release was associated with enhanced encoding of emotional memories (Southwick et al., 2002). Vasopressin and oxytocin have been shown to modulate memory formation in both animals (McGaugh, 2000) and human subjects (including those with PTSD) (Pitman, Orr, & Lasko, 1993).

Glucocorticoids also affect learning and memory. Elevations of glucocorticoids within the physiological range result in reversible deficits in memory function in animals (Bodnoff et al., 1995; Oitzl & de Kloet, 1992) as well as human subjects (de Quervain, Roozendaal, Nitsch, McGaugh, & Hock, 2000; Kirschbaum, Wolf, May, Wippich, & Hellhammer, 1996; Lupien, Gillin, & Hauger, 1999; Lupien et al., 1997; Lupien et al., 2002; Newcomer, Craft, Hershey, Askins, & Bardgett, 1994; Newcomer et al., 1999; Wolf, Schommer, Hellhammer, McEwen, & Kirschbaum, 2001). Glucocorticoids released during stress, possibly acting through the hippocampus, may explain in part the acutely reversible as well as chronic effects that stress has on declarative memory (de Kloet et al., 1999; Kirschbaum et al., 1996; Porter & Landfield, 1998; Wolf, 2003). Greater deficits are seen in younger subjects in comparison to older subjects, hypothesized to be secondary to age-related decreases in glucocorticoid receptor density (Newcomer, Selke, Kelly, Paras, & Craft, 1995). Impairment of working memory by glucocorticoids may require noradrenergic stimulation to have its effect (Elzinga & Roelofs, 2005). We used a protocol of 1 mg of dexamethasone, followed by 2 mg one day later, and found an impairment in declarative memory function (percent retention of a paragraph after a delay) in healthy subjects but not in patients with depression (Bremner, Vythilingam, Vermetten, Newcomer, & Charney, 2004) or PTSD (Bremner et al., 2005b). We hypothesized that this might be due to disease-related decreases in glucocorticoid receptor function. This is consistent with the idea of PTSD as an "accelerated aging" (Bremner & Narayan, 1998) related to common theories of progressive hippocampal atrophy and dysfunction in both processes. We have also shown that endogenous cortisol release stimulated by a cognitive stress challenge in healthy subjects impaired delayed recall of words and a spatial memory task (Elzinga, Bakker, & Bremner, 2005). Some studies have shown, however, that endogenous cortisol levels in healthy subjects who became upset during a social speech task were correlated with enhanced delayed memory recall of unpleasant pictures (Abercrombie, Speck, & Monticelli, 2005). These discrepant findings may be related to different effects of endogenous cortisol on recall of verbal versus visual materials.

Stress-related release of neurohormones can influence recall of childhood abuse memories. As noted above, the stress hormones catecholamines and cortisol influence the encoding and retrieval of memory. These neurohormones can be released at varying levels at the time of stress, thus influencing the encoding of traumatic memory. Also, they can be released at varying concentrations in an unpredictable manner at the time of memory retrieval. In addition, as reviewed above, release of these stress hormones is altered in patients with stress-induced mental disorders, which may lead to different outcomes than in healthy subjects.

Conclusions

This chapter has reviewed the neurobiology of stress and memory as it applies to traumatized children and questions related to delayed recall of childhood abuse. Studies of the effects of memory have shown that stressful events are remembered differently than normal events. For instance, evidence from "flashbulb" memory studies showed that emotional events are remembered better than neutral events. Other studies showed that the central features of emotional events are remembered better than peripheral details. Studies in normal children have shown that stressful memories in general are remembered accurately and are typically more resistant to suggestion.

Results from studies of abuse victims related to their ability to remember their abuse events have been varied. Due to the complex nature of abuse, underreporting, and the difficulties of verification, research in this area has been very difficult.

Studies have shown that memory is subject to distortion. However, implausible memories are more difficult to "implant" than plausible memories, making it less likely that individuals can have memories of traumatic memories "implanted." On the other hand, abuse-related patients with mental disorders have greater memory impairment, making it more likely that they may have "source memory" errors. Consistent with this are studies showing that abused PTSD patients are more susceptible to suggestion on the Deese/Roediger-McDermott paradigm. For these reasons, therapists should proceed with caution in discussions of early abuse and not provide suggestions about abuse that the patient is not aware of.

Neurobiological studies have implications for the recall of abuse. Patients with abuse-related mental disorders have a wide range of memory impairments. At its most extreme, patients with early abuse and DID have a complete breakdown of autobiographical memory, making the accurate recall of personal life experiences more difficult. Patients with abuse-related mental disorders also have smaller hippocampal volume, which we hypothesize is stress related. Altered hippocampal function can be associated with an impairment of memory recall, or the accurate integration of individual elements of memory.

Abuse-related PTSD is also associated with increased amygdala function and decreased function of the medial prefrontal cortex/anterior cingulate. Increased amygdala function is associated with enhanced fear responses, while a failure of medial prefrontal function is associated with a failure of extinction, or inability to turn off the fear response. Deficits in medial prefrontal function are also seen in women with early abuse and BPD. Given the enhanced brain responsiveness to reminders of the trauma, it is anticipated that patients with early-abuse-related psychopathology will avoid reminders of the abuse, which may lead to the development of amnesia.

Changes in stress-responsive hormonal systems may also have an effect on memory in patients with abuse-related mental disorders. Traumatic memories can be both enhanced and impaired depending on release of stress hormones such as cortisol and norepinephrine, as well as the effects of stress on brain areas involved in memory and emotion such as the hippocampus, amygdala, and prefrontal cortex.

Understanding how stress affects memory and the brain will have important implications for the treatment of traumatized children throughout their lives. This area also has implications for public health and for promoting the health of children.

Future studies should examine normal and stress-related memory in children and adults with early childhood abuse–related mental disorders.

Other studies should continue to assess brain circuits and systems involved in memory and the stress response and the effects of treatments on these brain systems. These studies need to expand beyond brain function to areas such as neuroreceptors and neurosignalling pathways. Finally, research should shift from exploring the consequences of abuse to investigating novel approaches toward prevention.

References

Abercrombie, E. D., & Jacobs, B. L. (1987). Single-unit response of noradrenergic neurons in the locus coeruleus of freely moving cats. II. Adaptation to chronically presented stressful stimuli. *Journal of Neuroscience, 7,* 2844–2848.

Abercrombie, H. C., Speck, N. S., & Monticelli, R. M. (2005). Endogenous cortisol elevations are related to memory facilitation only in individuals who are emotionally aroused. *Psychoneuroendocrinology, 31,* 187–196.

Alexander, K. W., Quas, J. A., Goodman, G. S., Ghetti, S., Edelstein, R. S., Redlich, A. D., et al. (2005). Traumatic impact predicts long-term memory for documented child sexual abuse. *Psychological Science, 16,* 33–40.

Anderson, C. M., Teicher, M. H., Polcari, A., & Renshaw, P. F. (2002). Abnormal t2 relaxation time in the cerebellar vermis of adults sexually abused in childhood: Potential role of the vermis in stress-enhanced risk for drug abuse. *Psychoneuroendocrinology, 27,* 231–244.

Arborelius, L., Owens, M. J., Plotsky, P. M., & Nemeroff, C. B. (1999). The role of corticotropin-releasing factor in depression and anxiety disorders. *Journal of Endocrinology, 160,* 1–12.

Bahrick, L. E., Parker, J. F., Fivush, R., & Levitt, M. (1998). The effects of stress on young children's memory for a natural disaster. *Journal of Experimental Psychology: Applied, 4*(4), 308–331.

Battle, C. L., Shea, M. T., Johnson, D. M., Yen, S., Zlotnick, C., Zanarini, M. C., et al. (2004). Childhood maltreatment associated with adult personality disorders: Findings from the collaborative longitudinal personality disorders study. *Journal of Personality Disorders, 18*(2), 193–211.

Bodnoff, S. R., Humphreys, A. G., Lehman, J. C., Diamond, D. M., Rose, G. M., & Meaney, M. J. (1995). Enduring effects of chronic corticosterone treatment on spatial learning, synaptic plasticity, and hippocampal neuropathology in young and mid-aged rats. *Journal of Neuroscience, 15,* 61–69.

Bohannon, J. N. (1988). Flashbulb memories for the space shuttle disaster: A tale of two theories. *Cognition, 29,* 179–196.

Bohannon, J. N., & Symons, V. L. (1992). Flashbulb memories: Confidence, consistency and quantity. In E. Winograd & U. Neisser (Eds.), *Affect and accuracy in recall: Studies in "flashbulb memories"* (pp. 65–94). New York: Cambridge University Press.

Bremner, J. D. (1999). Traumatic memories lost and found: Can lost memories of abuse be found in the brain? In L. M. Williams & V. L. Banyard (Eds.), *Trauma & memory* (pp. 217–228). London: SAGE.

Bremner, J. D. (2001). A biological model for delayed recall of childhood abuse. *Journal of Aggression, Maltreatment, and Trauma, 4*(2), 165–183.

Bremner, J. D. (2002). *Does stress damage the brain? Understanding trauma-related disorders from a mind-body perspective.* New York: W. W. Norton.

Bremner, J. D. (2003a). Functional neuroanatomical correlates of traumatic stress revisited 7 years later, this time with data. *Psychopharmacology Bulletin, 37*(2), 6–25.

Bremner, J. D. (2003b). Long-term effects of childhood abuse on brain and neurobiology. *Child and Adolescent Psychiatric Clinics of North America, 12*(2), 271–292.

Bremner, J. D. (2005a). *Brain imaging handbook.* New York: W. W. Norton.

Bremner, J. D. (2005b). The neurobiology of childhood sexual abuse in women with posttraumatic stress disorder. In K. A. Kendall-Tackett (Ed.), *Handbook of women, stress and trauma* (pp. 181–206). New York: Brunner-Routledge.

Bremner, J. D., Krystal, J. H., Charney, D. S., & Southwick, S. M. (1996a). Neural mechanisms in dissociative amnesia for childhood abuse: Relevance to the current controversy surrounding the "false memory syndrome." *American Journal of Psychiatry, 153*(7), 71–82.

Bremner, J. D., Krystal, J. H., Southwick, S. M., & Charney, D. S. (1996b). Noradrenergic mechanisms in stress and anxiety: I. Preclinical studies. *Synapse, 23,* 28–38.

Bremner, J. D., Krystal, J. H., Southwick, S. M., & Charney, D. S. (1996c). Noradrenergic mechanisms in stress and anxiety: II. Clinical studies. *Synapse, 23,* 39–51.

Bremner, J. D., & Narayan, M. (1998). The effects of stress on memory and the hippocampus throughout the life cycle: Implications for childhood development and aging. *Development & Psychopathology, 10,* 871–886.

Bremner, J. D., Narayan, M., Staib, L. H., Southwick, S. M., McGlashan, T., & Charney, D. S. (1999a). Neural correlates of memories of childhood sexual abuse in women with and without posttraumatic stress disorder. *American Journal of Psychiatry, 156,* 1787–1795.

Bremner, J. D., Randall, P. R., Capelli, S., Scott, T. M., McCarthy, G., & Charney, D. S. (1995). Deficits in short-term memory in adult survivors of childhood abuse. *Psychiatry Research, 59,* 97–107.

Bremner, J. D., Randall, P. R., Vermetten, E., Staib, L., Bronen, R. A., Mazure, C. M., et al. (1997). MRI-based measurement of hippocampal volume in posttraumatic stress disorder related to childhood physical and sexual abuse: A preliminary report. *Biological Psychiatry, 41,* 23–32.

Bremner, J. D., Shobe, K. K., & Kihlstrom, J. F. (2000). False memories in women with self-reported childhood sexual abuse: An empirical study. *Psychological Sciences, 11,* 333–337.

Bremner, J. D., Soufer, R., McCarthy, G., Delaney, R. C., Staib, L. H., Duncan, J. S., et al. (2001). Gender differences in cognitive and neural correlates of remembrance of emotional words. *Psychopharmacology Bulletin, 35,* 55–87.

Bremner, J. D., Southwick, S. M., Darnell, A., & Charney, D. S. (1996d). Chronic PTSD in Vietnam combat veterans: Course of illness and substance abuse. *American Journal of Psychiatry, 153,* 369–375.

Bremner, J. D., Staib, L., Kaloupek, D., Southwick, S. M., Soufer, R., & Charney, D. S. (1999b). Neural correlates of exposure to traumatic pictures and sound in Vietnam combat veterans with and without posttraumatic stress disorder: A positron emission tomography study. *Biological Psychiatry, 45,* 806–816.

Bremner, J. D., Steinberg, M., Southwick, S. M., Johnson, D. R., & Charney, D. S. (1993). Use of the structured clinical interview for *DSM-IV*-dissociative disorders for systematic assessment of dissociative symptoms in posttraumatic stress disorder. *American Journal of Psychiatry, 150,* 1011–1014.

Bremner, J. D., & Vermetten, E. (2001). Stress and development: Behavioral and biological consequences. *Development & Psychopathology, 13,* 473–489.

Bremner, J. D., Vermetten, E., & Kelley, M. E. (in press). Cortisol, dehydroepiandrosterone, and estradiol measured over 24 hours in women with childhood sexual abuse-related posttraumatic stress disorder. *Journal of Nervous and Mental Disease.*

Bremner, J. D., Vermetten, E., Nafzal, N., & Vythilingam, M. (2004). Deficits in verbal declarative memory function in women with childhood sexual abuse-related posttraumatic stress disorder (PTSD). *Journal of Nervous and Mental Disease, 192*(10), 643–649.

Bremner, J. D., Vermetten, E., Schmahl, C., Vaccarino, V., Vythilingam, M., Afzal, N., et al. (2005a). Positron emission tomographic imaging of neural correlates of a fear acquisition and extinction paradigm in women with childhood sexual abuse-related posttraumatic stress disorder. *Psychological Medicine, 35*(6), 791–806.

Bremner, J. D., Vermetten, E., Vythilingam, M., Afzal, N., Schmahl, C., Elzinga, B. E., et al. (2003a). Neural correlates of the classical neutral and emotional Stroop in women with abuse-related posttraumatic stress disorder. *Biological Psychiatry, 55,* 612–620.

Bremner, J. D., Vythilingam, M., Vermetten, E., Adil, J., Khan, S., Nazeer, A., et al. (2002). Cortisol response to a cognitive stress challenge in posttraumatic stress disorder (PTSD) related to childhood abuse. *Psychoneuroendocrinology, 28,* 733–750.

Bremner, J. D., Vythilingam, M., Vermetten, E., Newcomer, J. W., & Charney, D. S. (2004). Effects of glucocorticoids on declarative memory function in major depression. *Biological Psychiatry, 55*(8), 811–815.

Bremner, J. D., Vythilingam, M., Vermetten, E., Newcomer, J. W., & Charney, D. S. (2005b). Effects of dexamethasone on declarative memory function in posttraumatic stress disorder (PTSD). *Psychiatry Research, 129*(1), 1–10.

Bremner, J. D., Vythilingam, M., Vermetten, E., Southwick, S. M., McGlashan, T., Nazeer, A., et al. (2003b). MRI and PET study of deficits in hippocampal structure and function in women with childhood sexual abuse and posttraumatic stress disorder (PTSD). *American Journal of Psychiatry, 160,* 924–932.

Brown, R., & Kulik, J. (1977). Flashbulb memories. *Cognition, 5,* 73–99.

Bruce, D., Wilcox-O'Hearn, L. A., Robinson, J. A., Phillips-Grant, K., Francis, L., & Smith, M. C. (2005). Fragment memories mark the end of childhood amnesia. *Memory & Cognition, 33,* 567–576.

Brunson, K. L., Eghbal-Ahmadi, M., Bender, R., Chen, Y., & Baram, T. Z. (2001). Long-term, progressive hippocampal cell loss and dysfunction induced by early-life administration of corticotropin-releasing hormone reproduce the effects of early-life stress. *Proceedings of the National Academy of Sciences USA, 98*(15), 8856–8861.

Brunson, K. L., Kramar, E., Lin, B., Chen, Y., Colgin, L. L., Yanagihara, T. K., et al. (2005). Mechanisms of late-onset cognitive decline after early-life stress. *Journal of Neuroscience, 25*(41), 9328–9338.

Buckley, T. C., Blanchard, E. B., & Neill, W. T. (2000). Information processing and PTSD: A review of the empirical literature. *Clinical Psychology Reviews, 28*(8), 1041–1065.

Cahill, L., Prins, B., Weber, M., & McGaugh, J. L. (1994). Beta-adrenergic activation and memory for emotional events. *Nature, 371,* 702–704.

Carrion, V. G., Weems, C. F., Eliez, S., Patwardhan, A., Brown, W., Ray, R. D., et al. (2001). Attenuation of frontal asymmetry in pediatric posttraumatic stress disorder. *Biological Psychiatry, 50,* 943–951.

Casey, B. J., Giedd, J. N., & Thomas, K. M. (2000). Structural and functional brain development and its relation to cognitive development. *Biological Psychiatry, 54,* 241–257.

Ceci, S. J., & Bruck, M. (1993). Suggestibility of the child witness: A historical review and synthesis. *Psychological Bulletin, 113,* 403–439.

Ceci, S. J., Caves, R. D., & Howe, M. J. A. (1981). Children's long-term memory for information that is incongruous with their prior knowledge. *British Journal of Psychology, 72,* 443–450.

Ceci, S. J., Ross, D. F., & Toglia, M. P. (1987). Suggestibility of children's memory: Psycholegal implications. *Journal of Experimental Psychology: General, 116,* 38–49.

Chen, E., Zeltzer, L. K., Craske, M. G., & Katz, E. R. (2000). Children's memories for painful cancer treatment procedures: Implications for distress. *Child Development, 71*(4), 933–947.

Christianson, S., & Loftus, E. F. (1987). Memory for traumatic events. *Applied Cognitive Psychology, 1,* 225–239.

Christianson, S., & Nilsson, L. (1984). Functional amnesia as induced by psychological trauma. *Memory & Cognition, 12,* 142–155.

Christianson, S.-A., & Loftus, E. F. (1991). Remembering emotional events: The fate of detailed information. *Cognition and Emotion, 5,* 81–108.

Christianson, S.-A., Loftus, E. F., Hoffman, H. G., & Loftus, G. R. (1991). Eye fixation and memory for emotional events. *Journal of Experimental Psychology: Learning, Memory and Cognition, 17,* 693–701.

Cicchetti, D., & Rogosch, F. A. (2001). The impact of child maltreatment and psychopathology on neuroendocrine functioning. *Development & Psychopathology, 13,* 783–804.

Cicchetti, D., & Walker, E. F. (2001). Stress and development: Biological and psychological consequences. *Development & Psychopathology, 13,* 413–418.

Clancy, S. A., Schacter, D. L., McNally, R. J., & Pitman, R. K. (2000). False recognition in women reporting recovered memories of sexual abuse. *Psychological Sciences, 11,* 26–31.

Czeh, B., Michaelis, T., Watanabe, T., Frahm, J., de Biurrun, G., van Kampen, M., et al. (2001). Stress-induced changes in cerebral metabolites, hippocampal volume, and cell proliferation are prevented by antidepressant treatment with tianeptine. *Proceedings of the National Academy of Sciences USA, 98,* 12796–12801.

D'Sa, C., & Duman, R. S. (2002). Antidepressants and neuroplasticity. *Bipolar Disorder, 4,* 183–194.

De Bellis, M. D., Baum, A. S., Keshavan, M. S., Eccard, C. H., Boring, A. M., Jenkins, F. J., et al. (1999a). A. E. Bennett research award: Developmental traumatology: Part I: Biological stress systems. *Biological Psychiatry, 45,* 1259–1270.

De Bellis, M. D., Chrousos, G. P., Dorn, L. D., Burke, L., Helmers, K., Kling, M. A., et al. (1994). Hypothalamic pituitary adrenal dysregulation in sexually abused girls. *Journal of Clinical Endocrinology & Metabolism, 78,* 249–255.

De Bellis, M. D., Hall, J., Boring, A. M., Frustaci, K., & Moritz, G. (2001). A pilot longitudinal study of hippocampal volumes in pediatric maltreatment-related posttraumatic stress disorder. *Biological Psychiatry, 50,* 305–309.

De Bellis, M. D., Keshavan, M. S., Clark, D. B., Casey, B. J., Giedd, J. N., Boring, A. M., et al. (1999b). A. E. Bennett research award: Developmental traumatology: Part II. Brain development. *Biological Psychiatry, 45,* 1271–1284.

De Bellis, M. D., Keshavan, M. S., Frustaci, K., Shifflett, H., Iyengar, S., Beers, S. R., et al. (2002). Superior temporal gyrus volumes in maltreated children and adolescents with PTSD. *Biological Psychiatry, 51*(7), 544–552.

De Bellis, M. D., Keshavan, M. S., Spencer, S., & Hall, J. (2000). N-acetylaspartate concentration in the anterior cingulate of maltreated children and adolescents with PTSD. *American Journal of Psychiatry, 157,* 1175–1177.

de Kloet, E. R., Oitzl, M. S., & Joels, M. (1999). Stress and cognition: Are corticosteroids good or bad guys? *Trends in Neurosciences, 22,* 422–426.

de Quervain, D. J.-F., Roozendaal, B., Nitsch, R. M., McGaugh, J. L., & Hock, C. (2000). Acute cortisone administration impairs retrieval of long-term declarative memory in humans. *Nature Neuroscience, 3*(4), 313–314.

DePrince, A. P., Allard, C. B., Oh, H., & Freyd, J. J. (2004). What's in a name for memory errors? Implications and ethical issues arising from the use of the term "false memory" for errors in memory for details. *Ethics and Behavior, 14,* 201–233.

Diamond, D. M., Fleshner, M., Ingersoll, N., & Rose, G. M. (1996). Psychological stress impairs spatial working memory: Relevance to electrophysiological studies of hippocampal function. *Behavioral Neuroscience, 110,* 661–672.

Dube, S. R., Felitti, V. J., Dong, M., Giles, W. H., & Anda, R. F. (2003). The impact of adverse childhood experiences on health problems: Evidence from four birth cohorts dating back to 1900. *Preventive Medicine, 37,* 268–277.

Duman, R. S. (2004). Depression: A case of neuronal life and death? *Biological Psychiatry, 56,* 140–145.

Duman, R. S., Heninger, G. R., & Nestler, E. J. (1997). A molecular and cellular theory of depression. *Archives of General Psychiatry, 54,* 597–606.

Duman, R. S., Malberg, J. E., & Nakagawa, S. (2001). Regulation of adult neurogenesis by psychotropic drugs and stress. *Journal of Pharmacology & Experimental Therapeutics, 299,* 401–407.

Durston, S., Hulshoff, P., Hilleke, E., Casey, B. J., Giedd, J. N., Buitelaar, J. K., et al. (2001). Anatomical MRI of the developing human brain: What have we learned? *Journal of the American Academy of Child & Adolescent Psychiatry, 40*(9), 1012–1020.

Eacott, M. J., & Crawley, R. A. (1998). The offset of childhood amnesia: Memory for events that occurred before age 3. *Journal of Experimental Psychology: General, 127,* 22–23.

Eisen, M. L., Qin, J., Goodman, G. S., & Davis, S. L. (2002). Memory and suggestibility in maltreated children: Age, stress arousal, dissociation, and psychopathology. *Journal of Experimental Child Psychology, 83,* 167–212.

Elzinga, B. M., Bakker, A., & Bremner, J. D. (2005). Stress-induced cortisol elevations are associated with impaired delayed, but not immediate recall. *Psychiatry Research, 134*(3), 211–223.

Elzinga, B. M., & Bremner, J. D. (2002). Are the neural substrates of memory the final common pathway in PTSD? *Journal of Affective Disorders, 70,* 1–17.

Elzinga, B. M., & Roelofs, K. (2005). Cortisol-induced impairments of working memory require acute sympathetic activation. *Behavioral Neuroscience, 119,* 98–103.

Elzinga, B. M., Schmahl, C. G., Vermetten, E., van Dyck, R., & Bremner, J. D. (in press). Increased cortisol responses to the stress of traumatic reminders in abuse-related PTSD. *Neuropsychopharmacology.*

Foa, E. B., Feske, U., Murdock, T. B., Kozak, M. J., & McCarthy, P. R. (1991). Processing of threat related information in rape victims. *Journal of Abnormal Psychology, 100,* 156–162.

Franklin, C. L., & Zimmerman, M. (2001). Posttraumatic stress disorder and major depressive disorder: Investigating the role of overlapping symptoms in diagnostic comorbidity. *Journal of Nervous and Mental Disease, 189*(8), 548–551.

Freyd, J. J., & DePrince, A. P. (Eds.). (2001). *Trauma and cognitive science: A meeting of minds, science, and human experience.* New York: Haworth Maltreatment & Trauma Press.

Garcia, R. (2002). Stress, metaplasticity, and antidepressants. *Current Molecular Medicine, 2,* 629–638.

Giedd, J. N., Blumenthal, J., & Jeffries, N. O. (1999a). Development of the normal human corpus callosum during childhood and adolescence: A longitudinal MRI study. *Progress in Neuropsychopharmacology and Biological Psychiatry, 23,* 571–588.

Giedd, J. N., Blumenthal, J., Jeffries, N. O., Castellanos, F. X., Liu, H., Zijdenbos, A., et al. (1999b). Brain development during childhood and adolescence: A longitudinal MRI study. *Nature Neuroscience, 2*(10), 861–863.

Giedd, J. N., Castellanos, F. X., Rajapakse, J. C., Vaituzis, A. C., & Rapoport, J. L. (1997). Sexual dimorphism of the developing human brain. *Progress in Neuropsychopharmacology and Biological Psychiatry, 21*(8), 1185–1201.

Giedd, J. N., Shaw, P., Wallace, G., Gogtay, N., & Lenroot, R. K. (2006). Anatomic brain imaging studies of normal and abnormal brain development in children and adolescents. In D. Cicchetti & D. J. Cohen (Eds.), *Developmental psychopathology* (Vol. 2, pp. 127–196). Hoboken, NJ: John Wiley & Sons.

Giedd, J. N., Snell, J. W., Lange, N., Rajapakse, J. C., Casey, B. J., Kozuch, P. L., et al. (1996a). Quantitative magnetic resonance imaging of human brain development: Ages 14–18. *Cerebral Cortex, 6*(4), 551–560.

Giedd, J. N., Vaituzis, A. C., Hamburger, S. D., Lange, N., Rajapakse, J. C., Kaysen, D., et al. (1996b). Quantitative MRI of the temporal lobe, amygdala, and hippocampus in normal human development: Ages 4–18 years. *Journal of Comparative Neurology, 366*(2), 223–230.

Gold, P. E., & van Buskirk, R. (1975). Facilitation of time-dependent memory processes with posttrial epinephrine injections. *Behavioral Biology, 13,* 145–153.

Goodman, G. S., & Aman, C. (1990). Children's use of anatomically detailed dolls to recount an event. *Child Development, 61,* 1859–1871.

Goodman, G. S., Ghetti, S., Quas, J. A., Edelstein, R. S., Alexander, K. W., Redlich, A. D., et al. (2003). A prospective study of memory for child sexual abuse: New findings relevant to the repressed-memory controversy. *Psychological Science, 14*(2), 113–118.

Goodman, G. S., Hirschman, J. E., Hepps, J. E., & Rudy, L. (1991). Children's memory for stressful events. *Merrill-Palmer Quarterly, 37,* 109–158.

Gould, E., Beylin, A., Tanapat, P., Reeves, A., & Shors, T. J. (1999). Learning enhances adult neurogenesis in the hippocampal formation. *Nature Neuroscience, 2,* 260–265.

Gould, E., Tanapat, P., McEwen, B. S., Flugge, G., & Fuchs, E. (1998). Proliferation of granule cell precursors in the dentate gyrus of adult monkeys is diminished by stress. *Proceedings of the National Academy of Sciences USA, 95,* 3168–3171.

Gunnar, M. R., Morison, S. J., Chisolm, K., & Schuder, M. (2001). Salivary cortisol levels in children adopted from Romanian orphanages. *Development & Psychopathology, 13,* 611–628.

Gunnar, M. R., & Vazquez, D. (2006). Stress neurobiology and developmental psychopathology. In D. Cicchetti & D. J. Cohen (Eds.), *Developmental psychopathology* (Vol. 2, pp. 533–577). Hoboken, NJ: John Wiley & Sons.

Hart, J., Gunnar, M., & Cicchetti, D. (1996). Altered neuroendocrine activity in maltreated children related to symptoms of depression. *Development & Psychopathology, 8,* 201–214.

Heim, C., Newport, D. J., Bonsall, R., Miller, A. H., & Nemeroff, C. B. (2001). Altered pituitary-adrenal axis responses to provocative challenge tests in adult survivors of childhood abuse. *American Journal of Psychiatry, 158,* 575–581.

Heim, C., Newport, D. J., Heit, S., Graham, Y. P., Wilcox, M., Bonsall, R., et al. (2000). Pituitary-adrenal and autonomic responses to stress in women after sexual and physical abuse in childhood. *Journal of the American Medical Association, 284,* 592–597.

Henn, F. A., & Vollmayr, B. (2004). Neurogenesis and depression: Etiology or epiphe-nomenon? *Biological Psychiatry, 56,* 146–150.

Howe, M. L., Cicchetti, D., & Toth, S. L. (2006). Children's basic memory processes, stress, and maltreatment. *Development and Psychopathology, 18,* 759–769.

Howe, M. L., Cicchetti, D., Toth, S. L., & Cerrito, B. M. (2004). True and false memories in maltreated children. *Child Development, 75*(5), 1402–1417.

Howe, M. L., & Courage, M. L. (1993). On resolving the enigma of infantile amnesia. *Psychological Bulletin, 113,* 305–326.

Howe, M. L., & Courage, M. L. (1997). The emergence and early development of autobiographical memory. *Psychological Review, 104,* 499–523.

Howe, M. L., Toth, S. L., & Cicchetti, D. (2006). Memory and developmental psy-chopathology. In D. Cicchetti & D. J. Cohen (Eds.), *Developmental psychopathology* (Vol. 2, pp. 629–655). Hoboken, NJ: John Wiley & Sons.

Hyman, I. E., Husband, T. H., & Billings, F. J. (1995). False memories of childhood experiences. *Applied Cognitive Psychology, 9,* 181–197.

Ito, Y., Teicher, M. H., Glod, C. A., Harper, D., Magnus, E., & Gelbard, H. A. (1993). Increased prevalence of electrophysiological abnormalities in children with psy-chological, physical and sexual abuse. *Journal of Neuropsychiatry & Clinical Neurosci-ence, 5,* 401–408.

Kaufman, J., Birmaher, B., Perel, J., Dahl, R. E., Moreci, P., Nelson, B., et al. (1997). The corticotropin-releasing hormone challenge in depressed abused, depressed nonabused, and normal control children. *Biological Psychiatry, 42,* 669–679.

Kempermann, G., Kuhn, H. G., & Gage, F. H. (1998). Experience-induced neurogen-esis in the senescent dentate gyrus. *Journal of Neuroscience, 18,* 3206–3212.

Kendall-Tackett, K. A. (Ed.). (2005). *Handbook of women, stress and trauma.* New York: Brunner-Routledge.

Kessler, R. C., Sonnega, A., Bromet, E., Hughes, M., & Nelson, C. B. (1995). Post-traumatic stress disorder in the national comorbidity survey. *Archives of General Psychiatry, 52,* 1048–1060.

Kihlstrom, J. F. (1995). The trauma-memory argument. *Consciousness and Cognition, 4,* 63–67.

Kirschbaum, C., Wolf, O. T., May, M., Wippich, W., & Hellhammer, D. H. (1996). Stress- and treatment-induced elevations of cortisol levels associated with impaired declarative memory in healthy adults. *Life Sciences, 58,* 1475–1483.

Kitayama, N., Vaccarino, V., Kutner, M., Weiss, P., & Bremner, J. D. (2005). Mag-netic resonance imaging (MRI) measurement of hippocampal volume in post-traumatic stress disorder: A meta-analysis. *Journal of Affective Disorders, 88*(1), 79–86.

Lemieux, A. M., & Coe, C. L. (1995). Abuse-related posttraumatic stress disorder: Evidence for chronic neuroendocrine activation in women. *Psychosomatic Medicine, 57,* 105–115.

Liang, K. C., Juler, R. G., & McGaugh, J. L. (1986). Modulating effects of post-training epinephrine on memory: Involvement of the amygdala noradrenergic system. *Brain Research, 368,* 125–133.

Liang, K. C., McGaugh, J. L., & Yao, H. Y. (1990). Involvement of amygdala pathways in the influence of post-training intra-amygdala norepinephrine and peripheral epinephrine on memory storage. *Brain Research, 508,* 225–233.

Lindsay, D. S. (1990). Misleading suggestions can impair eyewitnesses' ability to remember event details. *Journal of Experimental Psychology: Learning, Memory and Cognition, 16,* 1077–1083.

Lindsay, D. S., & Johnson, M. K. (1989). The eyewitness suggestibility effect and memory for source. *Memory & Cognition, 17,* 349–358.

Liu, D., Diorio, J., Day, J. C., Francis, D. D., & Meaney, M. J. (2000). Maternal care, hippocampal synaptogenesis and cognitive development in rats. *Nature Neuroscience, 8,* 799–806.

Loftus, E. F., & Burns, T. E. (1982). Mental shock can produce retrograde amnesia. *Memory & Cognition, 10,* 318–323.

Loftus, E. F., Garry, M., & Feldman, J. (1994). Forgetting sexual trauma: What does it mean when 38% forget? *Journal of Consulting and Clinical Psychology, 62,* 1177–1181.

Loftus, E. F., Miller, D. B., & Burns, H. J. (1978). Semantic integration of verbal information into a visual memory. *Journal of Experimental Psychology: Human Learning and Memory, 4,* 19–31.

Loftus, E. F., & Palmer, J. C. (1974). Reconstruction of automobile destruction: An example of the interaction between language and memory. *Journal of Verbal Learning and Verbal Behavior, 13,* 585–589.

Luby, J. L., Heffelfinger, A., Mrakotsky, C., Brown, K., Hessler, M., & Spitznagel, E. (2003). Alterations in stress cortisol reactivity in depressed preschoolers relative to psychiatric and no-disorder comparison groups. *Archives of General Psychiatry, 60*(12), 1248–1255.

Lucassen, P. J., Fuchs, E., & Czeh, B. (2004). Antidepressant treatment with tianeptine reduces apoptosis in the hippocampal dentate gyrus and temporal cortex. *European Journal of Neuroscience, 14,* 161–166.

Luine, V., Villages, M., Martinex, C., & McEwen, B. S. (1994). Repeated stress causes reversible impairments of spatial memory performance. *Brain Research, 639,* 167–170.

Lupien, S. J., Gaudreau, S., Tchiteya, B. M., Maheu, F., Sharma, S., Nair, N. P., et al. (1997). Stress-induced declarative memory impairment in healthy elderly subjects: Relationship to cortisol reactivity. *Journal of Clinical Endocrinology & Metabolism, 82,* 2070–2075.

Lupien, S. J., Gillin, C. J., & Hauger, R. L. (1999). Working memory is more sensitive than declarative memory to the acute effects of corticosteroids: A dose-response study in humans. *Behavioral Neuroscience, 113,* 420–430.

Lupien, S. J., Wilkinson, C. W., Briere, S., Ng Ying Kin, N. M. K., Meaney, M. J., & Nair, N. P. V. (2002). Acute modulation of aged human memory by pharmacological manipulation of glucocorticoids. *Journal of Clinical Endocrinology & Metabolism, 87*(8), 3798–3807.

MacMillan, H. L., Fleming, J. E., Trocme, N., Boyle, M. H., Wong, M., Racine, Y. A., et al. (1997). Prevalence of child physical and sexual abuse in the community: Results from the Ontario health supplement. *Journal of the American Medical Association, 278,* 131–135.

Magarinos, A. M., McEwen, B. S., Flugge, G., & Fluchs, E. (1996). Chronic psychosocial stress causes apical dendritic atrophy of hippocampal ca3 pyramidal neurons in subordinate tree shrews. *Journal of Neuroscience, 16,* 3534–3540.

Malberg, J. E., Eisch, A. J., Nestler, E. J., & Duman, R. S. (2000). Chronic antidepressant treatment increases neurogenesis in adult rat hippocampus. *Journal of Neuroscience, 20,* 9104–9110.

McCauley, J., Kern, D. E., Kolodner, K., Dill, L., Schroeder, A. F., DeChant, H. K., et al. (1997). Clinical characteristics of women with a history of childhood abuse: Unhealed wounds. *Journal of the American Medical Association, 277,* 1362–1368.

McCloskey, M., & Zaragoza, M. (1985). Misleading postevent information and memory for events: Arguments and evidence against memory impairment hypotheses. *Journal of Experimental Psychology, 114,* 1–16.

McEwen, B. S., Angulo, J., Cameron, H., Chao, H. M., Daniels, D., Gannon, M. N., et al. (1992). Paradoxical effects of adrenal steroids on the brain: Protection versus degeneration. *Biological Psychiatry, 31,* 177–199.

McEwen, B. S., & Chattarji, S. (2004). Molecular mechanisms of neuroplasticity and pharmacological implications: The example of tianeptine. *European Neuropsychopharmacology, 14 Suppl 5,* S497–S502.

McGaugh, J. L. (2000). Memory—a century of consolidation. *Science, 287,* 248–251.

Meaney, M. J., Aitken, D., van Berkel, C., Bhatnager, S., & Sapolsky, R. M. (1988). Effect of neonatal handling on age-related impairments associated with the hippocampus. *Science, 239,* 766–769.

Melia, K. R., & Duman, R. S. (1991). Involvement of corticotropin-releasing factor in chronic stress regulation of the brain noradrenergic system. *Proceedings of the National Academy of Sciences USA, 88,* 8382–8386.

Milrod, B., Leon, A. C., Busch, F., Rudden, M., Schwalberg, M., Clarkin, J., et al. (2007). A randomized controlled clinical trial of psychoanalytic psychotherapy for panic disorder. *American Journal of Psychiatry, 164,* 265–272.

Moradi, A. R., Doost, H. T., Taghavi, M. R., Yule, W., & Dalgleish, T. (1999). Everyday memory deficits in children and adolescents with PTSD: Performance on the rivermead behavioural memory test. *Journal of Child Psychology and Psychiatry, 40,* 357–361.

Moradi, A. R., Taghavi, R., Neshat-Doost, H. T., Yule, W., & Dalgleish, T. (2000). Memory bias for emotional information in children and adolescents with posttraumatic stress disorder: A preliminary study. *Journal of Anxiety Disorders, 14*(5), 521–534.

Morgan, C. A., & LeDoux, J. E. (1995). Differential contribution of dorsal and ventral medial prefrontal cortex to the acquisition and extinction of conditioned fear in rats. *Behavioral Neuroscience, 109,* 681–688.

Neisser, U., & Harsch, N. (1992). Phantom flashbulbs: False recollections of hearing the news about *Challenger.* In E. Winograd & U. Neisser (Eds.), *Affect and accuracy in recall: Studies in "flashbulb memories"* (pp. 9–31). New York: Cambridge University Press.

Newcomer, J. W., Craft, S., Hershey, T., Askins, K., & Bardgett, M. E. (1994). Glucocorticoid-induced impairment in declarative memory performance in adult humans. *Journal of Neuroscience, 14,* 2047–2053.

Newcomer, J. W., Selke, G., Kelly, A. K., Paras, L., & Craft, S. (1995). Age-related differences in glucocorticoid effect on memory in human subjects. *Society for Neuroscience Abstracts, 21*(1), 161.

Newcomer, J. W., Selke, G., Melson, A. K., Hershey, T., Craft, S., Richards, K., et al. (1999). Decreased memory performance in healthy humans induced by stress-level cortisol treatment. *Archives of General Psychiatry, 56*(6), 527–533.

Nibuya, M., Morinobu, S., & Duman, R. S. (1995). Regulation of BDNF and trkB mRNA in rat brain by chronic electroconvulsive seizure and antidepressant drug treatments. *Journal of Neuroscience, 15,* 7539–7547.

Oakes, M. A., & Hyman, I. E. (2001). The role of the self in false memory creation. In J. J. Freyd & A. P. DePrince (Eds.), *Trauma and cognitive science: A meeting of minds, science and human experience* (pp. 87–103). Binghamton, NY: The Haworth Maltreatment & Trauma Press.

Oitzl, M. S., & de Kloet, E. R. (1992). Selective corticosteroid antagonists modulate specific aspects of spatial orientation learning. *Behavioral Neuroscience, 106*(1), 62–71.

Paus, T., Zijdenbos, A., Worsley, K., Collins, D. L., Blumenthal, J., Giedd, J. N., et al. (1999). Structural maturation of neural pathways in children and adolescents: In vivo study. *Science, 283*(5409), 1908–1911.

Pezdek, K. (2007). Reply: It's just not good science. *Consciousness and Cognition, 16,* 29–30.

Pezdek, K., Finger, K., & Hodge, D. (1997). Planting false memories: The role of event plausibility. *Psychological Science, 8,* 437–441.

Pezdek, K., & Lam, S. (2007). What research paradigms have cognitive psychologist used to study "false memory," and what are the implications of these choices? *Consciousness and Cognition, 16,* 2–17.

Pfefferbaum, A., Mathalon, D. H., Sullivan, E. V., Rawles, J. M., Zipursky, R. B., & Lim, K. O. (1994). A quantitative magnetic resonance imaging study of changes in brain morphology from infancy to late adulthood. *Archives of Neurology, 34,* 71–75.

Pillemer, D. (1984). Flashbulb memories of the assassination attempt on President Reagan. *Cognition, 16,* 63–80.

Pitman, R. K. (2001). Investigating the pathogenesis of posttraumatic stress disorder with neuroimaging. *Journal of Clinical Psychiatry, 62,* 47–54.

Pitman, R. K., Orr, S. P., & Lasko, N. B. (1993). Effects of intranasal vasopressin and oxytocin on physiologic responding during personal combat imagery in Vietnam veterans with posttraumatic stress disorder. *Psychiatry Research, 48,* 107–117.

Porter, N. M., & Landfield, P. W. (1998). Stress hormones and brain aging. *Nature Neuroscience, 1,* 3–4.

Prigerson, H. G., Maciejewski, P. K., & Rosenheck, R. A. (2001). Combat trauma: Trauma with highest risk of delayed onset and unresolved posttraumatic stress disorder symptoms, unemployment, and abuse among men. *Journal of Nervous and Mental Disease, 189*(2), 99–108.

Putnam, F. W., Guroff, J. J., Silberman, E. K., Barban, L., & Post, R. M. (1986). The clinical phenomenology of multiple personality disorder: A review of 100 recent cases. *Journal of Clinical Psychiatry, 47,* 285–293.

Quas, J. A., Goodman, G. S., Bidrose, S., Pipe, M.-E., Craw, S., & Ablin, D. S. (1999). Emotion and memory: Children's long-term remembering, forgetting, and suggestibility. *Journal of Experimental Child Psychology, 72,* 235–270.

Quirk, G. J., Garcia, R., & Gonzalez-Lima, F. (2006). Prefrontal mechanisms in extinction of conditioned fear. *Biological Psychiatry, 60*(4), 337–343.

Radley, J. J., Sisti, H. M., Hao, J., Rocher, A. B., McCall, T., Hof, P. R., et al. (2004). Chronic behavioral stress induces apical dendritic reorganization in pyramidal neurons of the medial prefrontal cortex. *Neuroscience, 125*(1), 1–6.

Rapoport, J. L., Giedd, J. N., Blumenthal, J., Hamburger, S. D., Jeffries, N. O., Fernandez, T., et al. (1999). Progressive cortical change during adolescence in childhood-onset schizophrenia: A longitudinal magnetic resonance imaging study. *Archives of General Psychiatry, 56*(7), 649–654.

Roediger, H. L., & McDermott, K. B. (1995). Creating false memories: Remembering words not presented in lists. *Journal of Experimental Psychology: Learning, Memory and Cognition, 21,* 803–814.

Rubin, D. C., & Kozin, M. (1984). Vivid memories. *Cognition, 16,* 81–95.

Rudy, L., & Goodman, G. S. (1991). Effects of participation on children's reports: Implications for children's testimony. *Developmental Psychology, 27,* 527–538.

Saigh, P. A., & Bremner, J. D. (1999). *Posttraumatic stress disorder: A comprehensive text.* Needham Heights, MA: Allyn & Bacon.

Saigh, P. A., Mroweh, M., & Bremner, J. D. (1997). Scholastic impairments among traumatized adolescents. *Behavioral Research and Therapy, 35,* 429–436.

Saigh, P. A., Yasik, A. E., Oberfield, R. A., Halamandaris, P. V., & Bremner, J. D. (2006). The intellectual performance of traumatized children and adolescents with or without posttraumatic stress disorder. *Journal of Abnormal Psychology,* 332–340.

Santarelli, L., Saxe, M., Gross, C., Surget, A., Battaglia, F., Dulawa, S., et al. (2003a). Requirement of hippocampal neurogenesis for the behavioral effects of antidepressants. *Science, 301*(5634), 805–809.

Santarelli, L., Saxe, M., Gross, C., Surget, A., Battaglia, F., Dulawa, S., et al. (2003b). Requirement of hippocampal neurogenesis for the behavioral effects of antidepressants. *Science, 301,* 805–809.

Sapolsky, R. M. (1996). Why stress is bad for your brain. *Science, 273,* 749–750.

Sapolsky, R. M., Uno, H., Rebert, C. S., & Finch, C. E. (1990). Hippocampal damage associated with prolonged glucocorticoid exposure in primates. *Journal of Neuroscience, 10,* 2897–2902.

Saywitz, K. J., Goodman, G. S., Nicholas, E., & Moan, S. F. (1991). Children's memories of a physical examination involving genital touch: Implications for reports of child sexual abuse. *Journal of Consulting and Clinical Psychology, 59,* 682–691.

Schacter, D. L. (1996). *Searching for memory: The brain, the mind, and the past.* New York: Basic Books.

Schacter, D. L., Coyle, J. T., Fischbach, G. D., Mesulam, M. M., & Sullivan, L. E. (1995). *Memory distortion: The brain, the mind, and the past.* Cambridge, MA: Harvard University Press.

Schiffer, F., Teicher, M. H., & Papanicolaou, A. C. (1995). Evoked potential evidence for right brain activity during the recall of traumatic memories. *Journal of Neuropsychiatry & Clinical Neuroscience, 7,* 169–175.

Schmahl, C. G., Elzinga, B. M., Vermetten, E., Sanislow, C., McGlashan, T. H., & Bremner, J. D. (2003a). Neural correlates of memories of abandonment in women with and without borderline personality disorder. *Biological Psychiatry, 54,* 42–51.

Schmahl, C. G., Vermetten, E., Elzinga, B. M., & Bremner, J. D. (2003b). Magnetic resonance imaging of hippocampal and amygdala volume in women with childhood abuse and borderline personality disorder. *Psychiatry Research: Neuroimaging, 122,* 193–198.

Schmahl, C. G., Vermetten, E., Elzinga, B. M., & Bremner, J. D. (2004). A positron emission tomography study of memories of childhood abuse in borderline personality disorder. *Biological Psychiatry, 55,* 759–765.

Shin, L. M., McNally, R. J., Kosslyn, S. M., Thompson, W. L., Rauch, S. L., Alpert, N. M., et al. (1999). Regional cerebral blood flow during script-driven imagery in childhood sexual abuse-related PTSD: A PET investigation. *American Journal of Psychiatry, 156,* 575–584.

Southwick, S. M., Horner, B., Morgan, C. A., Bremner, J. D., Davis, M., Cahill, L., et al. (2002). Relationship of enhanced norepinephrine activity during memory consolidation to enhanced long-term memory in humans. *American Journal of Psychiatry, 159,* 1420–1422.

Sowell, E. R., Thompson, P. M., Holmes, C. J., Batth, R., Jernigan, T. L., & Toga, A. W. (1999). Localizing age-related changes in brain structure between childhood and adolescence using statistical parametric mapping. *NeuroImage, 9,* 587–597.

Stein, M. B., Hanna, C., Vaerum, V., & Koverola, C. (1999). Memory functioning in adult women traumatized by childhood sexual abuse. *Journal of Traumatic Stress, 12*(3), 527–534.

Stein, M. B., Koverola, C., Hanna, C., Torchia, M. G., & McClarty, B. (1997). Hippocampal volume in women victimized by childhood sexual abuse. *Psychological Medicine, 27,* 951–959.

Stein, M. B., Yehuda, R., Koverola, C., & Hanna, C. (1997). Enhanced dexamethasone suppression of plasma cortisol in adult women traumatized by childhood sexual abuse. *Biological Psychiatry, 42,* 680–686.

Thompson, P. M., Giedd, J. N., Woods, R. P., MacDonald, D., Evans, A. C., & Toga, A. W. (2000). Growth patterns in the developing brain detected by using continuum mechanical tensor maps. *Nature, 404*(6774), 190–193.

Usher, J. N., & Neisser, U. (1993). Childhood amnesia and the beginnings of memory for four early life events. *Journal of Experimental Psychology: General, 122,* 155–165.

Vermetten, E., & Bremner, J. D. (2002a). Circuits and systems in stress. I. Preclinical studies. *Depression & Anxiety, 15,* 126–147.

Vermetten, E., & Bremner, J. D. (2002b). Circuits and systems in stress. II. Applications to neurobiology and treatment of PTSD. *Depression & Anxiety, 16,* 14–38.

Vermetten, E., Schmahl, C., Lindner, S., Loewenstein, R. J., & Bremner, J. D. (2006). Hippocampal and amygdalar volumes in dissociative identity disorder. *American Journal of Psychiatry, 163,* 1–8.

Vermetten, E., Vythilingam, M., Southwick, S. M., Charney, D. S., & Bremner, J. D. (2003). Long-term treatment with paroxetine increases verbal declarative memory and hippocampal volume in posttraumatic stress disorder. *Biological Psychiatry, 54*(7), 693–702.

Wade, K. A., Sharman, S. J., Garry, M., Memon, A., Mazzoni, G., Merckelbach, H., et al. (2007). False claims about false memory research. *Consciousness and Cognition, 16,* 18–28.

Watanabe, Y., Gould, E., Daniels, D. C., Cameron, H., & McEwen, B. S. (1992). Tianeptine attenuates stress-induced morphological changes in the hippocampus. *European Journal of Pharmacology, 222,* 157–162.

Watanabe, Y. E., Gould, H., Cameron, D., Daniels, D., & McEwen, B. S. (1992). Phenytoin prevents stress and corticosterone induced atrophy of ca3 pyramidal neurons. *Hippocampus, 2,* 431–436.

Widom, C. S., & Morris, S. (1997). Accuracy of adult recollections of childhood victimization: Part 2. Childhood sexual abuse. *Psychological Assessment, 9*(1), 34–46.

Williams, L. M. (1994). Recall of childhood trauma: A prospective study of women's memories of child sexual abuse. *Journal of Consulting and Clinical Psychology, 62,* 1167–1176.

Williams, L. M., & Banyard, V. L. (Eds.). (1999). *Trauma and memory.* London: SAGE.

Wolf, O. T. (2003). HPA axis and memory. *Best practice & research. Clinical endocrinology and metabolism, 17,* 287–299.

Wolf, O. T., Schommer, N. C., Hellhammer, D. H., McEwen, B. S., & Kirschbaum, C. (2001). The relationship between stress induced cortisol levels and memory differs between men and women. *Psychoneuroendocrinology, 26,* 711–720.

Yen, S., Shea, M. T., Battle, C. L., Johnson, D. M., Zlotnick, C., Dolan-Sewell, R., et al. (2002). Traumatic exposure and posttraumatic stress disorder in borderline, schizotypal, avoidant, and obsessive-compulsive personality disorders: Findings from the collaborative longitudinal personality disorders study. *Journal of Nervous and Mental Disease, 190*(8), 510–518.

Zola-Morgan, S. M., & Squire, L. R. (1990). The primate hippocampal formation: Evidence for a time-limited role in memory storage. *Science, 250,* 288–290.

2

Trajectories of Neurobehavioral Development

The Clinical Neuroscience of Child Abuse

CARRYL P. NAVALTA, AKEMI TOMODA,
AND MARTIN H. TEICHER

Over the past 20 years, our research has focused on elucidating the developmental effects of child abuse (CA) at the behavioral and neurobiological levels. In parallel, a cadre of behavioral scientists and neuroscientists has collectively established a substantial body of work on the etiology, course, and outcome of CA (for reviews, see Glaser, 2000; Heim & Nemeroff, 2002; Kaufman & Charney, 2001; Putnam, 2003; Tarullo & Gunnar, 2006; Teicher et al., 2003; Teicher, Tomoda, & Andersen, 2006). From a nosological perspective, CA is considered a traumatic stressor and precursor to the development of post-traumatic stress disorder (PTSD) as defined in the *Diagnostic and Statistical Manual of Mental Disorders* (4th ed., text rev.) *(DSM-IV-TR)* (American Psychiatric Association, 2000). In addition, several other psychiatric conditions are associated with CA—most notably depression, anxiety, borderline personality disorder, dissociation, and substance use disorders. The central tenet to our work (and that of others) is that the stress that results from CA has an unfavorable effect on neurodevelopment and, consequently, behavioral development.

In this chapter, we will review what is known about the clinical neuroscience of CA and provide new findings on neuroanatomical effects of CA and their relation with memory processes.

Child abuse is but one of many forms of early adverse experiences. Sigmund Freud (1896/1959) outlined one of the first theories of the causal role that sexual abuse during childhood plays in the development of psychopathology. Historically, CA has also included physical abuse and neglect. Precise definitions notwithstanding, these types of maltreatment are common worldwide and are the primary problems that child protective/social services address. More recently, researchers have a renewed interest in understanding the impact of emotional abuse—typically manifested as either verbal abuse/aggression or the witnessing of domestic violence—on mental health. In fact, initial evidence suggests that emotional abuse also functions as a traumatic stressor; is a marked risk factor for later psychopathology; and may prove to have more detrimental effects than the traditional forms of CA (Grilo & Masheb, 2001; Kaplan & Klinetob, 2000; Simeon, Guralnik, Schmeidler, Sirof, & Knutelska, 2001; Teicher, Samson, Polcari, & McGreenery, 2006).

Our research endeavors have been predicated on the conjecture that stress in the form of CA negatively affects neurodevelopment, which in turn can result in disordered behavior, thought, and emotion. In support of this contention, a vast array of preclinical studies have demonstrated that brain development is sculpted by early experience and that specific brain regions are particularly sensitive to the effects of early stress (Kaufman, Plotsky, Nemeroff, & Charney, 2000; Teicher, Tomoda, et al., 2006). For example, initial work by Berrebi, Fitch, Ralphe, Denenberg, Friedrich, and Denenberg (1988) showed that early handling influences corpus callosum development, particularly in male rats. Not surprisingly, human studies have provided evidence that the corpus callosum is particularly sensitive to the effects of CA (De Bellis et al., 1999; De Bellis et al., 2002; Teicher et al., 2004; Teicher et al., 1997). Utilizing a hypothetico-deductive approach, we proposed a clinical model in which a cascade of events produces CA effects and that this succession is primarily mediated by stress that results in the release of stress hormones (cortisol, adrenalin, and vasopressin) and enhances the turnover of neurotransmitters (e.g., dopamine, serotonin, and norepinephrine) in key brain regions (Teicher, 2000; Teicher, Andersen, Polcari, Anderson,& Navalta,2002;Teicher et al.,2003). Such stress-induced neurochemical alterations effect modifications in myelination, synaptogenesis, and neurogenesis. This model hinges on the premise that CA is perceived and responded to as a stressor, regardless of the parameters of the adverse experience, which directly impacts neurodevelopment.

Our Earlier Studies

We first began exploring the neurobiological underpinnings of CA by examining individuals with borderline personality disorder who had (a) symptoms indicative of temporal lobe epilepsy (TLE), (b) abnormal electroencephalograms (EEG) consisting of spike and sharp waves, and (c) findings of temporal mesial sclerosis or dilated temporal horns as observed with magnetic resonance imaging or computed tomography (Teicher, Glod, Surrey, & Swett, 1993). Given that these individuals all had a history of CA—together with animal models of kindling—we hypothesized that CA exerts a deleterious effect on limbic system electrophysiology or development. Using the Limbic System Checklist (LSCL-33) to assess symptoms typically encountered by persons with TLE during seizures with 253 consecutive admissions to an adult outpatient clinic, we found that scores were significantly elevated in subjects with a self-reported history of childhood sexual or physical abuse. For those subjects who experienced both physical and sexual abuse, LSCL-33 scores were comparable to subjects with documented TLE. In a subsequent study with 115 consecutive admissions to a child and adolescent center, the incidence of clinically significant EEG abnormalities (i.e., spike waves, sharp waves, and paroxysmal slowing) was observed to be markedly greater in children with abuse histories than those who were never exposed to abuse (Ito et al., 1993). Furthermore, children with a documented history of severe physical and/or sexual abuse had a 72% incidence of abnormal EEG readings. Contrary to the premise that the EEG abnormalities were preexisting, preclinical studies provide evidence that exposure to early stress can indeed induce such anomalies. For example, Heath and colleagues (Heath, 1973; Heath & Harper, 1974) studied monkeys raised in isolation by Harry Harlow and documented spike waves in the hippocampus and fastigial nuclei, which project from the cerebellar vermis to a variety of brain structures such as the hippocampus.

As a follow-up, we used EEG coherence to assess cortical maturation and differentiation (Ito, Teicher, Glod, & Ackerman, 1998) and found that the left cortex of 15 healthy right-handed children was more developed than their right cortex, which is consistent with what is known about the anatomy of the dominant hemisphere (Galaburda, 1991). In contrast, EEG coherence revealed that the right hemispheres were significantly more developed than the left hemispheres in 15 child psychiatric inpatients with a documented history of CA, even though all subjects were right-handed. Although coherence measures indicated that the right hemisphere of CA subjects was comparable to that of control subjects, their left hemisphere lagged substantially behind the left hemisphere of the healthy children. This lateralized effect of CA was further supported in a study by Schiffer, Teicher, and Papanicolaou (1995).

As previously noted, the corpus callosum is one brain area that has received recent attention in the CA literature. Advancing the pioneering preclinical contributions of Denenberg (Denenberg, 1983; Denenberg, Garbanati, Sherman, Yutzey, & Kaplan, 1978; Denenberg & Yutzey, 1985), Sanchez, Hearn, Do, Rilling, and Herndon (1998) observed diminished corpus callosal size, in particular the midsaggital area, of male rhesus monkeys that were raised in relative isolation compared to monkeys living in a seminatural environment. In parallel, we examined the corpus callosum in children hospitalized for psychiatric disorders and also found a substantial reduction in the midsaggital area of those children who additionally had a history of abuse or neglect, especially in males (Teicher et al., 1997). This finding was replicated in a more comprehensive study of children with abuse-related PTSD (De Bellis et al., 1999). Although the clinical consequences of reduced corpus callosum area are not fully understood, some preliminary work from our research program illustrates how this brain alteration might influence emotional memory (see below).

To more fully understand our limbic findings, we used T2 relaxometry—a noninvasive means of ascertaining resting regional cerebral blood volume (Teicher et al., 2000)—to examine the relationship between cerebellar vermis functionality and limbic irritability symptoms in young adults (Anderson, Teicher, Polcari, & Renshaw, 2002). A strong correlation was observed between T2 relaxation time and the degree of limbic irritability on the LSCL-33 in all subjects. However, at any level of limbic symptomatology, a marked decrease in the relative perfusion of the vermis appeared specific to those individuals who had CA histories. Consequently, we interpreted this finding as indicative of a functional impairment of cerebellar vermis activity. This conclusion is consistent with preclinical studies demonstrating that isolation-reared monkeys with behavioral disturbances have epileptiform spike and sharp-wave activity in their fastigial nucleus (output nucleus of the cerebellar vermis) and hippocampus (Heath, 1973; Heath & Harper 1974).

Other Studies

Emerging evidence about the effects of stress on the hippocampus suggests that a unique developmental trajectory exists. For example, two initial, separate studies conducted by De Bellis and colleagues (1999, 2002) using independent samples of children with PTSD secondary to CA indicate that the hippocampus is unaltered, at least in terms of volumetric size. More recent work has demonstrated that the hippocampus may actually be larger in children who have been abused (Tupler & De Bellis, 2006). However, studies with adults have painted a different picture, methodological limitations notwithstanding (Jelicic & Merckelbach, 2004). A decade ago, reports of reduced left hippocampal volume in adults with childhood trauma and a current diagnosis of PTSD or dissociative identity disorder first appeared in the literature (Bremner et al., 1997; Stein, 1997). Subsequently, significant reductions in hippocampal volume were observed in women with borderline personality disorder and a history of childhood abuse (Driessen et al., 2000) as well as in adult females with a history of prepubertal physical and/or sexual abuse and depression (Vythilingam et al., 2002). To our knowledge, no comparable studies have been conducted solely with adolescent youth who have CA histories.

In concert with other work found in the present book, a developmental psychopathology approach incorporating a longitudinal design is warranted to ascertain how the hippocampus, specifically, and the brain, in general, transform across childhood and adolescence toward adult maturity. One useful and important means of effecting this type of research is preclinical animal-modeling studies. In particular, rats have been successfully utilized in relatively brief time periods (i.e., days to weeks) to document brain changes longitudinally due to their protracted rate of development (Andersen, 2003). Such a model is also needed to support a causal role of the effects of stressful experiences, such as CA, on neurodevelopment. Retrospective clinical studies of CA cannot prove that alterations in brain morphology or function are actually a consequence of the abuse. Ethically, children also cannot (and should not ever!) be randomly assigned to an experimental group that is exposed to CA and compared to a group of children who do not receive such maltreatment. In contrast, animal research enables scientists to randomly assign juvenile rats to either an experimental stress exposure group or a control group and compare them at later stages of development. Specifically in rodents, the manipulation of levels of maternal care (an important species-relevant stressor) has been documented to affect brain structure and function. This type of handling has included the removal of the nursing dam from the pups for varying amounts of time (Andersen & Teicher, 2004; Kehoe, Shoemaker, Triano, Callahan, & Rappolt, 1998; Levine, 1967), the use of surrogate mothers (Harlow, Dodsworth, & Harlow, 1965), and the selection of population extremes of high- and low-quality maternal behaviors (Caldji, Diorio, & Meaney, 2000).

Recently, we conducted one such study to test the hypothesis that CA might exert an effect on neurodevelopment (i.e., smaller hippocampus) that only emerges at a much later stage of brain maturation (Andersen & Teicher, 2004). This postulate differs from ones stating that reduced hippocampal size is the culminating end product of years or decades of PTSD or depressive symptoms or that such a reduction is a preexisting risk factor associated with the emergence of psychopathology that persists into adulthood (Bremner, 2003; Gilbertson et al., 2002). Specifically, developing rats were stressed by periods of maternal separation and isolation that occurred between 2 and 20 days of age. Following this early stress exposure, the rats were sacrificed at weaning, peripubertal, young adult, or full adult ages. Using synaptophysin via immunohistochemistry as a marker of synaptic density, we found no significant difference in synaptophysin measures at weaning and peripubertal ages, but a marked rise (overproduction) in synaptic density at the young adult age in normal control rats that was not observed in rats exposed to early stress. Synaptic density declined at subsequent ages, presumably as a result of pruning, but differences in synaptic density remained between normal control rats versus those exposed to early stress. In parallel, our clinical work has elucidated significant bilateral reductions in hippocampal volume in subjects aged 18 to 22 years who were exposed to repeated childhood sexual abuse (unpublished observations).

The amygdala is another brain region that has received attention from stress and trauma researchers given its crucial role in fear conditioning, the formation and recollection of emotional memory, the learning of nonverbal motor patterns, and the triggering of fight-or-flight responses (Lang & Davis, 2006; LeDoux, 1996, 2003). Structural imaging studies of amygdala volume in abuse survivors with PTSD found no differences compared to control subjects (Bremner et al., 1997; De Bellis et al., 1999; Stein, 1997). Although an initial study by Driessen et al. (2000) reported an 8% reduction in bilateral amygdaloid volume in women with a history of CA and a diagnosis of borderline personality disorder (BPD), this finding was not independently replicated in a separate study of individuals with BPD (Brambilla et al., 2004). A smaller amygdala, however, has been documented in individuals with dissociative identity disorder (Vermetten, Schmahl, Lindner, Loewenstein, & Bremner, 2006)—a condition associated with a history of severe CA. In addition, increased activation of the left amygdala was recently observed during the acquisition phase of a conditioned fear paradigm in women with CA-related PTSD (Bremner et al., 2005). Because amygdala overactivation appears to be a critical factor in PTSD (Rauch et al., 2000; Shin, Rauch, & Pitman, 2006), we have hypothesized that a smaller amygdala provides protection from the emergence of PTSD following CA or facilitates recovery from the disorder.

Since our initial EEG coherence findings, subsequent studies by other investigators have provided further evidence that CA alters cortical neuronal development in humans. The anterior cingulate cortex seems especially vulnerable, even across developmental stages. For example, in 11 children and adolescents who met *DSM-IV* criteria for PTSD secondary to CA, a significant reduction in the N-acetylaspartate:creatine ratio (an index of neuronal density and viability) was detected via magnetic resonance spectroscopy, which is indicative of neuronal loss and dysfunction in this brain area (De Bellis, Keshavan, Spencer, & Hall, 2000). In addition, Bremner and colleagues (2005) have documented decreased volume of the right anterior cingulate cortex in adults with CA-related PTSD as well as diminished anterior cingulate function during the extinction phase of a conditioned fear paradigm. Declines in functioning have also been seen in the right temporal pole/anterior fusiform gyrus, left precuneus, and posterior cingulate cortex of adults with histories of CA and a current diagnosis of borderline personality disorder (Lange, Kracht, Herholz, Sachsse, & Irle, 2005). Additional developmental effects were reported by Carrion et al. (2001), who found attenuated frontal lobe asymmetry and smaller total brain and cerebral volumes in 24 children (7 to 14 years of age) with a history of CA and PTSD symptoms. Together, these studies suggest that the effects of CA alter the normal developmental trajectory of the neocortex.

Expanded Neurobioevolutional Model

Simply put, our initial guiding hypothesis was that CA is a substantial stressor that serves as an antecedent to a succession of developmental brain modifications and associated behavioral dysfunction. Subsequently, this stance was held and expressed by other investigators (Bremner, 1999; Nelson & Carver, 1998; Penza, Heim, & Nemeroff, 2003). Our recent theorizing, however, expands upon this original position and couches the consequences of CA in an evolutionary framework that also incorporates the types of sensory and perceptual stimulation that are experienced as well as windows of sensitivity (Teicher, 2002; Teicher et al., 2003; Teicher, Tomoda, et al., 2006). The following postulates encapsulate our current thinking:

1. The brain goes through one or more sensitive periods in post-natal life when exposure to high levels of stress hormones selects for an alternative pathway of neurodevelopment.
2. The ensuing developmental trajectory is an adaptive one.
3. Exposure to corticosteroids is a keystone element in organizing the brain to develop in this manner.
4. Disparate brain systems are affected by different forms of abuse (e.g., sexual, physical, verbal), particularly the primary and secondary sensory systems that may be especially involved in perceiving or recalling the trauma.

Implications for the Development of Memory

With this updated model, early stress in the form of CA induces neurodevelopmental modifications that are triggered by the nature of the experiences during critical, sensitive stages. These changes are, in effect, an adaptive response that is intended to allow individuals who are exposed to such stress to become accustomed to elevated levels of stress or deprivation throughout life. Assuming that the development of memory hinges on certain brain regions and systems (e.g., hippocampus), memory processes are thus predicted to be negatively impacted when CA occurs during those time frames of sensitivity for those very regions and systems. In other words, depending in part on the chronological or developmental age when CA happens, disparate memorial outcomes will arise. If an individual is born into a harsh, cruel, and stress-ridden environment, the sequelae of CA on later development may serve as an adaptation whereby the individual can call upon memory processes and skills to guide behavior for survival. In contrast, these modifications are less optimal for thriving in more benevolent circumstances in which memory is needed to succeed in prosocial endeavors.

The consequences of corticosteroids are also hypothesized to be a primary mechanism for this altered trajectory of neurodevelopment. Not surprisingly, the hippocampus possesses a high density of glucocorticoid receptors (Patel et al., 2000) and plays, in concert, a major role in memory processing, specifically the encoding and retrieval of episodic information (Desgranges, Baron, & Eustache, 1998; Squire & Zola-Morgan, 1991). This brain region has been shown to be particularly vulnerable to prolonged exposure to stress hormones (Sapolsky, Krey, & McEwen, 1985). Pyramidal cell morphology alterations, pyramidal cell death, and suppression of new granule cell production can all be effected by exposure to stress or corticosteroids (Gould & Tanapat, 1999; Sapolsky, Uno, Rebert, & Finch, 1990). Conversely, evolution may have played a role in keeping the maturing hippocampus intact. Known as the "stress hyporesponsive" period in rodents (Oliver, Boudouresque, Lacroix, Anglade, & Grino, 1994), this early, postnatal developmental window prohibits a sizeable glucocorticoid response to a large number of stressors, which in turn protects the hippocampus from overexposure to glucocorticoids. Thus, memory processes that rely on hippocampal function may be safeguarded developmentally from the effects of CA—evidence to date supports this premise (see further on)—although deficits in memory may become unmasked at a later point in time.

Lastly, we postulate that CA influences neurodevelopment specific to the sensory modalities to which the abuse is delivered and received. That is, neural systems unique to auditory (including verbal), visual, tactile, olfactory, and kinesthetic stimulation are hypothesized to be negatively impacted depending on which stimuli are encoded. In a coming section, we provide preliminary evidence that the effects of exposure to CA preferentially rely on different sensory modalities for encoding experiences and environments.

Specifically, the left primary and secondary visual cortices seem especially sensitive to the consequences of childhood sexual abuse, which apparently is associated with a decrement in visual recognition memory.

Memory, Its Systems, and Their Development

At its most basic level, memory has been conceptualized as a process in which events influence the brain and its future activity (Siegel, 2001). However, memory is presently understood as a multifactorial phenomenon that includes, but is not limited to, the timing of the remembered event (immediate, recent, remote), the type of processing that is activated (encoding, storage, retrieval), strategies used to enhance processing (e.g., rehearsal), the sensory modalities that are impinged upon (e.g., auditory, visual), and context-dependent factors (e.g., physical setting parameters). Notwithstanding, all of memory is memory of our own mental activity. That is, what is remembered is our processing of external events in the environment, not the events themselves (Siegler, 2004).

The current zeitgeist holds that "memory" is an overall descriptor for multiple memory types and that several neurobiological systems underlie them (Eichenbaum, 2001; Schacter, 2000; Squire, 2004). One major type of memory is known as declarative (or explicit) memory, which refers to the capacity to consciously recall facts and events. Declarative memory is typically divided into semantic memory (i.e., facts about the world) and episodic memory (i.e., the capacity to reexperience an event in the context in which it originally occurred; Tulving, 1983). This type of memory, which is representational in that the memories model the external world—whether it be true or false, is the kind that is impaired in amnesia, and is dependent on structures in the medial temporal lobe and midline diencephalon. Laterally, semantic recall is centered more on left hippocampal activation, whereas autobiographical recall is more right-lateralized (Wheeler, Stuss, & Tulving, 1997).

Nondeclarative memory, on the other hand, is an umbrella term referring to several additional memory systems (Schacter & Tulving, 1994; Squire & Zola-Morgan, 1988). In contrast, nondeclarative memory is dispositional and nonreportable, involves multiple acquisition trials, is expressed through performance rather than recollection, is neither true nor false, and may not involve the self. At an elementary level, associative learning represents this type of memory. In fact, neurobiological studies of Pavlovian conditioning illustrate that at least three disparate memory systems are engaged: (1) a sensorimotor system that depends on cerebellar circuitry, (2) an affective system that is intimately tied to amygdala circuitry, and (3) a cognitive system that is dependent on the hippocampus (Stanton, 2000). Regardless of the true number, the various memory systems operate in parallel to support behavior.

With human developmental studies, declarative and nondeclarative memories have been shown to be distinguishable early in life (Nelson & Carver, 1998; Nelson & Webb, 2003). The emergence of declarative memory coincides with the maturation of the medial temporal lobe, which includes the hippocampus and the orbitofrontal cortex (Kelley et al., 1998; Mishkin, Suzuki, Gadian, & Vargha-Khadem, 1997; Mishkin, Vargha-Khadem, & Gadian, 1998; Perner & Ruffman, 1995). Specifically in infants, this type of memory largely reflects response to novelty, which is subserved by the hippocampus (Bachevalier, Brickson, & Hagger, 1993; Zola et al., 2000). After the first year, the inferotemporal and rhinal cortices improve their connectivity with the hippocampus, which allows for greater proficiency in more demanding memory tasks as well as longer retention intervals (Nelson & Webb, 2003). Moreover, Bachevalier and Vargha-Khadem (2005) have proposed that the hippocampus processes the encoding and retrieval of context-rich episodes and events while the perirhinal and entorhinal cortices underlie the formation of context-free cognitive memories.

Historically, nondeclarative memory has been presumed to be functional at an earlier age and to have a different developmental trajectory than declarative memory. In humans, a visual-perceptual representation system appears to be functional by 4 months of age and allows infants to notice perceptual similarities across time (Nelson & Webb, 2003). Even at birth, infants seem guided by rule-based behavior and early on demonstrate various motor, perceptual, and cognitive skills (DiGiulio, Seidenberg, O'Leary, & Raz, 1994). Both of these systems mature across several developmental stages as contingencies become more complex and motor tasks are more demanding. We have speculated that the underpinning neurobiological process is a refinement of neural connections via synaptic elimination/pruning (Andersen, Thompson, Rutstein, Hostetter, & Teicher, 2000; Teicher, Andersen, & Hostetter, 1995). Motorically, the affected brain areas would include the striatum and cerebellum. In addition, improvements in working memory would allow for behavior to be governed by more complex rule-based contingencies and for predicting possible outcomes of such responding (Nelson & Webb, 2003). The dorsolateral prefrontal cortex has been implicated as the neural substrate of working memory (Andreasen et al., 1995; Arnsten, 2000). Because rules for behavior are often made and upheld by adult authority figures (e.g., parents, teachers), a better understanding of socialization practices and the social environment where children's memory skills emerge and become consolidated is needed (Ornstein & Haden, 2001; Ornstein, Haden, & Hedrick, 2004).

Stress Effects on Memory

In essence, neural and behavioral development have an interdependent relationship that relies on reciprocal processing activities. Thus, one postulate is that if the process is somehow dramatically perturbed (either endogenously or exogenously), then the associated memory systems would take an altered developmental trajectory. Early damage to the hippocampus, including perinatal, results in a substantial loss of context-rich memory abilities (Bachevalier & Vargha-Khadem, 2005). High-dose prednisone treatment for children with asthma is associated with lower verbal memory skills than low-dose treatment (Bender, Lerner, & Poland, 1991). Given such findings, Nelson and Carver (1998) hypothesized that the developing nervous system is vulnerable to the deleterious chronic effects of stress on memory. Specifically, these investigators predicted that hippocampal-dependent memory should be negatively affected by substantial stress because of the effects of stress hormones on cell birth and death in the hippocampus, especially when this region is exposed to such stress during immature and vulnerable periods. Andersen and Teicher (2004) found in rats that early severe stress is associated with reduced synaptic numbers in the hippocampal region. Other developmental studies in rats indicate that fear conditioning with auditory versus visual stimuli has different ontogenetic profiles (Hunt & Campbell, 1997; Moye & Rudy, 1987), which suggests that an interaction exists between the developing hippocampus and the memory systems mediating auditory and visual learning (Stanton, 2000). However, the process in which early experience in humans influences the neurodevelopment that underlies the development of memory remains unclear (Howe, Cicchetti, & Toth, 2006; Howe, Toth, & Cicchetti, 2006).

Reduced memory performance has been shown to be more closely associated with chronic rather than acute stress (Jelicic & Bonke, 2001) as well as severe stress (Anda et al., 2006; Bremner, Vermetten, Afzal, & Vythilingam, 2004). In the study by Anda and colleagues (2006) with an epidemiological sample of 8,708 adult HMO members, a 4.4-fold increase in risk for impaired autobiographical memory of childhood was observed for persons who endorsed four or more adverse childhood experiences (e.g., abuse, witnessing domestic violence, serious household dysfunction). In addition, a dose-response relationship was seen between the extent of adverse childhood experiences and the number of age periods affected for memory disturbance. Such deficits in memory do not appear to be a function of decreased intellectual capacity (Bremner et al., 2004; but see Perez & Widom, 1994). Adult studies have also demonstrated that stress-related, glucocorticoid exposure effects possess an inverted U-shape function with memory (Andreano & Cahill, 2006). That is, stress appears to have opposite effects on memory depending on the duration and chronicity. Consolidation—a process that effects a more stable and consistent form of memory—is typically found to be enhanced by low doses of glucocorticoids (Roozendaal, 2002, 2003). However, a recent study in healthy females suggests that the glucocorticoid cortisol, induced by an acute stress challenge, negatively influences long-term consolidation of declarative memories—at least with a 24-hour retention interval (Elzinga, Bakker, & Bremner, 2005).

Because the hippocampus has a high density of glucocorticoid receptors, is particularly vulnerable to the effects of stress hormones and plays an integral role in the encoding and retrieval of declarative memory, this brain region has received significant attention from investigators of chronic and traumatic stress, especially in adults. Elzinga and Bremner (2002), for example, recently conceptualized PTSD as a memory disorder in which the intrusive memories and declarative memory function deficits (as well as the stress response) are intimately tied to the hippocampus. To date, few studies of the brain and memory have been conducted in traumatized individuals (Howe, Toth, & Cicchetti, 2006). Although findings thus far are suggestive, hippocampal abnormalities are not necessarily associated with memory deficits in individuals with PTSD (Jelicic & Merckelbach, 2004).

Bremner and colleagues have provided much of the evidence to support the association between hippocampal anomalies and memory impairment.

In one of the earliest studies in this field, Bremner et al. (1997) examined 17 adults with histories of CA and current PTSD and 17 control subjects matched for age, demographic characteristics, and alcohol abuse. The authors found that subjects with PTSD had a 12% smaller left hippocampal volume than control subjects and performed poorer on several verbal memory tasks. However, no memory tests were correlated with hippocampal volume. A follow-up study was conducted using positron emission tomography (PET) in 22 women with histories of child sexual abuse (Bremner et al., 1999). Their findings demonstrated that abuse memories (reactivated via auditory, personalized event scripts) are associated with decreased blood flow in right hippocampus (as well as fusiform/inferior temporal and supramarginal gyri and visual association cortex) in women with PTSD relative to those without PTSD. Further support for the association between hippocampal-related memory dysfunction and PTSD comes from a more recent study by Bremner et al. (2003). In their study, women with CA-related PTSD showed greater decreases in blood flow in several brain areas, including the left hippocampus, during retrieval of emotionally valenced word pairs, but not with neutral word pairs. Moreover, the manifest memory deficits appear to be specific to the verbal (versus visual) domain, independent of intelligence, but negatively correlated with PTSD symptom levels and severity of CA (Bremner et al., 2004).

CA-related borderline personality disorder (BPD) is another condition documented to be related to memory impairments. In an earlier study by O'Leary, Brouwers, Gardner, and Cowdry (1991), 16 research outpatients with BPD were compared to a group of 16 healthy volunteers using a battery of neuropsychological tests. The individuals with BPD were significantly impaired on memory tests requiring uncued recall of complex, recently learned material, which was not attributable to attentional problems, psychomotor impairment, current major depression, or history of alcohol abuse. In 21 females with BPD, Driessen et al. (2000) found 16% and 8% bilateral volume reductions of the hippocampus and amygdala, respectively. However, memory performance for this group was related to depressive symptoms rather than hippocampal volume. Two studies by Schmahl and colleagues (2003, 2004) used PET on women with and without BPD and found blood flow differences in the anterior cingulate and dorsolateral prefrontal cortex that were dependent on the types of memory reactivated. That is, hypometabolism was observed in these brain regions while subjects listened to personal CA scripts whereas memories of abandonment were associated with increased blood flow in bilateral dorsolateral prefrontal cortex. In addition, abandonment memories were associated with greater decreases in right anterior cingulate. Lastly, Lange et al. (2005) found regional hypometabolism in temporal and medial parietal cortical regions—areas intimately tied to episodic memory consolidation and retrieval—as well as strong correlations between impaired memory performance and metabolic activity in ventromedial and lateral temporal cortices in individuals with BPD.

Evidence from our research program suggests that the effects of CA-related stress on memory do not necessarily hinge upon the presence of a current psychiatric diagnosis. First, support for this hypothesis comes from an electrophysiological study utilizing probe auditory evoked potentials (Schiffer et al., 1995). Adults with a history of CA who were all currently well-functioning and had no active *DSM-IV* Axis I diagnosis were asked to actively recall a neutral or work-related memory, and then a disturbing memory from childhood with related affect. For psychologically healthy individuals with no trauma histories, both hemispheres appeared to be equally involved in the recall of these memories. In contrast, adults with a history of CA demonstrated a marked suppression of the evoked potential response over the left hemisphere during recall of the neutral memory, which is indicative of increased left hemispheric processing. In addition, a robust shift in laterality was observed, with the evoked potential response being suppressed over the right hemisphere during recall of the disturbing memory, indicating enhanced right hemispheric activation. These findings are consistent with the contention that CA is associated with an increase in hemispheric laterality together with a decrease in hemispheric integration. A recent follow-up study by Schiffer et al. (2007) suggests that the emotional valence of individuals with histories of CA can be lateralized in either hemisphere, but that the laterality of negative emotions in the left hemisphere, in particular, is associated with poorer memory (especially for visual information).

Second, Navalta, Polcari, Webster, Boghossian, and Teicher (2006) examined 26 young women (mean age = 20.0 years) with histories of childhood sexual abuse—most of whom (73%) had no current *DSM-IV* Axis I diagnosis. We found a strong graded association between duration of CA by the most closely related perpetrator (parent > sibling > uncle > other family > friend > authority figure > stranger/acquaintance) and memory function. Specifically, 2-point reductions in short-term, verbal, visual, and global memory scores were observed for every year that abuse occurred (standard scores; mean = 100, standard deviation [SD] = 15). Neither current symptoms of depression, anxiety, or PTSD nor a history of these disorders had a significant influence on this strong relationship. Although no difference between CA subjects and the contrast group was found on overall global memory, the CA group did exhibit lower visual span, but they also displayed superior verbal span. If the findings that childhood sexual abuse produces a duration-dependent decrease in memory function were true, then some of the CA subjects might actually have had quite high memory scores if they had never been abused.

In contrast to studies with adults, findings from child studies on the relationship between stress exposure and memory are scant and negative overall. Recent comprehensive reviews by Howe, Cicchetti, et al. (2006) and Howe, Toth, et al. (2006) clearly illustrate that evidence to date does not support the premise that stress causes memory deficits in children. Specific to children with abuse histories, basic memory performance does not distinguish them from demographically similar comparison children who have not been abused. For example, children with abuse histories apparently perform as well as (and possibly better than) nonabused children on daily memory tasks (Howe, Cicchetti, Toth, & Cerrito, 2004). Eisen, Qin, Goodman, and Davis (2002) evaluated children's memory and suggestibility about a medical examination and clinical assessment and found that children who were abused were just as likely to confuse details about the examination as children without abuse histories. In a study by Howe et al. (2004), children who were abused and from low socioeconomic backgrounds were assessed for the development of false memories. Similar to the findings of Eisen and colleagues (2002), both children with and without abuse histories demonstrated false memories, and the number of such memories increased with age at an equivalent rate. Overall, children from lower socioeconomic backgrounds had the poorest memory performance, regardless of abuse status. In addition, abuse-related PTSD (Beers & De Bellis, 2002; Moradi, Doost, Taghavi, Yule, & Dalgleish, 1999), dissociation (Eisen et al., 2002), and depression (Orbach, Lamb, Sternberg, Williams, & Dawud-Noursi, 2001) do not appear to be associated with memory deficits in children.

Recently, Porter, Lawson, and Bigler (2005) conducted a well-designed study examining memory and intellectual functioning in 24 children who were sexually abused compared to 24 physically and behaviorally healthy children with no abuse histories, matched for demographic characteristics. Five subtests of the Wechsler Intelligence Scale for Children (3rd ed.) and the Test of Memory and Learning (TOMAL) were administered. Mean scores illustrate that the CA group was functioning within the average range of memory and intellectual functioning. First-pass analyses indicate that the children with abuse histories scored lower than comparison children on several of the TOMAL indices, including verbal memory, attention/concentration, sequential recall, and free recall—even when statistically controlling for socioeconomic status. However, these differences were no longer apparent between the two groups after controlling for both socioeconomic status and intelligence. In addition, the presence of PTSD did not have a differential effect on cognitive function between CA subjects who currently had the disorder from those who did not. Porter and colleagues (2005) concluded that this sample of children who were sexually abused did not possess a distinct pattern of memory impairment.

Recent Findings

The following is preliminary evidence obtained from a group of young adults with histories of childhood sexual abuse who underwent a comprehensive diagnostic interview, neuropsychological testing, and brain magnetic resonance imaging.

Method and Participants

Subjects selected for study were right-handed, healthy, unmedicated young adults (18 to 22 years of age), with excellent hearing and visual acuity, recruited from the community by advertisements targeted toward college students. They were selected based on (a) a complete absence of exposure to trauma or (b) a self-reported history of exposure to repeated childhood sexual abuse (CSA, defined as at least three episodes of forced sexual contact accompanied by threats of harm to self or others and feelings of fear or terror, which occurred before age 18 years and at least 2 years prior to enrollment). Subjects were excluded who had any history of substance abuse, any recent substance use, brain injury with loss of consciousness, significant fetal exposure to alcohol or drugs, perinatal or neonatal complications, neurological disorders, or medical conditions that could adversely affect growth and development. Control subjects had no history of Axis I psychopathology (*DSM-IV*). The McLean Hospital Institutional Review Board approved all procedures. The purpose and meaning of this study were explained to subjects, who gave their written informed consent. Screenings were conducted on 720 volunteers to recruit 30 subjects with CSA and 30 control subjects for MRI evaluation. A disproportionate number of subjects with CSA were female. Hence, we limited this study to 23 females with CSA (mean age = 19.1 years; SD = 1.1 years) and to 14 female control subjects (mean age = 20.1 years; SD = 1.3 years) with complete MRI scans. The detailed selection process is published elsewhere (Navalta et al., 2006).

Four subjects with CSA had current major depressive disorder (MDD), 4 had post-traumatic stress disorder (PTSD), and 1 had depersonalization disorder. Abuse and control subjects were predominantly middle class or higher (96%); both groups had similar measures of parental socioeconomic status (SES; Hollingshead, 1975; $F[1, 35] = 0.35, p = .26$), and cognitive abilities as evaluated using the Memory Assessment Scale (MAS; Williams, 1991; global memory = 117 ± 10.1 versus $114 \pm 14.2; F[1, 35] = 0.36, p = .46$), and subjects' reports of Scholastic Aptitude Test (SAT) scores (scores = 1246 ± 145 versus $1299 \pm 103; F[1, 29] = 2.1, p = .26$).

MRI images were acquired on a General Electric Medical Systems (Milwaukee, WI) 1.5T Horizon LX Echo Speed scanner (Level 8.4) with a prototype Pathway MRI quadrature, receive-only, volume head coil. The Pathway coil provides an approximately 35% improvement in signal-to-noise ratio over the standard quadrature head coil. The anatomical image series consisted of T1-weighted sagittals, T2-weighted sagittals, T2-weighted axials, volumetric T1-weighted coronals, and anatomical dual echo axials (proton and T2-weighted). Parameters for the volumetric T1-weighted coronal images were three-dimensional, Fourier transform, spoiled gradient recalled acquisition (3DFT, SPGR) pulse sequence (TR = 35, TE = 5 ms/Fr; Flip angle = 45 degrees, FOV = 22×16 cm, 1.5 mm slice with no skip, 256×192 matrix, 1 NEX). Voxel-based morphometry (VBM) was performed using SPM2 for imaging processing (Ashburner & Friston, 2000; Good et al., 2001; Okada, Tanaka, Kuratsune, Watanabe, & Sadato, 2004) running in MATLAB 6.5 (The MathWorks Inc., Natick, MA, USA). VBM is a fully automated whole-brain morphometric technique that detects regional structural differences between groups on a voxel-by-voxel basis. Briefly, images were segmented into

gray matter, white matter, cerebrospinal fluid, and skull/scalp compart-
ments, then normalized to standard space and resegmented. Any volume
changes induced by normalization were adjusted. The spatially normalized segments of gray and white matter were smoothed using a 12 mm,
full-width, half-maximum, isotropic Gaussian kernel. Statistical analysis
of regional differences between groups was performed using a permutation test for decreased probability of a particular voxel containing gray or
white matter. Potential confounding effects of SES and whole segment
gray matter volume (GMV) differences were modeled. Variances attributable to them were excluded from analysis. The significance levels for
statistics estimated by permutation tests were set at $p < 0.05$, corrected
for multiple comparisons. Within the areas showing a significant volume
reduction in subjects, linear correlates between volume reduction and the
neuropsychiatric assessment and evaluation of neuropsychological and
cognitive functions were examined under the threshold of $p < 0.001$
to compensate for multiple comparisons. VBM is a potentially powerful
technique for identifying morphometric differences between groups, but
hinges on a number of assumptions, particularly the accuracy of image
coregistration (Bookstein, 2001).

Psychometric evaluation included the Structured Clinical Interview
for *DSM-IV* (First, Spitzer, Gibbon, & Williams, 1997) for diagnoses
of MDD, PTSD, and other psychiatric disorders. We also administered
the MAS (Williams, 1991), which comprises 12 subtests based on the
following seven memory tasks: verbal span, verbal list learning, verbal prose memory, visual span, visual recognition, visual reproduction,
and names-faces (a verbal-visual, paired-associates task). The resultant
global memory and summary scale scores provided measures of overall
memory performance, short-term memory, verbal memory, and visual
memory.

Results and Discussion

The most prominent finding was a highly significant reduction in
GMV in the left primary visual (LV-1) and visual association cortices
(LV-2) (Brodmann's Area [BA] 17 to 18; Talairach's coordinates x = −27
through 14, y = −90 through 86, z = −10 through 1; $p < 0.0001$, corrected cluster level; Fig. 2.1) (also see color insert). Compared with
healthy control subjects, a 14.1% lower average GMV was observed in

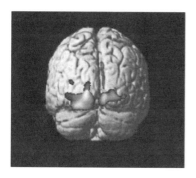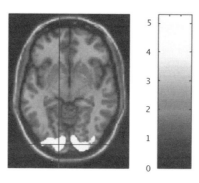

FIGURE 2.1. Differences in gray matter volume between abuse and control subjects. Significantly lower gray matter densities in abuse subjects were observed in the left visual cortex. Crosshairs placed at x = –14, y = –90, z = –1 (left lingual gyrus). Color scale (0–5) represents *t* values.

these regions for the abuse subjects. Within these areas, a strong correlation existed between visual memory and GMV of BA 17 ($r = 0.68$, $p < 0.00001$; x = 10, y = –91, z = –5; Fig. 2.2; Tables 2.1–2.3) (also see color insert). The MAS subscale with the strongest correlation to BA 17 GMV was visual recognition ($r = 0.65$, $p < 0.00005$; Talairach's coordinates x = 9, y = –90, z = –4). A significant correlation was also seen between GMV of BA 17 and an overall index of short-term memory ($r = 0.46$, $p < .005$; Talairach's coordinates x = 19, y = –101, z = –8). Within the occipital region, verbal memory correlated with GMV of BA 19 ($r = 0.43$, $p < 0.01$; Talairach's coordinates x = 45, y = –75, z = 0).

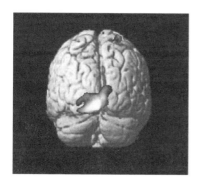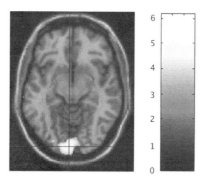

FIGURE 2.2. Correlations between brain volume and visual memory in the left primary visual cortex (LV-1). Crosshairs placed at x = –3, y = –90, z = –3 (left lingual gyrus). The color scale (0–6) indicates *t* values.

TABLE 2.1. Correlations Between Visually Based Memory Assessment Scale (MAS) Subtests and Left Visual Cortex Among All Subjects ($N = 37$)

MAS Subtest	p	r	Talairach Coordinates			t value	Region
			x	y	z		
Visual memory	0.005	0.45	−3	−90	−3	5.26	Left lingual gyrus
Visual span	0.027	0.36	−23	−93	−13	2.79	Left lingual gyrus
Visual reproduction	0.096	0.28	−19	−87	−7	5.42	Left lingual gyrus
Visual recognition	0.005	0.45	−3	−90	−3	4.19	Left lingual gyrus
Visual recognition (delayed recall)	0.034	0.35	−14	−88	−1	1.81	Left lingual gyrus
Verbal memory (controlling for visual memory)	0.004	0.47	−41	−89	3	4.07	Left middle occipital gyrus

The findings of reduced GMV in brain areas known to process visual stimuli are intriguing, especially in light of the fact that the reductions are correlated with visual memory—visual recognition in particular—but not verbal memory. We interpret these data as evidence to support the

TABLE 2.2. Correlations Between Visually Based Memory Assessment Scale (MAS) Subtests and Left Visual Cortex in Abuse Subjects ($N = 23$)

MAS Subtest	p	r	Talairach Coordinates			t value	Region
			x	y	z		
Visual memory	0.24	0.25	−3	−90	−3	5.26	Left lingual gyrus
Visual span	0.87	0.04	−23	−93	−13	2.79	Left lingual gyrus
Visual reproduction	0.26	0.24	−19	−87	−7	5.42	Left lingual gyrus
Visual recognition	0.25	0.25	−3	−90	−3	4.19	Left lingual gyrus
Visual recognition (delayed recall)	0.43	0.17	−14	−88	−1	1.81	Left lingual gyrus
Verbal memory (controlling for visual memory)	0.005	0.58	−41	−89	3	4.07	Left middle occipital gyrus

TABLE 2.3. Correlations Between Visually Based Memory Assessment Scale (MAS) Subtests and Left Visual Cortex in Control Subjects ($N = 14$)

MAS Subtest	p	r	Talairach Coordinates			t value	Region
			x	y	z		
Visual memory	0.0003	0.82	−3	−90	−3	5.26	Left lingual gyrus
Visual span	0.02	0.61	−23	−93	−13	2.79	Left lingual gyrus
Visual reproduction	0.01	0.66	−19	−87	−7	5.42	Left lingual gyrus
Visual recognition	0.0001	0.85	−3	−90	−3	4.19	Left lingual gyrus
Visual recognition (delayed recall)	0.03	0.57	−14	−88	−1	1.81	Left lingual gyrus
Verbal memory (controlling for visual memory)	0.005	0.58	−41	−89	3	4.07	Left middle occipital gyrus

proposition that disparate forms of CA can differentially influence the sensorium and its associated neurobiology. Thus, one prediction is that if the abuse that was experienced involved substantial visual perception, then perhaps those brain systems subserving visual information and processing were maladaptively impacted. Given that the neural substrates of visual perception overlap those of visual memory (e.g., occipital, inferior temporal, and parietal cortices; Slotnick, 2004), the possibility that visual stimuli perceived as external stressors (e.g., a child literally seeing an abuser perpetrating the abusive act[s]) could have adverse effects on the developing visual system seems plausible.

Conclusion

The jury is still out on the extent to which severe stress in the form of CA has true negative sequelae on the development of memory and its function. Thus far, research has shown that children who have been abused perform as well as other children on basic memory tasks (Howe, Cicchetti, et al., 2006, Howe, Toth, et al., 2006). Global brain-volume differences that have been observed also have not been associated with differences in children's memory performance (De Bellis & Thomas, 2003). However, a growing body of evidence from adult studies suggests that memory deficits do exist for individuals with abuse histories, and that these deficiencies are related to neuroanatomical anomalies. One explanation for this discrepancy is that the effects of CA on neurodevelopment and the development of memory are delayed and become unmasked at a later point in maturation. Longitudinal studies would allow investigators to test this hypothesis by evaluating, over several time points, children who have been abused. Ornstein et al. (2004) cogently argued that such a study design is warranted to ascertain the mechanisms that drive the development of memory. Of course, this developmental approach to memory testing would necessitate that comprehensive, reliable, and valid measures be available for use that are developmentally sensitive as well.

Sex differences is another area that has been ignored in this line of research. For example, because the vast majority of patients diagnosed with BPD are women, the reported memory findings in BPD remain unclear as to whether the effects are specific to women. We believe that manifest sex-related differences in memory function stem from the interaction of three factors: (1) sex differences in the nature of adverse early experience, (2) sexually dimorphic effects of early experience on brain development, and (3) sex differences in brain laterality and hormonal milieu (Teicher, Feldman, et al., 2002). For instance, our findings that sexual abuse is associated with diminished corpus callosum size in girls, while diminished corpus callosum size in boys is associated with neglect (Teicher et al., 2004), underscore the possibility that memory abilities that rely on interhemispheric neurotransmission may be adversely affected differentially across sex.

Lastly, we strongly side with those investigators who take a developmentally grounded, hypothetico-deductive approach toward CA research. Such an approach is imperative to provide a logical, comprehensive, and structured framework for conducting studies that are both developmentally and clinically meaningful. One such example comes from Howe and colleagues (Howe, Cicchetti, et al., 2006, Howe, Toth, et al., 2006), who have proposed that retrieval, rather than encoding, storage/consolidation, and retention, is deficient in individuals with abuse histories and that memory processes differ only in how the information is semantically organized. Nelson and Carver (1998) hypothesized that deficient long-term potentiation is the mechanism whereby the development of the explicit memory system is impacted by exposure to high levels of cortisol. We provided above a neurobioevolutional model as to how CA might influence the development of memory and its neurobiology. Future models will be enhanced by incorporating the "gene-environment interplay" notions delineated by Rutter and colleagues (2006). For instance, evidence indicates that polymorphism of the monoamine oxidase A (MAOA) gene moderates the development of antisocial behavior after exposure to physical abuse and that this relationship is more robust in males with the genotype conferring low versus high MAOA activity (Kim-Cohen et al., 2006). Given such findings, one speculation is that CA effects on the expression of certain genes might lead to the types of memory impairments that have been documented in the literature. To conclude, this subject is "ripe for the pickin' "—how well we decipher the short- and long-term effects of CA on memory is in our hands.

Acknowledgments

Partial funding for this chapter was provided by R01 awards MH-53636 and MH-66222 from the National Institute of Mental Health and DA-016934 and DA-017846 from the National Institute on Drug Abuse to MHT.

References

American Psychiatric Association. (2000). *Diagnostic and statistical manual of mental disorders* (4th ed., text rev.) Washington, DC: American Psychiatric Publishing.

Anda, R. F., Felitti, V. J., Bremner, J. D., Walker, J. D., Whitfield, C., Perry, B. D., Dube, S. R., & Giles, W. H. (2006). The enduring effects of abuse and related adverse experiences in childhood: A convergence of evidence from neurobiology and epidemiology. *European Archives of Psychiatry and Clinical Neurosciences, 256*(3), 174–186.

Anderson, C. M., Teicher, M. H., Polcari, A., & Renshaw, P. F. (2002). Abnormal T2 relaxation time in the cerebellar vermis of adults sexually abused in childhood: Potential role of the vermis in stress-enhanced risk for drug abuse. *Psychoneuroendocrinology, 27*(1–2), 231–244.

Andersen, S. L. (2003). Trajectories of brain development: Point of vulnerability or window of opportunity? *Neuroscience & Biobehavioral Reviews, 27*(1–2), 3–18.

Andersen, S. L., & Teicher, M. H. (2004). Delayed effects of early stress on hippocampal development. *Neuropsychopharmacology, 29*(11), 1988–1993.

Andersen, S. L., Thompson, A. T., Rutstein, M., Hostetter, J. C., & Teicher, M. H. (2000). Dopamine receptor pruning in prefrontal cortex during the periadolescent period in rats. *Synapse, 37*(2), 167–169.

Andreano, J. M., & Cahill, L. (2006). Glucocorticoid release and memory consolidation in men and women. *Psychological Science, 17*(6), 466–470.

Andreasen, N. C., O'Leary, D. S., Arndt, S., Cizadlo, T., Hurtig, R., Rezai, K., Watkins, G. L., Ponto, L. L., & Hichwa, R. D. (1995). Short-term and long-term verbal memory: A positron emission tomography study. *Proceedings of the National Academy of Sciences U S A, 92*(11), 5111–5115.

Arnsten, A. F. (2000). Through the looking glass: Differential noradenergic modulation of prefrontal cortical function. *Neural Plasticity, 7*(1–2), 133–146.

Ashburner, J., & Friston, K. J. (2000). Voxel-based morphometry—the methods. *Neuroimage, 11*(6 Pt 1), 805–821.

Bachevalier, J., Brickson, M., & Hagger, C. (1993). Limbic-dependent recognition memory in monkeys develops early in infancy. *Neuroreport, 4*(1), 77–80.

Bachevalier, J., & Vargha-Khadem, F. (2005). The primate hippocampus: Ontogeny, early insult and memory. *Current Opinions in Neurobiology, 15*(2), 168–174.

Beers, S. R., & De Bellis, M. D. (2002). Neuropsychological function in children with maltreatment-related posttraumatic stress disorder. *American Journal of Psychiatry, 159*(3), 483–486.

Bender, B. G., Lerner, J. A., & Poland, J. E. (1991). Association between corticosteroids and psychologic change in hospitalized asthmatic children. *Annals of Allergy, 66*(5), 414–419.

Berrebi, A. S., Fitch, R. H., Ralphe, D. L., Denenberg, J. O., Friedrich, V. L. Jr., & Denenberg, V. H. (1988). Corpus callosum: Region-specific effects of sex, early experience and age. *Brain Research, 438*(1–2), 216–224.

Bookstein, F. L. (2001). "Voxel-based morphometry" should not be used with imperfectly registered images. *Neuroimage, 14*(6), 1454–1462.

Brambilla, P., Soloff, P. H., Sala, M., Nicoletti, M. A., Keshavan, M. S., & Soares, J. C. (2004). Anatomical MRI study of borderline personality disorder patients. *Psychiatry Research, 131*(2), 125–133.

Bremner, J. D. (1999). Does stress damage the brain? *Biological Psychiatry, 45*(7), 797–805.

Bremner, J. D. (2003). Long-term effects of childhood abuse on brain and neurobiology. *Child & Adolescent Psychiatric Clinics of North America, 12*(2), 271–292.

Bremner, J. D., Narayan, M., Staib, L. H., Southwick, S. M., McGlashan, T., & Charney, D. S. (1999). Neural correlates of memories of childhood sexual abuse in women with and without posttraumatic stress disorder. *American Journal of Psychiatry, 156*(11), 1787–1795.

Bremner, J. D., Randall, P., Vermetten, E., Staib, L., Bronen, R. A., Mazure, C., et al. (1997). Magnetic resonance imaging-based measurement of hippocampal volume in posttraumatic stress disorder related to childhood physical and sexual abuse—a preliminary report. *Biological Psychiatry, 41*(1), 23–32.

Bremner, J. D., Vermetten, E., Afzal, N., & Vythilingam, M. (2004). Deficits in verbal declarative memory function in women with childhood sexual abuse-related posttraumatic stress disorder. *Journal of Nervous & Mental Disease, 192*(10), 643–649.

Bremner, J. D., Vermetten, E., Schmahl, C., Vaccarino, V., Vythilingam, M., Afzal, N., et al. (2005). Positron emission tomographic imaging of neural correlates of a fear acquisition and extinction paradigm in women with childhood sexual-abuse-related post-traumatic stress disorder. *Psychological Medicine, 35*(6), 791–806.

Bremner, J. D., Vythilingam, M., Vermetten, E., Southwick, S. M., McGlashan, T., Staib, L. H., et al. (2003). Neural correlates of declarative memory for emotionally valenced words in women with posttraumatic stress disorder related to early childhood sexual abuse. *Biological Psychiatry, 53*(10), 879–889.

Caldji, C., Diorio, J., & Meaney, M. J. (2000). Variations in maternal care in infancy regulate the development of stress reactivity. *Biological Psychiatry, 48*(12), 1164–1174.

Carrion, V. G., Weems, C. F., Eliez, S., Patwardhan, A., Brown, W., Ray, R. D., et al. (2001). Attenuation of frontal asymmetry in pediatric posttraumatic stress disorder. *Biological Psychiatry, 50*(12), 943–951.

De Bellis, M. D., Keshavan, M. S., Clark, D. B., Casey, B. J., Giedd, J. N., Boring, A. M., et al. (1999). Developmental traumatology. Part II: Brain development. *Biological Psychiatry, 45*(10), 1271–1284.

De Bellis, M. D., Keshavan, M. S., Shifflett, H., Iyengar, S., Beers, S. R., Hall, J., et al. (2002). Brain structures in pediatric maltreatment-related posttraumatic stress disorder: A sociodemographically matched study. *Biological Psychiatry, 52*(11), 1066–1078.

De Bellis, M. D., Keshavan, M. S., Spencer, S., & Hall, J. (2000). N-Acetylaspartate concentration in the anterior cingulate of maltreated children and adolescents with PTSD. *American Journal of Psychiatry, 157*(7), 1175–1177.

De Bellis, M. D., & Thomas, L. A. (2003). Biologic findings of post-traumatic stress disorder and child maltreatment. *Current Psychiatry Reports, 5*(2), 108–117.

Denenberg, V. H. (1983). Lateralization of function in rats. *American Journal of Physiology, 245,* R505-R509.

Denenberg, V. H., Garbanati, J., Sherman, G., Yutzey, D. A., & Kaplan, R. (1978). Infantile stimulation induces brain lateralization in rats. *Science, 201,* 1150–1152.

Denenberg, V. H., & Yutzey, D. A. (1985). Hemispheric laterality, behavioral asymmetry, and the effects of early experience in rats. In S. D. Glick (Ed.), *Cerebral lateralization in nonhuman species* (pp. 109–133). Orlando: Academic Press.

Desgranges, B., Baron, J. C., & Eustache, F. (1998). The functional neuroanatomy of episodic memory: The role of the frontal lobes, the hippocampal formation, and other areas. *Neuroimage, 8*(2), 198–213.

DiGiulio, D. V., Seidenberg, M., O'Leary, D. S., & Raz, N. (1994). Procedural and declarative memory: A developmental study. *Brain and Cognition, 25*(1), 79–91.

Driessen, M., Herrmann, J., Stahl, K., Zwaan, M., Meier, S., Hill, A., et al. (2000). Magnetic resonance imaging volumes of the hippocampus and the amygdala in women with borderline personality disorder and early traumatization. *Archives of General Psychiatry, 57*(12), 1115–1122.

Eichenbaum, H. (2001). The long and winding road to memory consolidation. *Nature Neuroscience, 4*(11), 1057–1058.

Eisen, M. L., Qin, J., Goodman, G. S., & Davis, S. L. (2002). Memory and suggestibility in maltreated children: Age, stress arousal, dissociation, and psychopathology. *Journal of Experimental Child Psychology, 83*(3), 167–212.

Elzinga, B. M., Bakker, A., & Bremner, J. D. (2005). Stress-induced cortisol elevations are associated with impaired delayed, but not immediate recall. *Psychiatry Research, 134*(3), 211–223.

Elzinga, B. M., & Bremner, J. D. (2002). Are the neural substrates of memory the final common pathway in posttraumatic stress disorder (PTSD)? *Journal of Affective Disorders, 70*(1), 1–17.

First, M. B., Spitzer, R. L., Gibbon, M., & Williams, J. B. W. (1997). *Structured clinical interview for* DSM-IV *axis I disorders—clinician version (SCID-CV)*. Washington, DC: American Psychiatric Press.

Freud S. (1896/1959). The aetiology of hysteria. In E. Jones (Ed.) and J. Riviere (Trans.), *Sigmund Freud: Collected papers* (Vol. 1, pp. 183–220). New York: Basic Books.

Galaburda, A. M. (1991). Asymmetries of cerebral neuroanatomy. *Ciba Foundation Symposia, 162,* 219–226.

Gilbertson, M. W., Shenton, M. E., Ciszewski, A., Kasai, K., Lasko, N. B., Orr, S. P., et al. (2002). Smaller hippocampal volume predicts pathologic vulnerability to psychological trauma. *Nature Neuroscience, 5*(11), 1242–1247.

Glaser, D. (2000). Child abuse and neglect and the brain—a review. *Journal of Child Psychology & Psychiatry, 41*(1), 97–116.

Good, C. D., Johnsrude, I. S., Ashburner, J., Henson, R. N., Friston, K. J., & Frackowiak, R. S. (2001). A voxel-based morphometric study of ageing in 465 normal adult human brains. *Neuroimage, 14*(1 Pt 1), 21–36.

Gould, E., & Tanapat, P. (1999). Stress and hippocampal neurogenesis. *Biological Psychiatry, 46*(11), 1472–1479.

Grilo, C. M., & Masheb, R. M. (2001). Childhood psychological, physical, and sexual maltreatment in outpatients with binge eating disorder: Frequency and associations with gender, obesity, and eating-related psychopathology. *Obesity Research, 9*(5), 320–325.

Harlow, H. F., Dodsworth, R. O., & Harlow, M. K. (1965). Total social isolation in monkeys. *Proceedings of the National Academy of Sciences of the United States of America, 54*(1), 90–97.

Heath, R. G. (1973). Fastigial nucleus connections to the septal region in monkey and cat: A demonstration with evoked potentials of a bilateral pathway. *Biological Psychiatry, 6*(2), 193–196.

Heath, R. G., & Harper, J. W. (1974). Ascending projections of the cerebellar fastigial nucleus to the hippocampus, amygdala, and other temporal lobe sites: Evoked potential and histological studies in monkeys and cats. *Experimental Neurology, 45*(2), 268–287.

Heim, C., & Nemeroff, C. B. (2002). Neurobiology of early life stress: clinical studies. *Seminars in Clinical Neuropsychiatry, 7*(2), 147–159.

Hollingshead, A. B. (1975). *Four factor index of social status.* New Haven, CT: Yale University Department of Sociology.

Howe, M. L., Cicchetti, D., & Toth, S. L. (2006). Children's basic memory processes, stress, and maltreatment. *Development and Psychopathology. Special issue: Risk, Trauma, and Memory, 18*(3), 759–769.

Howe, M. L., Cicchetti, D., Toth, S. L., & Cerrito, B. M. (2004). True and false memories in maltreated children. *Child Development, 75*(5), 1402–1417.

Howe, M. L., Toth, S. L., & Cicchetti, D. (2006). Memory and developmental psychopathology. In D. Cicchetti & D. J. Cohen (Eds.), *Developmental psychopathology: Vol. 2. Developmental neuroscience* (2nd ed., pp. 629–655). Hoboken, NJ: John Wiley & Sons, Inc.

Hunt, P. S., & Campbell, B. A. (1997). Developmental dissociation of the components of conditioned fear. In M. E. Bouton & M. S. Fanselow (Eds.), *Learning, motivation, and cognition: The functional behaviorism of Robert C. Bolles* (pp. 53–74). Washington, DC: American Psychological Association.

Ito, Y., Teicher, M. H., Glod, C. A., & Ackerman, E. (1998). Preliminary evidence for aberrant cortical development in abused children: A quantitative EEG study. *Journal of Neuropsychiatry & Clinical Neurosciences, 10*(3), 298–307.

Ito, Y., Teicher, M. H., Glod, C. A., Harper, D., Magnus, E., & Gelbard, H. A. (1993). Increased prevalence of electrophysiological abnormalities in children with psychological, physical, and sexual abuse. *Journal of Neuropsychiatry and Clinical Neurosciences, 5,* 401–408.

Jelicic, M., & Bonke, B. (2001). Memory impairments following chronic stress? A critical review. *European Journal of Psychiatry, 15*(4), 225–232.

Jelicic, M., & Merckelbach, H. (2004). Traumatic stress, brain changes, and memory deficits: A critical note. *Journal of Nervous & Mental Disease, 192*(8), 548–553.

Kaplan, M. J., & Klinetob, N. A. (2000). Childhood emotional trauma and chronic posttraumatic stress disorder in adult outpatients with treatment-resistant depression. *Journal of Nervous & Mental Disease, 188*(9), 596–601.

Kaufman, J., & Charney, D. (2001). Effects of early stress on brain structure and function: Implications for understanding the relationship between child maltreatment and depression. *Development and Psychopathology, 13*(3), 451–471.

Kaufman, J., Plotsky, P. M., Nemeroff, C. B., & Charney, D. S. (2000). Effects of early adverse experiences on brain structure and function: Clinical implications. *Biological Psychiatry, 48*(8), 778–790.

Kehoe, P., Shoemaker, W. J., Triano, L., Callahan, M., & Rappolt, G. (1998). Adult rats stressed as neonates show exaggerated behavioral responses to both pharmacological and environmental challenges. *Behavioral Neuroscience, 112*(1), 116–125.

Kelley, W. M., Miezin, F. M., McDermott, K. B., Buckner, R. L., Raichle, M. E., Cohen, N. J., et al. (1998). Hemispheric specialization in human dorsal frontal cortex and medial temporal lobe for verbal and nonverbal memory encoding. *Neuron, 20*(5), 927–936.

Kim-Cohen, J., Caspi, A., Taylor, A., Williams, B., Newcombe, R., Craig, I. W., et al. (2006). MAOA, maltreatment, and gene-environment interaction predicting children's mental health: New evidence and a meta-analysis. *Molecular Psychiatry, 11*(10), 903–913.

Lang, P. J., & Davis, M. (2006). Emotion, motivation, and the brain: Reflex foundations in animal and human research. *Progress in Brain Research, 156,* 3–29.

Lange, C., Kracht, L., Herholz, K., Sachsse, U., & Irle, E. (2005). Reduced glucose metabolism in temporo-parietal cortices of women with borderline personality disorder. *Psychiatry Research, 139*(2), 115–126.

LeDoux, J. (1996). Emotional networks and motor control: A fearful view. *Progress in Brain Research, 107,* 437–446.

LeDoux, J. (2003). The emotional brain, fear, and the amygdala. *Cellular and Molecular Neurobiology, 23*(4–5), 727–738.

Levine, S. (1967). Maternal and environmental influences on the adrenocortical response to stress in weanling rats. *Science, 156*(772), 258–260.

Mishkin, M., Suzuki, W. A., Gadian, D. G., & Vargha-Khadem, F. (1997). Hierarchical organization of cognitive memory. *Philosophical Transactions of the Royal Society B: Biological Sciences, 352*(1360), 1461–1467.

Mishkin, M., Vargha-Khadem, F., & Gadian, D. G. (1998). Amnesia and the organization of the hippocampal system. *Hippocampus, 8*(3), 212–216.

Moradi, A. R., Doost, H. T., Taghavi, M. R., Yule, W., & Dalgleish, T. (1999). Everyday memory deficits in children and adolescents with PTSD: Performance on the Rivermead Behavioural Memory Test. *Journal of Child Psychology & Psychiatry, 40*(3), 357–361.

Moye, T. B., & Rudy, J. W. (1987). Ontogenesis of trace conditioning in young rats: Dissociation of associative and memory processes. *Developmental Psychobiology, 20*(4), 405–414.

Navalta, C. P., Polcari, A., Webster, D. M., Boghossian, A., & Teicher, M. H. (2006). Effects of childhood sexual abuse on neuropsychological and cognitive function in college women. *Journal of Neuropsychiatry & Clinical Neurosciences, 18*(1), 45–53.

Nelson, C. A., & Carver, L. J. (1998). The effects of stress and trauma on brain and memory: A view from developmental cognitive neuroscience. *Development and Psychopathology. Special issue: Risk, Trauma, and Memory, 10*(4), 793–809.

Nelson, C. A., & Webb, S. J. (2003). A cognitive neuroscience perspective on early memory development. In M. De Haan & M. H. Johnson (Eds.), *Cognitive neuroscience of development* (pp. 99–126). New York: Taylor & Francis, Inc.

Okada, T., Tanaka, M., Kuratsune, H., Watanabe, Y., & Sadato, N. (2004). Mechanisms underlying fatigue: A voxel-based morphometric study of chronic fatigue syndrome. *BioMedCentral Neurology, 4*(1), 14.

O'Leary, K. M., Brouwers, P., Gardner, D. L., & Cowdry, R. W. (1991). Neuropsychological testing of patients with borderline personality disorder. *American Journal of Psychiatry, 148*(1), 106–111.

Oliver, C., Boudouresque, F., Lacroix, O., Anglade, G., & Grino, M. (1994). Effect of POMC-derived peptides on corticosterone secretion during the stress hypo-responsive period in rat. *Endocrine Regulations, 28*(2), 67–72.

Orbach, Y., Lamb, M. E., Sternberg, K. J., Williams, J. M., & Dawud-Noursi, S. (2001). The effect of being a victim or witness of family violence on the retrieval of autobiographical memories. *Child Abuse & Neglect, 25*(11), 1427–1437.

Ornstein, P. A., & Haden, C. A. (2001). Memory development or the development of memory? *Current Directions in Psychological Science, 10*(6), 202–205.

Ornstein, P. A., Haden, C. A., & Hedrick, A. M. (2004). Learning to remember: Social-communicative exchanges and the development of children's memory skills. *Developmental Review. Special issue: Memory Development in the New Millennium, 24*(4), 374–395.

Patel, P. D., Lopez, J. F., Lyons, D. M., Burke, S., Wallace, M., & Schatzberg, A. F. (2000). Glucocorticoid and mineralocorticoid receptor mRNA expression in squirrel monkey brain. *Journal of Psychiatric Research, 34*(6), 383–392.

Penza, K. M., Heim, C., & Nemeroff, C. B. (2003). Neurobiological effects of childhood abuse: Implications for the pathophysiology of depression and anxiety. *Archives of Women's Mental Health, 6*(1), 15–22.

Perez, C. M., & Widom, C. S. (1994). Childhood victimization and long-term intellectual and academic outcomes. *Child Abuse & Neglect, 18*(8), 617–633.

Perner, J., & Ruffman, T. (1995). Episodic memory and autonoetic consciousness: Developmental evidence and a theory of childhood amnesia. *Journal of Experimental Child Psychology, 59*(3), 516–548.

Porter, C., Lawson, J. S., & Bigler, E. D. (2005). Neurobehavioral sequelae of child sexual abuse. *Child Neuropsychology, 11*(2), 203–220.

Putnam, F. W. (2003). Ten-year research update review: Child sexual abuse. *Journal of the American Academy of Child & Adolescent Psychiatry, 42*(3), 269–278.

Rauch, S. L., Whalen, P. J., Shin, L. M., McInerney, S. C., Macklin, M. L., Lasko, N. B., et al. (2000). Exaggerated amygdala response to masked facial stimuli in posttraumatic stress disorder: A functional MRI study. *Biological Psychiatry, 47*(9), 769–776.

Roozendaal, B. (2002). Stress and memory: Opposing effects of glucocorticoids on memory consolidation and memory retrieval. *Neurobiology of Learning and Memory, 78*(3), 578–595.

Roozendaal, B. (2003). Systems mediating acute glucocorticoid effects on memory consolidation and retrieval. *Progress in Neuropsychopharmacology and Biological Psychiatry, 27*(8), 1213–1223.

Rutter, M., Moffitt, T. E., & Caspi, A. (2006). Gene-environment interplay and psychopathology: Multiple varieties but real effects. *Journal of Child Psychology & Psychiatry, 47*(3–4), 226–261.

Sanchez, M. M., Hearn, E. F., Do, D., Rilling, J. K., & Herndon, J. G. (1998). Differential rearing affects corpus callosum size and cognitive function of rhesus monkeys. *Brain Research, 812*(1–2), 38–49.

Sapolsky, R. M., Krey, L. C., & McEwen, B. S. (1985). Prolonged glucocorticoid exposure reduces hippocampal neuron number: Implications for aging. *Journal of Neuroscience, 5*(5), 1222–1227.

Sapolsky, R. M., Uno, H., Rebert, C. S., & Finch, C. E. (1990). Hippocampal damage associated with prolonged glucocorticoid exposure in primates. *Journal of Neuroscience, 10*(9), 2897–2902.

Schacter, D. L. (2000). Memory: Memory systems. In A. E. Kazdin (Ed.), *Encyclopedia of psychology* (Vol. 5, pp. 169–172). Washington, DC: American Psychological Association.

Schacter, D. L., & Tulving, E. (1994). What are the memory systems of 1994? In D. L. Schacter & E. Tulving (Eds.), *Memory systems 1994* (pp. 1–38). Cambridge, MA: MIT Press.

Schiffer, F., Teicher, M. H., Anderson, C., Tomoda, A., Polcari, A., Navalta, C. P., et al. (2007). Determination of hemispheric emotional valence in individual subjects: A new approach with research and therapeutic implications [Electronic version]. *Behavioral and Brain Functions, 3*(1), 13.

Schiffer, F., Teicher, M. H., & Papanicolaou, A. C. (1995). Evoked potential evidence for right brain activity during the recall of traumatic memories. *Journal of Neuropsychiatry & Clinical Neurosciences, 7*(2), 169–175.

Schmahl, C. G., Elzinga, B. M., Vermetten, E., Sanislow, C., McGlashan, T. H., & Bremner, J. D. (2003). Neural correlates of memories of abandonment in women with and without borderline personality disorder. *Biological Psychiatry, 54*(2), 142–151.

Schmahl, C. G., Vermetten, E., Elzinga, B. M., & Bremner, J. D. (2004). A positron emission tomography study of memories of childhood abuse in borderline personality disorder. *Biological Psychiatry, 55*(7), 759–765.

Shin, L. M., Rauch, S. L., & Pitman, R. K. (2006). Amygdala, medial prefrontal cortex, and hippocampal function in PTSD. *Annals of the New York Academy of Sciences, 1071,* 67–79.

Siegel, D. J. (2001). Memory: An overview, with emphasis on developmental, interpersonal, and neurobiological aspects. *Journal of the American Academy of Child & Adolescent Psychiatry, 40*(9), 997–1011.

Siegler, R. S. (2004). Turning memory development inside out. *Developmental Review. Special issue: Memory Development in the New Millennium, 24*(4), 469–475.

Simeon, D., Guralnik, O., Schmeidler, J., Sirof, B., & Knutelska, M. (2001). The role of childhood interpersonal trauma in depersonalization disorder. *American Journal of Psychiatry, 158*(7), 1027–1033.

Slotnick, S. D. (2004). Visual memory and visual perception recruit common neural substrates. *Behavioral and Cognitive Neuroscience Reviews, 3*(4), 207–221.

Squire, L. R. (2004). Memory systems of the brain: A brief history and current perspective. *Neurobiology of Learning and Memory, 82*(3), 171–177.

Squire, L. R., & Zola-Morgan, S. (1988). Memory: Brain systems and behavior. *Trends in Neurosciences, 11*(4), 170–175.

Squire, L. R., & Zola-Morgan, S. (1991). The medial temporal lobe memory system. *Science, 253*(5026), 1380–1386.

Stanton, M. E. (2000). Multiple memory systems, development and conditioning. *Behavioral Brain Research, 110*(1–2), 25–37.

Stein, M. B. (1997). Hippocampal volume in women victimized by childhood sexual abuse. *Psychological Medicine, 27*(4), 951–959.

Tarullo, A. R., & Gunnar, M. R. (2006). Child maltreatment and the developing HPA axis. *Hormones and Behavior, 50*(4), 632–639.

Teicher, M. H. (2000). Wounds that time won't heal: The neurobiology of child abuse. *Cerebrum, 4*(2), 50–67.

Teicher, M. H. (2002). Scars that won't heal: The neurobiology of child abuse. *Scientific American, 286*(3), 68–75.

Teicher, M. H., Andersen, S. L., & Hostetter, J. C., Jr. (1995). Evidence for dopamine receptor pruning between adolescence and adulthood in striatum but not nucleus accumbens. *Brain Research Developmental Brain Research, 89*(2), 167–172.

Teicher, M. H., Andersen, S. L., Polcari, A., Anderson, C. M., & Navalta, C. P. (2002). Developmental neurobiology of childhood stress and trauma. *Psychiatric Clinics of North America, 25*(2), 397–426.

Teicher, M. H., Andersen, S. L., Polcari, A., Anderson, C. M., Navalta, C. P., & Kim, D. M. (2003). The neurobiological consequences of early stress and childhood maltreatment. *Neuroscience & Biobehavioral Reviews, 27*(1–2), 33–44.

Teicher, M. H., Anderson, C. M., Polcari, A., Glod, C. A., Maas, L. C., & Renshaw, P. F. (2000). Functional deficits in basal ganglia of children with attention-deficit/hyperactivity disorder shown with functional magnetic resonance imaging relaxometry. *Nature Medicine, 6*(4), 470–473.

Teicher, M. H., Dumont, N. L., Ito, Y., Vaituzis, C., Giedd, J. N., & Andersen, S. L. (2004). Childhood neglect is associated with reduced corpus callosum area. *Biological Psychiatry, 56*(2), 80–85.

Teicher, M. H., Feldman, R., Polcari, A., Anderson, C. M., Andersen, S. L., Webster, D. M., et al. (2002). Early adverse experience and the neurobiology of borderline personality disorder: Gender differences and implications for treatment. In K. H. Pearson, S. B. Sonswalla, & J. F. Rosenbaum (Eds.), *Women's Health and Psychiatry* (pp. 9–26). New York: Lipincott, Williams & Wilkins.

Teicher, M. H., Glod, C. A., Surrey, J., & Swett, C., Jr. (1993). Early childhood abuse and limbic system ratings in adult psychiatric outpatients. *Journal of Neuropsychiatry & Clinical Neurosciences, 5*(3), 301–306.

Teicher, M. H., Ito, Y., Glod, C. A., Andersen, S. L., Dumont, N., & Ackerman, E. (1997). Preliminary evidence for abnormal cortical development in physically and sexually abused children using EEG coherence and MRI. *Annals of the New York Academy of Sciences, 821,* 160–175.

Teicher, M. H., Samson, J. A., Polcari, A., & McGreenery, C. E. (2006). Sticks, stones, and hurtful words: Relative effects of various forms of childhood maltreatment. *American Journal of Psychiatry, 163*(6), 993–1000.

Teicher, M. H., Tomoda, A., & Andersen, S. L. (2006). Neurobiological consequences of early stress and childhood maltreatment: Are results from human and animal studies comparable? *Annals of the New York Academy of Sciences, 1071,* 313–323.

Tulving, E. (1983). *Elements of episodic memory.* Oxford: Clarendon Press.

Tupler, L. A., & De Bellis, M. D. (2006). Segmented hippocampal volume in children and adolescents with posttraumatic stress disorder. *Biological Psychiatry, 59*(6), 523–529.

Vermetten, E., Schmahl, C., Lindner, S., Loewenstein, R. J., & Bremner, J. D. (2006). Hippocampal and amygdalar volumes in dissociative identity disorder. *American Journal of Psychiatry, 163*(4), 630–636.

Vythilingam, M., Heim, C., Newport, J., Miller, A. H., Anderson, E., Bronen, R., et al. (2002). Childhood trauma associated with smaller hippocampal volume in women with major depression. *American Journal of Psychiatry, 159*(12), 2072–2080.

Wheeler, M. A., Stuss, D. T., & Tulving, E. (1997). Toward a theory of episodic memory: The frontal lobes and autonoetic consciousness. *Psychological Bulletin, 121*(3), 331–354.

Williams, J. M. (1991). *Memory Assessment Scales: Professional Manual.* Odessa, FL: Psychological Assessment Resources.

Zola, S. M., Squire, L. R., Teng, E., Stefanacci, L., Buffalo, E. A., & Clark, R. E. (2000). Impaired recognition memory in monkeys after damage limited to the hippocampal region. *Journal of Neuroscience, 20*(1), 451–463.

3

Maltreatment, Event-Related Potentials, and Memory

DANTE CICCHETTI AND W. JOHN CURTIS

Event-Related Potentials and Memory in Nonclinical Populations

Over the past three decades, research utilizing event-related potentials (ERPs) has greatly advanced knowledge concerning the neural under-pinnings of a variety of cognitive processes in both children and adults. In addition, this methodology has allowed an examination of changes in the neural processes associated with cognitive development from early in-fancy through young adulthood. The vast majority of the ERP literature in children has been focused on investigating normative processes of cognitive development, with very few studies to date employing ERPs to examine the impact of social experience on brain development and func-tioning. Nonetheless, the wealth of knowledge obtained from the use of ERPs concerning the neural bases of normative cognitive development can potentially inform ERP research investigating the neural correlates of the experience of child maltreatment.

Reciprocally, employing ERPs to examine the neural mechanisms underlying memory processes in children who have experienced mal-treatment could provide valuable knowledge concerning the effects of

83

maltreatment on neural functioning. It may be of great importance in understanding the sequelae of maltreatment to demonstrate how ERPs may be associated with aberrations in the development and functioning of memory at the level of analysis of the brain, and in what way such aberrant neural processes may, to some degree, mediate the behavioral and developmental disturbances associated with maltreatment.

Although our focus in the current chapter is on how ERPs have been utilized to examine memory in children who have experienced maltreatment, we first briefly review what is known about ERPs and memory in children who are considered to be on a typical developmental trajectory and who have not been exposed to maltreatment. This approach is consistent with one of the fundamental tenets of the discipline of developmental psychopathology—namely, that the study of normality and pathology are mutually informative (e.g., Cicchetti, 1984, 1990a, 1993; Cicchetti & Sroufe, 2000; Rutter & Sroufe, 2000; Sroufe, 1990). Cicchetti (1990a) has described developmental psychopathology as a discipline that is the product of an integration of various fields of study, including genetics, embryology, neuroscience, epidemiology, psychoanalysis, psychiatry, and psychology, the efforts of which had previously been separate and distinct. Multiple theoretical perspectives and diverse research strategies and findings have contributed to developmental psychopathology. In fact, contributions to this field have come from virtually every corner of the biological and social sciences (Cicchetti & Cohen, 2006a, 2006b, 2006c; Cicchetti & Sroufe, 2000).

In addition, developmental psychopathology has made great strides in recent years to incorporate a "multiple levels of analysis" approach into its conceptual and empirical framework (Cicchetti & Blender, 2004; Cicchetti & Dawson, 2002); in part as a consequence, understanding of the development of psychopathology generally has made great advances by employing findings from basic neuroscience and normal brain development (e.g., Cicchetti & Curtis, 2006; Cicchetti & Posner, 2005; for a detailed historical review of this topic, see Cicchetti, 2002a). In particular, knowledge of normal development can and should inform the study of deviant developmental trajectories eventuating in psychopathology. This principle also is embraced by developmental neuroscientists (see, e.g., Cicchetti, 1990a, 2002a; Cicchetti & Cannon, 1999; Goldman-Rakic, 1987; Johnson, 1998). Developmental psychopathologists and developmental neuroscientists both emphasize the importance of understanding normal developmental patterns so that we may begin to investigate the ways in which deviant development may eventuate (Cicchetti & Posner, 2005).

Goals of the Chapter

Adopting a theoretical approach emphasizing the integration of the study of normal and atypical development utilizing multiple levels of analysis, we begin this chapter with a brief technical and historical overview of ERP methodology, followed by a survey of the major findings of ERP studies examining normative memory functioning in infants and children. In the penultimate section, the review of ERP and memory in normal populations will serve to set the stage for a more comprehensive understanding of the patterns of findings in ERP research with children who have experienced maltreatment. Finally, we suggest future research directions on ERPs and memory in samples of maltreated and nonmaltreated infants and children and discuss how such investigations could inform the design and implementation of randomized prevention and intervention trials with children who have experienced maltreatment.

Event-Related Potentials: A Brief General Overview

Physiological Bases of the Signal

Event-related potentials (ERPs) are an index of central nervous system (CNS) functioning thought to reflect the underlying processing of discrete stimuli (Hillyard & Picton, 1987). ERPs are scalp-derived changes in brain electrical activity over time, obtained by averaging time-locked segments of the electroencephalogram (EEG) that are synchronized to the presentation of a stimulus (Donchin, Karis, Bashore, Coles, & Gratton, 1986). In general, the physical basis of the ERP signal derives from transient changes in electrical activity occurring in the brain, and reflects the summation of excitatory and inhibitory postsynaptic potentials (EPSPs and IPSPs) across large numbers of synchronously firing neurons (Allison, Woods, & McCarthy, 1986).

The primary neural generators of the postsynaptic potentials underlying the ERP signal are believed to be pyramidal cells in the cerebral cortex. Among the most common neurons in the cortex and named for their relatively large (10 to 70 μm in diameter), pyramid-shaped cell bodies, they have a single prominent apical dendrite, small basal dendrites, and a lone basal axon (Pritchard & Alloway, 1999). Pyramidal cells are located primarily in Layer III (the external pyramidal layer) and Layer V (the internal pyramidal layer) of the cortex, with some pyramidal cells, projecting to the thalamus, residing in Layer VI (the multiform layer). The single apical dendrite of the pyramidal cell arborizes through more superficial cortical layers (i.e., those closer to the cortical surface, signified by lower numerical designations, e.g., Layers I, II), while the short basal dendrites ramify within deeper cortical layers. The basal axon may ramify locally within the cortical layer, or may project to remote cortical and even subcortical targets (Pritchard & Alloway, 1999). Pyramidal cells are often characterized as the efferent neurons of the cerebral cortex, with the medium and large pyramidal cells in Layer V making up its primary output layer.

It is generally agreed that action potentials are not the source of electrical activity reflected by ERPs. Action potentials are discrete voltage spikes that travel along the axon until the potential reaches an axon terminal. Action potentials occur relatively quickly (1 to 2 ms), and more importantly, the highly asynchronous nature of action potentials across groups of neurons tends to cancel out the voltage produced, and thus makes detection of voltage from action potentials at the scalp virtually impossible. In fact, the only way to record action potentials from a large number of neurons is to place an electrode very near the cell bodies (i.e., intracranially).

Rather, electrical activity detected at the scalp that is represented by ERPs originates from the summation of extracellular changes in ion concentrations that result from chemically mediated EPSPs and IPSPs, occurring across large groups of thousands or even millions of neurons. Postsynaptic potentials typically have a duration of 10 to 250 ms (da Silva & van Rotterdam, 1982) and involve the movement of potassium, sodium, and chloride across the neurocellular membrane. The probable sequence of specific events is as follows: In the case of an EPSP, an excitatory neurotransmitter is released at the apical dendrite of a cortical pyramidal cell. Subsequently, an electrical current will flow from the extracellular space into the cell, resulting in a net negativity (or negative charge) outside of the cell in the region immediately surrounding the apical dendrite. To complete the process, current will also flow out of the cell body and basal dendrites, yielding a net positive charge in this area. This co-occurrence of discrete areas of negative and positive charge in extracellular space, separated by a small distance, creates what is termed a dipole.

A single dipole associated with a single neuron would not be detectable from an electrode placed on the scalp. In order for this process to be detected as voltage at the scalp, the summated dipoles from thousands or millions of neurons must occur at approximately the same time, and the dipoles from individual neurons must be spatially aligned. Fortunately, large populations of pyramidal cells in the cortex are indeed aligned parallel to one another (and perpendicular to the scalp). Thus, the synchronous activation and parallel spatial arrangement of cortical pyramidal cells results in the summation of many dipoles, and the subsequent current moves through the extracellular space between the surface of the cortex and the skull, finally reaching the surface of the scalp, and the experimenter's waiting electrode, by volume conduction.

Beyond these fundamental electrophysiological properties of the generation of the ERP signal, inferring what is ongoing in the brain (and where) from minutely small electrical potentials measured at the scalp is often associated with a great degree of methodological complexity and some degree of uncertainty. One major challenge, for example, is that ERPs spread out as they travel through the brain and the skull, thus resulting in distortion or blurring of the surface distribution of voltage, with a resultant uncertainty about the actual source of the observed voltage. However, the recent advent of high-density electrode arrays that provide ever-increasing coverage of the scalp, and sophisticated software algorithms designed to correct for blurring of the surface distribution of voltage, have greatly reduced many of the uncertainties that surround the analysis and interpretation of ERPs (e.g., Tucker, 1993; Tucker, Liotti, Potts, Russell, & Posner, 1994). More importantly, in-depth technical knowledge of such details that compose much of the methodological challenges in the field of electrophysiology is not a prerequisite for understanding the results of ERP research, and the reader with an interest in ERPs and the knowledge they provide should not be discouraged by the often esoteric and seemingly unfathomable details specific to this area of study.[1]

---

1. A technically detailed description of the neural origins of ERPs is beyond the scope of this chapter. The interested reader is referred to Nelson & Monk (2001) and Luck (2005) for excellent, in-depth discussion of the neural bases of ERPs.

Event-Related Potential Data

Despite the wide variety of questions addressed by ERP researchers, and the many different experimental paradigms employed to answer them, there are several characteristics of ERP data that are seen as common across diverse studies. ERP data consist of the series of positive and negative changes in voltage across the time segment comprising the experimental trial (see Figure 3.1 for sample ERP data). The relative amplitudes and latencies of these voltage changes comprise what are referred to as waveforms (e.g., P300, Nc, etc.), the broad unit of analysis of the ERP (more specific details on the nature and meaning of these waveforms will follow in subsequent sections of this chapter). The length of the averaged time-locked segments of the EEG comprising the ERP data typically ranges from 1 to 2 seconds (this segment corresponds to an experimental trial) and is determined by several parameters, largely dependent on the type of stimuli, the length of time the stimuli is to be presented, and the amount of time allotted to recording after the stimulus has been presented. However, given that brain electrical potentials are being recorded in "real time" and the relative rapidity of neural responses to quickly presented,

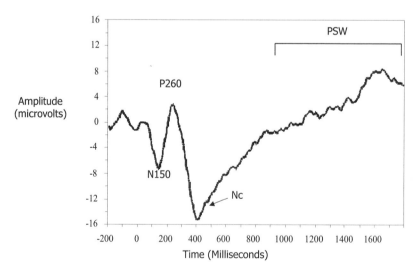

FIGURE 3.1. Sample grand mean illustrating event-related potential (ERP) data. Waveforms shown were elicited from 30-month-olds as they viewed face stimuli. Nc: negative central; PSW: positive slow wave.

discrete stimuli, the maximum useful time for recording a given trial typically does not exceed 2 to 3 seconds.

In most ERP investigations, these segments of EEG signal are averaged
together for each participant, across multiple trials from a given condition,
and each electrode site separately, to make up what are usually referred to
as individual averages. Typically, each participant in an ERP experiment
will have several individual averages, each representing data collected during one or more types of trials. For example, in a simplified hypothetical ERP experiment where the participant is shown two types of visual
stimuli (faces, objects), each participant would have two individual averages, one representing an average of the ERP responses for all of the trials where faces were shown and another for the trials that consisted of
objects. Data derived from the individual averages typically make up the
unit of analysis in ERP studies. Very generally, for each individual average,
the amplitudes (usually reported in microvolts) of the peaks of relevant
waveforms are determined through a combination of software algorithm
and manual inspection. Likewise, the latencies (i.e., time of occurrence) of
the peak amplitudes of the waveforms are also determined. These values
are then submitted to appropriate statistical analyses.

Although data at the level of individual averages are utilized for statistical analyses, the grand mean is typically what is illustrated in write-ups of
ERP experiments (see Fig. 3.1). The grand mean is a mean of the individual averages from each relevant group or condition. Thus, continuing
the hypothetical experiment from above, the authors of this study would
most likely include two grand means in their write-up, one illustrating the
face condition and one of the object condition. The grand mean is useful in illustrating the morphology of waveforms and, as an average over
many participants, is less "noisy" and provides a composite picture of the
waveforms elicited by the ERP paradigm.

Application of ERP Methodology

ERP methodology is ideal for use in younger populations and is well suited
for assessment of neural function even in young infants; in contrast, the
use of other, more invasive imaging techniques such as functional magnetic resonance imaging (fMRI) or positron emission tomography (PET)
are typically only justified in infants and young children when medically necessary. In addition, although other, less invasive methods such as

magnetoencephalography (MEG) could potentially be used with younger children, the typical task demands associated with the use of these imaging methods as well as the need for the participant to sit still and sustain attention for long periods of time restrict their use for young children. In contrast, ERP experiments can be designed to require little if any motor response from the participant. Also, whereas participants in ERP experiments do need to minimize motor activity during data collection, as large muscle movements will introduce movement artifact (EMG) into the data, there is no need to remain absolutely still during data collection. While it is possible to correct for a relatively small degree of head movement during an fMRI experiment, the degree of movement allowed in an ERP experiment is generally greater and more easily corrected. The need for participants to remain very still during fMRI, in addition to ethical considerations concerning the use of this technology in younger, non-clinical samples, generally precludes the use of fMRI in children under the age of 8 years. In contrast, however, ERPs can be practically utilized beginning in the neonatal period.

Although metabolic-based procedures for brain imaging such as fMRI do provide superior spatial resolution and lend themselves ideally to the localization of brain function, ERPs are still unmatched in their ability to provide millisecond-level temporal resolution of neural functioning. Historically, however, ERPs have provided very poor spatial resolution. As recently as 15 years ago, it was not uncommon for published ERP studies to have utilized as few as 3 or 4 electrodes, and up until merely 10 years ago a 32-channel electrode array was considered state of the art. However, with the recent advent of high-density EEG electrode arrays, allowing experimenters to record from 128 and even 256 electrodes simultaneously (e.g., Geodesic Sensor Net [GSN], Tucker, 1993), and the application of newly developed sophisticated source localization software algorithms to these data (e.g., Brain Electrical Source Analysis [BESA], Berg & Scherg, 1994; Scherg, 1990), it is now possible to localize the source of ERP signal to a much greater degree of accuracy and certainty than ever before. In dipole-source modeling, complex mathematical models are applied to scalp-recorded electrical activity, whereby location (source) and the relative strength of the EEG signal can be inferred across the scalp.

This ability to localize neural function fairly well with ERPs, combined with their high degree of temporal resolution, makes them an ideal tool with which to study neural functioning in infants and young children. In addition, given the relatively noninvasive procedure required to place electrodes on the scalp and record ERPs, this methodology is ideally suited for use with children who have experienced trauma and for whom enduring more invasive brain imaging procedures may exacerbate their potentially stressful reactions to participating in research of this nature. In sum, although ERPs do not represent a type of functional neuroimaging technique per se (in the strict sense that ERPs do not yield a direct "image" of the brain), the data provided by this methodology can provide an invaluable addition to knowledge about the neurofunctional characteristics of many aspects of cognition and memory.

A Brief Historical Context for ERPs

In 1929, Hans Berger reported the results of the first experiment in which he demonstrated that electrical activity could be recorded from the human brain by placing an electrode on the scalp, amplifying the signal, and plotting the change in voltage over time (Berger, 1929). Initially, the existence of this signal, called the electroencephalogram (EEG), was met with some skepticism, although over the next few years others confirmed the existence of this ongoing electrical activity produced by the brain (e.g., Adrian & Matthews, 1934; Gibbs, Davis, & Lennox, 1935; Jasper & Carmichael, 1935). The measure of ongoing brain electrical activity represented by the EEG proved to be useful in a variety of research and clinical applications in subsequent years. However, the development of the ERP, a more specific measure of the brain's response to discrete stimuli that is embedded within a brief time frame of the EEG (e.g., 1 to 2 seconds), was not developed until some years later. Luck (2005) reported that the first ERP recordings from awake humans were reported by Davis (1939). ERP research began to come into its own in the 1950s, although most of this early work involved recordings of basic sensory responses and did not examine neural processes underlying what would be considered higher-order cognitive functioning (i.e., memory, attention).

The first experiment investigating a cognitive-based ERP waveform was published by Walter, Cooper, Alkdridge, McCallum, and Winter (1964). These investigators recorded an ERP waveform, which they called the contingent negative variation (CNV), that was linked with a preparatory cognitive response associated with pressing a button upon detection of a particular visual stimulus. Shortly thereafter, the P3 (or P300) component was discovered by Sutton, Braren, Zubin, and John (1965). This was a large, positive waveform that peaked approximately 300 ms after the presentation of a nonpredictable stimulus. In the two decades following the publication of that paper, hundreds of empirical studies were published examining this particular waveform, and in addition a large body of work was devoted to identifying a multitude of other ERP waveforms. Further, a great deal of research was dedicated to developing methods for recording and analyzing ERPs, as well as experimental methodologies for eliciting different types of cognitively based ERP waveforms. Much of this work from the 1970s and 1980s was devoted to discovering and understanding different ERP waveforms, and, until very recently, little work has focused on applying knowledge of ERPs to attempt to answer questions of broad scientific interest, in particular those about human development and the effect of social experience on neural processes (Luck, 2005).

While an extensive literature utilizing ERPs to study a wide range of cognitive processes in adults has developed since the discovery of the P3, employing ERPs to study the neural bases of cognitive developmental processes in infants and children has only more recently occurred. As articulated by Nelson (1995) and Nelson and Bloom (1997), the relative lack of study of neurodevelopmental processes in children during an era in which the field of cognitive neuroscience was established and flourishing was due, in part, to a firmly entrenched approach in developmental psychology to examining human behavior at a level of analysis largely confined to behavioral description of psychological phenomena (see also Cicchetti, 2002a Goldman-Rakic, 1987; Segalowitz, 1994). In addition, the approach of neuroscience was viewed by many in the field of developmental psychology as too reductionistic to be fruitfully applied to answer questions about human development.

However, beginning in the 1980s and continuing to the present time, many researchers in developmental psychology have incorporated neuroscientific methodology into the study of development, and in particular have applied brain imaging techniques to the study of cognitive developmental processes (Amso & Casey, 2006; Casey, Tottenham, Liston, & Durston, 2005; Nelson & Monk, 2001; Nelson, Thomas, & de Haan, 2006; Thomas & Cicchetti, in press). Event-related potentials have proven to be a particularly useful tool in the study of memory and memory development in infants and children, and a relatively large body of work exists that has identified the nature and morphology of ERP waveforms associated with memory processes in infants and young children (see Nelson, 1994, 1995, and Nelson & Webb, 2003, for detailed reviews of the work in this area). Thus, ERPs have now been used extensively to examine normative cognitive developmental processes in infancy and childhood, and have increased our understanding of the neural processes underlying the development of memory, attention, and other realms of cognition.

In the following section, we provide a review of the relevant literature on the neural correlates of memory development as revealed by the use of ERPs. We first provide a brief overview of experimental paradigms that have been employed in ERP memory research conducted with normal infants and children. Next, we examine the morphology and development of specific ERP waveforms that have been found to be associated with memory functioning and related cognitive processes in normally developing samples of infants and children. In keeping with a developmental psychopathology perspective, the knowledge gleaned from investigations on the neural correlates of memory derived from basic research with typical infants and children is used to suggest ways in which the experimental study of ERPs and memory can provide a valuable entrée into the mechanisms whereby maltreatment affects the developmental processes underlying memory.

ERPs and Memory: An Overview of Experimental Paradigms

A number of investigators have employed ERPs over the past several decades to examine early cognitive and linguistic development (e.g., Alho, Sainio, Sajaniemi, Reinikainen, & Naatanen, 1990; Molfese & Molfese, 1985). To date, however, the large majority of ERP research with infants and young children has investigated recognition memory (see Nelson, 1994, 1996, and Nelson et al., 2006, for a comprehensive review of this area).

Such cognitive research employing ERP methodology with infants examined neurofunctional processes associated with discrimination and recognition memory, primarily utilizing either a standard version of the adult "oddball" paradigm or a combination of infant habituation and the oddball paradigm (Nelson, 1994), with the first such studies published in the early 1980s (Courchesne, Ganz, & Norcia, 1981; Hofmann & Salapatek, 1981; Hofmann, Salapatek, & Kuskowski, 1981). This experimental procedure involves the sequential presentation of stimuli (usually visual or auditory), some of which occur more frequently than others, with a typical ratio of frequent to infrequent of 80% versus 20%. While an adult subject would be instructed to attend and/or respond to one stimulus or another, for infants this paradigm involves "passive" viewing of (or listening to) the stimuli with no overt response required. In addition to work employing a direct adaptation of the adult oddball paradigm, other investigators have modified the oddball procedure to make it comparable to the infant habituation paradigm, thus including a preliminary familiarization period consisting of the presentation of a single stimulus over repeated trials followed by a sequence of trials in which the familiar stimulus is then presented in conjunction with an unfamiliar, or novel, stimulus (e.g., Bornstein, 1985; Nelson & Collins, 1991; Nelson & deRegnier, 1992; Nelson & Salapatek, 1986).

The rationale for this experimental approach to the study of recognition memory with ERPs dates to early work by Fantz (1961, 1963) that utilized a paired comparison procedure in which it was found that infants looked longer at novel stimuli than at familiar stimuli. This experimental paradigm has been employed in hundreds of behavioral studies examining recognition memory in infants (for reviews, see Aslin, 1987, and Kellman & Arterberry, 2006). The adaptation of this paradigm and modifications of it for use in ERP studies has provided a wealth of data concerning the ontogeny of recognition memory, as well as theoretical models of the neural processes underlying recognition memory (Nelson, 1994). Behavioral measures of the time spent looking in the visual paired comparison task index what decision an infant has made concerning the compared stimuli, but ERPs, on the other hand, have been able to provide a great deal of additional information from data received from electrical activity of the brain, such as when the decision was reached, the neural processes underlying the decision, and what areas of the brain are employed in reaching a decision (Nelson, 1994).

As adapted for the investigation of recognition memory in infants utilizing ERPs, the assumption underlying the oddball paradigm is that, over enough trials, the high-probability events will become relatively more familiar to the infant than the low-probability trials, and thus the two types of events (familiar and unfamiliar) will elicit different cognitive and brain responses. It is presumed that the more frequently seen stimulus will be encoded into memory, while the less frequently seen stimulus will be "less" encoded (i.e., the memory will not be firmly established). Consequently, when the infrequent stimulus is viewed, a neurocognitive operation typically referred to as "updating" must take place in order to more firmly encode this stimulus into memory. Thus, recognition memory is inferred based on differential cortical responses to each of the memory-stimulus types.

In infants, this paradigm typically elicits a middle-latency negative ERP component over central scalp electrodes referred to as Negative Central (Nc; see Fig. 3.1), which is assumed to reflect a general orienting response associated with attention. The Nc has been found to be greater in amplitude following novel stimulus presentations. Late slow waves proposed to reflect recognition memory include the negative slow wave (NSW, associated with novelty detection) and the positive slow wave (PSW, associated with an updating of recognition memory) (see next section of this chapter for more detailed summaries of these waveforms).

The particular modality (visual, auditory) and form (voice, tone, pictures of objects, faces) of the stimulus in this paradigm have many variations, as do the ratio of familiar to unfamiliar and degree of habituation. ERP studies of recognition memory continue to incorporate the oddball paradigm, in part due to its widespread prevalence, reproducibility, simplicity, and applicability across sensory modalities. One adaptation in particular has involved a line of research utilizing faces as visual stimuli in several variations of the oddball paradigm. This approach has particular relevance for ERP studies of infants and children who have experienced maltreatment, in that the use of faces as stimuli—in particular those with expressions of emotion—can potentially tap into not only recognition memory per se but also memory that involves perception and encoding of emotion.

ERP Waveforms and Memory

When studying infants and children, researchers have documented numerous ERP waveforms that appear to be correlates of underlying neurocognitive processes related to memory. As a result, great progress has been made in understanding the neural processes underlying the behavioral manifestations of memory as well as memory development (e.g., Nelson, 1995). An important consideration in examining the impact of maltreatment is the effect it may have on the developing brain (Cicchetti, 2002b; Cicchetti & Tucker, 1994; DeBellis, 2001). It is particularly important to utilize a developmental perspective in considering the effect of maltreatment on ERPs and memory, as there are morphological changes in many ERP waveforms across development that may reflect both maturational changes in the brain and development of the underlying cognitive processes. In addition, it would be quite useful to employ ERPs to investigate environmental influences on brain functioning and development, in particular those brought about by the experience of maltreatment. Although some of the waveforms to be reviewed are not necessarily directly related to memory processing per se, they nonetheless appear to represent neural processing indirectly related to memory. As such, examining these ERP waveforms may provide important insight into the effects of maltreatment on memory.

P300

The P300 (also referred to as the P3b or "classical" P3), perhaps the most extensively studied ERP component, is a positive waveform that peaks between 300 and 900 ms after stimulus presentation, and in adults is typically maximal in electrode sites over the parietal lobe. This waveform is elicited by an infrequent stimulus presented in the context of an oddball paradigm and is believed to represent neural processes involved in context updating (i.e., updating one's representation of the current environment) or revising the contents of recognition or working memory (Donchin, 1981; Rugg, 1995). Source modeling of the P300 has localized its origin specifically to the hippocampal and parietal cortical regions, and possibly the temporal lobe as well (Nakajima, Miyamoto, & Kikuchi, 1994). Studies of individuals with physical lesions in the brain corroborate these findings, with damage to tissue in the temporal–parietal junction inducing a loss of the P300 waveform (e.g., Knight, 1990).

   The hallmark of the P300 is its sensitivity to stimulus probability; the amplitude of this waveform reliably increases as stimulus probability decreases (see Duncan-Johnson & Donchin, 1977, for the classic work on this topic). In addition to its relation to stimulus probability, the amplitude of the P300 is also generally greater the more a particular stimulus deviates from the ongoing stream of familiar stimuli (e.g., Fabiani, Karis, & Donchin, 1990). Distinct from the P300 is another subcomponent referred to as the P3a (an earlier occurring component believed to be generated by an automatic, nonmemory related response to novel stimuli (Knight &

Scabini, 1998). Many studies examining the nature of the P300 itself have shown a multitude of factors that have an effect on the amplitude of the P300, including presentation probability (Duncan-Johnson & Donchin, 1977), stimulus sequence (Duncan-Johnson & Donchin, 1982), stimulus quality, attention, and task relevance of the stimulus (Coles, Smid, Scheffers, & Otten, 1995).

This wide variety of experimental conditions under which the P300 can be elicited has resulted in this waveform being implicated in a range of cognitive processes, and the debate concerning its exact psychological meaning is far from over (Luck, 2005). However, its association with recognition memory through the oddball paradigm has been consistent in the literature, and the general consensus appears to be that the context-updating interpretation of the P300 originally put forth by Donchin (1981), and its relation to updating of working memory (e.g., Rugg, 1995), is the best first approximation to its significance. Aside from the many methodological variations involved in the study of the P300 per se and the disagreement in the literature concerning the exact cognitive process(es) represented by the P300 and the neural generators that give rise to it, there is a vast body of literature supporting its association with updating and/or revising the contents of memory.

Despite the vast literature describing the characteristics and function of the P300 in adults, little work has been done examining the development and nature of this waveform in children. Although some work has shown an auditory P300 produced in the second year of life (e.g., Hoffman & Salapatek, 1981; Hoffman, Salapatek, & Kuskowski, 1981; McIsaac & Polich, 1992), there is some contention that the wave identified as a P300 in this work was not analogous to an adult P300 (see Nelson, 1994, for a critical review). However, early studies by Courchesne (1977, 1978) demonstrated that in children as young as 6 years of age, a P300 elicited by rare, target stimuli in an oddball paradigm was apparent, with a peak latency of approximately 700 ms. The latency of the peak amplitude of the P300 steadily decreased in older children (i.e., the waveform occurred earlier or more quickly), and declined to 400 to 500 ms in young adults. In a study comparing ERP waveforms in adults and a group of 8-year-olds, Thomas and Nelson (1996) demonstrated that the infrequent stimulus in an oddball paradigm elicited a robust P300 in both groups. The findings from this study were consistent with those in the Courchesne (1977, 1978) studies, with the children's P300 waveform broader in shape (less sharply peaked) and occurring later than the P300 observed in the adults.

The P300 waveform appears to develop beginning in middle childhood, with pronounced shifts in characteristics, such as latency, occurring into adulthood. However, it is unclear exactly when (and how) this waveform appears. Thomas and Nelson (1996) demonstrated the P300 in children 8 years old, but the P300 is generally not observed in ERP studies utilizing visual stimuli in infants and young children. A cross-sectional ERP study that included infants, 4-year-old children, and adults demonstrated that while face stimuli elicited a robust P300 in the adults, there was not evidence of a P300 in the 4-year-olds (Scott, Luciana, Wewerka, & Nelson, 2005). However, an earlier study by Nelson and Nugent (1990) demonstrated a waveform with positive peak at approximately 700 ms in a sample of 5-year-olds that was similar in morphology and function to an adult P300. Nelson and colleagues (e.g., Nelson, Thomas, de Haan, & Wewerka, 1998) have speculated that the positive slow wave (PSW; see next section of this chapter) consistently observed in ERP studies of infant memory, and believed to represent the updating of working memory, may be the developmental precursor of the P300. However, to date there are no longitudinal studies of children spanning the period from infancy through middle childhood that could reveal the emergence of the P300 waveform and the morphological changes in ERPs that might accompany this developmental process.

Study of the P300 in the context of maltreatment and memory would allow direct neurofunctional examination of possible memory deficits associated with the experience of maltreatment. Neurobehavioral studies of children who have been maltreated and manifest symptoms of post-traumatic stress disorder (PTSD) report memory deficits in this population (DeBellis, 2001). Thus relevant questions would be whether behavioral evidence of memory deficits in children who have experienced maltreatment is associated with anomalies in the P300 and, more specifically, whether the experience of maltreatment delays the emergence of the P300 waveform. Such research would elucidate the neurofunctional process by which maltreatment may lead to deficits in memory functioning.

ERP studies of school-age maltreated children (Pollak, Cicchetti, Klorman, & Brumaghim, 1997; Pollak, Klorman, Thatcher, & Cicchetti, 2001; Pollak & Tolley-Schell, 2003) have examined the P300 as an index of selective attention as it may be associated with context updating;

however, these investigators have not directly interpreted their findings in the context of memory functioning. An examination of the P300 in children who have experienced maltreatment, particularly the development of the P300 and its relation to memory processes, would be an especially fruitful area of study. Longitudinal examination of the emergence of the P300 from early to middle childhood would provide an unprecedented opportunity to investigate the effects of maltreatment on the development of the brain and neural correlates of memory.

Positive Slow Wave

This waveform was first reported in early work by Courchesne and colleagues examining changes in ERP waveforms from childhood to adulthood (Courchesne, 1977, 1978; Courchesne et al., 1981). It is a long-latency, positive slow wave that begins approximately 1000 ms after stimulus onset and continues for up to another 1000 ms (see Figure 3.1 for an example of the morphology of this component). The designation "slow wave" indicates that this waveform does not exhibit a sharp peak but rather encompasses a broad temporal window, slowly increasing in amplitude and then gradually decreasing (see Fig. 3.1). In Courchesne's work, the PSW occurred in 4- to 7-month-old infants in response to infrequently presented stimuli (see Courchesne et al., 1981). The PSW has been primarily examined in infants older than 6 months of age, but it has recently been observed in 4-month-old infants (Webb, Long, & Nelson, 2005). It is generally evoked in response to a single, repeated novel stimulus embedded in a sequence of familiar stimuli (oddball paradigm). This waveform appears somewhat ubiquitous and is nearly always observed in ERP studies of infants and young children, but it does not appear in ERPs elicited by recognition memory tasks in adults (e.g., Nelson et al., 1998). However, there are no specific studies indicating at what age the PSW ceases to be apparent.

Based on an extensive line of ERP research on the development of recognition memory in infants and young children, Nelson and colleagues have concluded that the PSW is elicited by stimuli that have only been partially encoded, and thus require updating in memory (e.g., deHaan & Nelson, 1997; Nelson, 1994; Nelson & Collins, 1991; Nelson & deRegnier, 1992; Nelson & Monk, 2001). Specifically, Nelson (1994) has suggested that the PSW reflects a process whereby infants have begun to form what he terms a somewhat unstable or tenuous "template" for a relatively novel stimulus that has been seen infrequently (but one that is not completely novel, as no template could exist for such a stimulus). According to this conceptualization, this template must be periodically updated in working memory, with the PSW representing the electrical byproduct of the neural process underlying this updating. Thus the PSW occurs in response to stimuli that have only been partially encoded by the infant, with a stimulus that has been fully encoded into memory generally yielding an ERP pattern that shows a return to baseline following the Nc.

Some investigators have theorized that the PSW represents a process that has generally been interpreted as reflecting the updating of working memory, or context updating, analogous to that described by Donchin regarding the adult P300 wave (e.g., Donchin, 1981; Donchin & Coles, 1988). However, it is critical to remember that the PSW is almost certainly not a P300 per se, due to a variety of anatomical and physiological reasons (Nelson, 1994). In sum, the PSW most certainly indexes some component of memory processes, with much of the evidence pointing toward the idea that it represents updating of memory for those stimuli that have been only partially encoded. Similar to the P300, study of the PSW in children who have experienced maltreatment provides a potential opportunity to examine the developmental course of an ERP waveform strongly associated with memory processes. As will be detailed in a later section of this chapter, Cicchetti and Curtis (2005) have demonstrated hemispheric differences in the PSW in a sample of maltreated and nonmaltreated 30-month-old children.

Negative Central

The Nc is a middle-latency ERP component that is manifested as a negative deflection in the ERP that is maximal between 400 and 800 ms following the onset of a stimulus (see Figure 3.1 for an example of the morphology of this component). Generally, this waveform is quite robust, with a well-defined negative peak, and is present regardless of the familiarity, probability, or type of stimuli presented. It has maximal amplitude over fronto-central scalp regions. In a recent study utilizing dipole source modeling, the Nc was found to be localized to the anterior cingulate and other regions in the frontal cortex (Reynolds & Richards, 2005). This waveform has been observed in infants as young as 4 to 7 weeks old (e.g., Karrer & Monti, 1995) and persists as a prominent ERP wave feature through middle childhood. However, this waveform is generally not seen in adult ERPs.

A variety of studies of the Nc in infants have provided seemingly contradictory results concerning its behavioral correlates. Some studies have shown Nc is of greater amplitude in response to unexpected or un-recognizable events and infrequently presented stimuli (e.g., Courchesne et al., 1981; Karrer & Ackles, 1987), while others have demonstrated greater-amplitude Nc in response to familiar stimuli (e.g., de Haan & Nelson, 1997, 1999; Nelson et al., 2000; Snyder, Webb, & Nelson, 2002; Webb & Nelson, 2001). In general, however, these inconsistent findings appear to be due to the degree of familiarity with the stimuli used to elicit the Nc waveform. Those studies showing greater Nc amplitude in response to infrequent (or rare) events have employed the conventional oddball paradigm, with infants having no prior exposure to any of the stimuli. However, the studies conducted by Nelson and colleagues show-ing greater Nc amplitude in response to familiar events (e.g., de Haan & Nelson, 1997) have utilized stimuli familiar to the infant prior to the ex-periment (e.g., the mother's face) that were quite dissimilar in appearance to the unfamiliar stimuli, and they presented the familiar and unfamiliar stimuli with equal frequency.

The Nc waveform has been characterized as an obligatory or auto-matic attentional response (e.g., Courchesne et al., 1981; Karrer & Ackles, 1987; Nelson, 1994; Nelson & Collins, 1992; Nelson & Monk, 2001). Because it is the most robust of ERP components seen during infancy (it can often be observed on single trials and is manifested regardless of type or frequency of stimulus), the Nc waveform is largely considered to be automatic. However, despite its seeming automaticity, the amplitude of Nc does vary within individuals depending on the type and/or frequency of the eliciting stimuli.

Consistent with typically observed developmental changes in ERP waveforms, the latency of the Nc peak primarily depends upon the age of the participant, with the peak, on average, occurring earlier in older children. For example, at 4 months, the Nc peak has been observed at around 700 to 800 ms post stimulus onset, with a fairly rapid decrease in latency to approximately 400 to 500 ms by 12 months of age. In addition to the expected normative decrease in peak latency, there appears to be a change in terms of what type of stimuli elicits the greater amplitude Nc from infancy to early childhood. Consistent with previous findings by Nelson and colleagues, Carver et al. (2003) demonstrated that children under 24 months of age demonstrated a larger Nc amplitude in response to a familiar face compared to an unfamiliar face. However, the reverse pattern was seen in children older than 45 months, with these older children exhibiting greater Nc amplitude in response to an unfamiliar face compared to a familiar face. It is unclear what the neurofunctional significance of this shift may be.

The association of the Nc ERP component with memory per se is not clear, and it appears that this waveform may generally be more correlated with some fundamental neurobehavioral aspects of attention than memory. However, this waveform's responsivity to stimulus familiarity (e.g., Carver et al., 2003; de Haan & Nelson, 1997; Webb et al., 2005), in particular those stimuli to which infants have been pre-exposed (e.g., mother's face, favorite toy), may suggest that it could be associated with broader neural processes related to recognition memory (e.g., Reynolds & Richards, 2005). In the sense that familiarity with a stimulus may indirectly index memory, the neural processes underlying the generation of the Nc waveform may be of interest in ERP research on memory with children who have been maltreated. Also, examining the developmental aspects of this waveform and its behavioral correlates may also help inform questions of how the experience of child maltreatment may effect brain development generally.

N400

The N400 waveform is most typically considered to be a language-related ERP component, indexing violations of semantic expectancies (Luck, 2005). It is a negative-going wave that displays maximal amplitude over central and parietal electrode sites, with its neural generator believed to be located in the left temporal lobe (Luck, 2005). In addition, the N400 also has been linked to memory processing (Halgren & Smith, 1987; Rugg & Doyle, 1994). For example, in tasks where new and old stimuli are presented, the new stimuli elicit a greater-amplitude N400. Also, the amplitude of the N400 decreases with stimulus repetition, further indicating that this waveform is sensitive to familiarity (Rugg & Doyle, 1994). Thus, some ERP researchers (e.g., Halgren & Smith, 1987) have theorized that the N400 indexes the ease with which the currently viewed stimulus is integrated into the current context, with greater facility (i.e., integrating a repeated stimulus versus one that does not "fit" into the context of other stimuli) associated with lower-amplitude N400.

There are no published reports concerning the developmental course of the N400. Nelson and Monk (2001) have speculated that the Nc observed in infants and toddlers may evolve into the N400 by age 4 or 5 years, but this idea remains untested. However, the N400 is another ERP component that could potentially be utilized to index some aspect of memory functioning in children who have experienced maltreatment, particularly in the context of examining the developmental course of the Nc.

Negative Slow Wave

This long-latency slow wave has been described in infant ERPs by Karrer and colleagues (e.g., Karrer & Ackles, 1987) and Nelson and colleagues (e.g., de Haan & Nelson, 1997; Nelson & Collins, 1992). The NSW has typically been observed to follow the Nc and occurs when infants detect the periodic appearance of an unfamiliar stimulus in a presentation of otherwise familiar stimuli (Nelson, 1994). The NSW may represent neural processes underlying the detection of novel events against a background of familiar events, under conditions where an unfamiliar stimulus has not been previously encoded into memory, but not the updating of memory for the unfamiliar stimulus (a process represented by the PSW) (Nelson, 1994).

Generally, the NSW has not been observed beyond the infancy period (Nelson & Monk, 2001).

Developmental Changes in ERPs

To date, much of what is known about the development of ERPs elicited by visual stimuli has been derived from studies of memory development in children less than a year old (for a recent, comprehensive review of this area, see DeBoer, Scott, & Nelson, 2004). In general, there are three broad ERP characteristics that change with development: (1) peak amplitude, (2) latency, and (3) the actual morphology (shape) of the waveforms and the types of waveforms that are manifested.

Overall, there is a decrease in the latency of the peaks of ERP waveforms with development. (see Figs. 3.2*A* through 3.2*D*). Often, as in the case of Nc, there is a rapid change in latency of the waveform peak in the first year of life. Webb et al. (2005), in a longitudinal investigation of the development of ERP waveforms from 4 months to 12 months of age in a recognition memory paradigm, showed that the most significant latency decreases for Nc occurred from 4 to 8 months. This decreased latency is almost certainly brought about by normative brain maturational processes, such as increased myelination and refinement of synapses, that result in decreases in processing speed. This phenomenon is illustrated in Figure 3.2, where the latency of the Nc waveform is elicited by identical experimental paradigms whereby a face is passively viewed, across samples of children at 6 months, 15 months, 30 months, and 45 months of age. As can be seen, the mean latency of Nc decreases by 126 ms across 39 months.

Cross-sectional studies have examined the development of the P300 evoked by visual stimuli. This waveform has not been observed in children younger than 4 years of age. However, to date, no longitudinal studies have documented the development of this waveform, and thus it is unknown exactly when, how, and under what experimental circumstances this waveform appears. Nelson and colleagues have made the convincing theoretical argument that the infant PSW is the precursor to the later-observed P300 (e.g., Nelson, 1994). Examining the development of ERP waveforms in children who have experienced maltreatment, given the probable association of changes in ERP waveform latency and morphology with development of the neural substrate, would potentially provide valuable information concerning the effects of maltreatment on the developing brain.

One important caveat in interpreting developmental ERP studies of infants and children is that, to date, with the exception of Webb et al. (2005), they are cross-sectional, typically comparing ERP waveforms among groups of individuals of different ages. In addition, many of the paradigms used in studying ERP waveforms in adults and school-aged children have involved active-task responses (e.g., pressing a button when a "target" stimulus is presented), while, of necessity, ERP studies of infants and young children have employed passive viewing paradigms (i.e., the infant simply looks at stimuli). Interestingly, some studies (e.g., Nelson et al., 1998) have compared adult ERPs in passive and active paradigms,

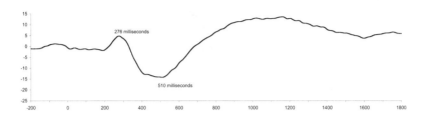

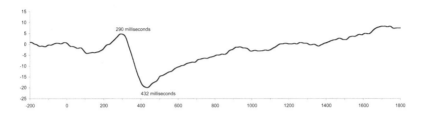

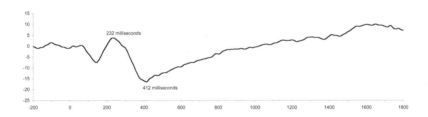

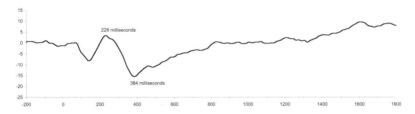

FIGURE 3.2. (From top) (*A*) Event-related potential (ERP) data (grand mean) from a sample of 6-month-old infants elicited while viewing face stimuli. (*B*) ERP data (grand mean) from a sample of 15-month-old infants elicited while viewing face stimuli. (*C*) ERP data (grand mean) from a sample of 30-month-old children elicited while viewing face stimuli. (*D*) ERP data (grand mean) from a sample of 45-month-old children elicited while viewing face stimuli. For all plots, data is from the Cz electrode (midline central scalp region), the vertical axis is amplitude is in microvolts, and the horizontal axis is time in milliseconds.

with both conditions eliciting P300 waveforms, with the active condition eliciting a greater-amplitude P300.

The next section of this chapter, following a brief review of the effects of maltreatment on the development of socioemotional and neuro-behavioral functioning, will critically examine the few existing studies of ERPs in children reared in atypical emotional environments. Although these studies have not employed ERPs to directly examine memory functioning in these at-risk children, they do provide some insight into the potential usefulness of ERP methodology for elucidating the associa-tion of maltreatment with memory deficits.

Child Maltreatment: Its Effect on Multiple Levels of Child Functioning

Extensive empirical investigations have provided ample evidence to impli-cate child maltreatment in the disruption of diverse areas of cognitive and socioemotional development, including emotion regulation and recogni-tion, the formation of secure attachment relationships, autonomy and inte-gration of the self system, effective peer relations, and successful adaptation to school (Cicchetti & Toth, 2005; Cicchetti & Valentino, 2006). Children who experience maltreatment and the associated disruptions in development often develop a profile of vulnerability factors that increases the probabil-ity of the emergence of maladaptation and psychopathology, accompanied by continued negative transactions with the environment (Cicchetti, 1989; Cicchetti & Lynch, 1995; Cicchetti & Toth, 1995, 2005).

Theoretical formulations and research investigations in the area of child maltreatment have examined and described the developmental outcomes associated with child maltreatment utilizing the domain of variables that focus primarily on the level of behavioral functioning of the individual, family, and community system. However, it has only been over the past decade that researchers investigating the consequences of child maltreat-ment have examined its impact on the brain and other neurobiological systems, as well as investigated the potential role that the alteration of these biological systems, in response to the experience of maltreatment, may have on the behavioral manifestation of atypical developmental and psychopathological outcomes.

There is a growing amount of evidence in the neuroscience litera-ture indicating that social experience alters brain structure, function, and organization across development (see, e.g., Black, Jones, Nelson, & Greenough, 1998; Cicchetti, 2002b; Greenough, Black, & Wallace, 1987; Nelson, 1999). Not surprisingly, research specifically examining the impact of adverse experience on humans and other animal species has clearly demonstrated the negative impact of such adversity on the brain and associated neurobiological systems (e.g., Gunnar & Vasquez, 2006; McEwen, 2000; Nelson, 2000a). In addition, recent work has begun to highlight the types of alterations of brain and biological functioning brought on by the experience of maltreatment (see Bremner, 2003; DeBellis, 2001, 2005; and Teicher, 2002, for reviews).

A more complete and integrated understanding of the vulnerability faced by maltreated children will be achieved only through examination of risk processes at multiple levels of analysis (see Cicchetti & Dawson, 2002). To date, studies that have directly examined brain structure and functioning in maltreated children have not explicitly tested the relation among biological systems, maladaptive developmental outcomes, and psychopathology. Nonetheless, the results from a number of these investigations have suggested possible linkages between some aspects of brain structure and functioning and the subsequent development of psychopathology (e.g., Cicchetti & Curtis, 2005; Cicchetti & Rogosch, 2001; DeBellis, Baum, et al., 1999; DeBellis, Keshavan, et al., 1999; Pollak et al., 1997). In addition, evidence from many of these studies has begun to suggest how the experience of maltreatment may effect memory functioning.

ERP Studies of Rearing in Atypical Environments

In this section, we review studies that have utilized ERPs to examine the effects of rearing in atypical emotional environments. The first investigations to be reviewed were carried out by Parker, Nelson, and their colleagues in the Bucharest Early Intervention Project Core Group (Parker & Nelson, 2005a, 2005b). These investigators conducted two studies with two groups of Romanian youngsters; one group was institutionalized and the other had never experienced institutional care. The researchers examined ERP waveforms evoked by facial expressions of emotion. Although not focused on child maltreatment by parents, these investigations have demonstrated the effects of institutional rearing and the associated emotional and physical neglect on brain functioning in young children.

Beginning with early studies by Spitz (1945a, 1945b), ample evidence has accumulated demonstrating the negative consequences of institutional rearing on the development and behavior of young children. While initial studies focused on intellectual development of children reared in institutions, finding drastic and permanent declines in intellectual functioning (Spitz, 1945a, 1945b), more recent work has shown that some aspects of functioning compromised by institutional rearing show recovery (e.g., Tizard, 1977). However, regardless of the degree of recovery of function and the circumstances under which this comes about, the consensus of findings across time and studies has consistently demonstrated the negative impact of institutionalization on all aspects of children's development, including intellectual, physical, behavioral, and socioemotional (for a comprehensive review of this area, see MacLean, 2003).

Researchers have not been able to clearly specify the mechanisms by which institutional upbringing is associated with the observed negative developmental outcomes. The specific factors or characteristics of institutions that are predictive of particular sets of deficits is not known, given the profound deprivation experienced by children across multiple realms (e.g., nutrition, emotional contact) that may each affect multiple areas of functioning and development. The studies by Parker and Nelson (2005a, 2005b) sought to examine the sequelae of institutional rearing on socioemotional development and functioning by utilizing ERPs to index institutionalized children's neural responses to facial expressions of emotion (Parker & Nelson, 2005a) and to familiar versus unfamiliar faces (Parker & Nelson, 2005b).

Parker and Nelson (2005a) worked with institutionalized Romanian infants between the ages of 7 and 32 months, examining the ERPs evoked by fearful, angry, happy, and sad facial expressions in order to ascertain whether these youngsters' deficits in processing emotional and social cues in behavioral interactions might have their origins in difficulties in the recognition of basic human emotions (see, e.g., O'Connor, Brendenkamp, & Rutter, 1999; O'Connor, Rutter, Beckett, Keaveney, & Kreppner, 2000; Rutter et al., 1999). Parker and Nelson (2005a) theorized that early institutional rearing, through its disruption of normal social interactions, may deprive the amygdala and its associated neural networks of vital experiences through which social and emotional stimuli are associated with internal states of pleasure and displeasure, thereby eventuating in deficits in the recognition of facial expressions of emotion. Specifically, these investigators examined four ERP waveforms elicited by these facial stimuli: (1) an early negative component (N170), believed to reflect early perceptual processes; (2) an early positive component (P250), reflecting later perceptual processes that may include recognition of the affective component of a face; (3) the Nc; and (4) the PSW.

Parker and Nelson (2005a) found that, compared to Romanian youngsters who had never resided in an institutional environment, children who were institutionalized manifested different patterns of responding in early-latency components of the ERP. Specifically, at both midline and lateral electrode sites, the never-institutionalized infants exhibited greater N170 amplitudes in response to the sad expression; in contrast, the institutionalized youngsters displayed greater N170 amplitudes elicited by the fearful expression. At the midline electrode site, never-institutionalized and institutionalized children manifested greater P250 amplitudes in response to the sad and fearful expressions, respectively.

In addition, Parker and Nelson (2005a) found that there were dramatic group differences in amplitude of all the ERP components when examined across average responses to all of the face stimuli. Relative to the institutionalized groups of children, the never-institutionalized comparison groups of youngsters displayed greater amplitudes of the N170, Nc and PSW ERP components, whereas, relative to the never-institutionalized group of children, the institutionalized group exhibited a larger amplitude of the P250. The group differences in ERP amplitude found in the Parker and Nelson (2005a) investigation provide support for the hypothesis that an early institutional upbringing may contribute to a long-lasting development of cortical hypoactivation, as well as dysfunction in emotion processing and brain function.

While this study was designed to assess neural responses to facial expressions of emotion and not memory per se, the results may have some bearing on memory processes. For example, some investigators have recently discussed the close relation between visual attention and recognition memory in infants (e.g., Reynolds & Richards, 2005; Richards, 2003). Richards (2003) argues that attention serves to enhance memory processes, and demonstrated that Nc was of greater amplitude in infants when they were indeed attending to a stimulus (as indexed by heart rate deceleration). More importantly, this increased Nc, directly tied to attentional processes, was associated with a higher probability of the occurrence of late slow waves in infant ERPs, associated with updating of memory.

Although the proposition that greater attentiveness to a stimulus is associated with enhancement of processes involved in updating memory for that stimulus may be self-evident, these co-occurring processes demonstrate the facilitative effect of attention on infant recognition memory. Thus, given that the institutionalized group of children displayed lower amplitudes of the Nc and PSW ERP components compared to the never-institutionalized group, it could be inferred that this general hypo-activation may reflect some general neurofunctional deficit in attention and memory processes. Also, early deficits in attentional processes revealed by ERPs (namely the Nc) may mark a vulnerability for these high-risk children to develop later deficits in memory functioning. Parker and Nelson (2005b) utilized the same sample of Romanian youngsters to examine neural processes involved in recognizing familiar and novel people, by recording ERPs elicited by images of caregivers' and strangers' faces. As in their other study (Parker & Nelson, 2005a), prominent amplitude differences between the institutionalized and never-institutionalized children were obtained in all of the ERP components examined (i.e., N170, P250, Nc, and PSW). With the exception of the P250 component, the amplitude of the other wave forms studied were larger in the never-institutionalized group, with the group of institutionalized children exhibiting a larger-amplitude P250.

Moreover, consistent with prior studies utilizing a similar paradigm (e.g., Carver et al., 2003; Dawson, Carver, Meltzoff, Panagiotides, McPartland, & Webb, 2002; de Haan & Nelson, 1997, 1999; Nelson & Collins, 1991), the amplitude of the Nc was greater in response to strangers' faces than to those of familiar caregivers for both the institutionalized and never institutionalized groups of children. In contrast, the institutionalized groups of youngsters displayed a greater PSW in response to the caregiver's face relative to the face of the stranger, suggesting that the faces of primary caregivers in institutionalized environments may not be fully encoded by the children assigned to their care.

The findings of deficits in recognition memory of faces of primary caregivers in this sample may have long-term consequences on several levels. Most basically, the findings may reflect general deficits (or at least delays) in neural processes related to recognition memory regardless of the type of stimuli or context. In addition, from a human-attachment perspective, these findings may have negative implications concerning the development of a secure attachment, which has as a prerequisite the ability to develop an internal working model of the attachment figure (Bowlby, 1980, 1988). The development of such a model almost certainly requires the ability to encode and easily remember the face (or some salient aspect) of the primary caregiver (Sroufe, 1996). The pattern of ERP evidence from Parker and Nelson (2005b) suggests that the ability to fully encode the face of the primary caregiver is compromised in the institutionalized children.

The next set of studies to be reviewed has examined ERP waveforms in children who have experienced child abuse and neglect. The bulk of this work has been conducted by Pollak and his colleagues, who have examined ERPs in response to various classes of emotion stimuli (Pollak et al., 1997; Pollak et al., 2001). This research has focused on elucidating the potential mechanisms through which the chronic stress experienced by children who have been maltreated could eventuate in problems in the processing of emotion (Pollak, Cicchetti, & Klorman, 1998), focusing on the construct of human attachment.

Attachment systems have been theorized to be constructed to permit flexible responses to environmental circumstances, to influence and be influenced by emotion-regulation abilities, and to function through internal working models that children hold of themselves and of their relationships with others (Bowlby, 1969/1982; Bretherton, 1990; Cassidy, 1994; Sroufe, 1996). In their ERP investigations, Pollak and colleagues have strived to ascertain whether the activation of these mental representations, which could be characterized as involving memory processes (i.e., retrieval), may be reflected through physiological activity as well as behavior. Pollak and colleagues reasoned that the P3b (P300) ERP component, which is believed to reflect neural processes involved in the updating of representations in working memory, may be useful in illuminating the cognitive processes that accompany the encoding of salient emotional stimuli.

In their first investigation, Pollak and colleagues (1997) looked at a group of school-aged children, comparing the ERPs of maltreated children to those of nonmaltreated children of comparable socioeconomic background and cognitive maturity. Across a variety of experimental conditions, different facial expressions of emotion (i.e., happy, angry, neutral) were utilized as stimuli, and the probability of occurrence (i.e., rare or frequent) and task relevance (i.e., target or nontarget) were manipulated. Children were instructed to respond to either an angry or a happy face, both of which appeared less frequently than the nontarget neutral face. The amplitude of the P3b ERP waveform of the nonmaltreated children was equivalent in both the happy and angry target conditions. In contrast, the P3b of the maltreated children was larger in the angry than in the happy target conditions. This pattern of results was interpreted by these investigators to reflect the neural correlates of a process whereby angry and happy targets activated affective representations differently for maltreated versus nonmaltreated children. Such activation may involve a process whereby experience with negative affect, likely to predominate in a maltreated child's environment, is remembered and becomes a predominant affective representation. Subsequent viewing of an angry facial expression may elicit memory processes, represented by the P3b seen in the Pollak et al. (1997) study.

In another study, conducted to determine the specificity of the relation between the ERP response of maltreated children and the nature of the eliciting stimuli, Pollak et al. (2001) examined and compared the ERP response of maltreated and nonmaltreated children to prototypic happy, angry, and fearful facial expressions. As was the case in their prior study, it was discovered that nonmaltreated children exhibited equivalent P3b amplitude in response to all of the target facial expressions of affect (e.g., anger, happiness, fear). However, the amplitude of the P3b waveform of the maltreated children exceeded that of the nonmaltreated children only in response to the angry target (Pollak et al., 2001). These investigators suggested that these findings demonstrated that there was specificity in maltreated children's differential processing of emotional information, and that maltreated children are uniquely sensitive to detecting anger over other facial expressions of emotion.

In ascribing psychological meaning to these psychophysiological results, Pollak et al. (1997; Pollak et al., 2001) conjectured that attention to negative versus positive affect activates mental representations in these children that are distinct from the patterns of activation observed in nonmaltreated children. Emotion systems have been postulated to function as associative networks wherein input that matches significant mental representations activates memory systems (Lang, 1994). P3b amplitude, in this context, may mark the match of facial stimuli with more complex emotional memories.

The results of the Pollak et al. (1997; Pollak et al., 2001) studies suggest that that the nature of experiences encountered by maltreated children during their lives has caused particular emotional stimuli to become more salient, based in part upon the stored mental representations (i.e., memories) that have been associated with the stimulus over time. Consequently, the prior experience of maltreated children is thought to be reflected in these children's psychophysiological response.

In a subsequent study, Cicchetti and Curtis (2005) conducted an investigation of maltreated toddlers' ERP responses to emotion stimuli. These investigators focused on neurofunctional processes in toddlerhood because it is a period when critical aspects of synaptogenesis, driven in large part by experience in the environment as well as continued myelination, are occurring (Cicchetti & Curtis, 2006; Huttenlocher, 2002; Thompson & Nelson, 2001). Moreover, development of higher cognitive functions primarily mediated by the prefrontal cortex, such as speech production and language, as well as advances in self-development and representational/symbolic processes, are taking place during the toddlerhood period (e.g., Cicchetti, 1990b; Thompson & Nelson, 2001).

Cicchetti and Curtis (2005) examined the association of maltreatment during the first year of life on the neural correlates of processing facial expressions of emotion at 30 months of age. ERPs evoked while maltreated and nonmaltreated children passively viewed standardized pictures of female models posing angry, happy, and neutral facial expressions were examined. Four ERP waveforms were derived in the study, including early perceptual waveforms (N150, P260), Nc, and a PSW.

As expected, the maltreated and nonmaltreated toddlers did not show latency or amplitude differences on the early perceptual negative component (N150). However, the maltreated toddlers displayed greater P260 amplitude at frontal leads compared to the nonmaltreated toddlers in response to viewing angry facial expressions. In addition, the scalp topography of the P260 differed between the two groups, as illustrated in Figure 3.3 (also see color insert). Specifically, within the maltreated group, the P260 showed equivalent maximal amplitude at frontal sites for all three emotion conditions (i.e., angry, happy, and neutral). However, for the nonmaltreated toddlers, P260 showed maximal amplitude at more central scalp sites while viewing angry faces but was maximal at frontal sites in response to happy and neutral faces.

Similar in morphology to the P250 waveform seen in the Parker and Nelson (2005a, 2005b) studies, the P260 waveform may represent a later perceptual process that includes recognition of the affective component of a face. Thus, the findings from the P260 may indicate a lack of early perceptual differentiation amongst the three facial expressions of emotion in the maltreated children, while, based on the differential scalp topography

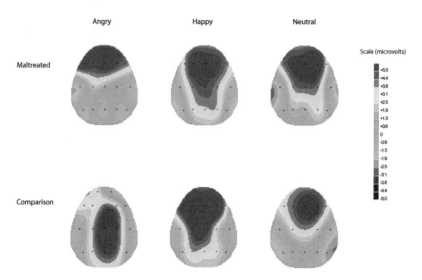

FIGURE 3.3. Topography of the P260 event-related potential (ERP) component across three emotion conditions for maltreated and nonmaltreated groups. Each map is constructed based on the latency of the P260 peak at Fz (midline frontal scalp region, where P260 was maximal) from the grand mean of that group and condition. Because of amplitude variations between groups and across emotions, the scales were adjusted for each condition separately in order to best illustrate the P260 component. *Source:* Cicchetti & Curtis, 2005.

of the P260, the nonmaltreated toddlers processed the angry facial expression "differently" than the happy or neutral facial expressions. Given its probable role in the early detection of affect, these findings could also indicate that the angry facial expression was more "novel" than the other expression for the nonmaltreated children.

A similar pattern of findings emerged for the Nc component, illustrated in Figure 3.4 (also see color insert). For this waveform, the maltreated toddlers showed greater Nc amplitude at the central midline scalp site while viewing angry faces, whereas no regional variations in Nc amplitude within the nonmaltreated comparison toddlers emerged. However, the nonmaltreated toddlers exhibited greater Nc amplitude at lateral parietal and temporal electrode sites while viewing pictures of happy faces compared to angry and neutral faces.

As reviewed earlier in the chapter, the Nc waveform is believed to represent the neurofunctional processes associated with the automatic allocation of attentional resources, theorized to be linked with an orienting

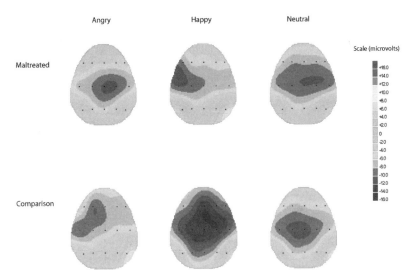

FIGURE 3.4. Topography of the Nc event-related potential (ERP) component across three emotion conditions for the maltreated and nonmaltreated groups. Each map is constructed based on the latency of the negative central (Nc) peak at Cz (midline central scalp region, where Nc was maximal) from the grand average of that group and condition. Because of amplitude variations between groups and across emotions, the scales were adjusted for each condition separately in order to best illustrate the Nc component. *Source:* Cicchetti & Curtis, 2005.

process (Nelson, 1994; Richards, 2003). In light of Richards' (2003) finding of an association between Nc amplitude and an objective measure of attention (i.e., greater Nc amplitude occurred during trials with greater attention), it is perhaps reasonable to interpret differences in Nc amplitude across stimulus categories as representing differences in the degree (or extent) of attention to those stimuli. Thus, maltreated toddlers in the Cicchetti and Curtis (2005) study may have been automatically allocating more attention to the angry faces relative to the happy and neutral faces, consistent with results from the Pollak et al. (1997; Pollak et al., 2001) studies of school aged maltreated children.

The relation of Nc to memory processes is less clear; the Nc has been shown to reflect some aspects of recognition independent of stimulus probability, with greater Nc amplitude observed in response to familiar stimuli in infants and young children (de Haan, Johnson, & Halit, 2003). Therefore, one inference that could be made is that angry facial expressions may be more familiar to maltreated children than happy or neutral facial expressions, as consistent with the findings from de Haan et al. (2003), where greater Nc amplitude was seen in response to familiar stimuli. Likewise, the increased Nc amplitude elicited by happy facial expressions in the nonmaltreated toddlers may be interpreted as reflecting increased attention to more familiar happy facial affect.

Finally, the nonmaltreated group in the Cicchetti and Curtis (2005) study showed a greater PSW area score in the right hemisphere in response to viewing angry facial expressions in comparison to the maltreated group. The PSW, as discussed in the overview of normative studies of ERP waveforms, is believed to represent updating of working memory for stimuli that have not been fully encoded. Thus it could be inferred from this finding that, for the nonmaltreated children, angry facial affect may be a less familiar stimulus and, as such, may require neural resources for updating in working memory.

Interpretation and Integration: Linkages Among Attachment, Memory, and Maltreatment

Although most of the studies utilizing ERPs to examine children raised in atypical environments have not been designed to specifically assess memory functioning (Parker & Nelson, 2005b, is the exception), some insights may be gleaned from these studies concerning the linkage between attachment processes and the relation between internal working models, affect, and memory. The extant body of literature on the relationship between children's memory and attachment orientation has been limited to normative samples of preschool-aged children, but their findings have been consistent in demonstrating that children's attachment has important implications for memory encoding, storage, and/or retrieval (e.g., Belsky, Spritz & Crnic, 1996; Goodman, Quas, Batterman-Faunce, Riddlesberger, & Kuhn, 1997; Kirsh & Cassidy, 1997; also see Alexander, Quas, & Goodman, 2002, for comprehensive review of this area). For example, the work of Belsky et al. (1996) suggests that children remember information best when it is consistent with their attachment schema or internal working models.

Several different developmental theories cohere to suggest that relational schemas, or representational models, are formed as a result of children's early interactions with their primary caregivers. Depending on the theoretical perspective, the internalizations of these early interaction experiences are labeled as representational models or internal working models (IWMs) within attachment theory (Bowlby, 1958; Bretherton & Munholland, 1999) and as schemas or scripts within social cognitive theory (Baldwin, 1992).

Despite differences in terminology for these constructs, both attachment and social/cognitive theorists agree that specific relationship experiences are encoded as cognitive representations of the self, other, and the self in relation to other, and are used to guide perception, attention, future expectations, and behavior within interpersonal contexts (Baldwin, 1992; Cicchetti, Cummings, Greenberg & Marvin, 1990; Main, Kaplan & Cassidy, 1985). As such, these cognitive representations serve as important organizing schemas for memory that can be used to facilitate encoding and recall (Markus, 1977; Rogers, 1981; Rogers, Kuiper, & Kirker, 1977). Representational models are also believed to guide an individual's attention, selecting for attachment-relevant information about the world, the self, and others in ways that allow the individual to process interpersonal information and to develop expectations about the future (Bowlby, 1980; Bretherton, 1990; Main et al., 1985). Unfortunately, early parent–child relationships within maltreating families are often characterized by negative interactions and have an adverse effect on children's representational models (see Azar, 2002, for review).

The findings of Cicchetti and Curtis (2005) concerning the Nc, an ERP component indexing attention, could be interpreted within an attachment and memory framework. Maltreated children may be primed to respond to negative affect (represented by the images of angry facial expressions utilized as stimuli) because these stimuli tapped their affective representations of early emotional experience, much of which is undoubtedly associated with anger and other negative affect. This process may in fact represent a primitive neurobiology of internal working models associated with the attachment system. This process may involve the tapping of an associative network of memory that is based on the affective valence of the particular stimuli, whereby early experience is "recognized" and memories of that experience are retrieved.

Comments and Caveats

In sum, the studies utilizing ERP methodology to examine the neural correlates of maltreatment have provided some evidence indicating that the experience of maltreatment, whether in the context of institutional rearing or neglect or abuse suffered at the hands of a parent, is manifested at the level of neurofunctional processes underlying memory. Although there are no studies to date specifically examining the ERP correlates of memory in children who have experienced maltreatment, the results of the ERP studies with maltreated children thus far have begun to suggest, at the very least, directions for future ERP studies of memory and maltreatment. Clearly, the experience of maltreatment early in development alters information processing systems related to recognition of emotion and attentional resources allocated to emotion recognition.

Although the studies conducted to date reveal a number of consistencies, these must be interpreted with caution given the different age ranges examined across investigations. For example, an overall pattern of hyper-responsivity in response to displays of angry facial affect among children who have experienced maltreatment has been observed. This heightened amplitude of ERP waveforms associated with angry affect is evident in the P260 waveform found in the Cicchetti and Curtis (2005) study, and in the P3b waveform observed by Pollak et al. (1997; Pollak et al., 2001). Although these two waveforms are not likely equivalent, and the ages of the participants in the studies by Pollak and colleagues (i.e., 6 to 12 years) and Cicchetti and Curtis (i.e., 28 to 36 months) are quite different, the processes underlying the heightened responsivity to angry facial affect in maltreated compared to nonmaltreated children may be parallel.

The ERP studies reviewed herein have, for the most part, tested hypotheses firmly grounded in theoretical and conceptual models of the development and functioning of emotional and attentional processes at both the behavioral and neural levels of analysis. In that sense, they represent an appropriate application of ERP methodology to answer questions tightly bound to well-explicated theoretical constructs. In addition, many of these theoretical constructions of neural processes have a great degree of face validity and "intuitive" appeal, and are grounded in comprehensive knowledge of neuroanatomical structure and functioning.

Nonetheless, it is important to note that knowledge concerning the linkage between the characteristics of ERP waveforms (i.e., morphology, amplitude) and neurobehavioral processes is far from complete. There is extensive empirical work demonstrating the neurobehavioral correlates of the most commonly observed ERP waveforms reviewed earlier in this chapter. However, the functional correlates of many waveforms observed in infants and children are less well understood (for example, the early positive component observed in Cicchetti & Curtis [2005] and Parker & Nelson [2005a, 2005b]). Of course, part of the functionality can be inferred from the latency of a particular component. For example, a component such as the P260, given that its peak amplitude occurs, on average, 260 ms after stimulus onset, is fairly early in the neurofunctional processing stream, and thus most likely reflects some perceptual process rather than later cognitive processing.

It is also important to keep in mind that inferences made from ERP data are correlational. Accordingly, this precludes making statements about whether any given observed ERP activity is necessary for the occurrence of a particular associated emotional or cognitive process (Otten & Rugg, 2001). In addition, it is crucial to temper any interpretation of the functional significance of ERP waveforms with the reality that the association of particular patterns of ERP activity with a given experimental condition is a necessary, but not sufficient, condition for concluding that distinct neurofunctional processes are engaged. Direct behavioral assessment of the particular function of interest is necessary, as exemplified by Richards's (2003) utilization of heart-rate changes in infants to index attention.

In the context of any research involving ERPs, careful consideration of what the meaning of amplitude differences in ERP waveforms may represent is of critical importance. From a purely electrophysiological standpoint, the amplitude of a waveform is an index of the degree to which its underlying neural generators are active (represented by voltage). This, in turn, is believed to reflect the degree of engagement of the associated perceptual, cognitive, or emotional processes, with greater amplitude representing "more" activity. However, inferences concerning the "psychological" meaning of between-group (or within-group, between-condition) differences in amplitude, such as those differences found in ERP waveforms elicited by facial expressions of emotion between maltreated and nonmaltreated children, must be done with some circumspection regarding the actual "psychophysiological" meaning of amplitude.

Although between-group or between-condition comparisons of latency of ERP waveforms can provide a straightforward index of the temporal characteristics of neural processing (one of the primary strengths of ERP methodology), few if any meaningful latency differences have been found in ERP studies of the effect of maltreatment. This lack of latency effect can most likely be attributed to the typically greater interindividual variability generally found in the latencies of ERP components, which in turn reduces the ability of conventional, analysis of variance (ANOVA)-based statistical analyses to reveal such effects (i.e., due to large standard deviations).

There are also methodological limitations that are important to note in some of the ERP studies of maltreatment. Although the findings reported in the Pollak et al. (1997; Pollak et al., 2001) studies are striking, it is necessary to acknowledge that the data for these studies were collected utilizing electrodes at only three midline scalp sites (i.e., Fz, Cz, and Pz). Though current standards call for high-density arrays of 128 and even 256 electrodes, at the time these data were being collected (i.e., the mid-1990s), ERP studies utilizing only a few electrodes were state of the art. Although this does not in any way diminish the validity of the findings from these investigations, it is nonetheless important to interpret the results from these early studies with this caveat in mind.

Conclusions

As we articulated earlier, we have brought a developmental psychopathology framework to bear on the topic of maltreatment, ERPs, and memory. Because of its emphasis on an interdisciplinary perspective, the mutually enriching interplay between work conducted with normal and atypical populations, and its focus on examining multiple domains of development concurrently, a developmental psychopathology approach is especially timely in providing a lens for increasing our understanding of the effects of maltreatment on neural functioning and memory (Howe, Toth, & Cicchetti, 2006).

Major advances have emerged in recent decades with respect to understanding memory. Perhaps most relevant for informing studies of maltreatment, brain functioning, and memory are conceptualizations that memory is comprised of various systems and subsystems that are separate but interacting (see Schacter & Tulving, 1994, for a review; also see Howe, 2000, and Rovee-Collier, 1997, for a different viewpoint). Because various kinds of memory are thought to be dependent on different brain structures and functions (Schacter, 1994), whether or not memory processes will be altered (either enhanced or impaired), as well as which types of memory may be positively or negatively affected, may be dependent on the status of an individual maltreated child's neurobiological development at the time traumatic experiences occurred. Views on memory and maltreatment that elucidate the importance of considering the developmental influences that are affecting memory processes are extremely compatible with a developmental psychopathology approach to assessing how experiences that occur at various developmental periods may affect biological and psychological functioning differently (Cicchetti & Tucker, 1994; Curtis & Cicchetti, 2003; Gunnar & Vasquez, 2006).

We next raise a number of issues that we believe must be addressed in future research in the area of maltreatment, ERPs, and memory. We also offer insights derived from developmental psychopathology on how best to address these issues.

1. *Additional studies of ERPs and memory must be conducted in normative samples.* A significant gap in the extant literature is the paucity of research on ERPs in samples of normal infants and children. The vast majority of research on ERPs and memory has been carried out with infants between 4 and 12 months of age. Furthermore, much of this work has focused on infants from middle socioeconomic status (SES) backgrounds. It is essential that future normative research on ERPs and memory focuses on ages beyond infancy and incorporates participants from the lower socioeconomic strata.

   Relatedly, there is a paucity of longitudinal research on ERPs and memory, with the existing longitudinal work focusing predominantly on the infancy period. If we are to discover whether early ERPs and memory are predictive of later memory functioning, either through utilizing electrophysiological or behavioral memory paradigms, the design and implementation of longitudinal investigations is crucial for future work in this area. We strongly recommend that longitudinal studies be conducted on samples of infants and children from the middle and lower SES. The conduct of longitudinal investigations of infants and children from lower-SES backgrounds will be extremely helpful in disentangling the effects (if any) that poverty may exert on neural functioning and memory, independent of the experiences of trauma, such as child abuse and neglect.

2. *Additional studies of ERPs and memory must be conducted with maltreated infants and children.* There has been a paucity of investigations of

ERPs and memory in maltreated infants and children. Although the findings from the extant studies have yielded interesting insights into the link between attention and memory in maltreated children, it is critical that researchers begin to carry out investigations of ERPs in maltreated children that are more directly tied to classic memory paradigms.

As was true for studies of ERPs and memory in normative samples, it is essential that future longitudinal investigations of ERP and memory be implemented with maltreated infants and children. Presently, we are in the process of conducting two such longitudinal studies in our laboratory. In one, we are investigating ERPs in maltreated and nonmaltreated infants from the lower SES. These infants are being seen at 6, 9, and 12 months. The goal of this investigation is to ascertain the effects of maltreatment within the first 6 months of life on neurobiological development and functioning and memory. In the second experiment, we also are following up a group of maltreated and nonmaltreated infants from low-SES backgrounds; however, in this study, ERPs of these children are examined at yearly intervals from age 1 year to 3 years. In both experiments, the infants and youngsters are viewing various prototypic emotion stimuli as their ERPs are being recorded.

Ideally, future investigations on ERPs and memory should take a comprehensive approach to evaluating the functioning of all memory systems in children who have experienced various types of maltreatment, even if a given system would not seem to be affected by trauma. Moreover, as more precise information is gathered about the specific nature of the trauma that subgroups of maltreated children have experienced, ERPs may be evoked by stimuli that more accurately reflect the actual traumatic event(s).

3. *It is essential that future research on maltreatment, neurobiological functioning, and memory incorporate a multiple-levels-of-analysis approach.* It is apparent that progress toward a process-level understanding of maltreatment, neural functioning, and memory will require research designs and strategies that emphasize and incorporate the simultaneous assessment of multiple domains of variables, both within and outside of the developing person. For example, investigations could include both electrophysiological (e.g., ERPs)

and behavioral measures in studies investigating neural functioning and memory in maltreated children, with and without concomitant psychopathological symptomatology/disorders (e.g., depression, dissociation). Moreover, future research could examine the relation between ERPs and functional magnetic resonance imaging (fMRI) in maltreated children's performance on memory paradigms. Such studies could employ coregistration of ERP and fMRI to obtain highly detailed data describing both the temporal and spatial aspects of neural function. Likewise, investigations that examine links among maltreatment, neuroendocrine functioning, and memory, as well as those that focus on elucidating the relations among maltreatment, genetic polymorphisms that have been found to have associations with memory processes (e.g., brain derived neurotrophic factor [BDNF] see Goldberg & Weinberger, 2004), structural and functional imaging of brain areas known to subserve aspects of memory (e.g., hippocampus, medial-temporal cortex), and behavioral tasks of memory, could contribute to a deeper understanding of the impact that abuse and neglect exert on memory.

Regardless of whether differences are found in maltreated children's memory performance across all levels of analysis, or if differences are shown at some levels of analysis but not others, or if no differences are revealed in memory functioning compared to demographically comparable nonmaltreated children, a more sophisticated and comprehensive understanding of memory will ensue from an examination of multiple levels of analysis within the same individual. Longitudinal investigations will be essential in order to ascertain whether, for example, maltreated children utilize different neural and/or behavioral processes but achieve the same level of memory performance as nonmaltreated children, and if so, whether employing compensatory mechanisms earlier eventuates in later memory problems. Because child abuse and neglect have been shown to affect multiple neurobiological systems (Cicchetti, 2002b; DeBellis, 2001; Teicher, 2002), the neurodevelopmental processes of multiple systems associated with memory may be altered, generating a cascade of effects through subsequent developmental periods, causing later problems in memory function.

Because different levels of analysis constrain other levels, as scientists learn more about multiple levels of analysis, researchers conducting their work at each level will need to develop theories about memory processes that are consistent across all levels. It is critical that an integrative framework be developed that incorporates all levels of analysis in investigating the effects that child maltreatment has on neural functioning and memory.

4. *It is important to consider diversity in process and outcome when examining ERPs and memory in maltreated children.* In the discipline of developmental psychopathology, the concepts of equifinality and multifinality are germane (Cicchetti & Rogosch, 1996). Equifinality indicates that there may be multiple pathways to the same outcome. Accordingly, various types of maltreatment experiences might result in similar ERP amplitudes and waveforms and neural functioning as well as in similar memory deficits or psychiatric symptomatology. Conversely, the principle of multifinality suggests that similar maltreatment experiences may not affect memory in the same way in different individuals. Thus, for example, it is unlikely that all physically or sexually abused children will evidence similar memory difficulties. Likewise, ERPs and other aspects of neural functioning are unlikely to be the same in all children with the same maltreatment experiences.

The concept of multifinality has broader implications for the effects of maltreatment on children's neurobiological development. It has been stated that "abuse ... induces a cascade of molecular and neurobiological effects that irreversibly alter neural development" (Teicher, 2002, p. 70). Although it is clear that child maltreatment exerts a deleterious impact on a variety of neurobiological systems (Cicchetti, 2002b; Cicchetti & Rogosch, 2001; DeBellis, Baum, et al., 1999; DeBellis, Keshavan, et al., 1999; Klorman, Cicchetti, Thatcher, & Ison, 2003; Teicher et al., 2003), based on the concept of multifinality we would predict that it is highly unlikely that all maltreated children will have the same structural or functional anomalies across all neurobiological systems. Indeed, it would not be at all surprising if some maltreated children, perhaps those who are functioning in a resilient fashion despite experiencing significant stress and adversity, would not have any detectable problems in neural structure, function, and memory.

5. *Can prevention and intervention alter the neurofunctional processes associated with memory deficits found in maltreated children?* A critical question that awaits long-term research investment is whether the early aberrations in neural functioning as they relate to memory or other developmental domains in maltreated children leave an indelible imprint on brain structure and function, or whether these altered brain systems and developmental processes can be improved through efficacious preventive and intervention strategies. There is increasing evidence that effective interventions can modify not only maladaptive behavior but also the cellular and physiological correlates of behavior (Cicchetti & Posner, 2005; Curtis & Cicchetti, 2003; Kandel, 1998, 1999). If targeted prevention programs and interventions are able to effect beneficial change in maltreated children's neural functioning and memory processes, then such results would suggest that neural plasticity can occur as a result of intervention and that the harmful effects of maltreatment are not indelible.

As prevention and intervention efforts increasingly begin to adopt a multiple-levels-of-analysis perspective, scientists and clinicians will be able to discover whether there is a psychobiology of hope and optimism for children who have experienced child maltreatment. Furthermore, research on preventive and treatment strategies can provide unprecedented and essential insights translatable to the making of further theoretical advances on the relation between ERPs and memory. If a negative behavioral and biological course is altered as a result of the implementation of a randomized prevention or intervention trial focused on improving memory in maltreated children, then this prevention and intervention research will have been shown to contribute to specifying the processes that were involved in the emergence of maladaptive ERP and memory functioning. Thus, in keeping with a major tenet of the developmental psychopathology perspective, the examination of both typical and atypical biological and psychological processes will have mutually informed theory about the course of normal and abnormal development.

Acknowledgments

Our work on this chapter was supported in part by grants from the National Institute of Mental Health (MH068413) and the Spunk Fund, Inc. to Dante Cicchetti.

References

Adrian, E. D., & Matthews, B. H. C. (1934). The Berger rhythm: Potential changes from the occipital lobes in man. *Brain, 57,* 355–385.

Alexander, K. W., Quas, J. A., & Goodman, G. S. (2002). Theoretical advances in understanding children's memory for distressing events: The role of attachment. *Developmental Review, 22,* 490–519.

Alho, K., Sainio, K., Sajaniemi, N., Reinikainen, K., & Naatanen, R. (1990). Event-related potentials of human newborns to pitch change of an acoustic stimulus. *Electroencephalography and Clinical Neurophysiology, 77,* 151–155.

Allison, T., Woods, C. C., & McCarthy, G. M. (1986). The central nervous system. In M. G. H. Coles, E. Donchin, and S. W. Porges (Eds.), *Psychophysiology: Systems, processes, and applications.* New York: Guilford Press.

Amso, D. & Casey, B. J. (2006). Beyond what develops when: Neuroimaging may inform how cognition changes with development. *Current Directions in Psychological Science, 15(1),* 24–29.

Aslin, R. N. (1987). Visual and auditory development in infancy. In J. D. Osofsky (Ed.), *Handbook of infant development* (pp. 5–97). New York: Wiley.

Azar, S. T. (2002). Parenting and child maltreatment. In M. H. Bornstein (Ed.), *Handbook of parenting* (Vol. 4, pp. 361–388). Mahwah, NJ: Lawrence Erlbaum Associates.

Baldwin, D. A. (1992). Clarifying the role of shape in children's taxonomic assumption. *Journal of Experimental Child Psychology, 54,* 392–416.

Belsky, J., Spritz, B., & Crnic, K. (1996). Infant attachment security and affective-cognitive information processing at age 3. *Psychological Science, 7,* 111–114.

Berg, P., & Scherg, M. (1994). *Brain Electrical Source Analysis (BESA), Version 2.0 Handbook.* Munich: Megis.

Berger, H. (1929). Ueber das Elektenkephalogramm des Mensschen. *Archives fur Psychiatrie Nervenkrankheiten, 87,* 527–570.

Black, J., Jones, T. A., Nelson, C. A., & Greenough, W. T. (1998). Neuronal plasticity and the developing brain. In N. E. Alessi, J. T. Coyle, S. I. Harrison, & S. Eth (Eds.), *Handbook of child and adolescent psychiatry* (pp. 31–53). New York: Wiley.

Bornstein, M. C. (1985). Habituation of attention as a measure of visual information processing in human infants: Summary, systematization, and synthesis. In G. Gottlieb & N. A. Krasnegor (Eds.), *Measurement of audition and vision in the first year of postnatal life: A methodological overview* (pp. 253–300). Norwood, NJ: Ablex.

Bowlby, J. (1958). The nature of the child's tie to his mother. *International Journal of Psychoanalysis, 39,* 350–373.

Bowlby, J. (1969/1982). *Attachment and loss* (Vol. 1). New York: Basic Books.

Bowlby, J. (1980). *Attachment and loss: Loss, sadness, and depression* (Vol. 3). New York: Basic Books.

Bowlby, J. (1988). *A secure base.* New York: Basic Books.

Bremner, J. D. (2003). Long-term effects of childhood abuse on brain and neurobiology. *Child and Adolescent Psychiatric Clinics of North America, 12,* 271–292

Bretherton, I. (1990). Open communication and internal working models: Their role in the development of attachment relationships. In R. Thompson (Ed.), *Nebraska symposium on motivation: Vol. 36. Socioeconomic development* (pp. 57–113). Lincoln, NE: University of Nebraska Press.

Bretherton, I., & Munholland, K. A. (1999). Internal working models in attachment relationships: A construct revisited. In J. Cassidy & P. R. Shaver (Eds.), *Handbook of attachment: Theory, research, and clinical applications* (pp. 89–111). New York: Guilford Press.

Carver, L. J., Dawson, G., Panagiotides, H., Meltzoff, A. N., McPartland, J., Gray, J., et al. (2003). Age-related differences in neural correlates of face recognition during the toddler and preschool years. *Developmental Psychobiology, 42*(2), 148–159.

Casey, B., Tottenham, N., Liston, C., & Durston, S. (2005). Imaging the developing brain: What have we learned about cognitive development? *Trends in Cognitive Science, 9*(3), 104–110.

Cassidy, J. (1994). Emotion regulation: Influences of attachment relationships. *Monographs of the Society for Research in Child Development, 59,* 228–283.

Cicchetti, D. (1984). The emergence of developmental psychopathology. *Child Development, 55,* 1–7.

Cicchetti, D. (1989). How research on child maltreatment has informed the study of child development: Perspectives from developmental psychopathology. In D. Cicchetti & V. Carlson (Eds.), *Child maltreatment: Theory and research on the causes and consequences of child abuse and neglect* (pp. 377–431). New York: Cambridge University Press.

Cicchetti, D. (1990a). A historical perspective on the discipline of developmental psychopathology. In J. Rolf, A. Masten, D. Cicchetti, K. Nuechterlein, & S. Weintraub (Eds.), *Risk and protective factors in the development of psychopathology* (pp. 2–28). New York: Cambridge University Press.

Cicchetti, D. (1990b). The organization and coherence of socioemotional, cognitive, and representational development: Illustrations through a developmental psychopathology perspective on Down syndrome and child maltreatment. In R. Thompson (Ed.), *Nebraska symposium on motivation: Vol. 36. Socioemotional development* (pp. 259–366). Lincoln, NE: University of Nebraska Press.

Cicchetti, D. (1993). Developmental psychopathology: Reactions, reflections, projections. *Developmental Review, 13,* 471–502.

Cicchetti, D. (2002a). How a child builds a brain: Insights from normality and psychopathology. In W. W. Hartup & R. A. Weinberg (Eds.), *The Minnesota symposia on child psychology: Vol. 32. Child psychology in retrospect and prospect* (pp. 23–71). Mawah, NJ: Lawrence Erlbaum Associates, Publishers.

Cicchetti, D. (2002b). The impact of social experience on neurobiological systems: Illustration from a constructivist view of child maltreatment. *Cognitive Development, 17,* 1407–1428.

Cicchetti, D., & Blender, J. A. (2004). A multiple-levels-of-analysis approach to the study of developmental processes in maltreated children. *Proceedings of the National Academy of Sciences, 101*(50), 17325–17326.

Cicchetti, D., & Cannon, T. D. (1999). Neurodevelopmental processes in the ontogenesis and epigenesis of psychopathology. *Development and Psychopathology, 11,* 375–393.

Cicchetti, D., & Cohen, D. (Eds.). (2006a). *Developmental Psychopathology* (2nd ed.)*: Vol. 1. Theory and Method.* New York: Wiley.

Cicchetti, D., & Cohen, D. (Eds.). (2006b). *Developmental Psychopathology* (2nd ed.): *Vol. 2. Developmental Neuroscience.* New York: Wiley.

Cicchetti, D., & Cohen, D. (Eds.). (2006c). *Developmental Psychopathology* (2nd ed.): *Vol. 3. Risk, Disorder, and Adaptation.* New York: Wiley.

Cicchetti, D., Cummings, E. M., Greenberg, M. T., & Marvin, R. (1990). An organizational perspective on attachment beyond infancy: Implications for theory, measurement, and research. In M. T. Greenberg, D. Cicchetti & E. M. Cummings (Eds.), *Attachment in the preschool years: Theory, research, and intervention* (pp. 3–49). Chicago: University of Chicago Press.

Cicchetti, D., & Curtis, W. J. (2005). An event-related potential study of the processing of affective facial expressions in young children who experienced maltreatment during the first year of life. *Development and Psychopathology, 17*(3), 641–677.

Cicchetti, D., & Curtis, W. J. (2006). The developing brain and neural plasticity: Implications for normality, psychopathology, and resilience. In D. Cicchetti & D. Cohen (Eds.), *Developmental Psychopathology: Vol. 2. Developmental Neuroscience* (2nd ed., pp. 1–64). New York: Wiley.

Cicchetti, D., & Dawson, G. (Eds.) (2002). Multiple levels of analysis [special issue]. *Development and Psychopathology, 14*(3), 417–666.

Cicchetti, D., & Lynch, M. (1995). Failures in the expectable environment and their impact on individual development: The case of child maltreatment. In D. Cicchetti & D. J. Cohen (Eds.), *Developmental psychopathology: Vol. 2. Risk, disorder, and adaptation* (pp. 32–71). New York: John Wiley & Sons, Inc.

Cicchetti, D., & Posner, M. I. (2005). Cognitive and affective neuroscience and developmental psychopathology. *Development and Psychopathology, 17*(3), 569–575.

Cicchetti, D., & Rogosch, F. A. (1996). Equifinality and multifinality in developmental psychopathology. *Development and Psychopathology, 8*(4), 597–600.

Cicchetti, D., & Rogosch, F. A. (2001). Diverse patterns of neuroendocrine activity in maltreated children. *Development and Psychopathology, 13,* 677–694.

Cicchetti, D., & Sroufe, L. A. (2000). Editorial: The past as prologue to the future: The times they've been a changin.' *Development and Psychopathology, 12*(3), 255–264.

Cicchetti, D., & Toth, S. L. (1995). A developmental psychopathology perspective on child abuse and neglect. *Journal of the American Academy of Child and Adolescent Psychiatry, 34,* 541–565.

Cicchetti, D., & Toth, S. L. (2005). Child maltreatment. *Annual Review of Clinical Psychology, 1,* 409–438.

Cicchetti, D., & Tucker, D. (1994). Development and self-regulatory structures of the mind. *Development and Psychopathology, 6*(4), 533–549.

Cicchetti, D., & Valentino, K. (2006). An Ecological Transactional Perspective on Child Maltreatment: Failure of the Average Expectable Environment and Its Influence Upon Child Development. In D. Cicchetti & D. J. Cohen (Eds.), *Developmental Psychopathology: Vol. 3. Risk, Disorder, and Adaptation* (2nd ed., pp. 129–201). New York, New York: Wiley.

Coles, M. G. H., Smid, H., Scheffers, M. K., & Otten, L. J. (1995). Mental chronometry and the study of human information processing. In M. D. Rugg and M. G. Coles (Eds.), *Electrophysiology of mind: Event-related brain potentials and cognition* (pp. 86–131). New York: Oxford University Press.

Courchesne, E. (1977). Event-related brain potentials: Comparison between children and adults. *Science, 197,* 589–592.

Courchesne, E. (1978). Neurophysiological correlates of cognitive development: Changes in long-latency event-related potentials from childhood to adulthood. *Electroencephalography and Clinical Neurophysiology, 45,* 468–482.

Courchesne, E., Ganz, L., & Norcia, A. M. (1981). Event-related brain potentials to human faces in infants. *Child Development, 52,* 804–811.

Curtis, W. J., & Cicchetti, D. (2003). Moving research on resilience into the 21st century: Theoretical and methodological considerations in examining the biological contributors to resilience. *Development and Psychopathology, 15,* 773–810.

da Silva, F. H. L., & van Rotterdam, A. (1982). A. Biophysical aspects of EEG and MEG generation. In E. Niedermeyer & F. H. L. da Silva (Eds.), *Electroencephalography* (pp. 15–26). Baltimore: Urban & Schwarzenberg.

Davis, P. A. (1939). Effects of acoustic stimuli on the waking human brain. *Journal of Neurophysiology, 2,* 494–499.

Dawson, G., Carver, L., Meltzoff, A. N., Panagiotides, H., McPartland, J. & Webb, S. J. (2002). Neural correlates of face and object recognition in young children with Autism Spectrum Disorder, developmental delay, and typical development. *Child Development, 73*(3), 700–717.

DeBellis, M. D. (2001). Developmental traumatology: The psychobiological development of maltreated children and its implications for research, treatment, and policy. *Development and Psychopathology, 13,* 539–564.

DeBellis, M. D. (2005). The psychobiology of neglect. *Child Maltreatment, 10,* 150—172.

DeBellis, M. D., Baum, A. S., Birmaher, B., Keshavan, M. S., Eccard, C. H., Boring, A. M., et al. (1999). Developmental traumatology part I: Biological stress systems. *Biological Psychiatry, 45,* 1259–1270.

DeBellis, M. D., Keshavan, M. S., Casey, B. J., Clark, D. B., Giedd, J., Boring, A. M., et al. (1999). Developmental traumatology: Biological stress systems and brain development in maltreated children with PTSD part II: The relationship between characteristics of trauma and psychiatric symptoms and adverse brain development in maltreated children and adolescents with PTSD. *Biological Psychiatry, 45,* 1271–1284.

DeBoer, T., Scott, L. S., & Nelson, C. A. (2004). Event-related potentials in developmental populations. In T. Handy (Ed.), Event-related potentials: A methods handbook (pp. 263–297). Cambridge, MA: MIT Press.

de Haan, M., Johnson, M. H., & Halit, H. (2003). Development of face-sensitive event-related potentials during infancy: A review. *International Journal of Psychophysiology, 51,* 45–58.

de Haan, M., & Nelson, C. A. (1997). Recognition of the mother's face by six-month-old infants: A neurobehavioral study. *Child Development, 68*(2), 187–210.

de Haan, M., & Nelson, C. A. (1999). Brain activity differentiates face and object processing in 6-month-old infants. *Developmental Psychology, 35,* 1113–1121.

Donchin, E. (1981). Surprise! . . . Surprise? *Psychophysiology, 18,* 493–513.

Donchin, E., & Coles, M. G. H. (1988). Is the P300 component a manifestation of context updating? *Behavioral and Brain Sciences, 11,* 355–372.

Donchin, E., Karis, D., Bashore, T. R., Coles, M. G. H., & Gratton, G. (1986). Cognitive psychophysiology and human information processing. In M. G. H. Coles, E. Donchin, & S. W. Porges (Eds.), *Psychophysiology* (pp. 244–267). New York: Guilford Press.

Duncan-Johnson, C. C., & Donchin, E. (1977). On quantifying surprise: The variation of event-related potentials with subjective probability. *Psychophysiology, 14,* 456–467.

Duncan-Johnson C., & Donchin, E. (1982). The P300 component of the event-related brain potential as an index of information processing. *Biological Psychology, 14,* 1–52

Fabiani, M., Karis, D., & Donchin, E. (1990). Effects of mnemonic strategy manipulation in a Von Restorff paradigm. *Electroencephalography and Clinical Neurophysiology, 75,* 22–35.

Fantz. R. L. (1961). The origin of form perception. *Scientific American, 204,* 66–72.

Fantz, R. L. (1963). Pattern vision in newborn infants. *Science, 140,* 296–297.

Gibbs, F. A., Davis, H., & Lennox, W. G. (1935). The electro-encephalogram in epilepsy and in conditions of impaired consciousness. *Archives of Neurology and Psychiatry, 34,* 1133–1148.

Goldberg, T. E., & Weinberger, D. R. (2004). Genes and the parsing of cognitive processes. *Trends in Cognitive Science, 8,* 325–335.

Goldman-Rakic, P. S. (1987). Development of cortical circuitry and cognitive function. *Child Development, 58,* 601–622.

Goodman, G. S., Quas, J. A., Batterman-Faunce, J. M., Riddlesberger, M. M., & Kuhn, J. (1997). Children's reactions to and memory for a stressful event: Influences of age, anatomical dolls, knowledge, and parental attachment. *Applied Developmental Science, 1,* 54–75.

Greenough, W., Black, J., & Wallace, C. (1987). Experience and brain development. *Child Development, 58,* 539–559.

Gunnar, M. R., & Vazquez, D. M. (2006). Stress neurobiology and developmental psychopathology. In D. Cicchetti & D. Cohen (Eds.), *Developmental*

Psychopathology: *Vol. 2. Developmental Neuroscience* (2nd ed., pp. 533–577). New York: Wiley.

Halgren, E., & Smith, M. E. (1987). Cognitive evoked potentials as modulatory processes in human-memory formation and retrieval. *Human Neurobiology, 6,* 129–139.

Hillyard, S. A., & Picton, T. W. (1987). Electrophysiology of cognition. In V. Mountcastle (Ed.), *Handbook of physiology: Vol. 5. Higher functions of the brain* (pp. 519–583). Bethesda, MD: American Physiological Society.

Hofmann, M. J., & Salapatek, P. (1981). Young infants' event-related potentials (ERPs) to familiar and unfamiliar visual and auditory events in a recognition memory task. *Electroencephalography and Clinical Neurophysiology, 52,* 405–417.

Hofmann, M. J., Salapatek, P., & Kuskowski, M. (1981). Evidence for visual memory in the averaged and single-trial evoked potentials in human infants. *Infant Behavior and Development, 4,* 401–421.

Howe, M. L. (2000). *The fate of early memories: Developmental science and the retention of childhood experiences.* Washington, DC: American Psychological Association.

Howe, M. L., Toth, S. L., & Cicchetti, D. (2006). Memory and Developmental Psychopathology. In D. Cicchetti & D. Cohen (Eds.), *Developmental Psychopathology: Vol. 2. Developmental Neuroscience* (2nd ed., pp. 629–655). New York: Wiley.

Huttenlocher, P. (2002). *Neural plasticity: The effects of environment on the development of the cerebral cortex.* Cambridge, MA: Harvard University Press.

Jasper, H. H., & Carmichael, L. (1935). Electrical potentials from the intact human brain. *Science, 81,* 51–53.

Johnson, M. H. (1998). The neural basis of cognitive development. In D. Kuhn & R. Siegler (Eds.), *Handbook of child psychology: Vol. 2. Cognition, perception, and language* (pp. 1–49). New York: Wiley.

Kandel, E. R. (1998). A new intellectual framework for psychiatry. *American Journal of Psychiatry, 155,* 475–469.

Kandel, E. R. (1999). Biology and the future of psychoanalysis: A new intellectual framework for psychiatry revisited. *American Journal of Psychiatry, 156,* 505–524.

Karrer, R., & Ackles, P. K. (1987). Visual event-related potentials of infants during a modified oddball procedure. In R. Johnson, J. W. Rohrbaugh, and R. Parasuraman (Eds.), *Current trends in event-related potential research* (EEG Supplement 40, pp. 603–608). Amsterdam: Elsevier.

Karrer, R. & Monti, L. A. (1995). Event-related potentials in 4–7 week-old infants in a visual recognition memory task. *Electroencephalography and Clinical Neurophysiology, 94,* 414–424.

Kellman, P. J., & Arterberry, M. E. (2006). Infant visual perception. In W. Damon & R. M. Lerner (Eds.), *Handbook of Child Psychology: Vol. 2, Cognition, Perception, and Language* (6th ed., pp. 109–160). New York: Wiley.

Kirsh, S. J., & Cassidy, J. (1997). Preschooler's attention to and memory for attachment-relevant information. *Child Development, 68,* 1143–1153.

Klorman, R., Cicchetti, D., Thatcher, J. E., & Ison, J. R. (2003). Acoustic startle in maltreated children. *Journal of Abnormal Child Psychology, 31,* 359–370.

Knight, R. T. (1990). Neural mechanisms of event-related potentials: Evidence from human lesion studies. In J. W. Rohrbaugh, R. Parasuraman, & R. Johnson (Eds.), *Event-related brain potentials: Basic issues and applications.* (pp. 3–18). New York: Oxford University Press.

Knight, R. T., & Scabini, D. (1998). Anatomic bases of event-related potentials and their relationship to novelty detection in humans. *Journal of Clinical Neurophysiology, 15,* 3–13.

Lang, P. J. (1994). The varieties of emotional experience: A mediation on James-Lange theory. *Psychological Review, 101,* 211–221.

Luck, S. J. (2005). An introduction to the event-related potential technique. Cambridge, MA: MIT Press.

MacLean, K. (2003). The impact of institutionalization on child development. *Development and Psychopathology, 15,* 853–884.

Main, M., Kaplan, N., & Cassidy, J. C. (1985). Security in infancy, childhood and adulthood: A move to the level of representation. In I. Bretherton & E. Waters (Eds.), *Growing points of attachment theory and research: Vol. 209* (pp. 66–104). MA: Society for Research in Child Development Monograph.

Markus, H. (1977). Self-schemas and processing information about the self. *Journal of Personality and Social Psychology, 35,* 63–78.

McEwen, B. S. (2000). Effects of adverse experiences for brain structure and function. *Biological Psychiatry, 48,* 721–731.

McIsaac, H., & Polich, J. (1992). Comparison of infant and adult P300 from auditory stimuli. *Journal of Experimental Child Psychology, 53,* 115–128.

Molfese, D. L., & Molfese, V. J. (1985). Electrophysiological indices of auditory discrimination in newborn infants: The bases for predicting later language development? *Infant Behavior and Development, 8,* 197–211.

Nakajima, Y., Miyamoto, K., & Kikuchi, M. (1994). Estimation of neural generators of cognitive potential P300 by dipole tracing method. *No to Shinkei—Brain & Nerve, 46,* 1059–1065.

Nelson, C. A. (1994). Neural correlates of recognition memory in the first postnatal year of life. In G. Dawson & K. Fischer (Eds.), *Human development and the developing brain* (pp. 269–313). New York: Guilford Press.

Nelson, C. A. (1995). The ontogeny of human memory: A cognitive neuroscience perspective. *Developmental Psychology, 31,* 723–738.

Nelson, C. A. (1996). Electrophysiological correlates of early memory development. In H. W. Reese & M. D. Franzen (Eds.), *Thirteenth West Virginia University Conference on Lifespan Developmental Psychology: Biological and Neuropsychological Mechanisms* (pp. 95–131). Hillsdale, NJ: Lawrence Erlbaum.

Nelson, C. A. (1999). Neural plasticity and human development. *Current Directions in Psychological Science, 8,* 42–45.

Nelson, C. A. (Ed.). (2002a). *The effects of early adversity on neurobehavioral development: Vol. 31. Minnesota Symposium on Child Psychology.* Mahwah, NJ: Lawrence Erlbaum Associates.

Nelson, C. A. (2002b). The neurobiological bases of early intervention. In J. Shonkoff & S. Meisels (Eds.), *Handbook of early childhood intervention* (2nd ed., pp. 204–227). New York: Cambridge University Press.

Nelson, C. A., & Bloom, F. E. (1997). Child development and neuroscience. *Child Development, 68*(5), 970–987.

Nelson, C. A., & Collins, P. F. (1991). Event-related potential and looking-time analysis of infants' responses to familiar and novel events: Implications for visual recognition memory. *Developmental Psychology, 27*(1), 50–58.

Nelson, C. A., & Collins, P.F. (1992). Neural and behavioral correlates of recognition memory in 4- and 8-month-old infants. *Brain and Cognition, 19,* 105–121.

Nelson, C. A., & deRegnier, R.A. (1992). Neural correlates of attention and memory in the first year of life. *Developmental Neuropsychology, 8,* 119–134.

Nelson, C. A., & Monk, C. S. (2001). The use of event related potentials in the study of cognitive development. In C. A. Nelson & M. Luciana (Eds.), *Handbook of Developmental Cognitive Neuroscience* (pp. 125–136). Cambridge, MA: Massachusetts Institute of Technology.

Nelson, C. A., & Nugent, K. (1990). Recognition memory and resource allocation as revealed by children's event-related potential responses to happy and angry faces. *Developmental Psychology, 26,* 171–179.

Nelson, C. A., & Salapatek, P. (1986). Electrophysiological correlates of infant recognition memory. *Child Development, 57,* 1483–1497.

Nelson, C. A., Thomas, K. M., & de Haan, M. (2006). Neural bases of cognition. In W. Damon, R. Lerner, D. Kuhn, & R. Siegler (Eds.), *Hand of Child Psychology: Vol. 2. Cognition Perception and Language* (6th ed., pp. 3–57). Hoboken, NJ: John Wiley & Sons.

Nelson, C. A., Thomas, K., de Haan, M., & Wewerka, S. (1998). Delayed recognition memory in infants and adults as revealed by event-related potentials. *International Journal of Psychophysiology, 29,* 145–165.

Nelson, C. A., & Webb, S. J. (2003). A cognitive neuroscience perspective on early memory development. In M. de Haan & M. H. Johnson (Eds.), *The cognitive neuroscience of development* (pp. 99–125). London: Psychology Press.

Nelson, C. A., Wewerka, S., Thomas, K. M., deRegnier, R., Tribbey-Walbridge, S., & Georgieff, M. (2000). Neurocognitive sequelae of infants of diabetic mothers. *Behavioral Neuroscience,* 114, 950–956.

O'Connor, T. G., Bredenkamp, D., & Rutter, M. (1999). Attachment disturbances and disorders in children exposed to early severe deprivation. *Infant Mental Health Journal, 20,* 10–29.

O'Connor, T. G., Rutter, M., Beckett, C., Keaveney, L., & Kreppner, J. M. (2000). The effects of global severe privation on cognitive competence: Extension and longitudinal follow-up. *Child Development, 71,* 376–390.

Otten, L. J., & Rugg, M. D. (2001). Electrophysiological correlates of memory encoding are task-dependent. *Cognitive Brain Research, 12,* 11–18.

Parker, S. W., & Nelson, C. A. (2005a). An event-related potential study of the impact of institutional rearing on face recognition. *Development and Psychopathology, 17*(3), 621–639.

Parker, S. W., & Nelson, C. A. (2005b). The impact of early institutional rearing on the ability to discriminate facial expressions of emotion: An event-related potential study. *Child Development, 76*(1), 54–72.

Pollak, S. D., Cicchetti, D., & Klorman, R. (1998). Stress, memory, and emotion: Developmental considerations from the study of child maltreatment. *Development and Psychopathology, 10,* 811–828.

Pollak, S. D., Cicchetti, D., Klorman, R., & Brumaghim, J. (1997). Cognitive brain event-related potentials and emotion processing in maltreated children. *Child Development, 68,* 773–787.

Pollak, S. D., Klorman, R., Thatcher, J. E., & Cicchetti, D. (2001). P3b reflects maltreated children's reactions to facial displays of emotion. *Psychophysiology, 38,* 267–274.

Pollak, S. D., & Tolley-Shell, S. A. (2003). Selective attention to facial emotion in physically abused children. *Journal of Abnormal Psychology, 1120,* 323–338.

Pritchard, T. C., & Alloway, K. D. (1999). *Medical neuroscience.* Madison, CT: Fence Creek Publishing.

Reynolds, G. D., & Richards, J. E. (2005). Familiarization, attention, and recognition memory in infancy: An ERP and cortical source localization study. *Developmental Psychology, 41,* 598–615.

Richards, J. E. (2003). Attention affects the recognition of briefly presented visual stimuli in infants: An ERP study. *Developmental Science, 6,* 312–328.

Rogers, T. B. (1981). A model of the self as an aspect of the human information processing system. In J. Cantor & N. Kihlstrom (Eds.), *Personality, cognition and social interaction.* Hillsdale, NJ: Erlbaum.

Rogers, T. B., Kuiper, N. A., & Kirker, N. A. (1977). Self-reference and the encoding of personal information. *Journal of Personality and Social Psychology, 35,* 677–688.

Rovee-Collier, C. (1997). Dissociations in infant memory: Rethinking the development of implicit and explicit memory. *Development and Psychopathology, 104*(3), 476–498.

Rugg, M. D. (1995). ERP studies of memory. In M. D. Rugg & M. G. H. Coles (Eds.), *Electrophysiology of mind: Event-related brain potentials and cognition* (pp. 133–170). New York: Oxford University Press.

Rugg, M. D., & Doyle, M. C. (1994). Event-related potentials and stimulus repetition in direct and indirect tests of memory. In H. J. Heinze, T. Munte, & G. R. Mangun (Eds.), *Cognitive electrophysiology.* Boston: Birkhauser.

Rutter, M., Andersen-Wood, L., Beckett, C., Bredenkamp, D., Castle, J., Groothues, C., et al. (1999). Quasi-autistic patterns following severe early global privation. *Journal of Child Psychology and Psychiatry and Allied Disciplines, 40,* 537–549.

Rutter, M., & Sroufe, L. A. (2000). Developmental psychopathology: Concepts and challenges. *Development and Psychopathology, 12,* 265–296.

Schacter, D. (1994). Priming and multiple memory systems: Perceptual mechanisms of implicit memory. D. L. Schacter & E. Tulving (Eds.), *Memory Systems* (pp. 233–268). Cambridge, MA: MIT Press.

Schacter, D., & Tulving, E. (1994). What are the memory systems of 1994? In D. L. Schacter & E. Tulving (Eds.), *Memory Systems of 1994* (pp. 1–38). Cambridge, MA: MIT Press.

Scherg, M. (1990). Fundamental of dipole source potential analysis. In F. Grandori, M. Hoke, and G. L. Romani (Eds.), *Advances in Audiology: Vol. 6. Auditory Evoked Magnetic Fields and Electrical Potentials* (pp. 40–69). Basel, Switzerland: Karger.

Scott, L. S., Luciana, M., Wewerka, S., & Nelson, C. A. (2005). Electrophysiological correlates of facial self-recognition in adults and children. *Cognitie Creier Comportament, 9,* 211–238.

Segalowitz, S. J. (1994). Developmental psychology and brain development: A historical perspective. In G. Dawson & K. W. Fischer (Eds.), *Human behavior and the developing brain* (pp. 67–92). New York: Guilford.

Snyder, K., Webb, S. J., & Nelson, C. A. (2002). Theoretical and methodological implications of variability in infant brain response during a recognition memory paradigm. *Infant Behavior and Development, 25,* 466–494.

Spitz, R. (1945a). Hospitalism: An inquiry into the genesis of psychiatric conditions in early childhood. *Psychoanalytic Study of the Child, 1,* 53–74.

Spitz, R. (1945b). Hospitalism: A follow-up report. *Psychoanalytic Study of the Child, 2,* 113–118.

Sroufe, L. A. (1990). Considering normal and abnormal together: The essence of developmental psychopathology. *Development and Psychopathology, 2,* 335–347.

Sroufe, L. A. (1996). *Emotional development: The organization of emotional life in the early years.* New York: Cambridge University Press.

Sutton, S., Braren, M., Zubin, J., & John, E. R. (1965). Evoked potential correlates of stimulus uncertainty. *Science, 150,* 1187–1188.

Teicher, M. (2002). Scars that won't heal: The neurobiology of child abuse. *Scientific American, 28*(3), 68–80.

Teicher, M. H., Anderson, S. L., Polcari, A., Anderson, C. M., Navalta, C. P., & Kim, D. M. (2003). The neurobiological consequences of early stress and childhood maltreatment. *Neuroscience and Biobehavioral Reviews, 27,* 33–44.

Thomas, K., & Cicchetti, D. (in press). Imaging brain symptoms in normality and psychopathology. *Development and Psychopathology.*

Thomas, K. M., & Nelson, C. A. (1996). Age-related changes in the electrophysiological response to visual stimulus novelty: A topographical approach. *Electroencephalography & Clinical Neurophysiology, 98,* 294–308.

Thompson, R. A., & Nelson, C. A. (2001). Developmental science and the media: Early brain development. *American Psychologist, 56,* 5-15.

Tizard, B. (1977). *Adoption: A second chance.* London: Open Books.

Tucker, D. M. (1993). Spatial sampling of head electrical fields: The geodesic sensor net. *Electroencephalography and Clinical Neurophysiology, 87,* 145–163.

Tucker, D. M., Liotti, M., Potts, G. F., Russell, G. S., & Posner, M. I. (1994). Spatio-temporal analysis of brain electrical fields. *Human Brain Mapping, 1,* 134–152.

Walter, W. G., Cooper, R., Alkdridge, V. J., McCallum, W. C., & Winter, A. L. (1964). Contingent negative variation: An electric sign of sensorimotor association and expectancy in the human brain. *Nature, 203,* 380–384.

Webb, S. J., Long, J. D., & Nelson, C. A. (2005). A longitudinal investigation of visual event-related potentials in the first year of life. *Developmental Science, 8,* 605–616.

Webb, S. J., & Nelson, C. A. (2001). Perceptual priming for upright and inverted faces in infants and adults. *Journal of Experimental Child Psychology, 79,* 1–22.

Part II
Cognitive Perspectives

4

Trauma and Autobiographical Memory Functioning

Findings from a Longitudinal Study of Family Violence

ANDREA F. GREENHOOT, SARAH L.
BUNNELL, JENNIFER S. CURTIS,
AND ALISA MILLER BEYER

Exposure to violence and abuse in the home can wreak havoc in the lives of children. Several decades of research have established that family violence and abuse are associated with atypical patterns of social, emotional, and cognitive development, including lower scores on language and intelligence assessments (Coster, Gersten, Beeghly, & Cicchetti, 1989; Hoffman-Plotkin & Twentyman, 1984; Oates, Peacock, & Forrest, 1984; Trickett, 1993), lower self-esteem (Arata, Langhinrichsen-Rohling, Bowers, & O'Farrill-Swails, 2005; Bolger, Patterson, & Kupersmidt, 1998; Kim & Cicchetti, 2004), and higher levels of aggression and psychopathology (Connor, Steingard, Cunningham, Anderson, & Melloni, 2004; Downey & Walker, 1992; Herrera & McCloskey, 2003; McCloskey, Figueredo, & Koss, 1995). A long-standing issue in the clinical literature is whether exposure to abuse during childhood also leads to disturbances in autobiographical memory development, as clinicians report that many adult survivors of child abuse have difficulty remembering large portions of their childhoods (e.g., Herman & Schatzow, 1987). Consistent with these observations, there is mounting empirical evidence of autobiographical memory impairments in adults who report childhood histories of abuse or other traumas (e.g., Henderson, Hargreaves, Gregory, & Williams, 2002; Hermans et al., 2004; Kuyken & Brewin, 1995). The clinical significance of autobiographical memory problems has served as the impetus for much of this research. It is generally agreed that our self-concepts and our relationships with other people are built, at least in part, on our memories of our past experiences (Fivush, Haden, & Reese, 1996; Fivush & Vasudeva, 2002; McAdams, 1993; Thorne, 2000). Moreover, autobiographical memory problems have been linked to deficits in interpersonal problem-solving and poorer outcomes for individuals in therapy (Brittlebank, Scott, Williams, & Ferrier, 1993; Evans, Williams, O'Loughlin, & Howells, 1992; Pollock & Williams, 2001; Sidley, Whitaker, Calam, & Wells, 1997). Thus, autobiographical memory dysfunctions may have serious implications for well-being.

In addition to the clinical implications, an understanding of trauma-related memory problems and their underlying mechanisms is of considerable relevance to the recent public and scientific debate over the impact of traumatic stress on memory and testimony for childhood experiences. Nonetheless, these issues have only recently been explored within the literature on memory development (e.g., see Eisen, Goodman, Davis, & Qin, 1999; Howe, Cicchetti, Toth, & Cerrito, 2004; Howe, Toth, & Cicchetti, 2006). In this chapter, we examine what is known about changes in autobiographical memory development or memory functioning that may be brought about by chronic exposure to stressful events such as abuse. We begin with a discussion of the empirical literature on autobiographical memory disturbances among adults who report having been abused as children, followed by a consideration of the major theoretical explanations for abuse-related impairments. We then present our own research on these issues, integrating findings from our longitudinal study of children exposed to various forms of domestic violence. Finally, we conclude with a treatment of the plausibility of competing explanations for the mechanisms contributing to these memory dysfunctions.

Child Abuse History and Autobiographical Memory

There is considerable evidence in the clinical literature that exposure to traumatic experiences in childhood, particularly physical or sexual abuse, is linked to autobiographical memory disturbances in adulthood. Many adults who have experienced childhood trauma report gaps in their memories of childhood (e.g., Edwards, Fivush, Anda, Felitti, & Nordenberg, 2001; Herman & Schatzow, 1987). For instance, a study conducted by Edwards et al. (2001) indicated that adult men and women who retrospectively reported histories of child sexual or physical abuse were significantly more likely than other adults to report that there were large parts of their childhoods (after age 4) that they could not remember. Other work has shown that a self-reported history of sexual abuse is related to poorer recall of personal facts from childhood, such as the name of one's elementary school (Hunter & Andrews, 2002). The most consistent findings, however, relate to the ability to remember or report specific episodes from one's past. In this regard, a number of studies have illustrated that adults who report histories of childhood trauma have difficulty recollecting specific autobiographical memories (e.g., Burnside, Startup, Byatt, Rollinson, & Hill, 2004; Henderson et al., 2002; Hermans et al., 2004; Kuyken & Brewin, 1995). In most of these studies, autobiographical memory is assessed with an autobiographical memory test (AMT) in which participants are asked to generate specific memories (i.e., personal memories that refer to single events lasting less than 24 hours) in response to cue words. Adults who report childhood trauma histories are more likely than control subjects to generate generic or "overgeneral" memories that reflect a category of events (e.g., "My mom and my stepdad argued all the time," in response to the cue "arguing") rather than one specific event in their lives (e.g., "I remember my mom and my aunt arguing about how I cut my head"). Moreover, the duration and severity of the trauma is negatively associated with memory specificity among trauma survivors (Burnside et al., 2004). Nevertheless, not all studies have found poor memory specificity among adults exposed to childhood trauma. In their longitudinal study of depressed outpatients, Peeters, Wessel, Merckelbach, and Boon-Vermeeren

(2002) found that reports of childhood trauma actually predicted *greater* memory specificity in response to negative cue words.

In the literature on memory and psychopathology, it is well established that difficulty retrieving and reporting specific autobiographical memories is also associated with depression. Compared to nondepressed control adults, depressed or suicidal adults show longer latencies when retrieving specific memories and are more likely to report inappropriately general memories when assessed with AMTs (Brittlebank et al., 1993; Park, Goodyer, & Teasdale, 2002; Watkins, Teasdale, & Williams, 2000; Williams & Broadbent, 1986; Williams & Dritschel, 1988). It does not seem to be the case, however, that trauma-related autobiographical memory problems are simply a reflection of elevated levels of depression among trauma survivors, as childhood trauma is related to difficulty recalling personal memories even when depression is statistically controlled (Edwards et al., 2001; Henderson et al., 2002; Hermans et al., 2004; Kuyken & Brewin, 1995).

Only a handful of studies have examined the autobiographical memory functioning of children and adolescents exposed to trauma, and the findings are less consistent than those observed with adults. In a sample of adolescent psychiatric inpatients, de Decker, Hermans, Raes, and Eelen (2003) found that teens' retrospective reports of a trauma history were associated with the production of more overgeneral memories on an AMT. In contrast, two studies using measures of autobiographical memory functioning other than the AMT have failed to find trauma-related memory deficits. Eisen et al. (1999) examined memory and suggestibility for a medical examination among maltreated children and found no differences in memory performance or susceptibility to suggestion between the abused children and nonabused controls. Similarly, in their study of adolescents with childhood exposure to family violence, Orbach, Lamb, Sternberg, Williams, and Dawud-Noursi (2001) found that neither witnessing nor being a target of family violence was related to the specificity of the adolescents' memories for family disagreements. The authors also noted, however, that children exposed to family violence were more likely than children in a control group to omit responses to questions; thus they avoided providing any responses, either generic or specific.

To summarize, there is reasonably strong evidence that a history of childhood trauma is associated with atypical patterns of autobiographical memory in adulthood, although whether these memory deficits appear during childhood or adolescence is unclear. Furthermore, it is not known whether trauma–related memory patterns are attributable to deficits in the encoding and storage of autobiographical memories, impairments in the retrieval of stored memories, or unwillingness to report memories that are retrieved. So how can trauma–related autobiographical memory problems be explained? In the next section, we turn to this issue.

Explanations for Abuse-Related Autobiographical Memory Patterns

Trauma and Cognitive Resources

One explanation for trauma–related autobiographical memory problems is that they reflect more general cognitive deficits caused by intrusive thoughts about traumatic experiences. Adults with histories of childhood trauma such as sexual or physical abuse frequently report having recurrent and intrusive negative thoughts about their victimization experiences (e.g., Kuyken & Brewin, 1994). Individuals who experience intrusive thoughts characterize them as unpleasant and report engaging in effortful attempts to avoid them (Kuyken & Brewin, 1994). Concerted efforts to block intrusive thoughts, however, are typically unsuccessful and often lead to even more frequent intrusions (Kuyken & Brewin, 1994, 1995; Wegner, Schneider, Carter, & White, 1987). Kukyen and Brewin (1995) have argued that this combination of intrusive memories and efforts to avoid them drains limited storage and processing resources in working memory. The depletion of cognitive resources, in turn, is thought to increase the likelihood that the autobiographical memory retrieval process will be interrupted before a specific episode or episodic details are accessed (Williams, Chan, Crane, & Barnhofer, 2006). In other words, specific memories may have been encoded and stored, but resource-demanding intrusive thoughts impair the ability to retrieve them.

Consistent with this argument, frequent intrusive thoughts seem to be associated with poor autobiographical memory specificity. For instance, post-traumatic stress disorder (PTSD), which is characterized by intrusive memories of negative events, is related to problems retrieving specific personal memories (McNally, Lasko, Macklin, & Pitman, 1995). Moreover, several studies using the Impact of Events Scale (IES) to measure the frequency of intrusive thoughts (as measured by the IES intrusion subscale) and conscious attempts to avoid trauma-related memories (as measured by the IES avoidance subscale) have illustrated direct associations between measures of intrusive thoughts and overgeneral memory on the AMT. In their study of adult psychiatric patients who were exposed to war atrocities as children, Wessel, Merckelbach, and Dekkers (2002) found that higher intrusion and avoidance scores on the IES were associated with more overgeneral memories. Similarly, research with depressed adults illustrated that overgeneral memory is predicted by high levels of intrusion (Brewin, Reynolds, & Tata, 1999) and avoidance (Kuyken & Brewin, 1995) as measured by the IES. Finally, Park, Goodyer, and Teasdale (2004) found that an experimental induction of rumination about negative thoughts in depressed adolescents leads to an increase in overgeneral memories.

These findings notwithstanding, the support for the cognitive deficit explanation for trauma-related autobiographical memory disturbances is not overwhelming. To date, very few studies have actually examined working memory or broader cognitive functioning to determine whether poor autobiographical memory specificity in trauma victims can be explained by a depletion of cognitive resources. The investigations that have included such measures suggest that cognitive resources do not account for the particular autobiographical memory deficits linked to trauma and depression (de Decker et al., 2003; Raes et al., 2006; Wessel, Merckelbach, & Dekkers, 2002). For instance, Wessel et al. (2002) found that performance on a general neuropsychological memory test failed to predict rates of overgeneral memory among adults with childhood exposure to war-related trauma. Similarly, de Decker et al. (2003) reported that neither a measure of working memory nor a test of non-autobiographical episodic memory, as measured by immediate and delayed story recall, accounted for the links between adolescent inpatients' trauma exposure and their performance on the AMT. Thus, although intrusive memories and avoidance of such memories may well be associated with poor memory specificity, it does not appear that the underlying mechanism for overgeneral memory in abused persons is a deficiency in cognitive resources.

Trauma and Hippocampal Function

Another explanation for trauma-related autobiographical memory problems is that they reflect more general memory deficits caused by the harmful physiologic effects of chronic or traumatic stress on the structure and function of the brain. Much of the research relevant to this hypothesis has focused on cortisol-related damage to the hippocampus, an area of the brain thought to be involved in the consolidation of memory traces into cohesive, context-rich episodic memories (Nelson, 2000; Nelson & Carver, 1998). This work suggests that under conditions of high stress, the hypothalamic-pituitary-adrenal (HPA) axis stimulates the release of excessive levels of the stress hormone cortisol (Stansbury & Gunnar, 1994), which then floods the hippocampus (Bremner, 1999; Nelson & Carver, 1998; Sapolsky, 1996, 2000; Squire, 1992). These elevated levels of cortisol impair the mechanisms that are thought to be involved in memory consolidation in the hippocampus (Fillipini, Gijsbers, Birmingham, & Dubrovsky, 1991; Gould, Tanapat, McEwen, Flugge, & Fuchs, 1998), presumably leading to the formation of highly fragmented memories (Nadel & Jacobs, 1998). Further, prolonged exposure to high levels of stress hormones may lead to a reduction in the volume of the hippocampus and more chronic memory dysfunctions (Bremner, 2005; Bremner & Narayan, 1998; Kitayama, Vaccarino, Kutner, Weiss, & Bremner, 2005; for a recent review of this literature, see Chapter 1 in this volume).

Consistent with these claims, manipulations that involve both direct application of cortisol to the brain and inductions of highly stressful events have been shown to result in hippocampal atrophy and learning impairments in nonhuman animals (Gould et al., 1998; Sapolsky & McEwen, 1986). However, empirical support for the argument that trauma itself impairs hippocampal functioning in humans is less conclusive. On the one hand, there is some evidence that exposure to child physical or sexual abuse is related to reduced hippocampal volume in adults (Bremner et al., 1997; Stein, Koverola, Hanna, Torchia, et al., 1997; Vythilingam et al., 2002). For instance, Vythilingam et al. (2002) found bilateral decreases in hippocampal volume in depressed women who reported childhood abuse histories, relative to both depressed nonabused women and healthy, nonabused controls. On the other hand, there is also evidence to suggest that hippocampal atrophy in adults with a history of trauma is more specifically associated with trauma-related psychological disorders such as PTSD (Bremner, 2001; Bremner et al., 1997; Bremner et al., 2003; Kitayama et al., 2005) and depression (Bremner et al., 2000; Sheline, Sanghavi, Mintun, & Gado, 1999), rather than the trauma itself. Bremner et al. (2003), for example, found that women with childhood

sexual abuse (CSA) histories and PTSD had significantly smaller hippocampal volume than women with CSA histories without PTSD diagnoses or nonabused control subjects. Some researchers, moreover, have
posited that smaller hippocampal volume is not a consequence of trauma
or psychopathology but rather is a preexisting risk factor for the development of psychopathology following exposure to trauma (Gilbertson
et al., 2002; Sapolsky, 1996; Stein et al., 1997). In addition, it is unclear
how early in development trauma-related alterations in brain structure
and function might occur, as most of this research has focused on adult
populations and there has been little corroborative research on this issue
with children. A study by DeBellis, Hall, Boring, Frustaci, and Moritz
(2001) found no neuroanatomical differences between children who had
developed PTSD in response to maltreatment and healthy, nonmaltreated
children when the children were tested either pre- or post-pubescently.
Nevertheless, the finding that high levels of glucocorticoids used to treat
child asthma patients are associated with memory problems suggests
that cortisol elevation could lead to deficits in memory function during childhood (Annett & Bender, 1994). Thus, even if trauma-related
hippocampal volume deficits are not observed during childhood, it is
possible that trauma-induced stress hormone dysregulation could lead to
memory problems during childhood and eventual cell death in the hippocampal structure in adulthood.

If hippocampal dysfunction is in fact one of the mechanisms involved in the autobiographical memory impairments that typify abuse
victims, it seems likely that these autobiographical memory problems
would be accompanied by a broad range of memory deficits. The hippocampus is thought to be central in the consolidation of verbal declarative memory traces (Bremner et al., 2003; Bremner, Vythilingam,
Vermetten, Vaccarino, & Charney, 2004; Elzinga, Bakker, & Bremner,
2005; Squire, 1992), and it has also been implicated in the retrieval of
declarative memories (de Quervain, Roozendaal, & McGaugh, 1998),
implicit memory processes (Chun & Phelph, 1999), and spatial memory
(Maguire, Frackowiak, & Frith, 1997). Thus individuals with trauma-
related autobiographical memory problems should also be expected to
show deficits in nonautobiographical memory, and they should show
evidence of impaired encoding and storage processes as well as retrieval
processes. Surprisingly few studies of trauma-related autobiographical
memory disturbances have actually addressed these possibilities. One

exception is the study by de Decker et al. (2003) that illustrated that immediate and delayed story recall were unrelated to trauma–associated memory problems in their sample of adolescent psychiatric inpatients. Although more research is needed in this area, there is currently a dearth of empirical evidence to confirm that stress–related hippocampal damage accounts for the autobiographical memory problems observed in traumatized individuals.

Trauma and Emotion Regulation

The prevailing explanation for trauma–related memory deficits is that they reflect emotion regulation processes that have their roots in early adverse experiences (e.g., Brittlebank et al., 1993; Burnside et al., 2004; Williams, 1996). According to this model, stressful experiences during childhood lead to the development of a trait-like cognitive style that involves avoiding the retrieval of specific details of past events to blunt potentially negative affect (Williams, 1996). Evidence for the claim that poor memory specificity reflects an enduring style comes from studies reporting that overgeneral memory persists several months after depression has remitted (e.g., Brittlebank et al., 1993; Williams & Dritschel, 1988). Moreover, a few recent findings are consistent with the claim that overgeneral memory reflects affect control processes: nontraumatized, nondepressed adults who retrieve fewer specific memories score higher on a measure of "repressive" coping style (Raes et al., 2006), and report less subjective distress following a negative event in the laboratory (Raes, Hermans, & Eelen, 2003; Raes et al., 2006), than individuals who are highly specific in their memories. The affect regulation hypothesis also suggests that while an avoidant cognitive style may reduce distress in the short term, it increases vulnerability to depression in the long term because the inability to recall specific past experiences impairs problem-solving ability (Williams, 1996). Consistent with these claims, a longitudinal study of depressed adults showed that higher rates of overgeneral memory at the outset of the study increased the likelihood that the individuals remained depressed over a 7-month period (Brittlebank et al., 1993). There is also evidence that a lack of memory specificity is a precursor to the onset of depression among nondepressed adults; Van Minnen, Wessel, Verhaak, and Smeenk (2005) reported that women's depressive symptoms following a failed in vitro fertilization treatment were negatively related to the number of specific memories they had produced on an AMT prior to the treatment. Furthermore, poor memory specificity has in fact been directly linked to difficulties in problem solving (Evans et al., 1992; Pollock & Williams, 2001; Raes et al., 2006; Williams, Barnhofer, Crane, & Duggan, 2006). Thus, depression may actually be an outcome, rather than a cause, of autobiographical memory difficulties.

Although there seems to be a growing consensus in the literature that trauma-related memory problems reflect an emotion regulation style adopted during childhood, there are some unaddressed issues that bear on the plausibility of this explanation. First, this model has focused primarily on childhood trauma, and the role of recent or current stressors in autobiographical memory problems has not been addressed. Yet it seems possible that current stressors could elicit a more transient strategic response that involves avoiding details to control affect, thus mimicking the trait-like style adopted in response to childhood traumata. In addition, childhood trauma is associated with negative outcomes and revictimization, and those more recent negative experiences may be correlated with memory functioning. The issue is further clouded by the reliance in previous research on retrospective self-reports of early trauma. Documentation of early experiences through retrospective reports is not independent of participants' current abilities or willingness to disclose trauma, making it difficult to distinguish between the impact of actual early experiences and current mental conditions or "frame of mind." Thus the memory problems that have been observed in adults with childhood abuse histories could actually reflect a more dynamic coping strategy adopted in response to current negative thoughts about childhood or recent abuse experiences. Indeed, Park, Goodyer, and Teasdale's (2004) finding that a rumination induction increased rates of overgeneral memories among depressed adolescents is consistent with the view that the current experiencing of negative thoughts might elicit a strategic avoidance of details to blunt affect.

Another limitation is that there is currently little convergent evidence that trauma-related memory patterns reflect disengagement from emotionally laden stimuli. The index of memory functioning has almost exclusively been the rate of production of specific or overgeneral memories on an AMT in which participants are asked to generate specific memories in response to cue words. Yet if the overgeneral memories typical of traumatized individuals reflect a desire to avoid potentially painful details about past events, it seems likely that this would also be evident in examinations of the disclosure of emotions in personal recollections, as well as the emotional valence of memories. Specifically, traumatized individuals who are attempting to avoid painful recollections might also avoid retrieving or reporting the emotional details of their memories and/or negatively valenced memories altogether. Furthermore, although the use of similar tasks and outcome measures facilitates cross-study comparisons, an additional consequence is that conclusions cannot be drawn regarding whether the memory patterns associated with childhood abuse are specific to the AMT or generalize to other assessments of autobiographical memory, such as untimed, more extensive narratives of personal memories.

We have been addressing some of these issues in our own research program by examining memory functioning in a subset of adolescents who were participating in a larger longitudinal study of family violence. Our investigations have been designed to extend previous research by examining the effects of both early and recent abuse experiences on autobiographical memory functioning. Because we documented the participants' exposure to various forms of abuse prospectively rather than retrospectively, we have been able to examine the effects of childhood abuse independently of current frame of mind or more recent stressors that may be correlated with child abuse histories. Compared to most of the previous studies, our research examines a far broader range of memory measures, including diverse characteristics of the memory narratives elicited by an AMT, performance on additional types of autobiographical memory assessments, and measures of nonautobiographical episodic memory. These multiple indicators not only provide information about the context specificity of trauma-related memory disturbances but might also shed new light on the mechanisms underlying these memory problems. In the sections that follow, we provide an overview of the longitudinal project and then describe a set of investigations of trauma-related memory patterns in the longitudinal sample.

A Longitudinal Study of Domestic Violence

The longitudinal project was originally designed to examine the impact of family violence, particularly spousal violence, on women and children's mental health (see McCloskey, Figueredo, & Koss, 1995, for further details). Our follow-up assessments on this sample, however, have provided a rich and unique opportunity for addressing questions about the operation of memory under conditions of severe stress. During the first year of the study (Year 1), McCloskey et al. (1995) recruited 363 battered and nonbattered women and one of their children to participate in a study on families. Battered women (n = 193) were recruited through advertisements (radio, newspaper, and shoppers' guides) and flyers posted at battered women's shelters and over 150 community establishments asking them to contact researchers if they had experienced abuse by a male partner in the previous year. For the nonbattered women (n = 170), flyers were posted in the same community establishments recruiting women and children for a study on families (and giving a different phone number). For each family, a "target child" (the participant for the studies described here) between 6 and 12 years of age (M = 9 years) was selected according to a procedure that alternated between male or female sex during the phone intake. Thus, approximately half of the target children were female (n = 179). Fifty-three percent of the participants were white, 35% were Hispanic, 6% were African American, 4% were Native American, and the remaining 2% were of other ethnicities or unclassified. Most of the participants were from low-income households.

The children and mothers took part in separate 3-hour interviews to assess abuse exposure and children's social, emotional, and cognitive functioning. Using the Conflict Tactics Scale (Straus, 1979), the children were questioned about the frequency with which they had been exposed to various forms of mother-directed spousal violence (e.g., the mother being beaten, kicked, threatened with a weapon) and child-directed physical punishment and abuse (e.g., the child being hit with an object, kicked, burned) in the previous year. Children were not asked about exposure to violence prior to this time period, as the goal was to obtain information about the children's recent family circumstances while minimizing the possible influence of memory distortion or forgetting on their reports. Although the primary focus of this study was family violence, participants were also questioned about whether they had ever been sexually abused. Descriptive data on the children's reports of exposure to family violence and sexual abuse during the first year of the project are presented in Table 4.1. Mothers were questioned about the same events (and more) in separate interviews, but for the analyses presented in this chapter, we relied on the teens' reports of violence to

TABLE 4.1. Descriptive Data on Children's Reports of Mother- and Child-Directed Aggression and Sexual Abuse at Years 1 and 6

Group	# of Reports	Mean Frequency in Previous Year	Range of Frequency Estimates
Year 1 (*N* = 363)			
Mother-directed aggression	194	18.6	0 to 150
Child-directed aggression	228	9.1	0 to 79
Sexual abuse	35	—	—
Year 6 (*N* = 299)			
Mother-directed aggression	100	1.1	0 to 17
Child-directed aggression	91	4.9	0 to 505
Sexual abuse	21	—	—

Note: Abuse categories for each year were not mutually exclusive; participants could report more than one type of aggression or abuse during any given year. Therefore, for any given year, the number of participants reporting different forms of abuse may exceed the total number of participants for that year.

measure their frequency of exposure to ensure that the events reported were events to which the children were actually exposed. Nevertheless, to reduce the possible impact of fabricated or unreliable reports of violence (or the absence of violence), only participants whose reports were independently corroborated by their mothers were selected for inclusion in the analyses presented here.

We conducted a follow-up assessment on this sample 6 years later (Year 6), when the participants were 12 to 18 years old (*M* = 15 years). Eighty-two percent of the sample (*n* = 296) was retained in this second wave of interviews. At the Year 6 interview, the teens' social, emotional, and cognitive functioning, as well as their recent exposure to spousal violence, physical abuse, and sexual abuse, was evaluated using a set of questions comparable to those used in the Year 1 interview. Table 4.1 also provides information regarding the participants' exposure to mother-directed violence and child-directed physical and sexual abuse during Year 6. Note that the frequency of mother-directed violence decreased at the follow-up assessment, in part because many of the mothers were no longer in abusive relationships at the time of the follow-up interviews. The Year 6 interview also included an evaluation of the teens' autobiographical memories for childhood experiences in general, as well as their recollections of any abusive events that had been documented at Year 1. Although we have conducted extensive analyses of the teens' memories of childhood exposure to family violence per se (e.g., Green-hoot, McCloskey, & Glisky, 2005), it is the measures of autobiographical memory for childhood in general that are the focus of the investigations described in this chapter.

Abuse and the Accessibility of Childhood Memories

In the first investigation of trauma-related memory problems in our labo-ratory, Johnson, Greenhoot, Glisky, and McCloskey (2005) examined the extent to which both early and recent abuse experiences, as well as current depression, predicted adolescents' memory functioning during Year 6 of the longitudinal study. The sample consisted of a subset of 134 partici-pants whose autobiographical memory assessments were transcribed and available for analysis and whose reports regarding family violence were corroborated by their mothers.[1] The participants reported a broad range of family violence and abuse exposure, from no exposure to moderate exposure to highly frequent exposure. For both Year 1 and Year 6, we col-lapsed the indicators of mother- and child-directed violence into overall measures of the frequency of family violence reported at each interview, capping a few extreme outliers to prevent them from skewing the results. Because sexual abuse was only reported for a small number of these par-ticipants at Year 1 ($n = 8$) and Year 6 ($n = 12$), and because some of the disclosed abuse had taken place in the distant past, we created a dichoto-mous indicator of whether the participant had *ever* been sexually abused for these analyses.

During Year 6, when they were between 12 and 18 years of age, the participants' autobiographical memories for childhood were assessed with an adaptation of the AMT in which they were presented two positive (playing, present), two negative (arguing, punishment), and two neutral (car, shopping) cue words in random order. They were given 3 minutes to generate specific childhood memories (from before age 9) in response to each cue. Consistent with previous research using the AMT, each mem-ory generated was coded as specific or overgeneral. But whereas most

---

1. This subset of participants did not differ from the remainder of the sample in family violence exposure or demographic characteristics.

previous research has focused almost exclusively on rates of overgeneral or specific memories, we examined two additional dimensions of the participants' AMT performance that might indicate an inability or unwillingness to recollect specific past experiences: the number of interviewer prompts required to elicit each memory and the mean length of each memory produced (indexed by the number of words in the narrative). Occasionally, portions of the audiotaped interviews were too muffled for the transcribers and coders to interpret, and memories for which more than two words were unintelligible were not included in the calculation of average memory length and were assigned a code of "unintelligible." We also examined the valence of the memories produced (i.e., negative or non-negative), as judged from the perspective of an objective observer; we thought that valence might provide additional information about whether memory problems reflect emotion regulation processes as opposed to broader cognitive or memory dysfunctions. To evaluate the possibility that abuse-related autobiographical memory problems reflect more general memory deficits, we also tested the adolescents' immediate and delayed recall of a list of 10 verbally presented paired associates. Finally, to measure depressive symptoms at Year 6, we administered the Center for Epidemiologic Studies Depression Scale (CES-D; Radloff, 1977) and calculated a dichotomous indicator of depression using the clinical cutoff recommended by Radloff (1977). Although the Year 6 assessment included several other measures of child well-being and psychopathology (e.g., anxiety, attachment, attention problems, externalizing symptoms, and aggressive and delinquent behavior), preliminary analyses revealed no associations between autobiographical memory performance and these other measures of mental health; thus they were excluded from the remaining analyses.

A series of general linear models predicting the measures of childhood autobiographical memory indicated that the frequency of both recent and childhood exposure to family violence, as well as depression, were associated with performance on the AMT, even when other important variables such as age and gender were included in the models. Table 4.2 presents the standardized regression coefficients resulting from these analyses. Note that the model predicting memory length controlled for the number of unintelligible memories because these memories were excluded from the calculation of the mean length of each memory. Additionally, the model predicting the number of overgeneral memories generated per

TABLE 4.2. Standardized Regression Coefficients from General Linear Models Predicting Measures of Memory Performance on Year 6 AMT

Variable	# Prompts	Memory Length	# Overgeneral Memories	% Negative Memories
Sex[a]	−.224*	.078	.094	−.014
Age	.062	.039	—	.165
Positive cues	—	—	.021	—
Negative cues	—	—	.180*	—
Neutral cues	—	—	.300***	—
Year 1 family violence	.253**	.096	−.158	−.037
Year 6 family violence	−.052	−.195*	—	—
Positive cues	—	—	−.126	.086
Negative cues	—	—	.064	.134
Neutral cues	—	—	.164 †	−.237*
Sexual abuse	−.037	.142	.074	.119
Depression	−.121	.004	.220*	.119
Unintelligible memories	—	−.177 †	—	—
Memory length	—	—	−.111	—
Prompts	—	—	.328***	—
Specific memories	—	—	−.060	—

Parameter estimates are presented by cue type only when there was a significant interaction between a predictor and cue type.
[a] Male = 0; female = 1.
$^{\dagger}p < .06$; $^{*}p < .05$; $^{**}p < .01$; $^{***}p < .001$.

cue included memory length, number of prompts, and number of specific memories as covariates, because these variables might affect the number of responses participants were able to produce during each 3-minute period. As indicated in Table 4.2, teens who were exposed to higher levels of recent (Year 6) family violence provided shorter childhood memory narratives across all cue types, fewer negatively valenced memories in response to neutral cues, and more overgeneral memories in response to neutral cues, although the latter effect did not quite reach significance.[2] Greater exposure to family violence during childhood (Year 1) was as-

---

2. Note that although the univariate tests indicated that the effect of recent family violence on overgeneral memories for neutral cues did not quite reach significance, the test of the interaction between recent family violence and cue type in the repeated measures model predicting overgeneral memories was statistically significant, $F(2, 119) = 4.15, p = 0.018$.

sociated with more interviewer prompts on the AMT, suggesting that interviewers had to work harder to elicit specific childhood memories from teens with traumatic childhoods. Moreover, consistent with the extensive literature on depression and memory functioning, teens who met the clinical cutoff for depression produced more overgeneral memories across all cue types than teens who were not depressed. In contrast to previous research, reports of childhood sexual abuse did not relate to autobiographical memory patterns in this study, but it should also be noted that only 14% of the sample reported histories of sexual abuse, and this may not have been a large enough group to detect an effect on autobiographical memory.

Importantly, performance on the paired associates test, our measure of nonautobiographical episodic memory, was not associated with family violence, depression, or any of the measures of AMT performance. Thus, as in previous work by de Decker et al. (2003), the links between trauma history and autobiographical memory functioning observed in this study do not seem to be explained by basic memory impairments. The overall pattern of results is more consistent with the argument that trauma-related memory problems reflect cognitive strategies for affect regulation that involve avoiding thinking and talking about the details of past experiences so as to blunt potentially negative emotions. The fact that teens exposed to recent (Year 6) family violence produced shorter and more generic memories, as well as *fewer* negative memories in response to neutral cues, than other teens provides convergent evidence that they may have been avoiding the retrieval of potentially painful memories, or that they were unwilling to report memories that were retrieved. Similarly, the link between childhood family violence and the need for more interviewer prompting to elicit specific memories suggests that participants with childhood abuse histories had encoded and stored specific memories but were reluctant to recollect them. Whether depression is a cause or an outcome of this apparent avoidance cannot be determined from this study. Our results also suggest that avoidance may be more easily applied under some conditions than others. For instance, the link between Year 6 abuse and the production of fewer negative memories on the AMT held only for neutral cues, which offer more latitude in the types of memories recalled than positive or negative cues. Similarly, Year 6 abuse was associated with overgeneral memories for neutral cues alone. We are not aware of any other study that has used neutral cues on the AMT, but previous findings of cue type effects (i.e., positive versus negative) on trauma-related specificity problems have been quite inconsistent (e.g., de Decker et al., 2003; Henderson et al., 2002; Kuyken & Brewin, 1995). Although we cannot draw any definitive conclusions about these divergent cue type effects, one interpretation is that the semantic (e.g., strength and extensiveness of associative networks) and emotional qualities of different cues may create different contexts for recall, which may influence the degree to which avoidance is utilized.

An additional implication of our findings is that this pattern of avoidance does not necessarily have to emerge out of early adverse experiences, as both recent and childhood exposure to family violence predicted performance on the AMT. Thus, even though the tendency to avoid childhood recollections might reflect an enduring style that develops in response to early adversity, this pattern could also reflect a more transient, strategic response to current stressors. Indeed, given that research on the development of emotion regulation suggests that cognitive strategies for affect regulation develop late in childhood, it is possible that the tendency to avoid details and blunt affect does not develop until later in life, in response to negative thoughts about past experiences.

Abuse and Emotional Language in Childhood Memories at Year 6

Additional evidence consistent with the emotion regulation hypothesis comes from a secondary analysis of the autobiographical memories produced at Year 6, in which Greenhoot, Johnson, and McCloskey (2005) examined the teens' use of internal states language, particularly emotional language. We were interested in the representation of internal states in participants' recollections because recalling how one felt during a past experience is seen as one way in which people make sense of and find personal significance in past experiences (see Chapter 6 in this volume; Bauer, Stennes, & Haight, 2003; Fivush, Berlin, Sales, Mennuti-Washburn, & Cassidy, 2003; Pennebaker, Mayne, & Francis, 1997), and little is known about how individuals with trauma histories evaluate and make sense of their pasts. This investigation involved recoding the narratives produced in response to each cue in the AMT for the frequency of emotional language and other internal-states language. Specifically, we coded words related to internal states into four categories using an adaptation of a coding scheme developed by Bauer et al. (2003): emotion terms (e.g., happy, scared), cognition terms (e.g., understand, know), perception terms (e.g., hear, smell), and physiological states terms (e.g., hurt, tired). In addition, emotion terms were further classified according to valence (i.e., positive terms, such as "excited"; negative terms, such as "worried"; and neutral terms, such as "didn't care"), explicitness (i.e., whether an emotion was explicitly referred to or implied), and experiencer (i.e., self-referent or referring to others).

We related the frequency of internal-states language in childhood recollections on the AMT to measures of childhood (Year 1) and recent (Year 6) abuse. Because we were interested in whether the effect of abuse on internal-states language might vary as a function of the type of memory cue (positive, negative, or neutral), we constructed dichotomous indicators of abuse at Year 1 and Year 6. This approach facilitated examination of interactions between cue valence and abuse exposure, and also permitted us to collapse across all forms of abuse, including mother-directed violence, child-directed violence, and childhood sexual abuse. For this analysis, we selected participants who at Year 1 reported either high levels of exposure to these forms of abuse (the Abuse Exposure group) or no exposure to abuse during childhood (the No Exposure group). Only children who reported frequent (i.e., 35 to 150 incidents) or severe (e.g., beating, choking) abuse and whose mothers corroborated their reports were included in the Abuse Exposure group ($n = 47$). The No Exposure group ($n = 24$) included children exposed to no family aggression whatsoever, according to either the child's or mother's Year 1 report. Participants who reported moderate levels of domestic violence or whose mothers failed to corroborate their Year 1 reports were excluded from the analyses. The resulting 71 participants were also classified according to their abuse exposure at Year 6 (Abuse Exposure and No Exposure); 21 adolescents reported abuse exposure at Year 6, and this included adolescents who were exposed to moderate (rather than only severe) violence, due to the overall drop in violence exposure at Year 6. Although we used this classification approach to simplify presentation of the findings, it should also be noted that the patterns of results were quite similar when we conducted the analyses using continuous measures of abuse exposure and included participants with moderate exposure.

The results revealed that patterns of emotional language in the teens' recollections differed as a function of childhood abuse exposure, whereas other forms of internal-states language did not. Specifically, there was an interaction between childhood abuse history and cue type in the model predicting the frequency of emotion terms, $F(2, 62) = 5.23$, $p = 0.008$, controlling for overall narrative length, as well as gender and age. As shown in Figure 4.1, adolescents with no childhood abuse histories used more emotional language in recollections related to negative cues than in memories elicited by positive or neutral cues. It is important to note that analyses of the content of the teens' recollections indicated that almost all of the memories generated in response to the negative cues were negative and highly related to the cues themselves (i.e., involved punishment or conflict), whereas almost none of the memories prompted by positive and neutral cues referred to such events. Thus the pattern observed among nonabused teens is consistent with the findings of other investigations suggesting that emotions may be more salient and relevant in children's recollections of stressful events than nonstressful events (Fivush, Hazzard, et al., 2003). Yet Figure 4.1 also illustrates that adolescents with childhood abuse histories showed no such increase in the use of emotion terms in their responses to negative cues, in spite of the fact that their childhood experiences related to *arguing* and *punishment* were probably even more emotionally arousing than those of adolescents without childhood abuse histories. Indeed, teens in the Year 1 Abuse Exposure group used significantly fewer emotion words in their narratives elicited by negative cues than teens in the Year 1 No Exposure group. These patterns, moreover, were observed across all categories of emotions terms; when discussing

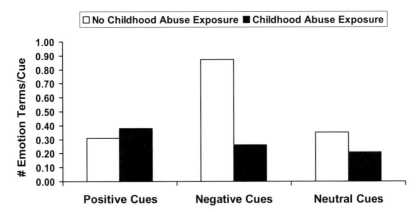

FIGURE 4.1. Mean number of emotion terms produced per memory as a function of childhood abuse exposure and cue type.

memories related to *punishment* and *arguing*, teens with childhood abuse histories produced fewer positive, negative, and neutral emotion terms; made fewer explicit and implicit references to emotion; and mentioned fewer self-referent and other-referent terms than teens without such a history. It is also worth mentioning that the lack of emotional content was not a direct consequence of overgeneral autobiographical memories, because the frequency of overgeneral memories was unrelated to the number of emotion terms elicited by each cue.

There are several potential explanations for the low levels of emotional language observed in the conflict-related memories of teens with childhood abuse histories. Conflict-related events may be especially confusing and difficult to appraise for children from abusive homes. Adults from abusive families, moreover, may be unlikely to talk about these events with their children, or perhaps might even actively discourage such discussion. It is also possible that children with Year 1 Abuse Exposure were desensitized to conflict, as there is evidence that abused children have dampened physiological responses to emotional stimuli (Carrey, Butter, Persinger, & Bialik, 1995). But the findings are also consistent with the prevailing explanation of other memory abnormalities seen among individuals with abuse histories: traumatic experiences might lead to a strategic avoidance of certain types of memory content in an attempt to regulate affect. Specifically, teens in the Year 1 Abuse Exposure group may have been reluctant to think or talk about their own and others' affective reactions to conflict-related experiences because they were likely to be unpleasant.

In contrast to childhood abuse exposure, recent (Year 6) exposure to abuse did not predict internal states language in childhood recollections. It is possible that tests of the effects of recent abuse were weaker than tests of childhood abuse in this study because we selected the sample based on childhood exposure, and recent exposure was far less frequent and severe. Yet when the analyses of emotional language were conducted on the entire sample for whom AMTs were available (in the alternative analyses using continuous abuse variables), recent abuse continued to be unrelated to emotional language. Moreover, recent abuse was a consistent predictor of specificity and related dimensions of performance on the AMT in Johnson et al. (2005). Therefore, it seems more likely that this pattern reflects age differences in the effects of abuse on affective processing, or that it is due to differences in the types of events being remembered, as the *childhood* experiences of teens with recent abuse exposure are not necessarily abuse-related and traumatic.

Conclusions

Our analyses of the longitudinal study thus far add to the growing literature showing that the personal recollections of adolescents and adults with trauma histories differ from those of individuals without such experiences. In contrast to previous research, we have documented individual participants' abuse exposure prospectively across childhood and adolescence, and our findings demonstrate that both early (i.e., childhood) experiences with abuse and very recent or concurrent stressors may lead to memory abnormalities. Thus, our work suggests that trauma-related memory problems may not necessarily reflect an enduring style or dysfunction that emerges out of early experience and could also be a more transient response to current conditions. We have also identified a broader range of abuse-related autobiographical memory problems than has been documented in the previous literature. Exposure to abuse, in both the recent past and childhood, predicted multiple indicators of the ability or willingness to recollect specific childhood memories. Childhood abuse exposure was also associated with lower levels of emotional language in participants' recollections generated on the AMT. Moreover, we have recently replicated this pattern of abuse-related deficits in emotional language in analyses of the teens' memory narratives obtained 2 years later in a third wave (Year 8) of the longitudinal project (Greenhoot, Tsethlikai, Beyer, and Johnson, 2005). During this assessment, the teens were given unlimited time to recollect family functioning and family experiences from Year 1 in response to open-ended prompts (e.g., "How did you and your dad/stepdad/mother's partner get along?" and "When your mom and your dad/stepdad/mother's partner fought or argued, what usually happened?"). As in the Year 6 analyses of responses to the AMT, childhood abuse exposure was associated with fewer references to emotions in these recollections. Thus, this particular abuse-related memory pattern does not seem to be limited to memories generated on an AMT but extends to untimed narratives about past life experiences. It is not clear, however, whether *all* of the trauma-related autobiographical memory patterns we have observed are attributable to the same underlying mechanisms.

The most frequently cited explanation for abuse-related memory specificity problems is the affect regulation hypothesis: poor specificity is the result of a coping style or strategy in which individuals avoid details to blunt potentially negative affect. The overall pattern of results from our first investigation seems to fit well with this argument. For example, teens exposed to higher levels of recent family violence produced shorter and more generic memories on the AMT, as well as fewer negative memories in response to neutral cues, suggesting that these adolescents may have been strategically avoiding potentially negative memory content. Additional indirect evidence in support of the affect regulation hypothesis comes from the observation that abuse-related memory patterns were unrelated to performance on a measure of nonautobiographical episodic memory. Thus, consistent with the findings of de Decker et al. (2003) and Wessel et al. (2002), trauma-related memory problems do not seem to be explained by either general episodic memory deficits that should be linked to hippocampal impairment or cognitive resource limitations associated with intrusive negative thoughts. Nonetheless, it would seem hasty to rule out these alternative explanations on the basis of a few null findings. For instance, given that the hippocampus is thought to be involved in memory consolidation (e.g., Elzinga et al., 2005), it is possible that the delays between encoding and recall in the tests of nonautobiographical episodic memory used in previous studies were not long enough to reveal trauma-related deficits. Moreover, because we did not obtain other measures of general cognitive functioning at the Year 6 assessment, we cannot eliminate the possibility that these memory patterns reflect other cognitive deficits (e.g., IQ or language deficits) known to be associated with child abuse (Coster et al., 1989; Hoffman–Plotkin & Twentyman, 1984; Oates et al., 1984; Trickett, 1993). A more comprehensive evaluation of the declarative memory and cognitive abilities of individuals with trauma histories therefore is warranted.

Perhaps more important, no one has looked at whether abuse-related memory problems are directly associated with measures of emotion regulation processes. If these memory patterns reflect strategic regulation of affect, abused individuals who have difficulty retrieving specific memories should be more likely than other people to use avoidant strategies (e.g., denial, mental disengagement) to cope with distressing events. Although a recent study reported by Hermans, Defranc, Raes, Williams, and Eelen (2005) revealed that nontraumatized individuals with less specific autobiographical memories on an AMT scored higher on measures of avoidance and thought suppression, researchers have not yet demonstrated that avoidance accounts for the poor specificity observed in individuals with trauma histories.

The emotional language findings also seem quite consistent with the emotion regulation hypothesis. On the other hand, the fact that patterns of memory specificity and emotional language were differentially associated with childhood and recent abuse suggests that different mechanisms could be responsible for these two deficits. Indeed, our recent analysis of the teens' Year 8 narratives about childhood family experiences provided results that are less consistent with a strategic avoidance of potentially negative memory content than the results related to specificity (Greenhoot, Tsethlikai, et al., 2005). Teens with childhood abuse histories disclosed less affective information but also provided *more* frequent and detailed memories of negative events than other teens. Of course, given that the participants were specifically asked to discuss family experiences from an unpleasant period in their childhoods (Year 1), teens with childhood abuse histories may have found it difficult to avoid memories of negative experiences altogether, even though they were able to avoid thinking or talking about how the experiences felt. But an alternative explanation is that deficits in emotional language may be due to atypical emotion socialization processes in the family, or to desensitization to emotional stimuli such that little affective detail was encoded in the first place.

One limitation of our longitudinal project is that memory assessments were not conducted at the outset of the study; therefore we do not know how early in development abuse-related autobiographical memory disturbances might emerge. Information about the developmental sequence of trauma-related memory problems might shed some additional light on the mechanisms that underlie them. For instance, the developmental literature on emotion regulation suggests that cognitive strategies emerge around middle to late childhood and increase with age (Brenner & Salovey, 1997). Thus, if these trauma-related memory patterns reflect a strategic tendency to avoid details and blunt affect, this tendency may not develop until later in childhood or adolescence, in response to unpleasant thoughts about past experiences.

An additional limitation is that the temporal locus of trauma-related memory deficits is not completely clear. Our own findings and those of others indicate that traumatized individuals do report some specific autobiographical memories, and that their memory specificity fluctuates according to retrieval conditions such as the type of memory cue (Johnson et al., 2005) or the presence of intrusive thoughts (e.g., Wessel et al., 2002). These patterns are consistent with the argument that abuse-related memory problems reflect atypical processes that occur at the time of recollection, although it is not clear whether they are due to difficulty retrieving memories or unwillingness to discuss them. Similarly, our finding that teens with childhood abuse histories required more prompting to recollect specific memories suggests that these individuals have encoded and stored specific memories but that they cannot or will not retrieve or share them. Nevertheless, encoding and storage deficits cannot be ruled out by these patterns alone, as individuals with weaker or sparser memory traces are likely to require more supportive conditions for successful retrieval. Furthermore, even if many abuse-related memory problems initially reflect an avoidance of painful memories during retrieval or reporting, it seems possible that over time such a strategy could be generalized to other levels of processing to affect the way new experiences are attended to, interpreted, and encoded.

In sum, it is clear that abuse-related disturbances in autobiographical memory functioning appear as early as adolescence, but further investigation is needed to establish the reasons for these disturbances, such as generalized stress-related cognitive dysfunctions or strategic disengagement from potentially negative stimuli. One additional possibility that has not been addressed in the extant literature is that these memory problems reflect an involuntary, automatic form of disengagement from stress-related information. Indeed, the dual process model of responses to stress developed by Compas and his colleagues (e.g., Compas & Boyer, 2001) suggests that individuals may engage or disengage from stress-related stimuli at both a voluntary and an involuntary level, and their data provide support for dissociations between these two response levels. In ongoing work in our laboratory, we are examining the relations between trauma-related memory patterns and disengagement at both of these levels.

We conclude by revisiting the scientific and clinical significance of this line of work. First, the research reviewed in this chapter illustrates that individual differences in exposure to abuse or sources of traumatic stress may be an important source of variation in memory for experiences, particularly stressful experiences. Models of the effect of stress on memory need to account for not only the degree of stress associated with a particular event, but each individual's history of experience with highly stressful events as well. Additionally, autobiographical memories that are devoid of emotional content or are overly generic may have negative consequences for well-being, as memories for past experiences are thought to be central to our self concept, our relationships, and our ability to solve interpersonal problems (e.g., Brittlebank et al., 1993; Evans et al., 1992; Fivush, Berlin, et al., 2003). Further research into the developmental course and underlying mechanisms of these problems may have important implications for the treatment of abuse victims.

References

Annett, R. D., & Bender, B. G. (1994). Neuropsychological dysfunction in asthmatic children. *Neuropsychology Review, 4*(2), 91–115.

Arata, C. M., Langhinrichsen-Rohling, J., Bowers, D., & O'Farrill-Swails, L. (2005). Single versus multi-type maltreatment: An examination of the long-term effects of child abuse. *Journal of Aggression, Maltreatment and Trauma, 11*(4), 29–52.

Bauer, P. J., Stennes, L., & Haight, J. C. (2003). Representation of the inner self in autobiography: Women's and men's use of internal states language in personal narratives. *Memory, 11*(1), 27–42.

Bolger, K. E., Patterson, C. J., & Kupersmidt, J. B. (1998). Peer relationships and self-esteem among children who have been maltreated. *Child Development, 69*(4), 1171–1197.

Bremner, J. D. (1999). Does stress damage the brain? *Biological Psychiatry, 45*(7), 797–805.

Bremner, J. D. (2001). Hypotheses and controversies related to effects of stress on the hippocampus: An argument for stress-induced damage to the hippocampus in patients with posttraumatic stress disorder. *Hippocampus, 11*(2), 75–81.

Bremner, J. D. (2005). Effects of traumatic stress on brain structure and function: Relevance to early responses to trauma. *Journal of Trauma and Dissociation, 6*(2), 51–68.

Bremner, J. D., & Narayan, M. (1998). The effects of stress on memory and the hippocampus throughout the life cycle: Implications for childhood development and aging. *Development and Psychopathology, 10*(4), 871–885.

Bremner, J. D., Narayan, M., Anderson, E. R., Staib, L. H., Miller, H. L., & Charney, D. S. (2000). Hippocampal volume reduction in major depression. *American Journal of Psychiatry, 157*(1), 115–117.

Bremner, J. D., Randall, P., Vermetton, E., Staib, L., Bronen, R. A., Mazure, C., et al. (1997). Magnetic resonance imaging-based measurement of hippocampal volume in posttraumatic stress disorder related to childhood physical and sexual abuse—a preliminary report. *Biological Psychiatry, 41,* 23–32.

Bremner, J. D., Vythilingam, M., Vermetten, E., Southwick, S. M., McGlashan, T., Nazeer, A., et al. (2003). MRI and PET study of deficits in hippocampal structure and function in women with childhood sexual abuse and posttraumatic stress disorder. *American Journal of Psychiatry, 160*(5), 924–932.

Bremner, J. D., Vythilingam, M., Vermetten, E., Vaccarino, V., & Charney, D. S. (2004). Deficits in hippocampal and anterior cingulate functioning during verbal declarative memory encoding in midlife major depression. *American Journal of Psychiatry, 161*(4), 637–645.

Brenner, E., & Salovey, P. (1997). Emotion regulation during childhood: Developmental, interpersonal, and individual considerations. In P. Salovey & D. Sluyter (Eds.), *Emotional literacy and emotional development* (pp. 168–192). New York: Basic Books.

Brewin, C. R., Reynolds, M., & Tata, P. (1999). Autobiographical memory processes and the course of depression. *Journal of Abnormal Psychology, 108*(3), 511–517.

Brittlebank, A. D., Scott, J., Williams, J. M., & Ferrier, I. N. (1993). Autobiographical memory in depression: State or trait marker? *British Journal of Psychiatry, 162,* 118–121.

Burnside, E., Startup, M., Byatt, M., Rollinson, L., & Hill, J. (2004). The role of overgeneral autobiographical memory in the development of adult depression following childhood trauma. *British Journal of Clinical Psychology, 43*(4), 365–376.

Carrey, N. J., Butter, H. J., Persinger, M. A., & Bialik, R. J. (1995). Physiological and cognitive correlates of child abuse. *Journal of the American Academy of Child and Adolescent Psychiatry, 34*(8), 1067–1075.

Chun, M. M., & Phelph, E. A. (1999). Memory deficits for implicit contextual information in amnesic subjects with hippocampal damage. *Nature Neuroscience, 2*(9), 844–847.

Compas, B. E., & Boyer, M. C. (2001). Coping and attention: Implications for child health and pediatric conditions. *Developmental and Behavioral Pediatrics, 22*(5), 323–333.

Connor, D. F., Steingard, R. J., Cunningham, J. A., Anderson, J. J., & Melloni, R. H. (2004). Proactive and reactive aggression in referred children and adolescents. *American Journal of Orthopsychiatry, 74*(2), 129–136.

Coster, W. J., Gersten, M. S., Beeghly, M., & Cicchetti, D. (1989). Communicative functioning in maltreated toddlers. *Developmental Psychology, 25*(6), 1020–1029.

De Bellis, M. D., Hall, J., Boring, A. M., Frustaci, K., & Moritz, G. (2001). A pilot longitudinal study of hippocampal volumes in pediatric maltreatment-related posttraumatic stress disorder. *Biological Psychiatry, 50*(4), 305–309.

de Decker, A., Hermans, D., Raes, F., & Eelen, P. (2003). Autobiographical memory specificity and trauma in inpatient adolescents. *Journal of Clinical Child and Adolescent Psychology, 32*(1), 22–31.

de Quervain, D. J.-F., Roozendaal, B., & McGaugh, J. L. (1998). Stress and glucocorticoids impair retrieval of long-term spatial memory. *Nature, 394,* 787–790.

Downey, G., & Walker, E. (1992). Distinguishing family-level and child-level influences on the development of depression and aggression in children at risk. *Development and Psychopathology, 4*(1), 81–95.

Edwards, V. J., Fivush, R., Anda, R. F., Felitti, V. J., & Nordenberg, D. F. (2001). Autobiographical memory disturbances in childhood abuse survivors. *Journal of Aggression, Maltreatment and Trauma, 4*(2), 247–263.

Eisen, M. L., Goodman, G. S., Davis, S. L., & Qin, J. (1999). Individual differences in maltreated children's memory and suggestibility. In L. M. Williams & V. L. Banyard (Eds.), *Trauma & memory* (pp. 31–46). Thousand Oaks, CA: SAGE Publications, Inc.

Elzinga, B. M., Bakker, A., & Bremner, J. D. (2005). Stress-induced cortisol elevations are associated with impaired delayed, but not immediate recall. *Psychiatry Research, 134*(3), 211–223.

Evans, J., Williams, J. M., O'Loughlin, S., & Howells, K. (1992). Autobiographical memory and problem-solving strategies of parasuicide patients. *Psychological Medicine, 22*(2), 399–405.

Fillipini, D., Gijsbers, K., Birmingham, M. K., & Dubrovsky, B. (1991). Effects of adrenal steroids and reduced metabolites on hippocampal long-term potentiation. *Journal of Steroid Biochemistry, 40,* 87–92.

Fivush, R., Berlin, L. J., Sales, J. M., Mennuti-Washburn, J., & Cassidy, J. (2003). Functions of parent-child reminiscing about emotionally negative events. *Memory, 11*(2), 179–192.

Fivush, R., Haden, C., & Reese, E. (1996). Remembering, recounting, and reminiscing: The development of autobiographical memory in social context. In D. C. Rubin (Ed.), *Remembering our past: Studies in autobiographical memory* (pp. 341–359). New York: Cambridge University Press.

Fivush, R., Hazzard, A., Sales, J. M., Sarfati, D., & Brown, T. (2003). Creating coherence out of chaos? Children's narratives of emotionally positive and negative events. *Applied Cognitive Psychology, 17*(1), 1–19.

Fivush, R., & Vasudeva, A. (2002). Remembering to relate: Socioemotional correlates of mother-child reminiscing. *Journal of Cognition and Development, 3*(1), 73–90.

Gilbertson, M. W., Shenton, M. E., Ciszewski, A., Kasai, K., Lasko, N. B., Orr, S. P., et al. (2002). Smaller hippocampal volume predicts pathologic vulnerability to psychological trauma. *Nature Neuroscience, 5*(11), 1242–1247.

Gould, E., Tanapat, P., McEwen, B. S., Flugge, G., & Fuchs, E. (1998). Proliferation of granule cell precursors in the dentate gyrus of adult monkeys is diminished by stress. *Proceedings of the National Academy of Sciences U S A, 95,* 3168–3171.

Greenhoot, A. F., Johnson, R., & McCloskey, L. A. (2005). Internal states language in the childhood recollections of adolescents with and without abuse histories. *Journal of Cognition and Development, 6*(4), 547–570.

Greenhoot, A. F., McCloskey, L., & Glisky, E. (2005). A longitudinal study of adolescents' recollections of family violence. *Applied Cognitive Psychology, 19*(6), 719–743.

Greenhoot, A. F., Tsethlikai, M., Beyer, A. M., & Johnson, R. (2005, April). *Childhood autobiographical memories in adolescents with and without abuse histories: Links to well-being.* Poster presented at the Biennial Meeting of the Society for Research in Child Development, Atlanta, GA.

Henderson, D., Hargreaves, I., Gregory, S., & Williams, J. M. G. (2002). Autobiographical memory and emotion in a nonclinical sample of women with and without a reported history of childhood sexual abuse. *British Journal of Clinical Psychology, 41*(2), 129–142.

Herman, J. L., & Schatzow, E. (1987). Recovery and verification of memories of childhood sexual trauma. *Psychoanalytic Psychology, 4*(1), 1–14.

Hermans, D., Defranc, A., Raes, F., Williams, J. M. G., & Eelen, P. (2005). Reduced autobiographical memory specificity as an avoidant coping style. *British Journal of Clinical Psychology, 44*(4), 583–589.

Hermans, D., Van den Broeck, K., Belis, G., Raes, F., Pieters, G., & Eelen, P. (2004). Trauma and autobiographical memory specificity in depressed inpatients. *Behaviour Research and Therapy, 42*(7), 775–789.

Herrera, V. M., & McCloskey, L. A. (2003). Sexual abuse, family violence, and female delinquency: Findings from a longitudinal study. *Violence and Victims, 18*(3), 319–334.

Hoffman-Plotkin, D., & Twentyman, C. T. (1984). A multimodal assessment of behavioral and cognitive deficits in abused and neglected preschoolers. *Child Development, 55*(3), 794–802.

Howe, M. L., Cicchetti, D., Toth, S., & Cerrito, B. (2004). True and false memories in maltreated children. *Child Development, 75,* 1402–1417.

Howe, M. L., Toth, S., & Cicchetti, D. (2006). Memory and developmental psychopathology. In D. Cicchetti & D. Cohen (Eds.), *Developmental psychopathology* (2nd ed.): *Vol. 2. Developmental neuroscience* (pp. 629–655). New York: Wiley.

Hunter, E. C. M., & Andrews, B. (2002). Memory for autobiographical facts and events: A comparison of women reporting childhood sexual abuse and non-abused controls. *Applied Cognitive Psychology, 16*(5), 575–588.

Johnson, R. J., Greenhoot, A. F., Glisky, E., & McCloskey, L. A. (2005). The relations among abuse, depression, and adolescents' autobiographical memory. *Journal of Clinical Child and Adolescent Psychology, 34*(2), 235–247.

Kim, J., & Cicchetti, D. (2004). A longitudinal study of child maltreatment, mother-child relationship quality and maladjustment: The role of self-esteem and social competence. *Journal of Abnormal Child Psychology, 32*(4), 341–354.

Kitayama, N., Vaccarino, V., Kutner, M., Weiss, P., & Bremner, J. D. (2005). Magnetic resonance imaging (MRI) measurement of hippocampal volume in post-traumatic stress disorder: A meta-analysis. *Journal of Affective Disorders, 88*(1), 79–86.

Kuyken, W., & Brewin, C. R. (1994). Intrusive memories of childhood abuse during depressive episodes. *Behaviour Research and Therapy, 32*(5), 525–528.

Kuyken, W., & Brewin, C. R. (1995). Autobiographical memory functioning in depression and reports of early abuse. *Journal of Abnormal Psychology, 104*(4), 585–591.

Maguire, E. A., Frackowiak, R. S. J., & Frith, C. D. (1997). Recalling routes around London: Activation of the right hippocampus in taxi drivers. *Journal of Neuroscience, 17*(18), 7103–7110.

McAdams, D. P. (1993). The stories we live by: Personal myths and the making of the self. New York: William Morrow & Co.

McCloskey, L. A., Figueredo, A. J., & Koss, M. P. (1995). The effects of systemic family violence on children's mental health. *Child Development, 66*(5), 1239–1261.

McNally, R. J., Lasko, N. B., Macklin, M. L., & Pitman, R. K. (1995). Autobiographical memory disturbance in combat-related posttraumatic stress disorder. *Behaviour Research and Therapy, 33*(6), 619–630.

Nadel, L., & Jacobs, W. J. (1998). Traumatic memory is special. *Current Directions in Psychological Science, 7*(5), 154–157.

Nelson, C. A. (2000). "Neural plasticity and human development: The role of early experience in sculpting memory systems": Response. *Developmental Science, 3*(2), 135–136.

Nelson, C. A., & Carver, L. J. (1998). The effects of stress and trauma on brain and memory: A view from developmental cognitive neuroscience. *Development and Psychopathology, 10*(4), 793–809.

Oates, R. K., Peacock, A., & Forrest, D. (1984). The development of abused children. *Developmental Medicine and Child Neurology, 26*(5), 649–656.

Orbach, Y., Lamb, M. E., Sternberg, K. J., Williams, J. M. G., & Dawud-Noursi, S. (2001). The effect of being a victim or witness of family violence on the retrieval of autobiographical memories. *Child Abuse and Neglect, 25*(11), 1427–1437.

Park, R. J., Goodyer, I. M., & Teasdale, J. D. (2002). Categoric overgeneral autobiographical memory in adolescents with major depressive disorder. *Psychological Medicine, 32*(2), 267–276.

Park, R. J., Goodyer, I. M., Teasdale, J. D. (2004). Effects of induced rumination and distraction on mood and overgeneral autobiographical memory in adolescent Major Depressive Disorder and controls. *Journal of Child Psychology and Psychiatry, 45*(5), 996–1006.

Peeters, F., Wessel, I., Merckelbach, H., & Boon-Vermeeren, M. (2002). Autobiographical memory specificity and the course of major depressive disorder. *Comprehensive Psychiatry, 43*(5), 344–350.

Pennebaker, J. W., Mayne, T. J., & Francis, M. E. (1997). Linguistic predictors of adaptive bereavement. *Journal of Personality and Social Psychology, 72*(4), 863–871.

Pollock, L. R., & Williams, J. M. G. (2001). Effective problem solving in suicide attempters depends on specific autobiographical recall. *Suicide and Life Threatening Behavior, 31*(4), 386–396.

Radloff, L. S. (1977). The CES-D Scale: A self-report depression scale for research in the general population. *Applied Psychological Measurement, 1*(3), 385–401.

Raes, F., Hermans, D., & Eelen, P. (2003). Rumineren bij depressie, of: Hoe stilstaan bij depressie eigenlijk achteruitgaan is. [Rumination in depression]. *Gedragstherapie, 36*(3), 147–163.

Raes, F., Hermans, D., Williams, J. M. G., Demyttenaere, K., Sabbe, B., Pieters, G., et al. (2006). Is overgeneral autobiographical memory an isolated memory phenomenon in major depression? *Memory, 14*(5), 584–594.

Sapolsky, R. M. (1996). Stress, glucocorticoids and damage to the nervous system: The current state of confusion. *Stress: The International Journal on the Biology of Stress, 1*(1), 1–19.

Sapolsky, R. M. (2000). The possibility of neurotoxicity in the hippocampus in major depression: A primer on neuron death. *Biological Psychiatry, 48*(8), 755–765.

Sapolsky, R. M., & McEwen, B. S. (1986). Stress, glucocorticoids, and their role in degenerative changes in the aging hippocampus. In T. Crook, R. Bartus, S. Ferris, & S. Gershon (Eds.), *Treatment development strategies for Alzheimer's disease* (pp. 151–171). Madison, CT: Mark Powley Associates.

Sheline, Y. I., Sanghavi, M., Mintun, M. A., & Gado, M. H. (1999). Depression duration but not age predicts hippocampal volume loss in medically healthy women with recurrent major depression. *Journal of Neuroscience, 19*(12), 5034–5043.

Sidley, G. L., Whitaker, K., Calam, R. M., & Wells, A. (1997). The relationship between problem-solving and autobiographical memory in parasuicde patients. *Behavioural and Cognitive Psychotherapy, 25*(2), 195–202.

Squire, L. R. (1992). Memory and the hippocampus: A synthesis from findings with rats, monkeys, and humans. *Psychological Review, 99*(2), 195–231.

Stansbury, K., & Gunnar, M. R. (1994). Adrenocortical activity and emotion regulation. *Monographs of the Society for Research in Child Development, 59*(2–3, Serial No. 240).

Stein, M. B., Koverola, C., Hanna, C., Torchia, M. G., et al. (1997). Hippocampal volume in women victimized by childhood sexual abuse. *Psychological Medicine, 27*(4), 951–959.

Straus, M. A. (1979). Measuring intrafamily conflict and violence: The Conflict Tactics (CT) Scales. *Journal of Marriage and the Family, 41*(1), 75–88.

Thorne, A. (2000). Personal memory telling and personality development. *Personality and Social Psychology Review, 4*(1), 45–56.

Trickett, P. K. (1993). Maladaptive development of school-aged, physically abused children: Relationships with the child-rearing context. *Journal of Family Psychology, 7*(1), 134–147.

Van Minnen, A., Wessel, I., Verhaak, C., & Smeenk, J. (2005). The relationship between autobiographical memory specificity and depressed mood following a stressful life event: A prospective study. *British Journal of Clinical Psychology, 44*, 405–415.

Vythilingam, M., Heim, C., Newport, J., Miller, A. H., Anderson, E., Bronen, R., et al. (2002). Childhood trauma associated with smaller hippocampal volume in women with major depression. *American Journal of Psychiatry, 159*(12), 2072–2080.

Watkins, E., Teasdale, J. D., & Williams, R. M. (2000). Decentering and distraction reduce overgeneral autobiographical memory in depression. *Psychological Medicine, 30*(4), 911–920.

Wegner, D. M., Schneider, D. J., Carter, S. R., & White, T. L. (1987). Paradoxical effects of thought suppression. *Journal of Personality and Social Psychology, 53*(1), 5–13.

Wessel, I., Merckelbach, H., & Dekkers, T. (2002). Autobiographical memory specificity, intrusive memory, and general memory skills in Dutch-Indonesian survivors
of the World War II era. *Journal of Traumatic Stress, 15*(3), 227–234.

Williams, J. M. (1996). Depression and the specificity of autobiographical memory.
In D. C. Rubin (Ed.), *Remembering our past: Studies in autobiographical memory* (pp.
244–267). New York: Cambridge University Press.

Williams, J. M., Barnhofer, T., Crane, C., & Duggan, D. S. (2006). The role of
overgeneral memory in suicidality. In T. E. Ellis (Ed.), *Cognition and suicide: Theory,
research, and therapy* (pp. 173–192). Washington, DC: American Psychological Association.

Williams, J. M., & Broadbent, K. (1986). Autobiographical memory in suicide attempters. *Journal of Abnormal Psychology, 95*(2), 144–149.

Williams, J. M., Chan, S., Crane, C., & Barnhofer, T. (2006). Retrieval of autobiographical memories: The mechanisms and consequences of truncated search.
Cognition and Emotion, 20(3/4), 351–382.

Williams, J. M., & Dritschel, B. H. (1988). Emotional disturbance and the specificity
of autobiographical memory. *Cognition and Emotion, 2*(3), 221–234.

5

Accuracy and Specificity of Autobiographical Memory in Childhood Trauma Victims

Developmental Considerations

CHRISTIN M. OGLE, STEPHANIE D. BLOCK,
LATONYA S. HARRIS, MICHELLE CULVER,
ELSE-MARIE AUGUSTI, SUSAN TIMMER,
ANTHONY URQUIZA, AND GAIL S. GOODMAN

1996, January 17th. The Northridge Earthquake. I was at my nanny's house where I was spending the night. It was about 4:30 in the morning. I had hardwood floors in my room. I heard a rumble. I had just got back from the bathroom, so I was kind of awake. The window in my room looked down to the backyard, and the pool splashed. I went to my window. I remember my bed moving across the room to the bedroom door. My nanny ran from down the hall. There were three closets between her room and my room. They were all opening and things were falling.

—"specific" autobiographical memory report

Before my father died. I was four and all I remember is a phone call. Then my mom started crying.

—"general" autobiographical memory report

All of us have undoubtedly experienced a multitude of events in childhood and adulthood that we now cannot remember in detail, whereas other events stand out in memory with particular clarity. However, for some individuals, difficulties in the ability to recall specific details of autobiographical experiences are especially pronounced (e.g., Williams et al., 2007). Such deficits in autobiographical memory *specificity* have been linked to childhood trauma, such as child maltreatment (Kuyken & Brewin,1995).

Despite an extensive body of research that now exists on deficits in autobiographical memory specificity, few studies have examined the *accuracy* of autobiographical memory in trauma victims. Scientific studies of trauma victims' accuracy on memory tasks have produced some surprising results, particularly for victims who suffer from post-traumatic stress disorder (PTSD). Of interest, although PTSD is associated with certain memory deficits on laboratory memory tasks (e.g., Bremner, Shobe, & Kihlstrom, 2000), trauma is associated with particularly strong and accurate memory for information relevant to past traumatic experiences, especially in individuals with symptoms of PTSD (e.g., Vrana, Roodman, & Beckham, 1995). An important question is whether such findings generalize to the accuracy of autobiographical memory. One goal of the present chapter is to review research on the specificity and accuracy of autobiographical memory, as well as to discuss research on general memory functioning, in individuals with trauma histories. In doing so, we explore relations between trauma, post-traumatic symptoms, and memory.

Current research on the impact of trauma on autobiographical memory is further limited by a lack of developmental investigation. Developmental examinations of trauma and memory are important not only to advance theory but also to guide intervention and application. For example, it is of interest whether adverse (or beneficial) effects of trauma on autobiographical memory begin in childhood or adolescence or are emergent only in adulthood. The present chapter reviews research on memory functioning in both children and adult trauma victims to explore the developmental trajectory of relations between trauma and memory.

Of particular relevance to our chapter is the traumatization associated with child sexual abuse. Memory in child sexual abuse victims has been a topic of much controversy, for instance, regarding "repressed memory." However, often absent from such controversies is a scientific understanding of basic autobiographical memory functioning in victims of childhood trauma. It is possible that child maltreatment and its emotional sequelae do not affect this special memory system. Alternatively, individuals who have suffered childhood maltreatment may be motivated to suppress conscious access to autobiographical memories (e.g., of abuse incidents or of childhood experiences in general), or at least to avoid public discussion of them, due to the negative affect involved. Such avoidance is believed to contribute to *overgeneral* memory (the opposite of memory specificity).

Another possibility, one explored in the present chapter, is that individuals with maltreatment histories, especially those with PTSD, might be hypervigilant to trauma and often consumed with thoughts of traumatic childhood incidents and their sequelae, including intrusive thoughts that are difficult to control. These intrusive thoughts may serve to increase the accuracy of childhood memories, for example, through rehearsal. At the same time, these individuals' heightened attention to trauma-related memories might come at the expense of attention to and memory of nontrauma-related information, for instance, as measured by standard laboratory tasks. We explore such possibilities in this chapter through our discussion of the role of attention in emotional processing and subsequent memory for trauma- and nontrauma-related information in maltreated populations,

Specifically, in this chapter, we review scientific theory and empirical research on (a) the development of autobiographical memory and an overgeneral autobiographical retrieval style, (b) attention to trauma-related versus nontrauma-related information as potentially relevant to memory, (c) memory for trauma-related information in traumatized individuals compared to (d) memory for neutral information in traumatized individuals, and (e) autobiographical memory specificity and accuracy in nontraumatized and traumatized adolescents and adults. We also present preliminary findings from an ongoing study that examines autobiographical memory development in documented child sexual abuse victims versus matched controls with no known history of child sexual abuse.

Theories of Autobiographical Memory and Its Development

Early Autobiographical Memory and Early Overgeneral Memory

In considering the effects of trauma on autobiographical memory, it is first important to review what is known from research and theory about the emergence of this specific memory function. Many diverse lines of research converge to suggest that children's ability to form and verbally recall enduring memories of specific, personal events develops at approximately 2.5 to 3 years of age, with some 2-year-olds able to accurately remember events dating back to age 1 (Peterson, 2002). Memory in adults and older children for the period prior to approximately 2.5 to 3 years is thought to be characterized by a psychological phenomenon called infantile amnesia, the inability to remember early childhood events. We know of few studies, however, that have examined the emergence of autobiographical memory in maltreated young children (for exceptions, see Eisen, Goodman, Qin, Davis, & Crayton, 2007; Eisen, Qin, Goodman, & Davis, 2002).

Despite general consensus among developmental researchers on the existence of infantile amnesia (but see Peterson, 2002), many diverse theories attempt to explain the cause of this memory phenomenon (e.g., neurological immaturity, storage failure, retrieval failure) and/or attempt to explain the development of autobiographical memory. Although such theories were not developed with maltreated children in mind, they may provide insight into possible memory advantages or deficits for such children and for adults who have child abuse histories.

The *personalization theory* of autobiographical memory states that the emergence of the cognitive self marks the onset of autobiographical memory and concurrently the end of infantile amnesia (Howe & Courage, 1993, 1997). According to this theory, children at approximately 18 to 24 months of age develop an internal representation of the self that allows experiences to take on personal meaning. A child's developing representation of the self facilitates the personalization of event memory by serving as the common element around which experiences are cognitively organized. However, in children who have been maltreated from an early age, the child's sense of self is likely to include feelings of being unworthy and unloved. Feelings of self-protection may also be particularly heightened. To the extent that negative experiences are especially memorable and retained with accuracy (e.g., Christianson, 1992; Goodman, Hirschman, Hepps, & Rudy, 1991), a relatively high percentage of negative but generally correct autobiographical memories may result. However, to the extent that such experiences are painful to the self system, and cognitively avoided (including at retrieval), a relatively high percentage of positive or neutral early memories might predominate for child abuse victims, with negative events retained poorly or reported infrequently.

A second theory of autobiographical memory development focuses on the role of language and socialization (Nelson, 1993). In this social interactionist theory, Fivush and Nelson (2004) propose that autobiographical memory is socially constructed through recounting past experiences with others (e.g., parents). According to this view, language is the medium through which children learn to understand and represent personal experiences. Children's autobiographical memory is therefore thought to develop concurrently with children's ability to use language at around 20 to 24 months of age. Children's emerging linguistic skills serve to structure and organize early personal experiences in memory, and allow children and adults to engage in conversation about past shared experences or about details of an ongoing event. Through these adult–child memory dialogues, children learn to form coherent linguistic narratives of their experiences that facilitate the future recall of these events. However, for maltreated children (particularly those who have suffered neglect or physical abuse), on average, language delays are common (e.g., Eigsti & Cicchetti, 2004; Gaudin, 1999). Such delays may result from lack of appropriate verbal stimulation from parents. Maltreating parents may spend less time, or may be less motivated toward or adept at, talking with their children about shared experiences. Thus, according to Fivush and Nelson's theory, children who have suffered maltreatment might be delayed in autobiographical memory development.

Nelson and Gruendel (1988) and Fivush (2002) further proposed that developmental advances in event representation/script formation facilitate children's autobiographical memory by enhancing the ability to understand and represent re-occurring and unique one-time events. However, young children's reports of repeated events have been shown to be more general and less detailed than their reports of single, distinctive events (e.g., Fivush, 1984). Although with sufficient prompting, specific memories of single and repeated events are possible in young children, their preferential retrieval seems to be at the general level. These findings play an important role in one recent theory of the effects of childhood trauma on later memory.

Specifically, it has been proposed that individuals who suffer repeated childhood trauma may, for motivational reasons, have difficulty advancing beyond the level of general memory retrieval that is characteristic of young children (Williams, 1996). According to this view, the lack of retrieval of detailed memories contributes later to overgeneral autobiographical memory (Williams & Broadbent, 1986). Adolescents and adults who exhibit such overgeneral memory report personal memories in broad terms without reference to time and place (e.g., "I used to play at the park, and once I lost my favorite necklace" as opposed to "I remember the afternoon—it was a Sunday in the summer—I played in the park behind my house and lost my favorite necklace. We looked all day for it, until sundown, when we finally found it by the playground").

The motivation underlying the development of overgeneral memory, according to Williams and colleagues (1986, 2007), is that children who have suffered negative childhood events retrieve information in generic form as a means of controlling negative affect. That is, traumatized children are said to learn a defensive style ("functional avoidance") for coping with negative memories. When memories of traumatic events are triggered, often automatically, such memories may be accompanied by strong negative affect, which activates executive control processes to truncate retrieval and thus dampen recall of specific, episodic memory (Dalgleish et al., 2007; Williams et al., 2007). Although in the short term, functional avoidance may be adaptive, in the long term it is associated with maladjustment (e.g., depression). Williams (1996) also makes the point that over time, functional avoidance affects what is encoded; that is, new events are encoded in a more schematic or less detailed form. One difficulty for Williams's model is distinguishing among several possible mechanisms underlying overgeneral memory, such as functional avoidance versus lack of willingness to discuss past experiences. Nevertheless, Williams's model has generated a growing body of research and discussion (e.g., see Brewin, 2007, and Chapter 4 in this volume).

In support of Williams's theory, Kuyken and Brewin (1995) found that adults with histories of child maltreatment and who reported posttraumatic symptoms produced overgeneral memories at particularly high rates (but see Kuyken, Howell, & Dalgleish, 2006; Moore & Zoellner, 2007). Of special interest from a developmental perspective, for an overgeneral autobiographical memory style to emerge, it appears that the adverse events must occur in childhood (e.g., see Stokes, Dritschel, & Bekerian, 2004): traumatic events in adulthood alone do not lead to overgeneral autobiographical memory (e.g., Kangas, Henry, & Bryant, 2005; McNally, Litz, Prassas, Shin, & Weathers, 1994).

Autobiographical and Overgeneral Memory in Adolescents and Adults

The theories reviewed so far focus mainly on the initial emergence or early stages of autobiographical memory in childhood. In the present chapter, we are primarily concerned with adolescents' and adults' autobiographical memory for childhood events, and thus theories of autobiographical memories in adolescents and adults are also relevant. Rubin (2006) has proposed the basic systems model. Taking this approach, Rubin contends that several basic systems are involved in autobiographical memory: memory and imagery systems (e.g., explicit memory, search and retrieval processes, spatial imagery), language and narrative systems, sensory systems (e.g., vision, audition, olfaction), emotion and pain systems, and vestibular/motor systems. In this model, each system is a separate network, and these networks interact to produce autobiographical memory (Rubin, 2006). Of interest for the present chapter, according to Rubin, emotions modulate memory encoding and recall. For individuals who have suffered maltreatment, one can imagine that systems such as the emotion/pain, language/narrative, and memory/imagery systems might be particularly affected. Although Rubin's view holds that the typical life script contains many positive events from adolescence and early adulthood (Berntsen & Rubin, 2002; Rubin & Berntsen, 2003), to our knowledge, no one has examined if that is so for adults with child maltreatment histories.

Conway and Pleydell-Pearce (2000) have also formulated a model of adult autobiographical memory, with such memory viewed as part of a larger, self-memory system. Within their model, three levels of hierarchically embedded representations exist: lifetime periods (e.g., "when I was a teenager"), which are at the most superordinate level; general event descriptions of repeated or one-time events (e.g., "walking to high school," "my interview with the social worker"), which are embedded in lifetime periods; and event-specific knowledge (e.g., "walking into the big building with a woman with red hair"), which contains more concrete sensory-perceptual information about unique events. Retrieval of a specific autobiographical memory occurs with coordinated activity at all three levels. However, information only enters autobiographical memory if the life experience is relevant to the individual's active goals. Within this model, if the traumatic event is relevant to ongoing goals but so strongly challenges self-coherence as to be unacceptable to the psychological self, lack of integration into autobiographical memory stores is possible. Moreover, overgeneral memory may be accounted for in the Conway and Pleydell-Pearce model as a truncated retrieval search ("dysfacilitation" of the retrieval process) that results from functional avoidance, whereas intrusive memories associated with PTSD are accounted for by a "direct retrieval" process that is involuntary.

In a further attempt to explain the phenomenon of overgeneral autobiographical memory in adults, Williams et al. (2007) recently proposed an extension of the Conway and Pleydell-Pearce model. This extension is termed the CaR-FA-X model (CaR stands for "capture and rumination," FA stands for "functional avoidance," and X stands for "impaired executive control"). Like Conway and Pleydell-Pearce, Williams and colleagues embrace the concept of functional avoidance of distressing memories, but these researchers add two additional processes based on research findings suggesting multiple possible contributions to overgeneral memory. In this model, capture and rumination, in addition to functional avoidance, can contribute to overgeneral memory. "Capture" refers to conceptual, abstract information about the self interfering with access to specific episodic memories, whereas "rumination" refers to repetitive thinking about one's symptoms and about the possible causes and consequences of these symptoms (Nolen-Hoeksema, 1991). Research suggests that overgeneral memory in depressed patients is less specific following rumination instructions (e.g., "Think about why you feel the way you do") than distraction instructions ("Think about the face of the Mona Lisa"; Watkins & Teasdale, 2001; Watkins, Teasdale, & Williams, 2000). Finally, according to the CaR-FA-X model, "impaired executive control" is a third contributor to overgeneral memory. Impaired executive control is associated both with failure to inhibit irrelevant information and reduced processing resources, both of which interfere with retrieval of specific autobiographical memory. In regard to traumatized individuals, the CaR-Fa-X model specifies that trauma-related intrusions, and effortful attempts to avoid and control such intrusions, lead to diminished executive resources to apply to retrieval of specific memories, thus resulting in overgeneral autobiographical memory.

Although these models are powerful and elegant, they mainly point to autobiographical memory deficits as a result of traumatization. Furthermore, support for these models is based primarily on a single type of autobiographical memory test, one that fails to assess autobiographical memory accuracy. As will be discussed later in the present chapter, there are reasons to suspect that autobiographical memory in traumatized individuals may at times be particularly accurate. To develop this thesis, we first turn to studies on attention in maltreated children and adults as they relate to autobiographical memory.

Attention to Trauma-Related Information in Maltreated Populations

Studying maltreated children can provide crucial information about mechanisms that underlie emotional processing and, by extension, autobiographical memory. It has been proposed that, in certain respects, maltreated children process emotional cues differently than do nonmaltreated children (see Pollak, 2003, for review). Specifically, Pollak (2003) contends that the processing of negative emotions can be heightened in maltreated children because negative emotional signals in their home environments are prominent and/or because children perceive evidence of threats in such signals. According to this view, abused children develop patterns of information processing that reflect priming for negative emotions.

Evidence of heightened attention to threat cues comes from a study by Pollak and Tolley-Schell (2003). These authors found that physically abused children disengaged from anger cues less easily than did nonabused children, although no differences were found for happy cues. This demonstrates a bias toward anger; maltreated children find it difficult to disengage their attention upon seeing anger cues.

Research has also shown that maltreated children, compared to non-maltreated children, are aroused for longer periods of time by anger in background situations (Pollak, Vardi, Bechner, & Curtin, 2005). Specifically, although physically abused and nonabused children did not significantly differ in initial arousal (as measured by skin conductance) to a background argument, once the anger was resolved, abused children's arousal did not return to baseline as quickly as did that of nonabused children. Pollak and colleagues interpreted this continued state of arousal as resulting from maltreated children's monitoring of the environment for any indications that the anger may continue. Physically abused children were also more concerned than nonabused children when the situation was unresolved and ambiguous, which may, in the abused children's home environments, foreshadow frightening events (Pollak et al., 2005). Overall, it appears that physically abused children are particularly primed to attend to expressions of anger and consequently devote considerable attentional resources to these emotional signals.

If physically abused children are primed to anger cues in the environment, one would expect to see heightened reactions in the brain to emotional stimuli. To examine this possibility, Pollak et al. (1997) examined the event-related potential component P300, which may reflect cognitive processes activated when an individual is presented with salient emotional stimuli. The authors found differences in P300 amplitude between maltreated and nonmaltreated children who were asked to attend to faces reflecting various emotional expressions (e.g., a happy expression, an angry expression): maltreated children showed a larger amplitude when asked to attend to angry (versus happy) faces. Pollak et al. (1997) suggest that this could be due in part to how maltreated compared to nonmaltreated children process negative versus positive emotional expressions. In another study, Pollak et al. (2001) found larger P3b amplitudes for maltreated children compared to nonmaltreated children when shown angry faces, although significant differences were not found for happy or fearful expressions. (The term "P3b" is used interchangeably with P300, and thus it is also an event-related potential of the brain that is associated with the valence of a stimulus.) This study supports Pollak's previous findings of differences in brain activity when maltreated children are shown angry faces and also supports the hypothesis that maltreated children's attention and sensitivity to negative emotions has become accentuated as a result of their traumatic experiences.

Although Pollak's studies mainly concern child physical abuse, similar findings would be expected for child sexual abuse. Specifically, victims of child sexual abuse may be particularly attuned to safety and threat cues relevant to sexuality and/or sexual aggression. This should result in greater attention to or less ability to withdraw attention from such cues.

To our knowledge, studies comparable to Pollak's (e.g., on abuse-induced hypervigilance) have not been carried out with child sexual abuse victims. However, it is possible that a related phenomenon is tapped by the modified Stroop task (also called the emotional Stroop task), which has been used to examine attentional processes of clinical and traumatized populations including child sexual abuse victims. Similar to the standard Stroop task (Stroop, 1935), the modified Stroop task measures participants' ability to inhibit prepotent responses, which has been linked to attention and executive function (Wright, Waterman, Prescott, & Murdoch-Eaton,

2003). However, the modified Stroop task does so by presenting emotional words in different colors of ink. The participant is asked to name as fast as possible the *color* in which each word is printed instead of reading the actual word. The extent to which the meaning of the word slows naming of the color is taken as a measure of interference, caused for instance by being unable to inhibit the prepotent response, by an inability to withdraw attention quickly, and/or by automatic processing of the word to the semantic level (see Algom, Chajut, & Lev, 2004, for alternative views).

In maltreated and other traumatized populations, the modified Stroop interference effect is especially pronounced for words that are highly associated with their specific trauma. For example, words related to sexual abuse caused greater interference than nonsexual abuse words for adults who as children suffered sexual abuse (Field et al., 2001). These findings, like Pollak's, appear to indicate priming connected to child maltreatment. In the case of the modified Stroop task, reactivated memory "networks" may contribute to a delay in response (Field et al., 2001). This research suggests that earlier traumatic experiences guide attention in adults even at the unconscious level, leading to heightened attention to threat or trauma-related cues (Michael, Ehlers, & Halligan, 2005).

Thus, the overattention to threat cues in children as described by Pollak appears to carry forward into adulthood. This persistence into adulthood seems to be particularly apparent if the individual develops PTSD. In modified Stroop tasks, it has been consistently found that adults with a diagnosis of PTSD (including if the PTSD symptoms are associated with past child sexual abuse) exhibit more interference for trauma-related than non-trauma-related words. Adults with PTSD take longer to color-name trauma-related words (versus neutral, positive, or negative words), demonstrating an attentional bias in favor of such words (McNally, Kaspi, Riemann, & Zeitlin, 1990). Further, McNally, Clancy, Schacter, and Pitman (2000) found that PTSD severity was the strongest predictor of modified Stroop interference for adults with self-reported child sexual abuse histories. Similar attentional bias effects have also been found for individuals with PTSD subsequent to war/combat (e.g., McNally, English, & Lipke, 1993), rape (e.g., Cassidy, McNally, & Zeitlin, 1992; Foa, Feske, Murdock, Kozak, & McCarthy, 1991), and traffic accidents (e.g., Harvey, Bryant, & Rapee, 1996).

Few studies have investigated performance on the modified Stroop test in children with trauma histories or trauma-related psychopathology (e.g., depression). Dubner and Motta (1999) were perhaps the first to show that adolescents with trauma histories, specifically histories of child abuse, show attentional bias to trauma-related words on the modified Stroop test. However, when Doost, Taghavi, Moradi, Yule, and Dalgleish (1997) examined Stroop interference in 9- to 18-year-olds with depression, using depression-related, trauma-related, threat, happy, and neutral words, although depressed children were slower at color-naming of words over-all, contrary to expectation, there was no significant difference in read-ing times for the depression- and trauma-related words as compared to happy and neutral words. In contrast, in a study on children (9 to 17 years of age) with PTSD, Moradi, Taghavi, Neshat-Doost, Yule, and Dalgleish (2000) found a significant difference in color-naming times for trauma-related compared to neutral words. Children with PTSD took longer to color-name trauma-related compared to neutral words. Also, children with PTSD showed more trauma-related interference than did children with no history of trauma or PTSD.

Overall, findings on attentional processing in child maltreatment vic-tims generally (though not invariably) support the hypothesis that infor-mation that is particularly relevant to one's life concerns may attract more attentional resources or more automatic processing than information that is less relevant. Maltreated children's attention to, and possible priming for, emotionally salient information in the environment may facilitate better encoding of such information. The cognitive resources devoted to detecting and processing trauma-related emotional experiences, as dem-onstrated in brain activation, may lead to better autobiographical memory of these experiences.

Memory for Trauma-Related Information in Traumatized Populations

Given attentional biases in favor of trauma-related information in child maltreatment victims and/or individuals with PTSD, one might expect particularly good memory for such information. Indeed there is sup-port for such findings in the adult literature. For instance, Vrana et al. (1995) examined modified Stroop interference for trauma-related (i.e., Vietnam-specific, Vietnam-general), negative, and neutral words in rela-tion to general free recall and recognition memory for these three word types in combat veterans with and without PTSD. Although veterans in general showed greater Stroop interference for trauma-related than for neutral words, veterans with PTSD evinced more interference across all word categories than veterans without PTSD. Of importance, veterans with PTSD also demonstrated better recall and more accurate recognition memory both overall and of emotional words than veterans without PTSD. In a similar study, Golier, Yehuda, Lupien, and Harvey (2003) tested elderly Holocaust survivors' memory for Holocaust-related words using paired-associate learning and word-stem completion tasks. Compared to matched controls, adult Holocaust survivors with PTSD recalled more Holocaust-related than neutral word pairs (but see Mathews & MacLeod, 1985; Mogg, Mathews, & Weinman, 1989).

Research with adult victims of child sexual abuse using the directed-forgetting paradigm reveals related findings. Specifically, McNally, Metzger, Lasko, Clancy, and Pitman (1998) found that compared to child sexual abuse victims without PTSD and a nonabused control group, child sexual abuse victims with PTSD exhibited recall memory deficits for positive and neutral words but not for trauma-related stimuli. For words that participants were instructed to forget, no differences were found in recall among groups by word type (e.g., trauma-related, neutral, or positive words), suggesting that, at least in this study, the adults demonstrated a bias in favor of trauma-related to-be-remembered items but not for trauma-related to-be-forgotten items. Furthermore, child sexual abuse victims' recall of nontrauma words, but not trauma words, was related to depression and anxiety levels. The increased attention of child sexual abuse victims with PTSD to trauma-related stimuli may have led to their comparatively better memory for trauma stimuli as compared to non-trauma stimuli.

Evidence of trauma-related memory biases also comes from research on children and adolescents. Moradi and colleagues (2000) examined memory for emotionally valenced and trauma-relevant material in children and adolescents (9 to 17 years of age) with PTSD resulting from traffic accidents or exposure to violence. Participants were presented with positive, negative (depression- and trauma-related, general threat), and neutral words and then completed a free recall and recognition memory test. Overall, the PTSD group correctly recalled fewer words than the control group, supporting the relation between memory deficits and PTSD. However, compared to control participants, the PTSD group demonstrated a memory bias for negative information by recalling more negative words (including trauma-related words) than neutral and positive words.

Such findings suggest that an attentional bias toward trauma-related information can result in better memory for such information. At times, trauma victims with PTSD evince better memory for trauma-related information than do nontraumatized controls; at other times, trauma victims show deficits in memory compared to the nontraumatized controls, except when trauma-related information is to be remembered. Although these studies do not directly concern autobiographical memory retrieval, their findings may have implications for such memory processes.

Memory for Nontrauma-Related Information in Traumatized Populations

The research reviewed so far would lead one to suspect that individuals with maltreatment histories and/or PTSD might be particularly accurate at remembering trauma-related information. After all, such individuals appear to pay particular attention to trauma-related cues. However, other research points to deficits in memory function in child sexual abuse victims, especially those who have developed PTSD.

Most of the latter research has concerned memory for information that is not trauma-related. For example, Bremner, Vermetten, Afzal, and Vythilingam (2004) investigated differences in verbal declarative memory among women with self-reported child sexual abuse experiences, both with and without PTSD, and a nonmaltreated control group. These authors found that verbal declarative memory deficits were specifically related to PTSD: adults with child sexual abuse histories who had child sexual abuse–related PTSD had worse verbal declarative memory compared to women with child sexual abuse histories without PTSD and to nonabused women without PTSD. No relation was found between development (age at abuse) and memory, but verbal memory deficits were related to child sexual abuse severity and PTSD symptom severity.

Additional lines of research on victims of war-related traumatic events suggest that general and declarative memory is negatively affected by PTSD. Golier, Harvey, Legge, and Yehuda (2006) examined general memory performance using the California Verbal Learning Test (CVLT) in older combat veterans and Holocaust survivors both with and without PTSD as well as nontrauma-exposed controls. The CVLT consists of a series of word lists presented over five trials and was used to examine free recall (after both short and long delays), cued recall, and recognition memory performance. Findings indicated that participants with trauma histories and PTSD demonstrated significantly worse performance on these explicit memory tasks. Specifically, Holocaust survivors with PTSD had significantly lower scores than non-trauma-exposed controls on measures of free recall, cued recall, and recognition memory. Moreover, PTSD Holocaust survivors performed worse than non-PTSD Holocaust survivors in free recall memory. Memory performance for the combat veterans showed similar patterns. Combat veterans with PTSD performed significantly worse than non-trauma-exposed controls on measures of total learning, short-delay free and cued recall, long-delay free and cued recall, and recognition memory. The authors of this study noted that the participants included older adults (mean age = 69 years) and that the detrimental effects of PTSD on memory may have been greater and more generalized than those typically seen in younger PTSD patients. It is unknown to what extent the effects were related to age or to the chronicity (i.e., duration) of PTSD, or even to childhood trauma experiences as precursors to PTSD.

Research employing other measures of general memory functioning has found similar deficits in verbal and nonverbal memory performance in adult participants with PTSD compared to trauma-exposed participants without PTSD (e.g., Uddo, Vasterling, Brailey, & Sutker, 1993; Vasterling, Brailey, Constans, & Sutker, 1998), and to non-trauma-exposed controls (e.g., Jelinek et al., 2006). Furthermore, Yasik, Saigh, Oberfield, and Halamandaris (2007) reported similar findings with children. In this study, compared to children exposed to trauma but without PTSD and non-trauma-exposed control participants, children with PTSD performed worse on a measure of general memory functioning (i.e., the Wide Range Assessment of Memory and Learning; Sheslow & Adams, 1990), thus replicating the relation between general memory impairment and PTSD reported in the adult literature. Taken together, these findings from the developmental and the adult literature suggest a specific association between memory impairment and PTSD rather than between memory impairment and trauma exposure in the absence of PTSD.

However, research using the Deese/Roediger-McDermott (DRM) paradigm (Deese, 1959; Roediger & McDermott, 1995) provides evidence of memory deficits for neutral stimuli in trauma victims with

PTSD as well as without PTSD. The DRM task produces false memories for words in adults and children (e.g., Brainerd, Reyna, & Forrest, 2002; Ghetti, Qin, & Goodman, 2002). The task involves presenting a list of semantically related words (e.g., bed, rest, awake, tired, dream, wake, snooze, blanket, doze, slumber), all of which are associates of a critical lure (e.g., sleep) that is not presented. On a subsequent memory task, participants will often falsely remember the critical lure as having been presented. When adults are asked if they had a vivid feeling of remembering the critical lure or if they had a less distinctive feeling of familiarity, they often report the former (i.e., report the word as having been previously presented).

Zoellner, Foa, Brigidi, and Przeworski (2002) investigated the susceptibility of trauma victims to false memories on the DRM task. In this study, adult sexual and nonsexual assault victims with and without PTSD were compared to controls using the standard DRM paradigm. Trauma victims with and without PTSD produced more false memories of the critical lure in comparison to controls. In addition, participants with PTSD falsely recalled significantly more critical lures than did both the trauma victims without PTSD and the control group.

Bremner, Shobe, and Kihlstrom (2000) found similar DRM memory impairments with adult victims of child sexual abuse. However, their findings again implicate PTSD more than trauma exposure. Women with self-reported histories of child sexual abuse and PTSD had significantly higher levels of false recognition rates for the critical lure in comparison to participants with self-reported child sexual abuse histories and no PTSD and control participants. In fact, women with PTSD falsely recognized the critical lure more often than they correctly recognized studied words. These findings suggest that women who develop PTSD subsequent to child sexual abuse are more prone to memory distortions and illusions compared to those who did not develop PTSD. Possible explanations of these results are that these women are more dissociative, or that they suffered hippocampal damage, as indicated by previous research on PTSD (Bremner, 1999). Although these findings have been used to support claims that women with abuse histories and PTSD may be particularly susceptible to false memories in general, the word lists used in this study were relatively neutral. Research investigating DRM memory for trauma-related word lists in abuse populations with and without PTSD is needed.

Developmental researchers recently examined false memory in mal-treated children (Howe, Cicchetti, Toth, & Cerrito, 2004). After pre-sentation of standard DRM word lists, which contain mainly neutral, nontrauma-related themes, children ages 5 to 7 or 10 to 12 years produced false memories on both recall and recognition memory tests. Of par-ticular interest, no difference was observed in false memory performance between maltreated and nonmaltreated children. This study is important because it was the first to examine DRM false memory in maltreated ver-sus nonmaltreated youth. It is possible, however, that the effects of trauma on memory processes could take time to develop and therefore may not be evident until adolescence or young adulthood. In addition, inclusion of measures of trauma-related psychopathology (e.g., PTSD, dissociation) and trauma-related DRM lists would be of interest as an addition to this type of study. Similar to research described above with adults, memory deficits observed with children on the DRM task using neutral word lists may not generalize to memory for trauma-related information.

The research reviewed in this section indicates that traumatized adults typically perform worse on standardized and laboratory memory tests than nontraumatized adults when the "to-be- remembered" information is neu-tral. However, not all investigations of general memory functioning have uncovered differences between individuals with PTSD and controls (e.g., Beers & DeBellis, 2002; Jenkins, Langlais, Delis, & Cohen, 2000). In addi-tion, research described in the previous section of this chapter indicated that traumatized individuals pay more attention to trauma-related information and at times evince better memory, or at least equally accurate memory, for such information, compared to nontraumatized controls. This research shows that trauma victims attend to and remember trauma-related infor-mation relatively well. If so, trauma victims might have particularly accurate autobiographical memory for trauma-related events in their lives. Of note, for some child victims, their childhoods in general are trauma-related.

Autobiographical Memory in Traumatized Populations

There is surprisingly little scientific research on autobiographical mem-ory in trauma victims, especially in regard to memory accuracy. Here we review extant research concerning, first, the accuracy of child maltreat-ment victims' autobiographical memory and, second, the specificity of such victims' memory.

Accuracy of Autobiographical Memory

Albeit scant in number, investigations of autobiographical memory accuracy in adults and children who have suffered child abuse point both to memory deficits as well as advantages. Evidence of a detrimental effect of trauma on autobiographical memory functioning is drawn from research with adult survivors of child sexual abuse. Edwards, Fivush, Anda, Felitti, and Nordenberg (2001) described autobiographical memory loss (i.e., gaps in memory) for childhood experiences in a nonclinical adult population, with sexually abused and physically abused participants twice as likely to self-report holes in their autobiographical memory compared to nonabused participants. Experiences of repeated abuse, abuse by a relative, and more severe abuse were especially powerful predictors of self-reported memory loss (see also Brown et al., 2007). Hunter and Andrews (2002) found autobiographical memory deficits for personal semantic childhood facts (e.g., names of friends and teachers, schools attended, home addresses) in participants with child sexual abuse histories compared to nonabused controls. However, further analysis revealed that this effect held only for participants who reported a period of having forgotten their abuse experiences (compared to those who reported continuous memory for abuse). No differences were found between abused and nonabused participants in autobiographical memory specificity for childhood events (see also Melchert, 1996; Melchert & Parker, 1997).

However, when child maltreatment victims are questioned about specific *documented* events, their memory is not necessarily more inaccurate or devoid of detail than that of nonmaltreated controls. In support of this assertion is a study by Eisen and colleagues (Eisen et al., 2002; Eisen et al., 2007) in which children's autobiographical memory for medical procedures (e.g., anogenital examination, venipuncture) was investigated. Most of the children, who ranged in age from 3 to 17 years, were child maltreatment victims, although a small comparison group of children with no known history of abuse was also included. Given this age range, it is no surprise that age differences in accuracy and completeness of report were prominent. In addition, type of maltreatment (and even maltreatment itself) was generally not associated with memory inaccuracy. There were a few exceptions, however. Children who had suffered neglect were somewhat less accurate than children who had suffered physical or sexual abuse. Other research has shown that neglected children are particularly likely to be from impoverished and non–intellectually stimulating environments (Gaudin, 1999), which could contribute to memory deficits. Of special interest for the present chapter, Eisen and colleagues found that child sexual abuse victims were more accurate compared to other child victims and to nonabused controls in their memory of the anogenital examination plus venipuncture, perhaps because the anogenital exam was particularly relevant to these children's abuse experiences. Surprisingly, PTSD *diagnosis* did not predict accuracy in this study.

Other evidence of a positive association between trauma and memory comes from a prospective memory study conducted by Greenhoot, McCloskey, and Glisky (2005). In this study, memory for abuse was examined in 12- to 18-year-olds who as children had either witnessed domestic violence against their mothers (by male partners) or suffered child physical abuse or punishment themselves, or both. They found that adolescents had better memory for previously disclosed personally experienced abuse versus previously disclosed abuse directed at their mothers. Furthermore, adolescents were less likely to completely forget or fail to report personally experienced abuse (20%) compared to witnessed abuse (34%). Among other interesting results, adolescents who as children had the most negative attitudes toward the abuser and blamed him more had the most accurate autobiographical memories for assaults, and had lower rates of complete forgetting (see also Chapter 4).

Research on autobiographical memory functioning in adult trauma victims, including victims of abuse, further suggests that traumatic experiences are well retained. Porter and Peace (2007) compared the consistency of traumatic memories with memories for highly positive emotional events over time. Results revealed that traumatic memories remained highly consistent years after their occurrence compared to positive memories, and that positive memories deteriorated over time in subjective ratings of vividness, overall quality, and sensory components, whereas memory for traumatic events did not. Although these authors did not assess autobiographical memory accuracy directly, their findings suggest that adults with trauma histories retain memories of their traumatic experiences better than memories of other highly positive emotional events. One explanation for this finding is that memories for traumatic events may be subject to more frequent memory rehearsal, which likely impacts the accuracy as well as the consistency of autobiographical memories. Indeed, Porter and Peace (2007) found that individuals reported thinking about their trauma experiences more frequently than the positive events tested.

Finally, Alexander, Quas, Goodman, Ghetti, Edelstein, Redlich, and colleagues (2005) conducted a prospective study of child sexual abuse victims. These researchers found that victims who, in adulthood and late adolescence, self-reported more PTSD symptoms had more accurate memories for the child sexual abuse when tested 12 to 21 years ($M =$ 14.3 years) after the assaults. The same results held for the victims who reported child sexual abuse as their most traumatic experience even if they reported little in the way of PTSD symptomatology. Although we know of few studies on this topic, and thus firm conclusions are premature, these findings support the idea of particularly accurate retention of traumatic childhood events and further suggest that child maltreatment and PTSD do not necessarily lead to memory gaps or extreme error when a specific autobiographical event is at issue, especially if the event relates to their trauma experience.

In summary, research on accuracy of autobiographical memory in victims of childhood trauma suggests that although such victims may report gaps in their memory, in fact their autobiographical memories of the trauma itself and of trauma-related information is particularly accurate. Although further research is needed, the empirical work to date suggests that symptoms of PTSD predict better rather than worse autobiographical memory for the trauma itself.

Specificity of Autobiographical Memory

The growing body of literature on the specificity of autobiographical recall is important to the study of trauma and autobiographical memory functioning. As mentioned earlier, "overgeneral" autobiographical memory, first reported by Williams and Broadbent (1986), refers to autobiographical memory reports that are categorical in nature and lacking in detail and vividness. Such overgeneral autobiographical memory has been found in individuals with a wide range of psychological disorders (e.g., major depression, PTSD, obsessive–compulsive disorder, acute stress disorder; Rubin, Feldman, & Beckham, 2004; Wessel, Merckelbach, & Dekkers, 2002). The opposite of overgeneral memory is memory specificity.

Investigations of autobiographical memory specificity have been conducted with adolescents and adults who experienced a traumatic event during childhood. Evidence for Williams' (1996) proposal that the experience of adverse events during childhood may disrupt the normal development of autobiographical memory specificity, causing children to maintain a categoric retrieval style that is typical for early memory functioning, was first reported by Kuyken and Brewin (1995). Depressed female patients with a history of child sexual abuse retrieved less specific memories to positive and negative cue words compared to depressed patients without abuse histories. A similar pattern of results was later reported by Henderson, Hargreaves, Gregory, and Williams (2002) with female adult victims of child sexual abuse.

However, failures to replicate significant relations between trauma and overgeneral memory also exist (Arntz, Meeren, & Wessel, 2002; Hermans et al., 2004; Kuyken et al., 2006; Orbach, Lamb, Sternberg, Williams, & Dawud-Noursi, 2001; Wessel, Meeren, Peeters, Arntz, & Merckelbach, 2001; Wilhelm, McNally, Baer, & Florin, 1997). Moreover, some studies have reported more specific memory for individuals with maltreatment histories and/or greater psychopathology symptoms. Regarding adults, for example, Peeters, Wessel, Merckelbach, and Boon-Vermeeren (2002) found that childhood trauma predicted greater memory specificity in response to negative cue words. Burnside, Startup, Byatt, Rollinson, and Hill (2004) reported that abused adult women with depression reported fewer overgeneral memories to negative cue words compared to abused women with no self-reported depression symptomology. Similarly, Hermans et al. (2004) examined the relation between autobiographical memory specificity and self-reported trauma in depressed adults. Although physical abuse was significantly associated with poor memory specificity, sexual abuse was not. In addition, a positive relation was found between frequency of memory intrusions and autobiographical memory specificity.

Research with adolescents has revealed similarly mixed patterns. Swales, Williams, and Wood (2001) examined autobiographical memory performance of inpatient adolescents with a mix of diagnoses to normative data from a school sample. Overall, the clinical group produced less specific memories than the control group. However, within the clinical group, a positive relation existed between autobiographical memory specificity, depression, and hopelessness. In Orbach et al.'s (2001) study of adolescents with childhood exposure to family violence, neither witnessing domestic violence nor being the target of family violence was related to the specificity of the adolescents' memories for family disagreements. Orbach and colleagues noted that, compared to children in a control group, children exposed to family violence were more likely to omit responses to questions. They thus avoided providing any responses, either overgeneral or specific. In addition, overgeneral memory was positively related to depression. Finally, Kuyken et al. (2006) reported greater specificity of autobiographical memory in adolescent trauma victims compared to controls.

These studies suggest that mere exposure to trauma is not a sufficient or consistent predictor of overgeneral memory. It is possible, however, that levels of trauma in the key groups of some of these studies were insufficient in strength to detect a trauma influence on autobiographical memory or to reverse the more typical trend. Other research suggests the relation between trauma and memory specificity may be influenced by more qualitative characteristics of abuse (e.g., age of onset, duration, relationship to the abuser). Negative relations have been reported between autobiographical memory specificity and abuse severity (de Decker, Hermans, Raes, & Eelen, 2003), duration of abuse (Burnside et al., 2004), age of onset (Hermans et al., 2004), subjective distress related to abuse (Hermans et al., 2004), and abuse perpetrated by close relatives (Henderson et al., 2002). Furthermore, in a study with Vietnam War veterans, some of whom had PTSD and some of whom did not, strong positive relations emerged between overgeneral memory and PTSD symptoms, but not combat exposure (McNally et al., 1994; but see McNally et al., 2006). This research suggests that the qualitative nature of traumatic experiences is potentially more important than the objective presence of trauma in determining the relation between trauma and autobiographical memory.

Conclusions from this body of research must be drawn with caution. Many of the studies are fraught with methodological limitations, such as the absence of essential control groups, inclusion of control or comparison groups that were not screened for psychopathology, broadly defined trauma groups that span myriad trauma categories, absence of measures of general verbal fluency, gender confounds, and retrospectively self-reported trauma histories without documentation of abuse. Moreover, overgeneral memory has primarily been tested using the Autobiographical Memory Test (Williams & Broadbent, 1986), so that the generalizability of the findings to other tasks is largely unknown. Williams et al. (2007) recently suggested that other tasks should be employed. Furthermore, the causal mechanisms underlying the reduced autobiographical memory specificity remain unclear, although impressive progress has been made in that regard (Williams et al., 2007).

Autobiographical Memory in Child Sexual Abuse Victims: Preliminary Findings

To examine issues of autobiographical memory for childhood events in adolescent and adult victims of child sexual abuse, we are currently conducting a study in which both autobiographical memory accuracy and specificity are examined (see Augusti et al., 2006; Block et al., 2006; Ogle et al., 2007). Among other questions, we are exploring whether child sexual abuse and PTSD are associated with more or less accurate autobiographical memory, and with more specific or more overgeneral autobiographical memory.

Child sexual abuse victims ranging in age from 14 to 37 years are participating in this study, along with a group of age- and gender-matched individuals with no known history of child sexual abuse. Tests of trauma-related psychopathology are also being administered. One advantage of this study over much of the previous research is that the reports of child sexual abuse are not retrospective; the participants were referred to our study from a child protection center, and we were granted access to therapists' and social workers' reports of the participants' abuse histories.

To tap autobiographical memory in this study, the Semantic Autobiographical Memory Task (SAMT; Meesters, Merckelbach, Muris, & Wessel, 2000) and the Autobiographical Memory Interview (AMI; Kopelman, Wilson, & Baddeley, 1989) are administered. For the SAMT, participants are asked to recall semantic information from when they were in third grade. For the AMI, participants are asked to describe a specific memory from each of the following time periods: prior to preschool, during elementary school, and during sixth grade. Both tasks are administered as interviews.

For the adolescents, parents' answers to the SAMT autobiographical memory test are obtained; this permits us to examine the accuracy of adolescents' autobiographical memory by comparing their reports with those of their parents. Results thus far reveal that adolescents with a history of child sexual abuse and who have more reexperiencing symptoms associated with PTSD have more accurate autobiographical memory than do adolescents with fewer reexperiencing symptoms (Ogle et al., 2007). This finding is consistent with research by Alexander et al. (2005), who found PTSD symptoms to be associated with more accurate memories of abuse in adolescents and young adult victims of child sexual abuse.

Degree of autobiographical memory specificity is measured in our study by participants' first responses on the autobiographical incident portion of the AMI. Responses are coded for details of time and place using a 4-point scale of 0 to 3. The following scoring criteria are employed: A score of 0 indicates no memory or a response based on semantic memory. A score of 1 is given for vague personal memories. A score of 2 indicates a personal but not specific (general) event, or a specific event lacking in details for time or place. An example of a memory with a specificity score of 2 is the following: "I remember the first time I saw snow in Alaska. I was sitting at the kitchen table looking out the window, and my mom was standing behind me, and she was pointing at the snow." This memory report describes a specific event and contains details of place (inside at a table in Alaska) but not time. The memory report quoted at the start of this chapter about, receiving a phone call with the awful news of the father's impending death also received a score of 2. Finally, a score of 3 is given for episodic memories specific in time and place. The following memory report received a specificity score of 3: "When I was about 4 years old we were living in Santa Rosa, and somebody had broken into a bunch of cars in our apartment complex. When my mom was talking to people, I was in charge of watching little kids, because I was a lot more mature when I was 4, like I am now. But I remember watching a 2-year-old. I don't remember his name, but after I felt very special because I had to watch over him and protect him and make sure nothing happened." As another example, we opened this chapter with a detailed autobiographical memory of the morning the Northridge Earthquake hit California in 1996, and of things falling out of the nanny's closet. This memory report also received a score of 3. Coding was completed by two coders blind to maltreatment status and with interrater reliability of 0.86 (proportion of agreement).

Preliminary findings from the AMI indicated that adults with child sexual abuse histories provided more specific autobiographical memories, especially for the preschool years, than did matched controls (Augusti et al., 2006). This pattern of results did not emerge for the adolescents, for whom no significant differences between the child sexual abuse and control participants have been found to date.

A DRM task for neutral, emotional (positive, negative), and trauma-related lists is also included in the present study (Block et al., 2006). For the subset of individuals who indicated a past traumatic experience (including individuals in the "no child sexual abuse" control group), the more PTSD symptoms the individual had, the more errors she or he made on DRM lists (Harris et al., 2007). Thus, consistent with previous studies, PTSD was associated with greater memory error on the DRM task, including for trauma-related words. These findings are similar to those of Brennen, Dybdahl, and Kapidži (2007), who found that PTSD subsequent to war trauma was also associated with greater error on war-related DRM lists. However, our sample size is especially small for this analysis; thus the results may change as participants are added to the study.

Overall, it tentatively appears that child maltreatment and PTSD are, at times, associated with more accurate and more specific autobiographical memory. Such findings begin to emerge in adolescence, at least for autobiographical memory accuracy. However, on a variety of standard laboratory tasks, including the DRM task with lists that are trauma-related, PTSD is associated with greater error.

Conclusion

Individuals with child maltreatment histories, especially if they have PTSD, may overfocus on trauma in their lives and in their pasts. This focus may make their autobiographical memories particularly accurate, especially when trauma-related information is at issue. Perhaps the trauma and related experiences become the focus of their lives, often in an intrusive and uncontrollable way, leading to better memory but also distracting the person on laboratory tasks (and perhaps other tasks as well) that require sustained attention. However, additional research is needed on whether child maltreatment and PTSD also contribute to certain distortions of autobiographical memory. If, for example, some victims overinterpret neutral information or experiences as trauma-related (Windmann & Krüger, 1998), autobiographical memory errors could result. To the extent that trauma predisposes victims to dissociation, especially under conditions of high stress, memory errors may arise (Eisen et al., 2007). Overall, our review and our preliminary findings imply that caution should be used in extrapolating and generalizing performance on laboratory tasks to autobiographical memory in victims of traumatic events such as child sexual abuse.

There is ample room for further research on autobiographical memory in trauma victims. For example, studies on the accuracy of autobiographical memory are needed not only for adolescents and adults who experienced childhood trauma but also for young children and the elderly with such experiences. Moreover, the precise age at which the trauma was suffered and the ages at which subsequent traumas occurred need to be taken into account, as do factors associated with the main trauma (e.g., removal from home and subsequent placement in a foster home). Regarding specificity, additional research aimed at refining existing theoretical accounts of memory specificity is needed to advance our understanding of the central mechanisms underlying impoverished autobiographical memory. Specific to Williams' (1996) theory, future research should examine relations between the age at which the trauma occurred and subsequent changes in degree of memory specificity for both trauma–related and non–trauma–related autobiographical experiences. Furthermore, future research is needed to differentiate the contribution of encoding versus retrieval processes to overgeneral autobiographical memory. Similarly, research that distinguishes between reduced willingness to discuss negative autobiographical events and actual memory impairment might clarify the role of nonmemorial factors related to affect regulation in overgeneral memory. Finally, regarding both accuracy and specificity, research examining the impact of therapy might elucidate whether reports of greater accuracy and specificity in trauma victims are due to rehearsal of autobiographical experiences during therapy. Overall, there is much still to learn in this important area of study.

References

Alexander, K. W., Quas, J. A., Goodman, G. S., Ghetti, S., Edelstein, R. S., Redlich, A. D., et al. (2005). Traumatic impact predicts long-term memory for documented child sexual abuse. *Psychological Science, 16,* 33–40.

Algom, D., Chajut, E., & Lev, S. (2004). A rational look at the Emotional Stroop phenomenon: A generic slowdown, not a Stroop effect. *Journal of Experimental Psychology: General, 133,* 323–338.

Arntz, A., Meeren, M., & Wessel, I. (2002). No evidence for overgeneral memories in borderline personality disorder. *Behaviour Research and Therapy, 40,* 1063–1068.

Augusti, E., Ogle, C. M., Block, S. D., Harris, L. S., Pineda, A. S., Urquiza, A., et al. (2006, May). *Relations between autobiographical memory and traumatization in adolescents and young adults.* Paper presented at the meeting of the Association of Psychological Science, New York, NY.

Beers, S. R., & DeBellis, M. D. (2002). Neuropsychological function in children with maltreatment-related posttraumatic stress disorder. *American Journal of Psychiatry, 159,* 483–486.

Berntsen, D., & Rubin, D. C. (2002). Emotionally charged autobiographical memories across the life span: The recall of happy, sad, traumatic and involuntary memories. *Psychology and Aging, 17,* 636–652.

Block, S. D., Goodman, G. S., Harris, L. S, Ogle, C. M., Timmer, S., Urquiza, A., et al. (2006, May). *Trauma processing in adolescents and adults: New DRM lists and false memory findings.* Paper presented at the meeting of the Association of Psychological Science, New York, NY.

Brainerd, C. J., Reyna, V. F., & Forrest, T. J. (2002). Are young children susceptible to the false-memory illusion? *Child Development, 73,* 1363–1377.

Bremner, J. D. (1999). Does stress damage the brain? *Biological Psychiatry, 45,* 797–805.

Bremner, J. D., Shobe, K. K., Kihlstrom, J. F. (2000). False memories in women with self-reported childhood sexual abuse: An empirical study. *Psychological Science, 11,* 333–337.

Bremner, J. D., Vermetten, E., Afzal, N., & Vythilingam, M. (2004). Deficits in verbal declarative memory function in women with childhood sexual abuse-related posttraumatic stress disorder. *The Journal of Nervous and Mental Disease, 192,* 643–649.

Brennen, T., Dybdahl, R., & Kapidžac, A. (2007). Trauma-related and neutral false memories in war-induced post-traumatic stress disorder. *Consciousness & Cognition, 16,* 877–885.

Brewin, C. R. (2007). Autobiographical memory for trauma: Update on four controversies. *Memory, 15,* 227–248.

Brown, D. W., Anda, R. F., Edwards, V. J., Felitti, V. J., Dube, S. R., & Giles, W. H. (2007). Adverse childhood experiences and childhood autobiographical memory disturbance. *Child Abuse & Neglect, 31,* 961–969.

Buckley, T. C., Blanchard, E. B., & Neill, W. T. (2000). Information processing and PTSD: A review of the empirical literature. *Clinical Psychology Review, 28,* 1041–1065.

Burnside, E., Startup, M., Byatt, M., Rollinson, L., & Hill J. (2004). The role of overgeneral autobiographical memory in the development of adult depression following childhood trauma. *British Journal of Clinical Psychology, 43,* 365–376.

Cassidy, K. L., McNally, R. J., & Zeitlin, S. B. (1992). Cognitive processing of trauma cues in rape victims with Post-traumatic Stress Disorder. *Cognitive Therapy and Research, 16,* 283–295.

Christianson, S.-A. (1992). Emotional stress and eyewitness memory: A critical review. *Psychological Bulletin, 112,* 284–309.

Conway, M. A., & Pleydell-Pearce, C. W. (2000). The construction of autobiographical memories in the self-memory system. *Psychological Review, 107,* 261–288.

Dalgleish, T., Golden, A. J., Barrett, L. F., Au Yeung, C., Murphy, V., Tchanturia, K., et al. (2007). Reduced specificity of autobiographical memory and depression: The role of executive control. *Journal of Experimental Psychology: General, 136,* 23–42.

de Decker, A., Hermans, D., Raes, F., & Eelen, P. (2003). Autobiographical memory specificity and trauma in inpatient adolescents. *Journal of Clinical Child and Adolescent Psychology, 32,* 22–31.

Deese, J. (1959). On the prediction of occurrence of particular verbal intrusions in immediate recall. *Journal of Experimental Psychology, 58,* 17–22.

Dewhurst, S. A., & Robinson, C. A. (2004). False memories in children, evidence for a shift from phonological to semantic associations. *Psychological Science, 15,* 782–786.

Doost, H. T. N., Taghavi, M. R., Moradi, A. R., Yule, W., & Dalgleish, T. (1997). The performance of clinically depressed children and adolescents on the modified Stroop paradigm. *Personality and Individual Differences, 23,* 753–759.

Dubner, A. E., & Motta, R. W. (1999). Sexually and physically abused foster care children and posttraumatic stress disorder. *Journal of Consulting and Clinical Psychology, 67,* 367–373.

Edelstein, R. S., Ghetti, S., Quas, J. A., Goodman, G. S., Alexander, K. W., Redlich, A. D., et al. (2005). Individual differences in emotional memory: Adult attachment and long-term memory for child sexual abuse. *Personality and Social Psychology Bulletin, 31,* 1537–1548.

Edwards, V. J., Fivush, R., Anda, R. F., Felitti, V. J., & Nordenberg, D. F. (2001). Autobiographical memory disturbances in childhood abuse survivors. *Aggression, Maltreatment, and Trauma, 4,* 247–263.

Eigsti, I., & Cicchetti, D. (2004). The impact of child maltreatment on expressive syntax at 60 months. *Developmental Science, 7,* 88–102.

Eisen, M. L., Goodman, G. S., Qin, J., Davis, S. L., & Crayton, J. (2007). Maltreated children's memory: Accuracy, suggestibility, and psychopathology. *Developmental Psychology, 43,* 1275–1294.

Eisen, M. L., Qin, J., Goodman, G. S., & Davis, S. L. (2002). Memory and suggestibility in maltreated children: Age, stress, arousal, dissociation, and psychopathology. *Journal of Experimental Child Psychology, 83,* 167–212.

Field, N. P., Classen, C., Butler, L. D., Koopman, C., Zarcone, J., & Spiegel, D. (2001). Revictimization and information processing in women survivors of childhood sexual abuse. *Journal of Anxiety Disorders, 15,* 459–469.

Fivush, R. (1984). Learning about school: The development of kindergartners' school scripts. *Child Development, 55,* 1697–1709.

Fivush, R. (2002). Scripts, schemas, and memory of trauma. In N. L. Stein, P. J. Bauer, & M. Rabinowitz (Eds.), *Representations, memory, and development. Essays in honor of Jean Mandler* (pp. 53–74). Mahwah, NJ: Lawrence Erlbaum Associates.

Fivush, R., & Edwards, V. J. (2004). Remembering and forgetting childhood sexual abuse. *Journal of Child Sexual Abuse, 13,* 1–19.

Fivush, R., & Nelson, K. (2004). The emergence of autobiographical memory: A social cultural developmental theory. *Psychological Review, 111,* 486–511.

Foa, E. B., Feske, U., Murdock, T. B., Kozak, M. J., & McCarthy, P. R. (1991). Processing of threat-related information in rape victims. *Journal of Abnormal Psychology, 100,* 156–162.

Gaudin, J. M. (1999). Child neglect: Short-term and long-term outcomes. In H. Dubowitz (Ed.), *Neglected children* (pp. 89–108). Thousand Oaks, CA: SAGE.

Ghetti, S., Qin, J., & Goodman, G. S. (2002). False memories in children and adults: Age, distinctiveness, and subjective experience. *Developmental Psychology, 38,* 705–718.

Golier, J. A., Harvey, P. D., Legge, J., & Yehuda, R. (2006). Memory performance in older trauma survivors: Implications for the longitudinal course of PTSD. *Annals of the New York Academy of Sciences, 1071,* 54–66.

Golier, J. A., Yehuda, R., Lupien, S. J., & Harvey, P. D. (2003). Memory for trauma-related information in Holocaust survivors with PTSD. *Psychiatry Research, 121,* 133–143.

Goodman, G. S., Hirschman, J. E., Hepps, D., & Rudy, L. (1991). Children's memory for stressful events. *Merrill-Palmer Quarterly, 37,* 109–158.

Greenhoot, A. F., McCloskey, L., & Glisky, E. (2005). A longitudinal study of adolescents' recollection of family violence. *Applied Cognitive Psychology, 19,* 719–743.

Harley, K., & Reese, E. (1999). Origins of autobiographical memory. *Developmental Psychology, 35,* 1338–1348.

Harris, L. S., Block, S. D., Ogle, C. M., Larson, R. P., Culver, M., Urquiza, A., et al. (2007, April). *Roediger-McDermott false memory in maltreated and nonmaltreated adolescents and adults with PTSD symptoms.* Paper presented at the biennial meeting of the Society of Research in Child Development, Boston, MA.

Harvey, A. G., Bryant, R. A., & Dang, S. T. (1998). Autobiographical memory in acute stress disorder. *Journal of Consulting and Clinical Psychology, 66,* 500–506.

Harvey, A. G., Bryant, R. A., & Rapee, R. M. (1996). Preconscious processing of threat in posttraumatic stress disorder. *Cognitive Therapy and Research, 20,* 613–623.

Hellawell, S. J., & Brewin, C. R. (2002). A comparison of flashbacks and ordinary autobiographical memories of trauma: Cognitive resources and behavioural observations. *Behaviour Research and Therapy, 40,* 1143–1156.

Henderson, D., Hargreaves, I., Gregory, S., & Williams, J. M. G. (2002). Autobiographical memory and emotion in a nonclinical sample of women with and without a reported history of childhood sexual abuse. *British Journal of Clinical Psychology, 41,* 129–142.

Hermans, H., Van den Broeck, K., Belis, G., Raes, F., Pieters, G., & Eelen, P. (2004). Trauma and autobiographical memory specificity in depressed inpatients. *Behaviour Research and Therapy, 42,* 775–789.

Howe, M. L., Chicchetti, D., Toth, S. L., & Cerrito, B. M. (2004). True and false memories in maltreated children. *Child Development, 75,* 1402–1417.

Howe, M. L., & Courage, M. L. (1993). On resolving the enigma of infantile amnesia. *Psychological Bulletin, 113,* 305–326.

Howe, M. L., & Courage, M. L. (1997). The emergence and early development of autobiographical memory. *Psychological Review, 104,* 499–523.

Hunter, E. C. M., & Andrews, B. (2002). Memory for autobiographical facts and events: A comparison of women reporting childhood sexual abuse and non-abused controls. *Applied Cognitive Psychology, 16,* 575–588.

Jelinek, L., Jacobsen, D., Kellner, M., Larbig, F., Biesold, K., Barre, K., et al. (2006). Verbal and nonverbal memory functioning in posttraumatic stress disorder (PTSD). *Journal of Clinical and Experimental Neuropsychology, 28,* 940–948.

Jenkins, M. A., Langlais, P. J., Delis, D., & Cohen, R. (2000). Attentional dysfunction associated with posttraumatic stress disorder among rape survivors. *The Clinical Neuropsychologist, 14,* 7–12.

Kangas, M., Henry, J. L., & Bryant, R. A. (2005). A prospective study of autobiographical memory and posttraumatic stress disorder following cancer. *Journal of Consulting and Clinical Psychology, 73,* 293–299.

Kopelman, M. D., Wilson, B. A., & Baddeley, A. D. (1989). The autobiographical memory interview: A new assessment of autobiographical and personal semantic memory in amnesic patients. *Journal of Clinical and Experimental Neuropsychology, 11,* 724–744.

Kuyken, W., & Brewin, C. R. (1995). Autobiographical memory functioning in depression and reports of early abuse. *Journal of Abnormal Psychology, 104,* 585–591.

Kuyken, W., Howell, R., & Dalgleish, T. (2006). Overgeneral autobiographical memory in depressed adolescents with, versus without, a reported history of trauma. *Journal of Abnormal Psychology, 115,* 387–396.

Mathews, A., & MacLeod, C. (1985). Selective processing of threat cues in anxiety states. *Behavior Research and Therapy, 23,* 563–569.

McNally, R. J., Clancy, S. A., Barrett, H. M., Parker, H. A., Ristuccia, C. S., & Perlman, C. A. (2006). Autobiographical memory specificity in adults reporting repressed, recovered, and continuous memories of childhood sexual abuse. *Cognition and Emotion, 20,* 527–535.

McNally, R. J., Clancy, S. A., Schacter, D. L., & Pitman, R. K. (2000). Cognitive processing of trauma cues in adults reporting repressed, recovered, or continuous memories of childhood sexual abuse. *Journal of Abnormal Psychology, 109,* 355–359.

McNally, R. J., English, G. E., & Lipke, H. J. (1993). Assessment of intrusive cognition in PTSD: Use of the modified Stroop paradigm. *Journal of Traumatic Stress, 6,* 33–41.

McNally, R. J., Kaspi, S. P., Riemann, B. C., & Zeitlin, S. B. (1990). Selective processing of threat cues in posttraumatic stress disorder. *Journal of Abnormal Psychology, 99,* 398–402.

McNally, R. J., Litz, B. T., Prassas, A., Shin, L. M., & Weathers, F. W. (1994). Emotional priming of autobiographical memory in post-traumatic stress disorder. *Cognition & Emotion, 8,* 351–367.

McNally, R. J., Metzger, L., Lasko, N. B., Clancy, S. A. & Pitman, R. K. (1998). Directed forgetting of trauma cues in adult survivors of childhood sexual abuse with and without posttraumatic stress disorder. *Journal of Abnormal Psychology, 107,* 596–601.

Meesters, C., Merckelbach, H., Muris, P., & Wessel, I. (2000). Autobiographical memory and trauma in adolescents. *Journal of Behavior Therapy and Experimental Psychiatry, 31,* 29–39.

Melchert, T. P. (1996). Childhood memory and a history of different forms of abuse. *Professional Psychology: Research and Practice, 27,* 438–446.

Melchert, T. P., & Parker, R. L. (1997). Different forms of childhood abuse and memory. *Child Abuse & Neglect, 21,* 125–135.

Michael, T., Ehlers, A., & Halligan, S. L. (2005). Enhanced priming for trauma-related material in posttraumatic stress disorder. *Emotion, 5,* 103–112.

Mogg, K., Mathews, A., & Weinman, J. (1989). Selective processing of threat cues in anxiety states: A replication. *Behaviour Research and Therapy, 27,* 317–323.

Moore, S. A., & Zoellner, L. A. (2007). Overgeneral autobiographical memory and traumatic events: An evaluative review. *Psychological Bulletin, 133,* 419–437.

Moradi, A. R., Taghavi, R., Neshat-Doost, H. T., Yule, W., & Dalgleish, T. (2000). Memory bias for emotional information in children and adolescents with posttraumatic stress disorder: A preliminary study. *Journal of Anxiety Disorders, 14,* 521–534.

Nelson, K. (1993). The psychological and social origins of autobiographical memory. *Psychological Science, 4,* 7–14.

Nelson, K., & Gruendel, J. M. (1988). At morning it's lunchtime: A scriptal view of children's dialogue. In M. B. Franklin & S. S. Barten (Eds.), *Child language: A reader.* (pp. 263–277). New York: Oxford University Press.

Nolen-Hoeksema, S. (1991). Responses to depression and their effects on the duration of depressive episodes. *Journal of Abnormal Psychology, 100,* 569–582.

Ogle, C. M., Block, S. D., Harris, L. S., Augusti, E., Pineda, R., Urquiza, A., et al. (2007, April). *PTSD severity and DRM recall predict adolescents' autobiographical memory accuracy.* Paper presented at the biennial meeting of the Society of Research in Child Development, Boston, MA.

Orbach, Y., Lamb, M. E., Sternberg, K. J., Williams, J. M. G., & Dawud-Noursi, S. (2001). The effect of being a victim or witness of family violence on the retrieval of autobiographical memories. *Child Abuse & Neglect, 25,* 1427–1437.

Peeters, F., Wessel, I., Merckelbach, H., & Boon-Vermeeren, M. (2002). Autobiographical memory specificity and the course of major depressive disorder. *Comprehensive Psychiatry, 43,* 344–350.

Peterson, C. (2002). Children's long-term memory for autobiographical events. *Developmental Review, 22,* 370–402.

Pollak, S. D. (2003). Experience-dependent affective learning and risk for psychopathology in children. *Annals of the New York Academy of Sciences, 1008,* 102–111.

Pollak, S. D., Cicchetti, D., Klorman, R., & Brumaghim, J. T. (1997). Cognitive brain event-related potentials and emotion processing in maltreated children. *Child Development, 68,* 773–787.

Pollak, S. D., Klorman, R., Thatcher, J. E., & Cicchetti, D. (2001). P3b reflects maltreated children's reactions to facial displays of emotion. *Psychophysiology, 38,* 267–274.

Pollak, S. D., & Tolley-Schell, S. A. (2003). Selective attention to facial emotion in physically abused children. *Journal of Abnormal Psychology, 112*(3), 323–338.

Pollak, S. D., Vardi, S., Bechner, A. M. P., & Curtin, J. J. (2005). Physically abused children's regulation of attention in response to hostility. *Child Development, 76,* 968–977.

Porter, S., & Peace, K. A. (2007). The scars of memory: A prospective, longitudinal investigation of the consistency of traumatic and positive emotional memories in adulthood. *Psychological Science, 18,* 435–441.

Roediger, H. L., & McDermott, K. B. (1995). Creating false memories: Remembering words not presented in lists. *Journal of Experimental Psychology: Learning, Memory, and Cognition, 21,* 803–814.

Rubin, D. C. (2006). The basic-systems model of episodic memory. *Perspectives on Psychological Science, 1,* 277–311.

Rubin, D. C., & Berntsen, D. (2003). Life scripts help to maintain autobiographical memories of highly positive, but not highly negative events. *Memory & Cognition, 31,* 1–14.

Rubin, D. C., Feldman, M. E., & Beckham, J. C. (2004). Reliving, emotions, and fragmentation in the autobiographical memories of veterans diagnosed with PTSD. *Applied Cognitive Psychology, 18,* 17–35.

Sheslow, D., & Adams, W. (1990). *Wide Range Assessment of Memory and Learning.* Wilmington, DE: Wide Range Inc.

Stokes, D. J., Dritschel, B. H., & Bekerian, D. A. (2004). The effect of burn injury on adolescents' autobiographical memory. *Behaviour Research and Therapy, 42,* 1357–1365.

Stroop, J. R. (1935). Studies of interference in serial verbal reactions. *Journal of Experimental Psychology, 18,* 643–662.

Swales, M. A., Williams, M. G., & Wood, P. (2001). Specificity of autobiographical memory and mood disturbance in adolescents. *Cognition and Emotion, 15,* 321–331.

Uddo, M., Vasterling, J. J., Brailey, K., & Sutker, P. B. (1993). Memory and attention in combat-related post-traumatic stress disorder (PTSD). *Journal of Psychopathology and Behavioral Assessment, 15,* 43–52.

Vasterling, J. J., Brailey, K., Constans, J. I., & Sutker, P. B. (1998). Attention and memory dysfunction in posttraumatic stress disorder. *Neuropsychology, 12,* 125–133.

Vrana, S. R., Roodman, A., & Beckham, J. C. (1995). Selective processing of trauma-relevant words in posttraumatic stress disorder. *Journal of Anxiety Disorders, 9,* 515–530.

Watkins, E., & Teasdale, J. D. (2001). Rumination and overgeneral memory in depression: Effects of self-focus and analytic thinking. *Journal of Abnormal Psychology, 110,* 353–357.

Watkins, E., Teasdale, J. D., & Williams, R. M. (2000). Decentering and distraction reduce overgeneral autobiographical memory in depression. *Psychological Medicine, 30,* 911–920.

Wessel, I., Meeren, M., Peeters, F., Arntz, A., & Merckelbach, H. (2001). Correlates of autobiographical memory specificity: The role of depression, anxiety, and childhood trauma. *Behaviour Research and Therapy, 39,* 409–421.

Wessel, I., Merckelbach, H., & Dekkers, T. (2002). Autobiographical memory specificity, intrusive memory, and general memory skills in Dutch Indonesian survivors of the World War II era. *Journal of Traumatic Stress, 15,* 227–234.

Wilhelm, S., McNally, R. J., Baer, L., & Florin, I. (1997). Autobiographical memory in obsessive-compulsive disorder. *British Journal of Clinical Psychology, 36,* 21–31.

Williams, J. M. G. (1996). Depression and the specificity of autobiographical memory. In D. C. Rubin (Ed.), *Remembering our past: Studies in autobiographical memory* (pp. 244–267). New York: Cambridge University Press.

Williams, J. M., Barnhofer, T., Crane, C., Hermans, D., Raes, F., Watkins, E., et al. (2007). Autobiographical memory specificity and emotional disorder. *Psychological Bulletin, 133,* 122–148.

Williams, J. M., & Broadbent, K. (1986). Autobiographical memory in suicide attempters. *Journal of Abnormal Psychology, 95,* 144–149.

Windmann, S., & Krüger, T. (1998). Subconscious detection of threat as reflected by an enhanced response bias. *Consciousness and Cognition, 7,* 603–633.

Wright, I., Waterman, M., Prescott, H., & Murdoch-Eaton, D. (2003). A new Stroop-like measure of inhibitory function development: Typical developmental trends. *Journal of Child Psychology and Psychiatry, 44,* 561–575.

Yasik, A. E., Saigh, P. A., Oberfield, R. A., & Halamandaris, P. V. (2007). Posttraumatic stress disorder: Memory and learning performance in children and adolescents. *Biological Psychiatry, 61,* 382–388.

Zoellner, L. A., Foa, E. B., Brigidi, B. D., & Przeworski, A. (2002). Are trauma victims susceptible to "false memories"? *Journal of Abnormal Psychology, 109,* 517–524.

6

Talking About Twisters

How Mothers and Children Converse About a Devastating Tornado

PATRICIA J. BAUER, MELISSA M. BURCH,
DANA L. VAN ABBEMA, AND JENNIFER K. ACKIL

A deeply rooted assumption is that highly stressful and even traumatic events are differentially remembered relative to events that are more affectively neutral or positive. In the present chapter, we evaluate this assumption using data from a study of children's reports of the experience of a tornado that devastated the town of St. Peter, Minnesota, in March of 1998. The evaluation is multifaceted, featuring analyses of how much the children reported, the type of information they included, and the extent to which their reports were affected by the narrative style of their conversational partners, namely their mothers. We turn to the evaluation after a brief review of the basis for expectation of differential memory for traumatic events and a description of the St. Peter, Minnesota, tornado and its aftermath.

Why Traumatic Events Should Be Differentially Remembered

One of the bases for the expectation of differences in memories of stressful or traumatic experiences and nontraumatic experiences is the classic

Yerkes-Dodson Law of optimal arousal (Yerkes & Dodson, 1908). Briefly, the law predicts a systematic relation between level of arousal and performance, such that when arousal is either too low or too high, performance will be impaired relative to when arousal level is optimal. Stressful or traumatic experiences are expected to increase arousal relative to more benign events. Assuming that the level of arousal associated with a traumatic experience is high, but not too high, application of the Yerkes-Dodson law leads to the prediction that the experience will be well remembered. If the level of arousal associated with the traumatic event exceeds the optimal level, then memory for the experience will be impaired (Easterbrook, 1959).

In addition to differences in how much may be remembered about traumatic relative to nontraumatic events, memories of the different event types may differ qualitatively (see Goodman & Quas, 1997, for discussion). On the one hand, memories of traumatic experiences may have a vivid "flashbulb" quality (e.g., Brown & Kulik, 1977; Winograd & Neisser, 1992). Others suggest that in traumatic circumstances, attention is focused on the central features of the event, with correspondingly poorer memory for more peripheral features (e.g., Christianson, 1992).

The question of whether there are differences in children's memories for traumatic and nontraumatic events is not easy to address. For obvious practical and ethical reasons, researchers cannot intentionally subject children to traumatic events in order to study their memories for them. Instead, we investigate the question by examining the retrospective reports of children who have experienced varying degrees of trauma during stressful medical procedures (e.g., Brown et al., 1999; Goodman, Hirschman, Hepps, & Rudy, 1991; Vandermaas, Hess, & Baker-Ward, 1993) or other negative events, such as hurricanes (e.g., Bahrick, Parker, Merritt, & Fivush, 1998). Most often, the comparisons are across studies or between groups of children. For example, Brown et al. (1999) investigated the influence of trauma on remembering by comparing the reports of children (3- to 5-year-olds) who experienced a painful and embarrassing catheterization procedure (a voiding cystourethrogram—VCUG) to children who experienced a substantially less stressful pediatric exam. Bahrick et al. (1998; see also Parker, Bahrick, Lundy, Fivush, & Levitt, 1998) examined Florida preschool children's recall of the events surrounding Hurricane Andrew, in 1992, as a function of the damage their family sustained during the storm. Overall, stressful events are recalled at least as well as, and in some cases better than, more benign experiences (e.g., Ornstein, 1995; see Fivush, 1998, 2002, for reviews). However, in some studies, children who experienced high levels of stress produced more memory errors relative to children who were less stressed (e.g., Goodman & Quas, 1997).

These investigations inform the question of whether memories for traumatic and nontraumatic events differ quantitatively, qualitatively, or both. However, because the studies were between, rather than within, subjects, they cannot address the question of whether apparent differences between types of events actually are differences between groups. The few studies that have featured within-subjects comparisons of reports of traumatic and nontraumatic events suggest both similarities and differences. For instance, Fivush, Hazzard, Sales, Sarfati, and Brown (2003) interviewed 5- to 12-year-old children about nontraumatic events, such as vacations, parties, and family outings, and stressful or traumatic events, such as parental separation, violent or minor interpersonal altercations, and serious illness or death. Overall, children's narratives about the stressful or traumatic and the nontraumatic events were comparable in length. However, the children mentioned more people and objects and included more descriptions (i.e., use of adjectives, adverbs, possessives, and modifiers) in their accounts of nontraumatic experiences than in their accounts of stressful or traumatic experiences. On the other hand, the children provided more information about internal states (i.e., emotional, cognitive, and volitional states of self or other) when recounting traumatic relative to nontraumatic experiences. In addition, researchers rated narratives about traumatic experiences as more narratively coherent than narratives about nontraumatic experiences. The results of this study suggest that memory narratives about traumatic and nontraumatic events differ, and that narratives about traumatic events are more complete and better integrated, and more internally focused, compared with narratives about nontraumatic events.

A somewhat different perspective on the question is provided by Sales, Fivush, and Peterson (2003). Sales and colleagues examined conversations between parents (primarily mothers) and their 3- to 5-year-old children about a positive event, such as a family vacation, and the stressful or traumatic experience of a medical emergency sufficient to require a trip to the emergency room for the child (e.g., lacerations requiring stitches, broken bones). The conversations about the traumatic experiences were longer than the conversations about the more positive experiences (in Fivush et al., 2003, conversational length did not differ across event types). In addition, both parents and children spent proportionally more time talking about emotions in their conversations about positive events relative to traumatic events (the opposite was observed in Fivush et al., 2003). Conversely, both parents and their children spent proportionally more time discussing the causes of behavior (e.g., "What did you do to get hurt?" p. 192) in their conversations about the traumatic events relative to positive events. The reasons for the somewhat different patterns of findings in Sales et al. and in Fivush et al. are unknown, but may relate to the ages of the children (3- to 5-year-olds and 5- to 12-year-olds, respectively) or the basis for recruitment into the study (in Sales et al., families were recruited precisely because their child had experienced a traumatic event).

Address of the question of whether memories of traumatic and nontraumatic events differ is limited in another way as well: few studies have compared children's memory reports of traumatic and nontraumatic experiences over time. Rather, the majority of research has employed one-time examinations of children's memory reports. Those studies that have included follow-up examinations of children's memory for traumatic events (e.g., Fivush, Sales, Goldberg, Bahrick, & Parker, 2004; Howe, Courage, & Peterson, 1994; Peterson & Whalen, 2001; Quas et al., 1999) have not compared children's reports of traumatic and nontraumatic events. As a result, it is difficult to know whether changes in children's reports over time are due to the traumatic nature of the event or are more event-general. Examination of children's reports of a tornado that devastated the town of St. Peter, Minnesota, permitted us to address both of these limitations, as well as initiate address of the question of whether children's reports were affected by the narrative style of their conversational partners, namely their mothers.

The Tornado and Its Aftermath

On Sunday, March 29, 1998, at approximately 5:20 p.m., a series of destructive tornadoes hit the small, rural town of St. Peter, Minnesota (population 9,500). The storm cluster carried winds in excess of 200 miles per hour and cut a 1.25-mile-wide path of destruction through the town.

The tornado took the life of a 6-year-old child who was known to most of the participants in the study. Seventy-five percent of the town's homes were damaged, with 28% completely destroyed or damaged to the point that they were uninhabitable (Murray, 1998). As quoted in our first report of data from the study (Ackil, Van Abbema, & Bauer, 2003), one mother described the scene she observed as she emerged from the basement after the storm:

> It just literally looked like a bomb had gone off.... I probably walked about a mile and a half through town over power lines, over people's roofs and dressers. I expected to walk over bodies, the streets were so littered you could not get through... you were just literally walking across shingles and walls. You couldn't even identify where you were in town because everything looked so completely different.... People were just milling around trying to find where their loved ones were, trying to make sure people were okay and stuff. Trying to get to other households to make sure that people had survived. (p. 289)

The effects of the tornado were felt long after the storm had passed. Homes that were not destroyed were without power for more than a week, and in some cases in excess of a month. The nearly 2,100 elementary and secondary school children in the town were out of school for 9 days. Upon their return, children of all ages attended the same school in shifts for the remainder of the academic year. In short, the tornado and resulting destruction had an immediate, pronounced, and prolonged impact on the residents of the town and, thus, the participants in the research summarized in the present chapter.

As we discussed in Ackil et al. (2003), there are other features of the St. Peter tornado that made the experience of it uniquely traumatic and different from the negative and traumatic experiences examined in previous studies of children's memory. First, the storm and its consequences were unexpected, coming as it did on an otherwise sunny Minnesota afternoon in late March. Warning sirens were sounded minutes before the touchdown of the tornado, but families were otherwise unprepared for the event, and they had no time to discuss expectations of it in advance. This contrasts with much of the research on children's memory for negative events in which the events were anticipated. Stressful medical procedures often are scheduled in advance, and children are prepared for them (e.g., Goodman, Quas, Batterman-Faunce, Riddlesberger, & Kuhn, 1997). Even in the case of emergency room treatment there may be time en route to the hospital or in the waiting room for parents to provide some preparation of their children for what is to come. Medical personnel involved in suturing and casting "walk through" the procedures as they administer treatment (see Peterson & Bell, 1996). This advanced preparation may impact children's immediate interpretation and subsequent representation of the experience (e.g., Goodman et al., 1997). Consistent with this suggestion, in the study of children's memory for Hurricane Andrew, one of the categories that varied as a function of stress was children's recall of storm preparation (Bahrick et al., 1998). The unanticipated nature of the St. Peter tornado meant that children could not benefit from prior preparation by parents and others about the upcoming experience.

Second, unlike many unfamiliar and stressful events, the tornado also prohibited *concurrent* interpretation by parents. None of the families who participated in the study had any prior personal experience with a destructive tornado. They certainly were not able to predict the storm's outcome. In addition, many mothers reported that as it became clear that the storm was severe and potentially life threatening, they exhibited negative coping behaviors such as crying, hyperventilating, praying for safety, and so forth. Even for mothers who were less obviously emotional, it was difficult if not impossible to engage in conversation. The families were crouched in small spaces (interior bathrooms) and under large pieces of furniture (desks) as the loud winds of the storm raged around them. Such circumstances virtually precluded the kind of conversations that are known to support children's subsequent recall (Haden, Ornstein, Eckerman, & Didow, 2001; Tessler & Nelson, 1994). In short, the event of the St. Peter, Minnesota, tornado was traumatic, unique, and unanticipated, and it was only after the fact that it could be "processed" by the children and their caregivers.

Study Design

To investigate the possibility of quantitative differences, qualitative differences, or both in children's reports of traumatic and nontraumatic events, approximately 4 months after the tornado, we asked mothers and their children to talk about the storm and about two events that were not related to the tornado: one that had taken place within 4 months prior to the tornado, and one that had taken place since the storm but that was not related to it. To evaluate whether any observed differences persisted over time, 6 months after the first interview (10 months after the storm), we asked the dyads to talk about the same three events again. We included two different nontraumatic experiences from the relatively recent and more distant past in order to evaluate the possibility that any differences between memories of the tornado and nontraumatic events might be the result of systematic differences in the retention interval between when the events occurred and when they were discussed. Contrary to this suggestion, the analyses revealed few differences between the nontraumatic events that took place before and after the tornado. For this reason, we collapsed across the two nontraumatic events and used the resulting means in analyses.

The Sample

The initial sample consisted of 29 mother–child dyads who were residents of St. Peter, Minnesota, at the time of the March 29, 1998, tornado. Twenty-eight of the dyads participated in the second interview. Eleven of the children were girls. Six mothers participated with more than one child (one mother participated with three of her children, and five mothers participated with two of their children). Thus, 22 mothers participated in 29 unique mother–child pairs. The analyses summarized in this chapter were carried out on the full sample of 29 dyads. Parallel analyses on the smaller sample that results when only the 22 unique mothers are included revealed the same patterns (Bohanek, Van Abbema, Ackil, & Bauer, in preparation). Additional details about the sample (as well as procedures followed in data collection, reduction, and analysis) are available in Ackil et al. (2003); Bauer, Burch, Van Abbema, and Ackil (in press); and Bauer et al. (2005).

At the first interview, the children ranged in age from 3 to 11 years. This very wide age range allowed us to test whether age might interact with the nature of the event (traumatic versus nontraumatic) children were asked to recollect. To facilitate this analysis, we grouped the children into three age groups: 7 children were included in the "youngest" age group ($M = 3.6$ years; range = 2.6 to 4.9 years), 12 children were included in the "middle" age group ($M = 6.3$ years; range = 5.3 to 6.9 years), and 10 children were included in the "oldest" age group ($M = 9.3$ years;

range = 7.2 to 11.8 years). In spite of the wide age range and the use of a large number of analyses that might have been expected to yield them, there were relatively few age-related differences. Because a major focus of this chapter is possible differences between reports of traumatic and nontraumatic events, and because most of the age differences were main effects rather than interactions with event type, we feature little in the way of discussion of age trends in the data (the one interaction of Age x Event type is discussed; see Ackil et al., 2003; Bauer, Stark, et al., 2005; and Bauer, Burch, et al., in press, for findings).

Approach to Data Collection: Mother–Child Conversations

The most typical approach to examination of children's memory for traumatic experiences is to engage them in structured interviews. In the present research, we examined memory within the context of joint mother–child reminiscing. We took this approach for two reasons. The first was to reduce any stress or discomfort that the children might feel as they talked about what might have been a truly terrifying experience. The second reason for the approach was that it permitted us to examine joint reminiscing in the context of a traumatic event. Since the mid-1980s, it has been apparent that parents—arguably the most significant conversational partners for young children—differ in the ways they support their children's contributions to conversations about past events. Although a number of labels are used to capture the differences, there is consensus that parents exhibit two styles that vary in terms of the parents' contributions to conversations (e.g., Engel, 1986; Farrant & Reese, 2000; Fivush & Fromhoff, 1988; Nelson, 1993; Nelson & Fivush, 2000, 2004). Parents who frequently engage in conversations about the past, provide rich descriptive information about previous experiences, and invite their children to "join in" on the construction of stories about the past are said to use an *elaborative* style. An example of a conversation between a mother and her 3-year-old child illustrates the elaborative style:

> MOTHER: Say, [child's name], what was at Lauren's house a long time ago at her birthday party?
> CHILD: [no response]
> MOTHER: What did you hold—they were so tiny—at Lauren's house? Remember?

CHILD: A baby.

MOTHER: A baby kitty.

CHILD: Yeah, a baby kitty.

MOTHER: That's right. Oh and it was so soft. How many kitties did she have?

CHILD: Um, five.

MOTHER: Uh-huh. That's right.

CHILD: And they got away.

MOTHER: And they got away from you. Yeah.

In contrast to the elaborative style, parents who provide fewer details about past experiences and instead pose specific questions to their children are said to use a *low-elaborative* or *repetitive* style, illustrated by another mother and her 3-year-old child:

MOTHER: [child's name], do you remember going to Sandy's house and playing at her house?

CHILD: [nods in agreement]

MOTHER: Did they have some kids at her house?

CHILD: Yeah.

MOTHER: What kinds of kids were at her house?

CHILD: David.

MOTHER: David. Was he the only child that was at her house?

CHILD: [nods in agreement]

MOTHER: What other kids were at her house?

Evidence that these differences reflect varying approaches to memory conversations comes from findings that levels of elaboration are correlated over time (e.g., Reese, Haden, & Fivush, 1993). In addition, mothers show similar patterns with multiple children in the family (Haden, 1998; Lewis, 1999; relevant studies with fathers have not been conducted). Stylistic differences are apparent not only when parents are eliciting memory reports from their children, such as in the examples provided here, but also as events are being experienced and, thus, laid down in memory (Bauer & Burch, 2004; Haden et al., 2001; Tessler & Nelson, 1994).

Both concurrently and over time, children of parents using a more elaborative style are more involved in conversations about past events than are children of parents using a less elaborative style (e.g., Bauer & Burch,

2004; Fivush, 1991; Fivush & Fromhoff, 1988; Peterson & McCabe, 1994). Both of these patterns are nicely illustrated in longitudinal research by Reese et al. (1993). The researchers examined conversations between mother–child pairs at four time points while the children were between roughly 3 and 6 years of age. There were concurrent correlations between maternal elaborations and children's memory responses at all four time points. That is, at each session, the more elaborations mothers provided, the more memory contributions their children made. There also were correlations over time. For instance, mothers who used more elaborations when their children were 3 years of age had children who at 5 and 6 years made more memory contributions. Largely absent were relations between children's behavior at earlier time points and mothers' behavior at later time points. In fact, the only such relation was between children's behavior at age 5 years and mothers' behavior when their children were aged 6 years. The pattern is consistent with the suggestion that through conversations about the past, children are socialized in the arts of creating and sharing autobiographical narratives (Nelson & Fivush, 2000, 2004).

There have been several replications of findings of differences in maternal approaches to joint conversations about the past, and of relations between variables that define maternal style and children's participation in autobiographical reminiscing (e.g., Bauer & Burch, 2004; Boland, Haden, & Ornstein, 2003; Fivush & Fromhoff, 1988; Hudson, 1990; Lewis, 1999; McCabe & Peterson, 1991; Welch-Ross, 2001). However, almost without exception, they have been examined in the context of conversations about emotionally positive or affectively neutral events. It is rare to find an examination of whether similar relations extend to children's memories of less positive and even traumatic experiences. In light of expectations of quantitative differences, qualitative differences, or both in recollection of traumatic and nontraumatic events, it is possible that we might observe different patterns of parent–child interaction in conversations about the two event types and, as a result, differential socialization.

To date, there has been only one other investigation of this question. The data from Sales et al. (2003) were obtained in the context of mother–child interviews. Sales and her colleagues took advantage of this feature of their design and examined parental verbal behavior across traumatic and more positive events. They found that parents were consistent in their style across the conversations. That is, parents who were elaborative when talking about the positive event also were elaborative when talking about the traumatic event. They also found relations between parental variability and children's behavior in conversations about both types of events. Consistent with previous research, parents who posed more elaborative questions had children who made more contributions to the conversations. Relations between parental style and children's behavior were stronger in the context of discussions of the medical emergencies, relative to more positive experiences (i.e., the correlations were larger in magnitude). The St. Peter tornado study provided us with an opportunity to test for replication of these patterns in another sample. Moreover, because we asked the dyads to converse about the events two times, the study allowed us the unique opportunity to examine not only concurrent relations but relations between maternal and child behavior over time.

Children's Reports of the Tornado and Nontraumatic Events

We used the data from the St. Peter tornado study to address the questions of whether reports of traumatic and nontraumatic events differed in terms of the amount of information provided, the type of information provided, or the degree of relation between maternal and child contributions to the conversations. We addressed each question in turn.

Do Children Report Different Amounts of Information About Traumatic and Nontraumatic Events?

Prior within-subjects examinations of whether children provide more (or less) information about traumatic and nontraumatic events have provided mixed results. In one of the two prior studies that featured a within-subjects comparison, Fivush and her colleagues (2003) did not find a difference in the length of the conversations about the two different event types. In the other—which also featured mother–child interviews—Sales and her colleagues (2003) found that reports of traumatic events were longer than those about nontraumatic events.

In the St. Peter tornado study, at both the first interview (4 months after the storm) and the second interview (10 months after the storm), we observed that conversations about the tornado were twice as long as conversations about the two nontraumatic events, which did not differ from each other. The lengths of the conversations did not differ between Sessions 1 and 2 for any of the events. At both time points, mothers and their children exchanged roughly 40 conversational turns when they were talking about the tornado and took roughly 20 turns for each of the nontraumatic events. As reflected in Figure 6.1, the children themselves contributed almost 2.5 times as many propositions to the tornado relative to the nontraumatic event conversations (Bauer et al., in press).

It is tempting to consider the differences in conversational length and in children's participation in the conversations as evidence of a difference in the memory representations of traumatic and nontraumatic events. However, it is always important to bear in mind that reports of events are only that: they are not a direct window on the representation itself. Moreover, as we have argued elsewhere (Bauer et al., 2005), the participants in this research were selected because they had experienced the event of the tornado. This raises the possibility that conversations about the storm were longer because, either implicitly or explicitly, participants were aware that the traumatic event was the focus of the research. Consistent with this suggestion, in other research in which participants were selected because they had experienced traumatic events (medical emergencies), conversations between mothers and their 3- to 5-year-old children were

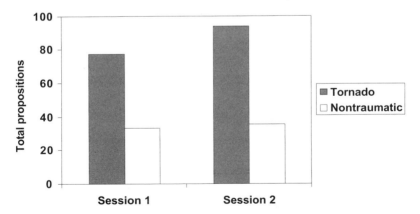

FIGURE 6.1. Children's contributions to conversations about the tornado and the nontraumatic events, as measured by the total number of propositions produced at Sessions 1 and 2.

substantially longer for the traumatic relative to the nontraumatic events (Sales et al., 2003). In contrast, in another within–subjects comparison in which recruitment was not based on experience of a particular type of trauma, narratives about the two different event types did not differ in length (Fivush et al., 2003).

Another possible reason why conversations about the storm might have been longer than conversations about the nontraumatic events is that there was simply more to talk about. The tornado was a particularly consequential event that impacted all aspects of life for residents of the St. Peter community (e.g., work, school, home, friends). As such, it provided a greater number of avenues readily available for discussion than the nontraumatic events the dyads chose to discuss. For all of these reasons, it seems ill advised to conclude that because the children in the sample reported more about the traumatic relative to the nontraumatic events, they remembered more about the traumatic event. Accordingly, all subsequent analyses reported were conducted with the sheer length of the conversations controlled statistically. This permitted us to determine whether the reports differed *per unit of conversation.*

Do Children Report Different Types of Information About Traumatic and Nontraumatic Events?

A "good narrative" includes several types of information, including the *who, what, where, when, why,* and *how* of the event. As we reported in Ackil et al. (2003), the breadth of the mother–children conversations differed as a function of whether they were talking about the tornado or the nontraumatic events. Specifically, tornado conversations were more likely to include contextual information (e.g., mention of being in a specific location during the event), information about the causes and consequences of elements of the event, and temporal connections within and between elements of the event. An example from one of the children in the study illustrates these features:

> I remember the sirens going off... and we all came downstairs to our
> TV room and watched the TV to see what was going on.... We kept on
> watching the news and it started to get dark in the sky. I remember you
> [the child's mother] were baking something and you told me to quickly go
> upstairs... to turn off the oven. Then I heard you scream at me to get back

down and you told me that you had heard like a high-pitched whistle. And
then we got under a desk in the TV room and, let's see ... we didn't have
a blanket because the blankets were at the other side of the room and you
were too scared to go across it because there was windows in between on
both sides.

The differences in the breadth of the conversations about the tornado
and the nontraumatic events were apparent even after we took into account the greater length of the conversations. Moreover, the differences
largely endured over the 6-month interval between sessions (Ackil et al.,
2003). Thus, in critical ways, conversations about the traumatic event
were more complete.

Although the conversations about the traumatic event included more
narrative categories, children's contributions to them were not markedly
more detailed. As discussed in Bauer et al. (in press), relative to the nontraumatic event conversations, in the tornado conversations children provided more *orientations* (information regarding who participated in the
event, physical objects that were part of the event, descriptions of objectively available features of objects or events, and information about
where and when the event occurred), *actions* (descriptions of what the
characters in the activity were doing during the event), *connections* (links
between aspects of events, typically conveyed through words such as *first*,
then, *before*, and *after*, and *because*, *if*, *so*, and *since*), and *evaluations* (subjective
experiences and impressions of the event, including subjective modifiers,
internal states, and intensifiers). However, once the greater length of the
tornado conversations was taken into account, the differences in the
amount of detail the children provided no longer were apparent, at either
session. That is, per unit of conversation, the children provided the same
number of *orientations*, *actions*, *connections*, and *evaluations* about the tornado
and the nontraumatic events. The only exception was for the oldest children in the sample (i.e., 7- to 11-year-olds) in terms of the specific type of
evaluation that conveys information about internal states (i.e., words that
describe emotional, cognitive, perceptual, and physiological states). At the
second session (10 months after the storm), the contributions that the
oldest children made to the tornado conversations were more saturated
with internal-states language relative to their contributions to the conversations about the nontraumatic events (Bauer et al., 2005). This difference
had not been apparent at the first session (4 months after the storm); it was

not apparent for either of the younger groups of children in the sample (i.e., 3- to 7-year-olds) at either session.

Is there Evidence of Differential Socialization of Narratives About Traumatic and Nontraumatic Events?

As just reviewed, there are some indications that children report more information about traumatic relative to nontraumatic events. The findings must be interpreted with caution, however, given other variables that vary across these event types (e.g., duration and impact of the event) and the basis for selection into some studies that afford direct comparison of the types of events. Indeed, with the length of the conversation controlled statistically, there is little evidence of differences in the level of detail children provide about traumatic and nontraumatic events. The one exception is the category of internal-states language, at least for older children. On the other hand, the mother–child conversations about the traumatic events featured greater narrative breadth relative to their conversations about the nontraumatic events. Learning to provide one's own perspective on an event and to tell the listener "the whole story" are major achievements in narrative development. They are also aspects of narrative development that are under the influence of socialization by children's conversational partners, most prominently their mothers. This raises the question of whether there is differential socialization of narratives about traumatic and nontraumatic events.

Differential socialization of narratives about traumatic and nontraumatic events may be particularly likely given the uniqueness of traumatic experiences and the strong emotions associated with them. Children may be especially dependent on parents or other caregivers to help them interpret such strong experiences and gain perspective on them. Because the children in the St. Peter tornado study engaged in conversation with their mothers, and because the dyads talked about both the traumatic event and nontraumatic events, we have the opportunity to examine this question. Our approach is to first discuss relations between maternal and child variables at each of the time points (4 months and 10 months after the storm) and then discuss relations over time (i.e., whether behavior at Session 1 was related to behavior at Session 2 in systematic ways). Within each of these sections, we first examined relations between the variables that define maternal style (relative degree of elaboration relative to repetition) and children's overall participation in the conversations (measured by the number of propositions they contributed). We then examined relations between maternal style variables and the amount of unique content that the children provided when talking about the tornado and the nontraumatic events (i.e., the number of unique *orientations*, *actions*, *connections*, and *evaluations* they provided).

Four Months After the Storm

Consistent with prior research, we found relations between mothers' and children's behavior in the conversations. The relations were stronger in the context of the tornado conversations than in the conversations about the nontraumatic events. The indices that are most defining of maternal style are the number of elaborations mothers make, the number of repetitions they produce, and the ratio of elaborations to repetitions (e.g., Fivush & Fromhoff, 1988; Reese et al., 1993). As might be expected, given the greater length of the tornado conversations, mothers provided more elaborations and more repetitions when engaged in conversations about the tornado relative to the nontraumatic events. However, with the total number of maternal utterances controlled statistically, there were not differences between the event types. Moreover, the *ratio* of elaborations to repetitions did not differ between the traumatic and nontraumatic events (*M* elaboration ratios at Session 1 = 7.99 and 8.65, respectively). Thus, mothers were equally elaborative and repetitive in their conversations about the two event types. In addition, mothers who were relatively more elaborative in conversations about the tornado also were relatively more elaborative in conversations about the nontraumatic events (correlations between the two event types were in the range of 0.54 to 0.80).

As reflected in Figure 6.2, mothers who were relatively more elaborative had children who were more participatory in conversations about both types of events. That is, mothers who produced a higher ratio of elaborations to repetitions had children who contributed larger numbers of propositions relative to children whose mothers were less elaborative. The relation was especially strong in the context of the tornado conversations. Maternal style was also related to the amount of unique content the children provided, especially in the context of conversations about the tornado. In the tornado conversations, children of more elaborative mothers provided more total unique content, and also more unique content in each of the

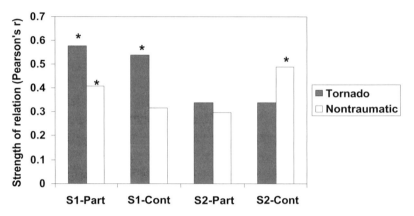

FIGURE 6.2. The strength of concurrent correlations (Pearson's *r*) between mothers and their children at Sessions 1 and 2 in terms of participation in the conversations ("Part") and the amount of unique content provided ("Cont"). Asterisks indicate that the correlation was statistically significant.

individual categories, relative to children of less elaborative mothers. Thus, to their conversations about the tornado, the children of more elaborative mothers contributed more orientations to the physical setting of the event, more descriptions of the activities that took place, and more temporal and causal connections. The children also contributed more information about how they (and others) thought and felt about the tornado (see Bauer et al., in press, for details). The relations were observed even though conversational length was controlled statistically. Overall, the pattern of concurrent relations between maternal behavior and child behavior were stronger for the tornado relative to the nontraumatic events.

Ten Months After the Storm

As was the case 4 months after the storm, 10 months later mothers were equally elaborative and repetitive in their conversations about the storm and the nontraumatic events. Unlike in Session 1, at Session 2 there were not strong relations between mothers' and children's participation in the conversations, and relations between mothers' behavior and the amount of unique content the children provided were only observed for the nontraumatic events. Specifically, with the total number of maternal utterances controlled statistically, there were not significant differences in the number of elaborations and repetitions mothers provided in their conversations about the tornado relative to the nontraumatic events. Nor were there differences in the *ratio* of elaborations to repetitions between the event types (M elaboration ratios for tornado and nontraumatic events at Session 2 = 7.89 and 7.41, respectively). Mothers who were relatively more elaborative in conversations about the tornado also were relatively more elaborative in conversations about the nontraumatic events (correlations between the two event types were in the range of 0.53 to 0.70).

At Session 2, relative to Session 1, measures of children's overall participation in the conversations were less strongly related to maternal style. As reflected in Figure 6.2, neither correlation reached the level of statistical significance. Nor was there a relation between maternal behavior and the amount of unique content the children provided about the tornado. For the nontraumatic events, however, the children of more elaborative mothers provided more unique content relative to children of less elaborative mothers. In their conversations about the nontraumatic events, the children of more elaborative mothers contributed more orientations to the physical setting, more descriptions of the activities that took place, and more temporal and causal connections (see Bauer et al., in press, for details). The weaker pattern of relation for the tornado relative to the nontraumatic events at Session 2 is the opposite of the pattern observed at Session 1. It is likely that differences in the patterns of relation from Session 1 to Session 2 for the mothers relative to the children, discussed in the next section, contributed to the relatively low degree of correlation observed at Session 2.

Relations Over Time: Within-Participant Groups

Overall, the mothers who participated in the study were not especially consistent in their approach to the conversations at the two time points, whereas the children were highly consistent. Specifically, as reflected in Figure 6.3, it was only in the context of the tornado conversations that mothers' ratios of elaborations to repetitions were correlated over time. In contrast to their mothers, for both types of events, the children in the sample were highly consistent across the 6-month interval between sessions. That is, for both the tornado and nontraumatic event conversations, children who had higher levels of participation and provided more unique content at the first session also participated more and provided more unique content at the second session.

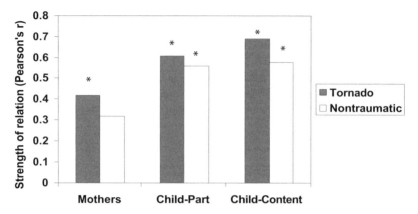

FIGURE 6.3. The strength of correlations (Pearson's *r*) from Session 1 to Session 2, within participant groups, for the tornado and nontraumatic-event conversations. The abbreviation "Child-Part" indicates children's participation in the conversations. Asterisks indicate that the correlation was statistically significant.

Relations Over Time: Children to Mothers

Consistent with prior research on conversations about nontraumatic events, there were few correlations between children's behavior at Session 1 and mothers' behavior at Session 2. As reflected in Figure 6.4, for the tornado, there were not significant cross-lag correlations between children's behavior 4 months after the storm and their mothers' behavior 6 months later (10 months after the storm). Thus, there was no evidence that children's earlier behavior in the context of conversations about the tornado influenced later maternal behavior. In the context of the non-traumatic events only, mothers had higher elaboration ratios at Session 2 with children who at the earlier session had provided more total unique content.

Relations Over Time: Mothers to Children

In contrast to the lack of prediction of maternal behavior in the tornado conversations by children's behavior 6 months earlier, there was evidence that the way mothers talked about the tornado at Session 1 influenced the way children talked about the storm at Session 2. As reflected in Figure 6.4, mothers who had higher ratios of elaborations to repetitions as they talked about the tornado had children who 6 months later were

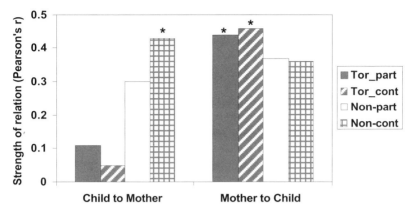

FIGURE 6.4. The strength of correlations (Pearson's *r*) from Session 1 to Session 2, across participant groups (i.e., child to mother and mother to child), for the tornado and nontraumatic-event conversations. The abbreviation "Tor_part" indicates children's participation in the tornado conversations. "Tor_cont" indicates the amount of content provided in the tornado conversations, "Non-part" indicates children's participation in the nontraumatic-event conversations, and "Non-cont" indicates the amount of content provided in the nontraumatic-event conversations. Asterisks indicate that the correlation was statistically significant.

more participatory in the conversations and also contributed more unique content. For the nontraumatic events, the correlations were not as strong and did not reach statistical significance.

To determine the relative contributions of concurrent and earlier maternal behavior, we conducted stepwise regression analyses with children's age in months, total maternal utterances at Session 1, and maternal elaboration ratios from both sessions as predictors of the child variables at Session 2. For the tornado event, maternal elaboration ratio at Session 1 emerged as the most significant predictor of the total number of propositions the children contributed at Session 2, accounting for 35% of the variance. Children's age brought the total variance accounted for to 47%. Maternal elaboration ratio at Session 1 also contributed unique variance to the total amount of content the children provided at Session 2: it added 13% of variance above the 40% accounted for by age. For the nontraumatic events, the largest predictor of the total number of propositions the children provided was age, which accounted for 31% of the variance. Maternal elaboration ratio at Session 1 contributed an additional 11% of variance. Maternal elaboration ratio at Session 1 did not add to prediction of the amount of unique content the children provided about the nontraumatic events at Session 2.

Summary and Interpretation of Major Findings

The first major question we addressed was whether there were differences in the amount of information that children ages 3 to 11 years provided about the tornado that devastated their town relative to the amount of information they provided about nontraumatic events that occurred before and after the tornado. Both 4 months and 10 months after the storm, conversations about the tornado were twice as long as conversations about the two nontraumatic events. The children themselves contributed more than twice the number of propositions to the tornado relative to the nontraumatic-event conversations (see Fig. 6.1). Whereas these patterns are consistent with the suggestion that children remembered more about the traumatic relative to the nontraumatic events, we caution against this interpretation. The conclusion is not warranted both because the verbal report and the event memory are not isomorphic, and because the basis for inclusion of the dyads in the study may have biased them to spend more time talking about the tornado than about the events before and after it. We suggest that the better question is the second that we addressed, namely whether the *type* of information the children provided about the traumatic and nontraumatic events differed.

There was clear evidence that the type of information included in conversations about traumatic and nontraumatic events differed. The differences were not apparent at the level of the details that the children provided about the events at either session, however. That is, per unit of conversation, the children provided the same amount of content about the tornado and the nontraumatic events. The only exception was among the oldest children, whose Session 2 contributions (but not their Session 1 contributions) were more infused with information about internal states (Bauer et al., 2005). Whereas, for the most part, children's contributions to the conversations about the tornado and the nontraumatic events did not differ in level of detail, there were differences between the event types in the breadth of the conversations. Tornado conversations were more likely to include contextual information, information about the causes and consequences of elements of the event, and temporal connections within and between elements of the event (Ackil et al., 2003). Thus the tornado conversations contained more of the features of a "good narrative" relative to the conversations about the nontraumatic events.

The third major question we addressed was whether there was evidence of differential socialization of contributions to conversations about the tornado relative to the nontraumatic events. The significant concurrent and cross-lagged correlations are schematically represented in Figure 6.5. At the first session (4 months after the storm) we observed concurrent correlations between maternal style (measured in terms of the ratio of elaborations to repetitions) and children's participation in both types of conversations. Correlations between maternal behavior and the amount of content that the children provided were strong enough to reach statistical significance only in the context of the tornado

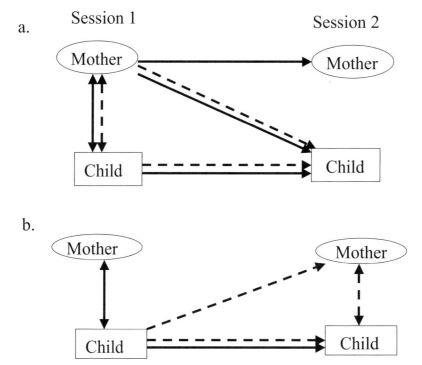

FIGURE 6.5. Schematic representation of statistically significant concurrent (i.e., within session) and cross-lagged (i.e., between sessions, over time) correlations within and between members of the dyads at Sessions 1 and 2. (*A*) is a representation of the relations for the tornado conversations, and (*B*) is a representation of the relations for the conversations about the nontraumatic events.

conversations (see also Fig. 6.2). That is, mothers who used a higher ratio of elaborations to repetitions had children who contributed more to the conversations. The ways mothers and their children worked together to co-construct the story of the tornado is nicely illustrated in this excerpt from a tornado conversation 4 months after the storm:

MOTHER: And then we went to Cub Foods and then what did we do?
CHILD: Go to St. Peter home. Tornado hit then.
MOTHER: Yeah.
CHILD: And I said there might be a tornado. And you said there is not going to be a tornado.
MOTHER: Did I say that? I don't remember that.
CHILD: [nods head yes]
MOTHER: And where did we go when we got in St. Peter?
CHILD: Jackie and [X] go in the basement and there was not very safe down there in the [X] so we went into the cedar closet.
MOTHER: Yep, and we had the radio.
CHILD: [nods head yes]
MOTHER: Yep, and do you remember when the radio went off?
CHILD: [nods head yes] 'Cause [X] was very very bad 'cause the line got cut.
MOTHER: And what did you think when you came upstairs?
CHILD: It looked different.
MOTHER: Yep.
CHILD: And it wasn't like it was before.
MOTHER: No, that is right. It looked really different.

Ten months after the storm, maternal behavior was no longer related to children's overall levels of participation in the conversations. The strength of the correlations between maternal elaboration ratios and the amount of content that the children provided about the tornado also had moderated substantially (and was no longer statistically significant). In contrast, the strength of the relation between maternal behavior when talking about the nontraumatic events and the amount of content the children provided about them had increased (see Figs. 6.2 and 6.5).

We suggest that the correlations over time within the participant groups are the key to understanding the finding of stronger concurrent relations between mothers and their children at the first, relative to the second, session (see Bauer et al., 2005, for further discussion). That is, it seems that the lower degree of concordance when talking about the tornado at Session 2 relative to Session 1 is due to changes in the ways that *mothers* talked about the events at the two sessions, in the face of consistency in the ways that the children talked about the events. For mothers, the degree of concordance between behavior at Session 1 and Session 2 was moderate (see Fig. 6.3) and significant only for the tornado conversations (see Fig. 6.5). In contrast, for children, the correlations were substantial and significant for both event types.

We also asked whether mothers' and children's contributions to the conversations were related over time (i.e., the 6-month interval between sessions). In the context of the conversations about the nontraumatic events, we found that the children's behavior at Session 1 was related to their mothers' behavior at Session 2 (see Fig. 6.5). This type of relation has been observed between mothers and their older children in the context of conversations about largely positive or affectively neutral events: significant cross-lagged relations have been observed between children and their mothers beginning when children are roughly 5 years of age (e.g., Reese et al., 1993). In contrast, in the context of the conversations about the tornado, there was very little evidence of relations between children's behavior at Session 1 and maternal behavior at Session 2. There was, however, evidence of relations between maternal behavior at the earlier session and children's behavior at the later session. Both in terms of general levels of participation and in terms of the amount of content that the children provided, the relations were stronger in the context of the tornado conversations than in the conversations about the nontraumatic events (see Fig. 6.4). It seems then that mothers' approaches to the tornado conversations at the first session were important determinants of the children's approaches 6 months later.

The results from the first session of the tornado study are a replication of the findings obtained by Sales et al. (2003). Specifically, Sales and her colleagues examined patterns of correlation between parental (mostly maternal) and child contributions to conversations about traumatic and nontraumatic events at a single point in time. They found that parents who adopted more elaborative (as opposed to repetitive) questioning styles had children who made more contributions to the conversations about both event types. Together, the two studies indicate that the findings of relations between maternal narrative style and children's contributions to conversations about past events extend beyond positive or neutral event contexts to discussions about traumatic events. Across the two studies, the findings can be said to obtain for children as young as 3 and as old as 11 years of age.

With the tornado study, we also extended the existing literature by testing relations over time as well as concurrent relations. This extension is significant because the strongest test of a socialization model of autobiographical narrative development comes not from observation of relations between maternal and child behavior at a single point in time but from relations over time. In the present research, we observed such relations. Importantly, they were apparent both at the level of overall participation in conversations about past events and at the level of the amount of content that the children contributed to the discussions. This suggests that maternal style operates not only to engage children in conversations about the past but also to focus children's attention on the elements that make for a good story about the experience, including general orienting information, information about the activities in events and how they are connected, and, perhaps in particular, information about the emotional and other reactions of event participants.

In both Sales et al. (2003) and in the present study, in general, the magnitudes of the correlations between maternal conversational style variables and children's contributions were greater in the context of conversations about the traumatic relative to the more positive events. In the present research, this was true at Session 1 and for the cross-lagged relations between sessions; it was not the case at Session 2, however. Why might relations be stronger for negative or traumatic relative to more positive or neutral events? One possibility is that there is something about the nature of the representations of traumatic experiences that makes them especially "susceptible" to socialization influences. Perhaps it is the emotional trauma associated with the event representation that renders them "special" and thus particularly amenable to socialization by others. Two things argue against this suggestion, however. The first is that if stronger relations were a result of special features of representations of such events, then we would have expected to see stronger relations at both time points in the present research. As noted, relations at Session 2 were not especially strong.

The second argument against the notion that memory representations of traumatic experiences have special features that render them particularly good candidates for socialization is that stronger relations are seen not only for events that we recognize as highly stressful and traumatic (medical emergencies and a tornado) but also for less extreme negative experiences, such as occur in the course of everyday activities. In Burch, Austin, and Bauer (2004), we reported an analysis of relations between maternal and child contributions to conversations about positive experiences, such as family vacations and birthdays parties, and to conversations that featured everyday trials and tribulations, such as going on a picnic and being stung by a bee or going on a hike and falling on a hill. By virtually no definition would such experiences be considered "traumatic." Nevertheless, we found stronger relations between maternal style variables and 3-year-old children's participation in conversations about these mildly negative experiences relative to conversations about affectively positive or neutral events.

We suggest that it is not necessary to appeal to special features of memory representations of traumatic events for explanation of the stronger pattern of relations between maternal and child contributions in the context of their discussion. Instead, we suggest that the difference be attributed to the fact that negative experiences are—thankfully—relatively uncommon. As such, children do not have a familiar frame of reference within which to understand and interpret them. Consequently, parental "intervention" in the process of construction of representations of such experiences becomes all the more important. This suggestion is consistent with the patterns of differential relations that have been observed across event types. For instance, in Sales et al. (2003), parents focused more on the causes of events when talking with their children about medical emergencies relative to the nontraumatic events. In Burch et al. (2004), maternal behavior was related to the number of subjective interpretations and suggestions of causal understanding that the children expressed in the context of discussions of negative, but not positive or neutral, experiences. Finally, in the St. Peter tornado study, both concurrent Session 1 and cross-lagged correlations between maternal style and children's behavior were especially strong for the category of evaluations expressed in the context of conversations about the tornado (see Bauer et al., in press, for details). These findings are consistent with the suggestion that patterns of correlation between maternal and child behavior may be tighter for negative or traumatic experiences because it is with these unique events that children require the most assistance in understanding, interpretation, and evaluation (see Fivush & Baker-Ward, 2005, for a similar argument).

The one exception to the general pattern of stronger relations between maternal and child behavior in the context of the conversations about traumatic relative to positive or nontraumatic events is the finding in the present research of generally weaker correlations between the members of the dyads in these conversations at Session 2. Although the interpretation is speculative, we suggest that the explanation for this pattern may be found in the public nature of the traumatic event that the children and their mothers experienced. That is, the tornado—and the devastation wrought by it—was shared and experienced by the entire community. Thus, the event was talked about by mothers and their children, but also by everyone else in the town of St. Peter, Minnesota. Especially over time, both mothers and children would be expected to participate in a number of conversations about the event, with a variety of conversational partners. It is not unreasonable to expect that the strength of relations between any two conversational partners might weaken under the influence of additional conversational partners, each with her or his own unique perspective on the event. Indeed, the different perspective that might be gained by frequent discussions of the event with different individuals may help to account for the relative lack of consistency in mothers' approaches to the conversations at the two sessions. Although these are post hoc interpretations of the findings of the present research, the suggestions could be tested empirically in future research.

Speculation about the public nature of the tornado event and how it might have influenced the pattern of findings in the St. Peter study also suggests an important qualifier on the generalizability of the results of the research. It is possible that the findings—including the pattern of relations between maternal and child behavior—would be different for more private events, such as maltreating experiences. To the extent that such events are talked about at all, they likely are talked about with fewer conversational partners. The partners may or may not lend credence to the child's account, thereby allowing or disallowing the child to own the experience. In addition, partners may attempt to work with the child to reevaluate and reconsider the significance of the experience (see Fivush, 2004, for discussion). Each of these possibilities has implications for the ways in which events are incorporated into the child's autobiography. The public versus private nature of experiences thus should be taken into consideration before extending the conclusions of any particular study beyond their bounds.

The Conspicuous Absence of Developmental Trends

Notable for its absence in this chapter is discussion of developmental trends in the data. This is not because we failed to detect them. Consistent with previous research on mother–child recollections of nontraumatic events (e.g., Fivush, Haden, & Reese, 1996; Haden, 1998), there were several instances where dyads' conversations varied with the age of the child. For example, as discussed in Ackil et al. (2003), overall, conversations with older children included more varied types of information than conversations with younger children. Specifically, Session 1 conversations with older children were more likely than those with children from both the middle and younger groups to include references to time, causes and consequences, temporal connections, and mention of comments made by others. Importantly, these differences did not interact with the type of event being discussed. The only exception to the pattern of main effects of age, rather than interactions of age and event type, was that when talking about the tornado, the oldest children in the sample included more internal-states terms relative to the children in the other two age groups (Bauer et al., 2005). Additional research is necessary to determine whether this observation replicates in other samples. Overall, it seems that retrospective memory conversations with older children were more inclusive than conversations with children in the younger groups regardless of whether the events being discussed were traumatic or nontraumatic. These differences likely reflect the more advanced language skills and greater knowledge base of older children. Whether they may also reflect differences in older children's memory is unclear.

Conclusions

The St. Peter, Minnesota, tornado study provides a unique perspective on the question of whether reports of traumatic and nontraumatic events differ. We found that conversations about the tornado were longer than those about the nontraumatic events. Conversations about the tornado also had more breadth than those about the nontraumatic events. On the other hand, the level of detail provided about the traumatic and nontraumatic events did not differ. Moreover, similar patterns of relations between maternal verbal behavior and children's contributions were apparent for the tornado and the nontraumatic events. The patterns of relations were, however, stronger when the dyads were talking about the traumatic event relative to when they were talking about nontraumatic events. Stronger relations in the context of traumatic relative to nontraumatic events may result from mothers' attempts to offer children greater assistance in understanding, interpreting, and evaluating these unusual experiences. The research provides a novel approach to the enduring question of whether stressful and even traumatic events are differentially remembered relative to events that are more affectively neutral or positive.

Acknowledgments

Support for this research was provided by a grant from the National Institutes of Health (HD-28425) to Patricia J. Bauer and by a grant from Gustavus Adolphus College to Jennifer K. Ackil. We also thank Jennie Waters for assistance with data collection; members of the Cognition in the Transition laboratory group (University of Minnesota) and the Memory and Cognition research group (Gustavus Adolphus College) for assistance with transcription; and Stephanie Bangston, Jean Burr, Jennifer Rademacher, Emily Stark, and Kathryn Struthers for assistance with data coding. We are especially grateful to the mothers and children who participated in this research; their generosity at what was a difficult time in their lives was truly remarkable.

References

Ackil, J. K., Van Abbema, D. L., & Bauer, P. J. (2003). After the storm: Enduring differences in mother-child recollections of traumatic and nontraumatic events. *Journal of Experimental Child Psychology, 84,* 286–309.

Bahrick, L., Parker, J., Merritt, K., & Fivush, R. (1998). Children's memory for Hurricane Andrew. *Journal of Experimental Psychology: Applied, 4,* 308–331.

Bauer, P. J. (2007). *Remembering the times of our lives: Memory in infancy and beyond.* Mahwah, NJ: Lawrence Erlbaum Associates.

Bauer, P. J., & Burch, M. M. (2004). Developments in early memory: Multiple mediators of foundational processes. In J. Lucariello, J. A. Hudson, R. Fivush, & P. J. Bauer (Eds.), *Development of the mediated mind: Culture and cognitive development.*

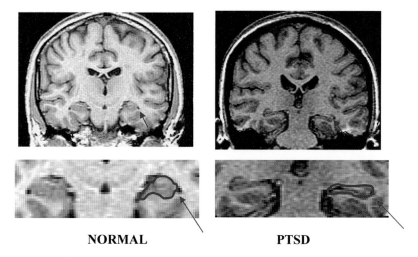

NORMAL   **PTSD**

FIGURE 1.3. Hippocampal volume reduction in PTSD on magnetic resonance imaging (MRI). There is smaller hippocampal volume in this patient with PTSD (right) compared to a control (left). *Source*: Bremner, J. D. Brain Imaging Handbook. Fig. 6.3, p. 101.

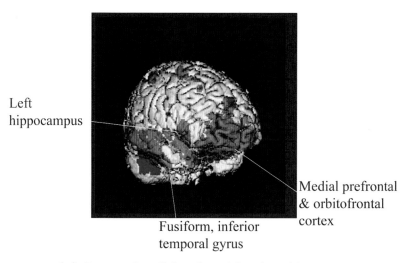

Left hippocampus

Fusiform, inferior temporal gyrus

Medial prefrontal & orbitofrontal cortex

FIGURE 1.4. Decreased medial prefrontal function with exposure to emotionally valenced words like "rape-mutilate." There was a decrease in medial prefrontal and hippocampal blood flow with exposure to trauma-related words in women with a history of early-childhood-abuse-related PTSD compared to controls. *Source:* Bremner et al., 2004.

Orbitofrontal cortex

Superior temporal gyrus

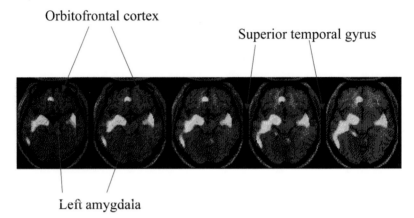

Left amygdala

FIGURE 1.5. Increased amygdala function during acquisition of conditioned fear responses in women with early childhood abuse and PTSD. Lighter areas represent bilateral amygdala activation. There was greater amygdala activation with acquisition of fear responses (pairing of conditioned stimulus and unconditioned stimulus) in women with PTSD compared to controls; z > 3.09, p < 0.001. *Source:* Bremner et al., 2005.

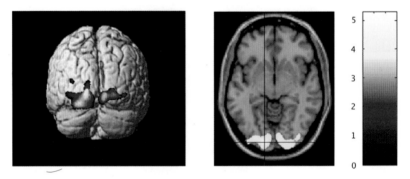

FIGURE 2.1. Differences in gray matter volume between abuse and control subjects. Significantly lower gray matter densities in abuse subjects were observed in the left visual cortex. Crosshairs placed at x = –14, y = –90, z = –1 (left lingual gyrus). Color scale (0–5) represents *t* values.

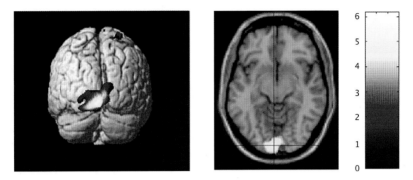

FIGURE 2.2. Correlations between brain volume and visual memory in the left primary visual cortex (LV-1). Crosshairs placed at x = –3, y = –90, z = –3 (left lingual gyrus). The color scale (0–6) indicates *t* values.

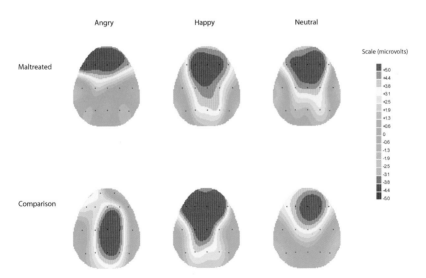

FIGURE 3.3. Topography of the P260 event-related potential (ERP) component across three emotion conditions for maltreated and nonmaltreated groups. Each map is constructed based on the latency of the P260 peak at Fz (midline frontal scalp region, where P260 was maximal) from the grand mean of that group and condition. Because of amplitude variations between groups and across emotions, the scales were adjusted for each condition separately in order to best illustrate the P260 component. *Source:* Cicchetti & Curtis, 2005.

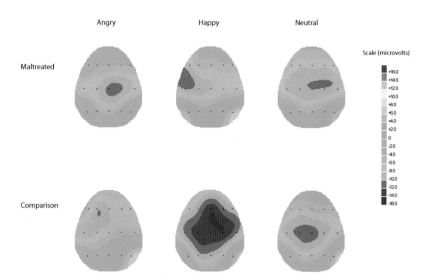

FIGURE 3.4. Topography of the Nc event-related potential (ERP) component across three emotion conditions for the maltreated and nonmaltreated groups. Each map is constructed based on the latency of the negative central (Nc) peak at Cz (midline central scalp region, where Nc was maximal) from the grand average of that group and condition. Because of amplitude variations between groups and across emotions, the scales were adjusted for each condition separately in order to best illustrate the Nc component. *Source:* Cicchetti & Curtis, 2005.

Essays in honor of Katherine Nelson (pp. 101–125). Mahwah, NJ: Lawrence Erlbaum Associates.

Bauer, P. J., Burch, M. M., Van Abbema, D. L., & Ackil, J. K. (In press). Talking about twisters: Relations between mothers' and children's contributions to conversations about a devastating tornado. *Journal of Cognition and Development.*

Bauer, P. J., Stark, E. N., Lukowski, A. F., Rademacher, J., Van Abbema, D. L., & Ackil, J. K. (2005). Working together to make sense of the past: Mothers' and children's use of internal states language in conversations about traumatic and non-traumatic events. *Journal of Cognition and Development, 6,* 463–488.

Bohanek, J., Van Abbema, D. L., Ackil, J. K., & Bauer, P. J. (In preparation). Parent-child narratives about a traumatic event: Implications for well-being.

Boland, A. M., Haden, C. A., & Ornstein, P. A. (2003). Boosting children's memory by training mothers in the use of an elaborative conversational style as an event unfolds. *Journal of Cognition and Development, 4,* 39–65.

Brown, D. A., Salmon, K., Pipe, M.-E., Rutter, M., Craw, S., & Taylor, B. (1999). Children's recall of medical experiences: The impact of stress. *Child Abuse and Neglect, 23,* 209–216.

Brown, R., & Kulik, J. (1977). Flashbulb memories. *Cognition, 5,* 73–99.

Burch, M. M., Austin, J., & Bauer, P. J. (2004). Understanding the emotional past: Relations between parent and child contributions in emotionally negative and neutral events. *Journal of Experimental Child Psychology, 89,* 276–297.

Christianson, S.-A. (1992). Emotional stress and eyewitness memory: A critical review. *Psychological Bulletin, 112,* 284–309.

Easterbrook, J. A. (1959). The effect of emotion on cue utilization and the organization of behavior. *Psychological Review, 66,* 183–201.

Engel, S. (1986). *Learning to reminisce: A developmental study of how young children talk about the past.* Unpublished doctoral dissertation, City University of New York Graduate Center.

Farrant, K., & Reese, E. (2000). Maternal style and children's participation in reminiscing: Stepping stones in children's autobiographical memory development. *Journal of Cognition and Development, 1,* 193–225.

Fivush, R. (1991). The social construction of personal narratives. *Merrill-Palmer Quarterly, 37,* 59–82.

Fivush, R. (1998). Gendered narratives: Elaboration, structure, and emotion in parent-child reminiscing across the preschool years. In C. P. Thompson, D. J. Herrmann, D. Bruce, J. D. Read, D. G. Payne, & M. P. Toglia (Eds.), *Autobiographical memory: Theoretical and applied perspectives* (pp. 79–103). Mahwah, NJ: Erlbaum.

Fivush, R. (2002). Scripts, schemas, and memory of trauma. In N. L. Stein, P. J. Bauer, & M. Rabinowitz (Eds.), *Representation, memory, and development: Essays in honor of Jean Mandler* (pp. 53–74). Mahwah, NJ: Erlbaum.

Fivush, R. (2004). Voice and silence: A feminist model of autobiographical memory. In J. M. Lucariello, J. A. Hudson, R. Fivush, & P. J. Bauer (Eds.), *The development of the mediated mind: Sociocultural context and cognitive development* (pp. 79–99). Mahwah, NJ: Erlbaum.

Fivush, R., & Baker-Ward, L. (2005). The search for meaning: Developmental perspectives on internal state language in autobiographical memory. *Journal of Cognition and Development, 6,* 455–462.

Fivush, R., & Fromhoff, F. (1988). Style and structure in mother–child conversations about the past. *Discourse Processes, 11,* 337–355.

Fivush, R., Haden, C. A., & Reese, E. (1996). Remembering, recounting, and reminiscing: The development of autobiographical memory in social context. In D. C. Rubin (Ed.), *Remembering our past: Studies in autobiographical memory* (pp. 341–359). New York: Cambridge University Press.

Fivush, R., Hazzard, A., Sales, J. M., Sarfati, D., & Brown, T. (2003). Creating coherence out of chaos? Children's narratives of emotionally positive and negative events. *Applied Cognitive Psychology, 17,* 1–19.

Fivush, R., Sales, J. M., Goldberg, A., Bahrick, L., & Parker, J. F. (2004). Weathering the storm: Children's long-term recall of Hurricane Andrew. *Memory, 12,* 104–118.

Goodman, G. S., Hirschman, J. E., Hepps, D., & Rudy, L. (1991). Children's memory for stressful events. *Merrill-Palmer Quarterly, 37,* 109–158.

Goodman, G. S., & Quas, J. A. (1997). Trauma and memory: Individual differences in children's recounting of a stressful experience. In N. L. Stein, P. A. Ornstein, B. Tversky, & C. Brainerd (Eds.), *Memory for everyday and emotional events* (pp. 267–294). Hillsdale, NJ: Erlbaum.

Goodman, G. S., Quas, J. A., Batterman-Faunce, J. M., Riddlesberger, M., & Kuhn, J. (1997). Children's reactions to and memory for a stressful event: Influences of age, anatomical dolls, knowledge, and parental attachment. *Applied Developmental Science, 1,* 54–75.

Haden, C. A. (1998). Reminiscing with different children: Relating maternal stylistic consistency and sibling similarity in talk about the past. *Developmental Psychology, 34,* 99–114.

Haden, C. A., Ornstein, P. A., Eckerman, C. O., & Didow, S. M. (2001). Mother–child conversational interactions as events unfold: Linkages to subsequent remembering. *Child Development, 72,* 1016–1031.

Howe, M. L., Courage, M. L., & Peterson, C. (1994). How can I remember when "I" wasn't there: Long-term retention of traumatic experiences and emergence of the cognitive self. *Consciousness and Cognition, 3,* 327–355.

Hudson, J. A. (1990). The emergence of autobiographical memory in mother–child conversation. In R. Fivush & J. A. Hudson (Eds.), *Knowing and remembering in young children* (pp. 166–196). Cambridge, MA: Cambridge University Press.

Lewis, K. D. (1999). Maternal style in reminiscing: Relations to child individual differences. *Cognitive Development, 14,* 381–399.

McCabe, A., & Peterson, C. (1991). Getting the story: A longitudinal study of parental styles in eliciting narratives and developing narrative skill. In A. McCabe & C. Peterson (Eds.), *Developing narrative structure* (pp. 217–253). Hillsdale, NJ: Erlbaum.

Murray, R. (1998, April 11). Extent of destruction is realized. *The Mankato Free Press,* p. 6S.

Nelson, K. (1993). The psychological and social origins of autobiographical memory. *Psychological Science, 4,* 7–14.

Nelson, K., & Fivush, R. (2000). Socialization of memory. In E. Tulving & F. I. M. Craik (Eds.), *The Oxford handbook of memory* (pp. 283–295). New York: Oxford University Press.

Nelson, K., & Fivush, R. (2004). The emergence of autobiographical memory: A social cultural developmental theory. *Psychological Review, 111,* 486–511.

Ornstein, P. A. (1995). Children's long-term retention of salient personal experiences. *Journal of Traumatic Stress, 8,* 581–605.

Parker, J. F., Bahrick, L., Lundy, B., Fivush, R., & Levitt, M. (1998). Effects of stress on children's memory for a natural disaster. In C. P. Thompson, D. J. Herrmann, J. D. Read, D. Bruce, D. G. Payne, & M. P. Toglia (Eds.), *Eyewitness memory: Theoretical and applied perspectives* (pp. 31–54). Mahwah, NJ: Lawrence Erlbaum Associates.

Peterson, C., & Bell, M. (1996). Children's memory for traumatic injury. *Child Development, 67,* 3045–3070.

Peterson, C., & McCabe, A. (1994). A social interactionist account of developing decontextualized narrative skill. *Developmental Psychology, 30,* 937–948.

Peterson, C., & Whalen, N. (2001). Five years later: Children's memory for medical emergencies. *Applied Cognitive Psychology, 15,* 7–24.

Quas, J. A., Goodman, G. S., Bidrose, S., Pipe, M.-E., Craw, S., & Ablin, D. S. (1999). Emotion and memory: Children's long-term remembering, forgetting, and suggestibility. *Journal of Experimental Child Psychology, 72,* 235–270.

Reese, E., Haden, C. A., & Fivush, R. (1993). Mother-child conversations about the past: Relationships of style and memory over time. *Cognitive Development, 8,* 403–430.

Sales, J. M., Fivush, R., & Peterson, C. (2003). Parental reminiscing about positive and negative events. *Journal of Cognition and Development, 4,* 185–209.

Tessler, M., & Nelson, K. (1994). Making memories: The influence of joint encoding on later recall by young children. *Consciousness and Cognition, 3,* 307–326.

Vandermaas, M. O., Hess, T. M., & Baker-Ward, L. (1993). Does anxiety affect children's reports of memory for a stressful event? *Applied Cognitive Psychology, 7,* 109–127.

Welch-Ross, M. (2001). Personalizing the temporally extended self: Evaluative self-awareness and the development of autobiographical memory. In C. Moore & K. Lemmon (Eds.), *The self in time: Developmental perspectives* (pp. 97–120). Mahwah, NJ: Erlbaum.

Winograd, E., & Neisser, U. (1992). *Affect and accuracy in recall.* New York: Cambridge University Press.

Yerkes, R. M., & Dodson, J. D. (1908). The relation of strength of stimulation to rapidity of habit formation. *Journal of Comparative Neurology of Psychology, 18,* 459–482.

7

Children's Memory
for Stressful Events

Exploring the Role of Discrete Emotions

ELIZABETH L. DAVIS, JODI A. QUAS,
AND LINDA J. LEVINE

Scientists and practitioners have long been interested in understanding how children remember emotionally significant, stressful personal experiences. This interest has been motivated by theoretical questions concerning the links between emotion and cognition in development and the nature of children's emerging event memories. Interest also has been motivated by applied questions concerning children's memory for traumatic experiences, the development of trauma-related disorders, and children's eyewitness capabilities (see Chapter 8). Indeed, numerous studies have examined children's memory for a range of stressful events (for reviews see Alexander, Quas, & Goodman, 2002; Fivush & Sales, 2004). Despite this extensive body of literature, few studies have focused on the nature of children's emotional experience during a to-be-remembered event. Instead, studies have largely considered how global indices of distress or arousal relate to children's memory. Yet there are several reasons why the specific emotions that arise during an event may affect the extent and content of children's later memory. In the present chapter, we outline these reasons and, in doing so, highlight the need for a new line of research that directly examines the relations between discrete emotions and children's memory for personal experiences.

Our chapter is organized as follows: First, we briefly review studies that have investigated children's memory for emotional, primarily stressful, events. Because several comprehensive reviews of this literature already exist (see Chapter 4; Fivush, 1998; Fivush & Sales, 2004; Howe, 1997; Howe, Cicchetti, & Toth, 2006; Howe, Toth, & Cicchetti, 2006; Ornstein, Manning, & Pelphrey, 1999; von Baeyer, Marche, Rocha, & Salmon, 2004), we focus here on the types of emotional events that have been studied and on the range of emotions children may have experienced during these events. Second, we discuss theoretical perspectives and empirical findings concerning the differing effects of discrete emotions on memory. To date, this research has primarily concerned adults' processing of and memory for emotional information. Third, we describe similarities and differences between children's and adults' appraisals of stressful events. Fourth and finally, we present testable hypotheses concerning how children's discrete emotional reactions to stressful events would likely affect their memories, and we review findings from the few studies that have considered how discrete emotions affect children's memory. We conclude by offering recommendations for pursuing this new, exciting line of inquiry.

Of note, most research concerning emotion and memory in children has investigated how well they remember distressing experiences. As such, our chapter focuses primarily on negative emotions, such as fear, anger, and sadness, each of which may be experienced to various degrees during a stressful event. In the future, it will be necessary to expand this area of research to examine how different positive as well as negative emotions affect children's memory for personal experiences. Also, in our review, we address how children's emotions at the time of encoding relate to their later memory. Of course, emotional experiences are not static states, and individuals' appraisals of situations, emotional responses, and adaptation to emotions continually change, often over extended periods following an event's occurrence (for a review, see Ellsworth & Scherer, 2003). These changing appraisals can affect memory (Baker-Ward, Eaton, & Banks, 2005; Levine, Prohaska, Burgess, Rice, & Laulhere, 2001) and certainly should be considered in future research. Finally, a separate body of research concerning mood-congruency effects on memory also exists. Because this research has not focused on the effects of discrete emotions on the content of children's memory, we will not discuss this topic in depth here. Instead, our review serves as a critical starting point from which we hope a larger body of research concerning discrete emotions and memory across development will emerge.

Children's Memory for Stressful Events

Studies concerning children's memory for stressful events can be heuristically divided into two general categories based on the type of event being remembered. One set of studies has focused on children's memory for naturally occurring stressful events (see Chapter 6), and the other has concerned children's memory for mildly arousing laboratory-based experiences. Across both types of studies, however, the central question has been the same: does stress help or hurt children's memory? Unfortunately, findings have not revealed a consistent pattern. Several studies have reported positive associations between stress and memory, both for naturally occurring stressors and arousing laboratory events (e.g., Alexander, Goodman, Schaaf, et al., 2002; Goodman, Hirschman, Hepps, & Rudy, 1991; Quas, Carrick, Alkon, Goldstein, & Boyce, 2006), but others have reported either no direct associations (e.g., Vaandermaas, Hess, & Baker-Ward, 1993) or negative associations (e.g., Bugental, Blue, Cortez, Fleck, & Rodriguez, 1992; Merritt, Ornstein, & Spicker, 1994; Quas, Bauer, & Boyce, 2004). What may be more useful than a simple description of the varying patterns of findings is an overview of the different types of to-be-remembered events that have been studied and a description of the range of possible emotions children may have experienced during these events. Insofar as children's emotional experiences vary, so may the content of their memories.

Naturalistic studies have capitalized on stressful events outside of the experimenters' control to which children have been exposed (e.g., Goodman, Quas, Batterman-Faunce, Riddlesberger, & Kuhn, 1997; Peterson, 1999). For instance, Fivush and colleagues assessed 3- to 4-year-old children's memory for Hurricane Andrew, a devastating hurricane that hit the Florida coast in the early 1990s (Fivush, Hazzard, Sales, Sarfati, & Brown, 2003; Fivush, Sales, Goldberg, Bahrick, & Parker, 2004). Children's proximity to the hurricane was related to the amount of damage to families' homes and to the amount of family displacement and disruption. Therefore, proximity was used as an index of children's stress during the hurricane to define high-, moderate-, and low-stress exposure groups. When children's memory was tested a few months after the hurricane, children in the moderate-stress group reported the most information, whereas children in the high- and low-stress groups reported less. When children's memory was examined 6 years afterward, children in the high-stress group again provided less information than children in the moderate-stress group, but only in free recall. With additional follow-up prompts, the high-stress children provided as much information as did the other children. Thus, even children in the high-stress group remembered the event after the long delay, but they were either unwilling or unable to describe their memories in detail without considerable prompting by the interviewer.

Other researchers have studied children's memory for medical experiences, including emergency room visits (Peterson, 1999; Peterson & Parsons, 2005; Peterson & Whalen, 2001) and prescheduled procedures (Alexander, Goodman, et al., 2002; Chen, Wang, Chen, & Liu, 2002; Merritt et al., 1994; Quas et al., 1999). Many of these events are distressing and painful, and some are highly standardized, providing researchers with objective information about what actually occurred to which children's reports can be compared for accuracy (Goodman, Quas, Batterman-Faunce, Riddlesberger, & Kuhn, 1994; Salmon, Price, & Pereira, 2002). Several teams of researchers, for instance, have studied children's memory for a scheduled radiological procedure involving urethral catheterization. The procedure, which is designed to identify a potentially serious kidney problem, requires that children be awake while their bladder is filled with a contrast medium. Afterward, children void while X-rays are taken. Children's memory for the procedure has been assessed immediately afterward (Merritt et al., 1994), several weeks later (Goodman et al., 1997; Merritt et al., 1994), and several years later (Quas et al., 1999). Merritt et al. (1994) found that medical staffs' ratings of child distress were negatively related to children's memory. Similarly, Quas et al. (1999) found that being more upset during the procedure, according to parental report, was associated with decreases in the amount of information children provided in free recall. However, Quas et al. (1999) also found that being more upset before the procedure was associated with increases in the number of correct responses to closed-ended, misleading questions. Thus, although the same stressful to-be-remembered event was examined across studies, the associations between child distress and memory varied, precluding clear patterns from being identified regarding the precise relations between stress and memory.

In contrast to the highly charged emotional events studied in naturalistic contexts, to-be-remembered events studied in laboratory contexts are typically mildly distressing events that children have either experienced or witnessed, such as brief fire-alarm incidents or negatively valenced video clips or pictures (Bugental et al., 1992; Quas et al., 2006). Because laboratory events can be controlled, objective records are nearly always available, and children can be randomly assigned to high- and low-stress conditions, allowing researchers to draw causal conclusions about the effects of mild distress or arousal on children's memory— conclusions not possible with naturalistic, correlational studies. Using this approach, Bugental et al. (1992) found that increases in 5-year-olds' heart rate while watching a video clip of a child visiting the doctor were associated with poorer memory (no relations between heart rate and memory were observed in older children, however). Yet, the opposite pattern was reported by Quas and Lench (2007). Arousal while watching a fear-eliciting video clip of four boys on a bridge as a train approaches was positively related to children's later memory. Thus, even in laboratory studies, findings continue to be mixed. Moreover, the extent to which findings from laboratory studies generalize to naturalistic contexts remains unknown.

As this brief review indicates, findings concerning the relations between stress and memory vary considerably. Stress often appears to inhibit children's performance when asked to recall stressful events, but this poor performance may be due to an unwillingness to talk about the events rather than poor memory per se. When direct questions are asked, stress often appears to enhance performance, although only in some studies. Of greater relevance to the present review, and another potentially important source of variation in studies' results, is the range of types of to-be-remembered events that have been investigated. Although all of the events have been labeled as stressful or arousing, children likely experienced one of several different emotions. For instance, during a hurricane, if children and their families are prepared and safe, children may not experience fear or distress. Instead, children may feel sad, but only later, upon returning to find devastation and significant changes to their lives (Fivush et al., 2004; Sales, Fivush, Parker, & Bahrick, 2002). During a medical procedure, some children may feel angry with the medical staff or their parents for inflicting pain. Others may feel frightened because they do not know what is happening or how to protect themselves. Still other children may be confused regarding why something designed to help them is painful. These emotions involve different appraisals and motivations and have different behavioral and physiological correlates. Further, children's ability to cope with these emotions changes over the course of development. Each of these factors has implications for the content, and possibly the accuracy, of children's later memory (Goodman et al., 1991).

Appraisals, Discrete Emotions, and Memory in Adults

Although little research has examined the potentially differing effects of discrete emotions on children's memories, these effects have begun to receive attention in theory and research on adults. Therefore, we now turn to a review of the adult literature to set the stage for generating hypotheses about how discrete emotions may affect children's memory for stressful events. In adults, studies have examined the links between emotion and memory, both when emotions are construed as general arousal and when discrete emotions are considered. A key finding has been that arousal enhances memory for central or emotionally salient information at the expense of peripheral details (e.g., Adolphs, Denburg, & Tranel, 2001; Berntsen, 2002; Burke, Heuer, & Reisberg, 1992; Cahill, Gorski, & Le, 2003; Safer, Christianson, Autry, & Osterlund, 1998; for a review see Reisberg & Heuer, 2004). For instance, in one early study, Christianson and Loftus (1987) presented participants with one of two matched slide sequences depicting either an emotional event (a boy hit by a car) or a neutral event (a boy walking beside a car). All participants wrote down the central feature of each slide. Participants who viewed the emotional slide sequence were better able to recall the central features than participants who viewed the neutral sequence, but they were less able to recognize details that allowed them to pinpoint the particular slides they had seen. Based on appraisal theories of emotion, Levine and Pizarro (2004) argued that the type of information an individual considers to be central should vary depending on his or her discrete emotional state, and hence the content of the individual's memory should vary. Thus, we next review the different appraisal processes associated with discrete emotions followed by empirical findings concerning the effects of discrete emotions on memory in adults.

Discrete Emotions and Appraisal Processes

According to appraisal theories, emotions such as happiness, fear, anger, and sadness are elicited by different interpretations of events and are associated with different physiological responses, motivational states, and problem-solving strategies. These characteristics of emotional experiences should influence the type of information people deem to be important or central and, therefore, the type of information they attend to and remember. Thus discrete emotions may serve as a powerful organizing force, not just for behavior but for perception and memory as well (Dalgleish, 2004; Frijda, 1986; Lerner & Keltner, 2000; Oatley & Johnson-Laird, 1987; Roseman, Wiest, & Swartz, 1994; Stein & Levine, 1987).

In general, appraisal theories hold that people continually evaluate the relevance of incoming information for their goals, with ongoing events being appraised along several dimensions that designate the events' relevance to those goals. Emotions are experienced when people perceive that a goal has been attained or obstructed and it becomes necessary for them to revise prior beliefs and construct new plans. The specific emotion experienced depends on the result of this appraisal process. Thus, when a potentially stressful event occurs, the extent to which people experience fear versus anger versus sadness, or some combination thereof, depends not only on objective features of the event but also on whether people feel personally threatened, whether the outcome is certain or uncertain, and whether they believe they have the resources available to overcome obstacles to their goals (e.g., Ellsworth & Scherer, 2003; Frijda, 1986; Levine, 1995, 1996; Roseman, Antoniou, & Jose, 1996; Smith & Lazarus, 1993; Stein & Levine, 1989; Stein, Trabasso, & Liwag, 2000; Weiner, 1985).

Moreover, once evoked, emotions are thought to direct subsequent cognitions, behaviors, and responses in a manner that is functional, or in other words, relevant for responding to the type of situation that evokes the emotion (Arnold, 1960; Lazarus, 1991; Lerner & Gonzalez, 2005; Lerner & Keltner, 2001; Oatley & Johnson-Laird, 1987; Scherer, 1998; Shaver, Schwartz, Kirson, & O'Connor, 1987; Stein & Levine, 1987). Thus appraisals, motivations, behaviors, and even physiological responses would be expected to vary depending on the discrete emotion elicited.

For example, happiness is elicited when people appraise events as conducive to the attainment of their goals. Happiness has been found to exert a variety of cognitive and behavioral effects that Fredrickson (1998) has characterized as "broaden-and-build" tendencies. That is, happiness promotes expansive thoughts and actions, such as affiliation, play, exploration, creative thinking, and the use of broad sources of information when making decisions.

Fear, in contrast, is elicited by the perception that goals are at risk and that one lacks control over the situation (e.g., Lerner & Gonzalez, 2005; Lerner & Keltner, 2001). Once elicited, fear motivates thoughts and behaviors directed toward avoiding the threat. Individuals must evaluate the situational information to assess the immediacy and severity of the threat, and identify methods of escaping or reducing the threat (e.g., whether "fight" or "flight" is the appropriate response or whether the assistance of another is needed). Consistent with this motivation, fear appraisals are often associated with increased physiological responses (e.g., Hamm, Cuthbert, Globisch, & Vaitl, 1997; Lerner, Gonzalez, Dahl, Hariri, & Taylor, 2005; Levenson, 1994, 1999). Thus, for example, fear-induced activation of the sympathetic nervous system leads to enhanced cardiovascular tone, increased blood flow to the skeletal muscles, and elevated blood glucose levels, all of which prepare an individual for the immediate action that may be necessary to avoid a threat (e.g., Christie & Friedman, 2004; Gray, 1994). To determine what action is necessary, people who are frightened would be expected to selectively attend to, encode, and retrieve information concerning the perceived threat and means of avoiding it.

Anger is elicited when people perceive that a goal is obstructed but also believe that they may be capable of overcoming that obstruction (Lerner & Tiedens, 2006; Levine, 1996). In contrast to fear, anger is not consistently associated with increased physiological arousal. For instance, although some studies show a positive association between anger and arousal (e.g., increased heart rate; Labouvie-Vief, Lumley, Jain, & Heinz, 2003), others find no significant associations (e.g., Porter, Stone, & Schwartz, 1999), or even negative associations (e.g., Carroll, Smith, Sheffield, Shipley, & Marmot, 1997; Smith & Houston, 1987). In addition, some researchers have found lower levels of cortisol and cardiovascular responses when anger is induced than when fear is induced (Lerner et al., 2005). The behavioral tendencies associated with anger are more clear-cut. Unlike fear, which is regarded as an avoidance emotion, anger is viewed as an approach emotion, because it motivates an individual to actively engage in a situation to eliminate perceived obstacles and reinstate goals (e.g., Gray, 1990). Thus angry people would be expected to selectively encode and retrieve information concerning goals and the agents or causes responsible for obstructing the goals. This focus on goals and the causes of failure serves an important function. People are most likely to construct effective plans to reinstate goals if they understand who or what caused the situation that they are trying to change.

A third negative emotion, sadness, is elicited when people appraise goal failure as irrevocable. When a goal cannot be reinstated, its failure affects all of the goals, beliefs, and plans associated with it. Further, with irrevocable loss, no action is necessary, leading to Gray's (1990, 1994) designation of sadness as an inhibition emotion or one that leads to a reduced likelihood of behavior. As such, sadness is not typically associated with increased physiological activation (Mauss, Levenson, McCarter, Wilhelm, & Gross, 2005), and a few studies have reported reduced autonomic, somatic, and electrodermal activity following the induction of sadness (e.g., Deichert, Flack, & Craig, 2005; Etzel, Johnsen, Dickerson, Tranel, & Adolphs, 2006). With regard to attention, for the sad person, information concerning the risks and potential causes of failure (central information for the fearful or angry person, respectively) would be irrelevant or peripheral, whereas understanding the outcomes and consequences of failure would be centrally important. Of note, although sadness may ultimately be followed by plans to substitute more attainable goals, in the midst of the emotional episode, the withdrawal and passivity commonly associated with sadness may reflect the difficult mental work of coming to terms with the need to revise prior goals and expectations (Levine, 1996). Thus, to effectively understand the outcomes associated with failed goals when feeling sad, people would be expected to attend to and focus on the losses that result from the goal failure.

Of course, fear, anger, and sadness are not the only emotions that a person may experience during a potentially stressful event. Yet, as the brief description above suggests, even across these three emotions that share a common negative valence, individuals' appraisals and motivations vary substantially. This variability likely affects the aspects of events to which individuals attend and, accordingly, what they remember about those events afterward. That is, in the service of responding to the circumstances that lead to their elicitation, discrete emotions should cause people to focus on and to search for information relevant to their current motivations. Thus the types of information that are of central importance, as opposed to peripheral details, should differ depending upon a person's specific emotional state (Lench & Levine, 2005; Levine & Bluck, 2004; Levine & Burgess, 1997; Levine & Pizarro, 2004; Levine, Pizarro, & Laney, 2006). Moreover, because the activation of one goal can inhibit the accessibility of alternative goals (Shah, Friedman, & Kruglanski, 2002), information peripheral to the motivational state of the discrete emotion being experienced may become less accessible.

Discrete Emotions and Memory

A growing body of research supports the view that discrete emotions have distinct effects on memory. Research on both adults and children suggests, for instance, that positive memories encompass a broad range of information whereas negative memories focus on specific information relevant to preventing (fear), reversing (anger), or adjusting to (sadness) goal failure. As one example, Berntsen (2002) had independent judges code the content of adults' most negative and positive autobiographical memories for central and peripheral information. Negative memories focused primarily on central information, as would be predicted by arousal-based models, but positive memories did not. Instead, positive memories tended to include a wide range of information. Other studies have shown that negative memories are less error-prone than positive memories. For example, Kensinger and Schacter (2006) had Boston Red Sox and New York Yankees fans recall the Sox's win in the American League playoff in October 2004 after 6 days and again approximately 6 months later. Although the fans of the winning Red Sox were more confident of their memories, the Yankees fans recalled details related to the game more accurately than did Red Sox fans (also see Levine & Bluck, 2004).

Turning to discrete negative emotional states and memory, several investigators have found that fearful people display enhanced memory for threat-related information and poorer memory for threat-irrelevant details. For example, Wessel and Merckelbach (1998) investigated the effects of fear on memory in a sample of spider-phobics. Phobic and low-fear control participants were shown a bulletin board to which central (pictures of spiders) and peripheral (pictures of babies and pens) stimuli were attached. Not only did the spider-phobics display an increase in physiological markers of fear when viewing the display, but when asked to recall the display, spider-phobics showed enhanced memory for the central, threatening information (i.e., the spider pictures) and impaired memory for peripheral, nonthreatening information (i.e., baby and pen pictures). A positive association between fear and memory for threatening stimuli also has been noted by investigators assessing the accuracy and completeness of eyewitness testimony. For instance, "weapon focus" refers to witnesses' tendency to focus on and remember the weapon used to commit a crime, often at the expense of memory for other, possibly more peripheral, information (e.g., Kramer, Buckhout, & Eugenio, 1990; Loftus, Loftus, & Messo, 1987; Steblay, 1992).

In another line of work, evidence indicates that chronically fearful individuals evince attentional and memory biases consistent with this discrete emotional state. Clinically anxious people have been found to exhibit hypersensitivity to threat-related information. Mathews and Klug (1993), for instance, used an emotional Stroop paradigm to assess color-naming latencies (a sign of greater attention) for positive and negative threat-related words, for positive and negative words unrelated to threat, and for neutral words. Participants included patients with a variety of anxiety disorders and controls. Anxious patients took longer to name the colors of both positive and negative threat-related words (but not positive or negative words unrelated to threat) than to name the colors of neutral words. Selective retrieval of threatening information also has been found (though less consistently) in studies using implicit memory measures (for reviews see MacLeod & Mathews, 2004; Mineka, Rafaeli, & Yovel, 2003). For example, Mathews, Richards, and Eysenck (1989) had clinically anxious people and controls listen to and write down homophones (words that sound alike but have different meanings and spellings). One of the homophones had a threatening meaning, and the other had a neutral meaning (e.g., *die* and *dye*). Anxious participants were more likely than controls to write down the threatening meaning upon hearing the word, suggesting that threatening information may be more accessible in memory for these people.

In contrast, people in a sad or depressed mood asked to recall autobiographical events tend to focus not on sources of threat but on negative outcomes such as personal losses and defeats. For example, Lyubomirsky, Caldwell, and Nolen-Hoeksema (1998) found that moderately sad or depressed people recalled more negative autobiographical events associated with loss (e.g., failing a test, losing a girlfriend, their parents' divorce) than did nondepressed people. Moreover, although depression and post-traumatic stress disorder (PTSD) are both characterized by the presence of intrusive memories, the content of the intrusive information for these two disorders differs. Consistent with the differing motivations associated with sadness and fear, depression is characterized by rumination on past negative outcomes and their consequences for the self, whereas PTSD is characterized by intrusive memories related to past threats to safety (e.g., Lyubomirsky et al., 1998; Reynolds & Brewin, 1999; Watkins & Teasdale, 2001).

Levine and Burgess (1997) conducted a study to test more directly the predictions derived from appraisal theories concerning the effects of discrete emotions on memory. The researchers contrasted discrete emotions in the same study to see if each emotion would lead to enhanced memory for particular kinds of information. Emotions were evoked in undergraduates by randomly assigning grades of A or D on a surprise quiz. Immediately afterward, students participated in what they believed to be an unrelated study during which they heard and later recalled a narrative. Finally, they rated how happy, angry, and sad they had felt when they received their quiz grade. Participants who received the A (and obviously reported being happy) demonstrated enhanced memory for the narrative as a whole. In contrast, participants who reported feeling primarily sad or primarily angry (all of whom received the D) tended to recall specific types of information. As predicted, those who reported feeling sad about their grade recalled significantly more information concerning event outcomes in the narrative than did participants who reported feeling angry about their grade. The latter individuals showed a nonsignificant tendency to recall more information about the protagonist's goals than did sad participants. Finally, a significant positive correlation was found between the intensity of anger reported and the amount of information that participants recalled about the goals of the lead character in the narrative.

Summary

Further research is clearly needed to identify the mechanisms underlying the effects of discrete emotions on memory, but the findings reported above support the view that discrete emotions evoke "appraisal tendencies" (Lerner & Keltner, 2000) as well as "action tendencies" (Frijda, 1986) that influence the processing, encoding, and retrieval of information in ways that are consistent with the differing functions of discrete emotions. Overall, negative emotions promote a focus on central information in the service of responding to potential goal failure. However, as argued by Levine and Pizarro (2004), the types of information deemed central appear to vary depending on the discrete negative emotion elicited. People tend to focus on and remember information about losses when sad, risks when fearful, and goal frustration and blame when angry. Next, we turn to the question of whether similar patterns emerge in children.

Appraisals, Discrete Emotions, and Memory in Children

To draw inferences from findings in the adult literature and make predictions about how discrete emotions affect children's memory, it is first necessary to establish that children experience the same range of discrete emotions as do adults and that children and adults are capable of similar appraisals in response to the same situations. It is also important, however, to acknowledge limitations in children's processing capacity, coping, and attentional resources. These limitations may have implications for differences between children and adults in their attention to, and memory for, stressful experiences.

Discrete Emotions, Appraisal Processes, and Emotion Regulation

Research on the development of emotional experience and understanding in childhood suggests considerable similarity between children's and adults' appraisals of events, although some key differences are also noteworthy. Regarding appraisal similarity, research shows continuity across development in the basic types of appraisals that elicit discrete emotions. For instance, in the first year of life, infants display facial expressions of happiness in response to success at instrumental attempts to attain a goal, anger when goals are obstructed, fear when danger is threatened (e.g., fear of heights), and sadness at losses (Alessandri, Sullivan, & Lewis, 1990; Campos, Bertenthal, & Kermoian, 1992; Lewis, Sullivan, Ramsay, & Alessandri, 1992; Sroufe & Waters, 1977; Stenberg, Campos, & Emde, 1983; for reviews see Lewis, 2000; Witherington, Campos, & Hertenstein, 2001).

Moreover, by the age of 3, children explain emotions in terms of whether goals have been attained or obstructed (Stein & Levine, 1989), and by the age of 5, children distinguish anger from sadness based in part on whether they believe that goal reinstatement is possible or not (Levine,

1995). Investigations of children's perceptions of provocation have shown that by 6 years of age, elementary school children have learned that other people may act with deliberately hostile intentions (Gifford-Smith & Rabiner, 2004). This understanding leads to an increase in aggressive responding when children perceive that another has harmed them intentionally, showing an increased focus on the agents and goals of anger-eliciting situations (Rule & Ferguson, 1986; Dodge et al., 2003). To some extent, the apparent similarity between children's and adults' understanding of emotional situations and appraisals is promoted by parents. For example, Fivush (1991) found that mothers tend to focus on agents (retaliation) and goals (repairing relationship damage) when talking to their children about anger.

Levine and colleagues directly compared children's and adults' appraisals of, and memories for, several emotional events (Levine, Stein, & Liwag, 1999). Parents of 2- to 6-year-olds recalled recent events that had made their child feel happy, sad, fearful, and angry. The children were then asked to describe those events and how the events had made them feel. Children remembered virtually all of the events their parents had described. Moreover, children's reported emotions often matched the emotions their parents had observed, with matches occurring most often for events that parents described as having elicited happiness or sadness, less often for fear, and least often for anger. Parents and children reported different emotional reactions most often when they focused on different goals or different temporal parts of the emotional episode. For example, a parent recalled her child's initial feelings of anger at being thwarted in his desire to bring a favorite toy to school. The child, focusing on the eventual outcome of being without his favorite toy, recalled having felt sad. Notably, however, when asked to recall familiar events of personal importance, even the youngest children were capable of generating a coherent account that included their goals or desires and how events impacted those goals (see also Izard, Levinson, Ackerman, Kogos, & Blumberg, 1998).

Despite these marked similarities, children's and adults' appraisals differ in complexity. Young children's appraisals of emotional situations tend to be less complex than the appraisals of older children and adults (see Stein & Levine, 1999, for a review; Bartsch & Wellman, 1995; Case, 1992; Harris, 1989). In particular, preschool children show limited understanding that people can feel emotional ambivalence and that individuals can experience two emotions concurrently (e.g., feeling sad about a pet's death and at the same time happiness that the pet's suffering has ended; Harris, 1989; Harter & Buddin, 1987). This limitation is most pronounced for emotions that vary in valence. Harter and Whitesell (1989) investigated children's understanding of the co-occurrence of multiple emotions within a single situation and found that children were not able to adequately coordinate dimensions of the emotional experience with opposing valence (e.g., one positive and one negative emotion) until they were about 10 years old. Younger children were not able to attend effectively to multiple facets of a situation. Instead, their attention was largely directed toward a single, emotionally relevant aspect of the event, and this aspect thus was central in guiding their appraisal. Of note, Stein et al. (2000) have argued that young children's appraisals are simpler than those of older children, but even young children—for instance, in the later preschool and early school-age years—have some appreciation of the experience of opposing emotions (e.g., feeling both good and bad about a single person or situation). However, the authors point out that this understanding is limited to feelings that occur *consecutively*, not extending to those that happen at the same time. For example, children can claim that they like someone while focusing on one salient goal (e.g., "I like her when she plays with me") and claim that they dislike that same person when they focus on a different goal (e.g., "I don't like her because she took my candy"). Nonetheless, evidence is consistent in highlighting a more limited appraisal process on the part of children relative to adults that focuses on single dimensions of an experience.

Another difference between children and adults that may affect children's memory concerns their more limited attentional and emotion regulation capabilities. Considerable developmental change occurs in children's capacity to engage in effective emotion regulation (for reviews see Aldwin, 1994; Campos, Frankel, & Camras, 2004; Compas, Connor-Smith, Saltzman, & Thomsen, 2001; Saarni, Campos, Camras, & Witherington, 2006; Skinner & Wellborn, 1994). For example, although during infancy children self-soothe (e.g., non-nutritive sucking) when faced with mild physiological distress (Kopp, 1989), children lack the skills required to deliberately regulate their own emotional responses to psychological distress through at least the early preschool years. They often rely on others, typically parents, to help them regulate their arousal (Miller, Klieweer, Hepworth, & Sandler, 1994; Valiente, Fabes, Eisenberg, & Spinrad, 2004). Indeed, parents, teachers, and older siblings typically intervene to assist distressed children by acting to change the distressing situation or, when this is not possible, by helping them redirect their attention to reduce arousal, providing further explanations to increase their understanding, physically comforting them, or modeling other coping behaviors that may reduce distress (e.g., Lopez & Little, 1996). Several studies have shown that supportive parenting is associated with improved coping abilities in young children (Eisenberg et al., 2001; Hardy, Power, & Jaedicke, 1993; Valiente et al., 2004), and parents often talk to children about distressing events, such as Hurricane Andrew, in ways that help children make sense of the events and their feelings (Fivush & Sales, 2004).

As children's understanding of events becomes more complex, so do their appraisals, as well as the range and frequency of strategies they use to regulate their emotional responses (Altshuler & Ruble, 1989). Compas, Connor-Smith, and Jaser (2004) reported that children who were temperamentally better able to control their attentional processes (e.g., had greater capacity for effortful control of their attention) were more likely to utilize advanced cognitive coping strategies, such as shifting attention and reappraising situations. The perception of an event's controllability is one important aspect of this developing sophistication. With age, children are better able to distinguish between stressors that are uncontrollable and those that are controllable, and children begin to use different types of emotion regulation strategies in these two cases (Aldwin, 1994). Uncontrollable situations, which tend to evoke sadness or fear, are more likely to motivate strategies such as cognitive reframing or distraction than are controllable situations (Aldwin, 1994; Brenner & Salovey, 1997; Marriage & Cummins, 2004). For instance, Hodgins and Lander (1997) found that among 5- to 13-year-olds undergoing a venipuncture, older children reported using a greater number of strategies to cope with the venipuncture, and these strategies increasingly reflected cognitive efforts, such as shifting attention. Thus, with age, children are able to attend to more facets of an emotional event (Harter & Whitesell, 1989; Stein et al., 2000), use a broader range of emotion regulation strategies (e.g., using cognitive strategies when a situation is perceived to be uncontrollable; Marriage & Cummins, 2004), and tailor their strategy choice to the situation at hand (Aldwin, 1994).

Discrete Emotions and Memory in Children

The research reviewed above indicates that children's emotional experience of events depends on how they appraise those events. The manner in which children appraise a potentially stressful incident has implications for what they consider to be central versus irrelevant (peripheral) during the incident and hence what they are likely to remember. Children's appraisals are similar to those of adults in many respects, but are less complex. Children also have more limited resources available to regulate their emotions when exposed to potential stressors. As a result, children are unlikely to have attentional resources available to monitor a broad range of information during an emotional experience and instead may direct their attention almost exclusively toward central information consistent with their appraisals. These ideas lay the foundation for our primary hypothesis concerning discrete emotions and memory in children. Specifically, we contend that effects of discrete emotions on memory will be stronger in children than in adults, with children primarily remembering information about a negative emotional experience that is consistent with their appraisals and goals to the exclusion of information not directly relevant to their appraisals and goals.

To date, this hypothesis has not been tested directly. In fact, only a paucity of scientific research has actually considered discrete emotions when investigating children's memory, and none has systematically considered whether discrete emotions differentially affect children's memory content. Nonetheless, a few studies have addressed the relation between emotional valence, or discrete emotions, and children's memory. The findings are consistent with the notion that the nature of children's emotional experience affects the types of information they attend to and recall.

In one investigation, Fivush et al (2003) compared 5- to 12-year-old children's memories of positive experiences (e.g., family vacations and school trips) and of stressful negative experiences (e.g., interpersonal violence, serious illness, medical procedures). Memory content was coded with respect to mention of persons, places, objects, actions, descriptions, and internal states. Although the overall amount of information recalled was equivalent across positive and negative experiences, the negative memory reports were more coherent and included more information about children's thoughts and emotions. Positive memories, in contrast, included a wide range of information about people, actions, and descriptions (also see Fivush & Sales, 2004). These findings are consistent with the research on adults showing that people experiencing positive emotions attend to, and remember, a broader range of information than do people experiencing negative emotions (e.g., Fredrickson, 1998).

In another study, Baker-Ward, Eaton, and Banks (2005) examined 10-year-old children's memory for a soccer tournament in which they had participated. Although objectively all children had experienced the same event, the outcomes and children's emotional reactions varied. That is, some children won, others lost. When children's memory was tested shortly after the game, the overall amount of information recalled did not differ between those who had won versus those who had lost. However, children who won reported more details about the game itself, whereas children who lost reported more interpretive or evaluative details (e.g., why the game was lost). Thus, children's emotional reactions to the outcome of the game appeared to differentially direct their recounting of the experience toward particular types of information. Of interest, Baker-Ward et al. (2005) commented that some of the children who lost the tournament reported feeling sad, whereas others reported being angry. The researchers did not examine whether the content of memory differed between these two groups of children. Because both of these groups lost but appraised the outcome differently, such an analysis would enable at least one test of whether and how children's attention and potential memory may vary depending on the discrete emotion experienced.

Turning to discrete negative emotions, Rice, Levine, and Pizarro (in press) examined the effects of sadness, and of instructions to regulate sadness, on children's memory for educational material. Seven- and 10-year-olds watched sad or neutral film clips. Those who watched the sad clips were then instructed either to emotionally disengage by suppressing their feelings and expression of sadness or to engage in problem solving concerning their feelings. A control group received no emotion-regulation instructions. Children then watched a neutral-toned, educational video and were later tested for their memory of the educational material. Finally, children who had watched the sad film clip were asked whether they had done anything to make themselves feel better while watching that film. Results indicated that children instructed to disengage from their feelings of sadness recalled more details concerning the educational video than did children receiving instructions directing their attention to the sad film (i.e., problem-solving instructions) or no emotion regulation instructions. In addition, children who reported having used a cognitive strategy to regulate their emotions during the sad film remembered more educational material than children who reported not having regulated emotion. Given that the content of the educational video was not relevant to motivations or appraisals associated with sadness and loss, the poorer memory of sad children who were not instructed to emotionally disengage is not surprising and is consistent with the view that memory for information peripheral to an emotional state is reduced.

In a study described briefly earlier, Quas and Lench (2007) assessed 5- and 6-year-olds' memory for a fear-eliciting video clip and found that increases in children's heart rate were positively related to the accuracy of their responses to closed-ended questions about the video. Virtually all of the questions about the video, which depicted four boys running on a bridge as a train approached, concerned central features of the event (e.g., how many boys were running, whether the train stopped, whether the boys saw the smoke from the approaching train). The finding that greater heart rate predicted better memory is thus consistent with the view that fear, induced as a result of observing the video, focused children's atten tion on information in the video concerning the source of the threat and the characters' strategy to escape the threat. Unfortunately, children's memory was not tested for peripheral information. Thus, there is no way of knowing whether a negative correlation would have emerged between children's heart rate during the video and their memory for information in the video that was unrelated to threat.

A final study, although not supportive of our hypothesis, remains noteworthy because the researchers in fact manipulated emotional state and tested children's memory for emotional information, even though the emotional state elicited and the emotion associated with the to-be-remembered event did not match. Potts, Morse, Felleman, and Masters (1986) induced emotion in 7- to 9-year-olds by having them think of a time that they had felt happy, sad, or neutral. Either before or after the emotion induction, children listened to a story in which two protagonists had negative (e.g., being yelled at by a neighbor) or positive (e.g., receiving a cookie from a friend's mother) experiences. Children's memory for the story was tested via free and cued recall and recognition. Overall, children recalled more emotional than neutral material; however, the specific emotion induced did not affect the amount of story information remembered. The researchers did not assess whether the content of children's memory varied based on the emotion induced, making it difficult to determine whether experiencing the particular emotion directed children's attention toward specific story details and therefore affected their memory.

Conclusion

The topic we introduce in this chapter—how discrete emotions affect children's memory—is ripe for systematic investigation. Based on several lines of research, we laid out a specific hypothesis, namely that children should remember information about a negative emotional experience that is consistent with their appraisals and goals to the relative exclusion of information not directly relevant to their appraisals and goals. Moreover, based on developmental limitations in children's appraisal processes and coping relative to that of adults, the effects of discrete emotions should be more pronounced in children than adults.

Insofar as this hypothesis is to be tested, we see two key issues that must be addressed. First, investigators must strive to create a match between the discrete emotion elicited during a to-be-remembered event and the content of the information for which memory is assessed. Studies of adults have focused on memory for emotional information both in the lab and in real-world situations; however, many of these studies, especially those conducted in the lab, have focused on the effects of inducing emotions on memory for neutral information. Studies of stress and memory in children, in contrast, have involved testing children's memory for the to-be-remembered event that actually had elicited the stress response in children. However, the specific or discrete emotion during the to-be-remembered event was not controlled. It is thus necessary to (a) identify events that target discrete emotional experiences and (b) test children's memory for the specific aspects of those experiences that are theoretically central and peripheral to the discrete emotion the experiences elicited. Once these studies are undertaken in a more direct, rigorous manner, researchers can better identify how the content of children's memory is affected by their specific experience of discrete negative emotions.

To have adequate control over the to-be-remembered events and specific questions asked during the memory interviews, the aforementioned types of issues are best addressed using laboratory events, which at most elicit mild levels of emotional arousal. Therefore, a second key issue in need of direct examination concerns the generalizability of laboratory to-be-remembered discrete emotional events to highly distressing real-world events that children at times encounter. In other words, of interest is how the discrete negative emotions experienced during highly traumatic experiences (like certain invasive medical procedures) affect children's memory. The more traumatic the event, the more likely it is that intense negative emotions will be elicited in children. However, studies focusing on children's distress currently do not assess children's own interpretations and reactions or the specific emotions children report experiencing. Gaining insight into children's own reactions and interpretations may explain, first, how children's general distress responses vary, and, second, when and how children's responses relate to the content and accuracy of their memory.

In closing, for the field often heuristically labeled "children's memory for stressful events" to continue to advance, it will be necessary to look beyond "distress" as a unitary construct and evaluate children's understanding or appraisals of those events that elicit distress, along with children's discrete emotional experiences and emotion regulation techniques. With age, children appraise situations and regulate their emotions in increasingly complex ways and become capable of attending to multiple dimensions of an event. We argue that younger children, with an appraisal process that is similar to but simpler than that of adults, and with limited emotion-regulation strategies, are likely to focus narrowly on the aspect of a situation that is more central and emotionally relevant to them. Such an intense singular attentional focus should in turn lead to enhanced memory for the aspects of an event that have direct relevance to the child's emotional state—memory for information about loss when feeling sad, agents and obstructed goals when feeling angry, and threats when feeling scared—at the expense of other, unrelated information. This possibility may well explain some of the variability in former studies, especially when a wide range of ages and events is included. Of importance, this possibility, if confirmed with continued empirical research, will further our understanding of the complex roles that emotions play across development in children's memory.

References

Adolphs, R., Denburg, N. L., & Tranel, D. (2001). The amygdala's role in declarative memory for gist and detail. *Behavioral Neuroscience, 115,* 983–992.

Aldwin, C. (1994). *Stress, coping, and development.* New York: Guilford Press.

Alessandri, S. M., Sullivan, M. W., & Lewis, M. (1990). Violation of expectancy and frustration in early infancy. *Developmental Psychology, 26,* 738–744.

Alexander, K. W., Goodman, G. S., Schaaf, J. M., Edelstein, R. S., Quas, J. A., & Shaver, P. R. (2002). The role of attachment and cognitive inhibition in children's memory and suggestibility for a stressful event. *Journal of Experimental Child Psychology, 83*, 262–290.

Alexander, K. W., Quas, J. A., & Goodman, G. S. (2002). Theoretical advances in understanding children's memory for distressing events: The role of attachment. *Developmental Review, 22,* 490–519.

Altshuler, J., & Ruble, D. (1989). Developmental changes in children's awareness of strategies for coping with uncontrollable stress. *Child Development, 60,* 1337–1349.

Arnold, M. B. (1960). *Emotion and personality: Vol. I. Psychological aspects.* New York: Columbia University Press.

Baker-Ward, L. E., Eaton, K. L., & Banks, J. B. (2005). Young soccer players' reports of a tournament win or loss: Different emotions, different narratives. *Journal of Cognition and Development, 6,* 507–527.

Bartsch, K., & Wellman, H. M. (1995). *Children talk about the mind.* New York: Oxford University Press.

Berntsen, D. (2002). Tunnel memories for autobiographical events: Central details are remembered more frequently from shocking than happy experiences. *Memory & Cognition, 16,* 1010–1020.

Brenner, E. M., & Salovey, P. (1997). Emotion regulation during childhood: Developmental, interpersonal, and individual considerations. In P. Salovey & D. Sluyter (Eds.), *Emotional development and emotional intelligence: Educational implications* (pp. 168–195). New York: Basic Books.

Bugental, D. B., Blue, J., Cortez, V., Fleck, K., & Rodriguez, A. (1992). Influences of witnessed affect on information processing in children. *Child Development, 63,* 774–786.

Burke, A., Heuer, F., & Reisberg, D. (1992). Remembering emotional events. *Memory & Cognition, 20,* 277–290.

Cahill, L., Gorski, L., & Le, K. (2003). Enhanced human memory consolidation with post- learning stress: Interaction with the degree of arousal at encoding. *Learning and Memory, 10,* 270–274.

Campos, J., Bertenthal, B., & Kermoian, R. (1992). Early experience and emotional development: The emergence of wariness of heights. *Psychological Science, 3,* 61–64.

Campos, J., Frankel, C., & Camras, L. (2004). On the nature of emotion regulation. *Child Development, 75,* 377–394.

Carroll, D., Smith, G. D., Sheffield, D., Shipley, M. J., & Marmot, M. G. (1997). The relationship between socioeconomic status, hostility, and blood pressure reactions to mental stress in men: Data from the Whitehall II study. *Health Psychology, 16,* 131–136.

Case, R. (1992). The role of the frontal lobes in the regulation of cognitive development. *Brain and Cognition, 20,* 51–73.

Chen, X., Wang, L., Chen, H., & Liu, M. (2002). Noncompliance and child-rearing attitudes as predictors of aggressive behaviors: A longitudinal study in Chinese children. *International Journal of Behavioral Development, 26,* 225–233.

Christianson, S.-A., & Loftus, E. F. (1987). Memory for traumatic events. *Applied Cognitive Psychology, 1,* 225–239.

Christie, I. C., & Friedman, B. H. (2004). Autonomic specificity of discrete emotion and dimensions of affective space: A multivariate approach. *International Journal of Psychophysiology, 51,* 143–153.

Compas, B. E., Connor-Smith, J., & Jaser, S. (2004). Temperament, stress reactivity, and coping: Implications for depression in childhood and adolescence. *Journal of Clinical Child and Adolescent Psychology, 33,* 21–31.

Compas, B. E., Connor-Smith, J., Saltzman, H., & Thomsen, A. H. (2001). Coping with stress during childhood and adolescence: Problems, progress, and potential in theory and research. *Psychological Bulletin, 127,* 87–127.

Dalgleish, T. (2004). Cognitive approaches to posttraumatic stress disorder: The evolution of multi-representational theorizing. *Psychological Bulletin, 130,* 228–260.

Deichert, N. T., Flack, W. F. Jr., & Craig, F. W. Jr. (2005). Patterns of cardiovascular responses during angry, sad, and happy emotional recall tasks. *Cognition & Emotion, 19,* 941–951.

Dodge, K. A., Lansford, J. E., Burks, V. S., Bates, J. E., Pettit, G. S., Fontaine, R., et al. (2003). Peer rejection and social information-processing factors in the development of aggressive behavior problems in children. *Child Development, 74,* 374–393.

Eisenberg, N., Gershoff, E., Fabes, R., Shepard, S., Cumberland, A., Losoya, S., et al. (2001). Mothers' emotional expressivity and children's behavior problems and social competence: Mediation through children's regulation. *Developmental Psychology, 37,* 475–490.

Ellsworth, P. C., & Scherer, K. R. (2003). Appraisal processes in emotion. In R. J. Davidson, K. R. Scherer, & H. H. Goldsmith (Eds.), *Handbook of affective sciences* (pp. 572–595). New York: Oxford University Press.

Etzel, J. A., Johnsen, E. L., Dickerson, J., Tranel, D., & Adolphs, R. (2006). Cardiovascular and respiratory responses during musical mood induction. *International Journal of Psychophysiology, 61,* 57–69.

Fivush, R. (1991). Gender and emotion in mother-child conversations about the past. *Journal of Narrative and Life History, 1,* 325–341.

Fivush, R. (1998). Children's recollections of traumatic and nontraumatic events. *Development and Psychopathology, 10,* 699–716.

Fivush, R., Hazzard, A., Sales, J., Sarfati, D., & Brown, T. (2003). Creating coherence out of chaos? Children's narratives of emotionally negative and positive events. *Applied Cognitive Psychology, 17,* 1–19.

Fivush, R., & Sales, J. M. (2004). Children's memories of emotional events. In D. Reisberg & P. Hertel (Eds.), *Memory and emotion* (pp. 242–271). Oxford, England: Oxford University Press.

Fivush, R., Sales, J. M., Goldberg, A., Bahrick, L., & Parker, J. (2004). Weathering the storm: Children's long-term recall of Hurricane Andrew. *Memory, 12,* 104–118.

Fredrickson, B. L. (1998). What good are positive emotions? *Review of General Psychology, 2,* 300–319.

Frijda, N. H. (1986). Emotion, cognitive structure, and action tendency. *Cognition and Emotion, 1,* 115–143.

Gifford-Smith, M. E., & Rabiner, D. L. (2004). Social information processing and children's social adjustment. In J. Kupersmidt & K. A. Dodge (Eds.), *Children's peer relations: From development to intervention* (pp. 69–84). Washington, DC: American Psychological Association.

Goodman, G. S., Hirschman, J. E., Hepps, D., & Rudy, L. (1991). Children's memory for stressful events. *Merrill-Palmer Quarterly, 37,* 109–157.

Goodman, G. S., Quas, J. A., Batterman-Faunce, J. M., Riddlesberger, M. M., & Kuhn, J. (1994). Predictors of accurate and inaccurate memories of traumatic events experienced in childhood. *Consciousness and Cognition, 3,* 269–294.

Goodman, G. S., Quas, J. A., Batterman-Faunce, J. M., Riddlesberger, M. M., & Kuhn, J. (1997). Children's reactions to and memory for a stressful event: Influences of age, anatomical dolls, knowledge, and parental attachment. *Applied Developmental Science, 1,* 54–75.

Gray, J. A. (1990). Brain systems that mediate both emotions and cognitions. In J. A. Gray (Ed.), *Psychobiological aspects of relationships between emotion and cognition* (pp. 269–288). Hillsdale, NJ: Erlbaum.

Gray, J. A. (1994). Three fundamental emotion systems. In P. Ekman & R. J. Davidson (Eds.), *The nature of emotion: Fundamental questions* (pp. 243–247). New York: Oxford University Press.

Hamm, A. O., Cuthbert, B. N., Globisch, J., & Vaitl, D. (1997). Fear and the startle reflex: Blink modulation and autonomic response patterns in animal and mutilation fearful subjects. *Psychophysiology, 34,* 97–107.

Hardy, D., Power, T., & Jaedicke, S. (1993). Examining the relation of parenting to children's coping with everyday stress. *Child Development, 64,* 1829–1841.

Harris, P. L. (1989). *Children and emotion: The development of psychological understanding.* Oxford, UK: Blackwell.

Harter, S., & Buddin, B. J. (1987). Children's understanding of the simultaneity of two emotions: A five-stage developmental acquisition sequence. *Developmental Psychology, 23,* 388–399.

Harter, S., & Whitesell, N. R. (1989). Developmental changes in children's understanding of single, multiple, and blended emotion concepts. In C. Saarni & P. Harris (Eds.), *Children's understanding of emotion* (pp. 81–116). Cambridge: Cambridge University Press.

Hodgins, M. J., & Lander, J. (1997). Children's coping with venipuncture. *Journal of Pain and Symptom Management, 13,* 274–285.

Howe, M. L. (1997). Children's memory for traumatic experiences. *Learning and Individual Differences, 9,* 153–174.

Howe, M. L., Cicchetti, D., & Toth, S. (2006). Children's basic memory processes, stress, and maltreatment. *Development and Psychopathology, 18,* 759–769.

Howe, M. L., Toth, S., & Cicchetti, D. (2006). Memory and developmental psychopathology. In D. Cicchetti & D. Cohen (Eds.), *Developmental psychopathology* (2nd ed.): *Vol. 2. Developmental neuroscience* (pp. 629–655). New York: Wiley.

Izard, C. E., Levinson, K. L., Ackerman, B. P., Kogos, J. L., & Blumberg, S. H. (1998). Children's emotional memories: An analysis in terms of differential emotions theory. *Imagination, Cognition, and Personality, 18,* 173–188.

Kensinger, E. A., & Schacter, D. L. (2006). When the Red Sox shocked the Yankees: Comparing negative and positive memories. *Psychonomic Bulletin and Review, 13,* 757–763.

Kopp, C. B. (1989). Regulation of distress and negative emotions: A developmental view. *Developmental Psychology, 25,* 343–354.

Kramer, T. H., Buckhout, R., & Eugenio, P. (1990). Weapon focus, arousal, and eyewitness memory: Attention must be paid. *Law and Human Behavior, 14,* 167–184.

Labouvie-Vief, G., Lumley, M. A., Jain, E., & Heinze, H. (2003). Age and gender differences in cardiac reactivity and subjective emotional responses to emotional autobiographical memories. *Emotion, 2,* 115–126.

Lazarus, R. S. (1991). Cognition and motivation in emotion. *American Psychologist, 46,* 352–367.

Lench, H. C., & Levine, L. J. (2005). Effects of fear on risk and control judgments and memory: Implications for health promotion messages. *Cognition & Emotion, 19,* 1049–1069.

Lerner, J. S., & Gonzalez, R. M. (2005). Forecasting one's future based on fleeting subjective experiences. *Personality and Social Psychology Bulletin, 31,* 454–466.

Lerner, J. S., Gonzalez, R., Dahl, R., Hariri, A., & Taylor, S. (2005). Facial expressions of emotion reveal neuroendocrine and cardiovascular stress responses. *Biological Psychiatry, 58,* 743–750.

Lerner, J. S., & Keltner, D. (2000). Beyond valence: Toward a model of emotion-specific influences on judgment and choice. *Cognition & Emotion, 14,* 473–493.

Lerner, J. S., & Keltner, D. (2001). Fear, anger, and risk. *Journal of Personality and Social Psychology, 81,* 146–159.

Lerner, J. S., & Tiedens, L. Z. (2006). Portrait of the angry decision maker: How appraisal tendencies shape anger's influence on cognition. *Journal of Behavioral Decision Making, 19,* 115–137.

Levenson, R. W. (1994). Human emotion: A functional view. In P. Ekman & R. J. Davidson (Eds.), *The nature of emotion: Fundamental questions* (pp. 123–126). New York: Oxford University Press.

Levenson, R. W. (1999). The intrapersonal functions of emotion. *Cognition & Emotion, 13,* 481–504.

Levine, L. J. (1995). Young children's understanding of the causes of anger and sadness. *Child Development, 66,* 697–709.

Levine, L. J. (1996). The anatomy of disappointment: A naturalistic test of appraisal models of sadness, anger, and hope. *Cognition & Emotion, 10,* 337–359.

Levine, L. J., & Bluck, S. (2004). Painting with broad strokes: Happiness and the malleability of event memory. *Cognition & Emotion, 18,* 559–574.

Levine, L. J., & Burgess, S. L. (1997). Beyond general arousal: Effects of specific emotions on memory. *Social Cognition, 15,* 157–181.

Levine, L. J., & Pizarro, D. A. (2004). Emotion and memory research: A grumpy overview. *Social Cognition, 22,* 530–554.

Levine, L. J., Pizarro, D. A., & Laney, C. (2006). Emotional valence, discrete emotions, and memory. In B. Uttl, N. Ohta, & A. L. Siegenthaler (Eds.), *Memory and emotions: Interdisciplinary perspectives.* New York: Blackwell.

Levine, L. J., Prohaska, V., Burgess, S. L., Rice, J. A., & Laulhere, T. M. (2001). Remembering past emotions: The role of current appraisals. *Cognition & Emotion, 15,* 393–417.

Levine, L. J., Stein, N. L., & Liwag, M. D. (1999). Remember children's emotions: Sources of concordant and discordant accounts between parents and children. *Developmental Psychology, 35,* 790–801.

Lewis, M. D. (2000). Emotional self-organization at three time scales. In M. D. Lewis & I. Granic (Eds.), *Emotion, development, and self-organization: Dynamic systems approaches to emotional development* (pp. 37–69). Cambridge, England: Cambridge University Press.

Lewis, M., Sullivan, M. W., Ramsay, D. S., & Alessandri, S. M. (1992). Individual differences in anger and sad expressions during extinction: Antecedents and consequences. *Infant Behavior & Development, 15,* 443–452.

Loftus, E. F., Loftus, G. R., & Messo, J. (1987). Some facts about "weapon focus." *Law and Human Behavior, 11,* 55–62.

Lopez, D. F., & Little, T. D. (1996). Children's action-control beliefs and emotional regulation in the social domain. *Developmental Psychology, 32,* 299–312.

Lyubomirsky, S., Caldwell, N. D., & Nolen-Hoeksema, S. (1998). Effects of ruminative and distracting responses to depressed mood on retrieval of autobiographical memories. *Journal of Personality and Social Psychology, 75,* 166–177.

MacLeod, C., & Mathews, A. (2004). Selective memory effects in anxiety disorders: An overview of research findings and their implications. In D. Reisberg & P. Hertel (Eds.), *Memory and emotion* (pp. 155–185). New York: Oxford University Press.

Marriage, K., & Cummins, R. (2004). Subjective quality of life and self-esteem in children: The role of primary and secondary control in coping with everyday stress. *Social Indicators Research, 66,* 107–122.

Mathews, A. M., & Klug, F. (1993). Emotionality and interference with color-naming in anxiety. *Behavior Research and Therapy, 29,* 147–160.

Mathews, A., Richards, A., & Eysenck, M. (1989). Interpretation of homophones related to threat in anxiety states. *Journal of Abnormal Psychology, 98,* 31–34.

Mauss, I. B., Levenson, R. W., McCarter, L., Wilhelm, F. H., & Gross, J. J. (2005). The tie that binds? Coherence among emotion experience, behavior, and physiology. *Emotion, 5,* 175–190.

Merritt, K. A., Ornstein, P. A., & Spicker, B. (1994). Children's memory for a salient medical procedure: Implications for testimony. *Pediatrics, 94,* 17–23.

Miller, P., Klieweer, W., Hepworth, J., & Sandler, I. (1994). Maternal socialization of children's postdivorce coping: Development of a measurement model. *Journal of Applied Developmental Psychology, 15,* 457–487.

Mineka, S., Rafaeli, E., & Yovel, I. (2003). Cognitive biases in emotional disorders: Information processing and social-cognitive perspectives. In R. J. Davidson, K. R. Scherer, & H. H. Goldsmith (Eds.), *Handbook of affective sciences* (pp. 976–1009). New York: Oxford University Press.

Oatley, K., & Johnson-Laird, P. N. (1987). Toward a cognitive theory of emotions. *Cognition & Emotion, 1,* 29–50.

Ornstein, P. A., Manning, E. L., & Pelphrey, K. A. (1999). Children's memory for pain. *Journal of Developmental & Behavioral Pediatrics, 20,* 262–277.

Peterson, C. (1999). Children's memory for medical emergencies: Two years later. *Developmental Psychology, 35,* 1493–1506.

Peterson, C., & Parsons, B. (2005). Interviewing former 1- and 2-year-olds about medical emergencies 5 years later. *Law and Human Behavior, 29,* 743–754.

Peterson, C., & Whalen, N. (2001). Five years later: Children's memory for medical emergencies. *Applied Cognitive Psychology, 15,* S7–S24.

Porter, L. S., Stone, A. A., & Schwartz, J. E. (1999). Anger expression and ambulatory blood pressure: A comparison of state and trait measures. *Psychosomatic Medicine, 61,* 454–463.

Potts, R., Morse, M., Felleman, E., & Masters, J. C. (1986). Children's emotions and memory for affective narrative content. *Motivation and Emotion, 10,* 39–57.

Quas, J. A., Bauer, A., & Boyce, W. T. (2004). Physiological reactivity, social support, and memory in early childhood. *Child Development, 75,* 797–814.

Quas, J. A., Carrick, N., Alkon, A., Goldstein, L., & Boyce, W. T. (2006). Children's memory for a mild stressor: The role of parasympathetic withdrawal and sympathetic activation. *Developmental Psychobiology, 48,* 686–702.

Quas, J. A., Goodman, G. S., Bidrose, S., Pipe, M.-E., Craw, S., & Ablin, D. S. (1999). Emotion and memory: Children's long-term remembering, forgetting, and suggestibility. *Journal of Experimental Child Psychology, 72,* 235–270.

Quas, J. A., & Lench, H. (2007). Arousal at encoding, arousal at retrieval, interviewer support, and children's memory for a mild stressor. *Applied Cognitive Psychology, 21,* 289–306.

Reisberg, D., & Heuer, F. (2004). Memory for emotional events. In D. Reisberg & P. Hertel (Eds.), *Memory and emotion.* New York: Oxford University Press.

Reynolds, M., & Brewin, C. R. (1999). Intrusive memories in depression and post-traumatic stress disorder. *Behaviour Research and Therapy, 37,* 201–215.

Rice, J. A., Levine, L. J., & Pizarro, D. A. (in press). "Just stop thinking about it": Effects of emotion suppression on children's memory for educational material. *Emotion.*

Roseman, I. J., Antoniou, A. A., & Jose, P. E. (1996). Appraisal determinants of emotions: Constructing a more accurate and comprehensive theory. *Cognition & Emotion, 10,* 241–277.

Roseman, I. J., Wiest, C., & Swartz, T. S. (1994). Phenomenology, behaviors, and goals differentiate discrete emotions. *Journal of Personality and Social Psychology, 67,* 206–221.

Rule, B. G., & Ferguson, T. J. (1986). The effects of media violence on attitudes, emotions, and cognitions. *Journal of Social Issues, 42,* 29–50.

Saarni, C., Campos, J. J., Camras, L. A., & Witherington, D. (2006). Emotional development: Action, communication, and understanding. In N. Eisenberg, W. Damon, & R. M. Lerner (Eds.), *Handbook of child psychology: Vol. 3. Social, emotional, and personality development* (6th ed., pp. 226–299). Hoboken, NJ: John Wiley & Sons.

Safer, M. A., Christianson, S.-A., Autry, M. W., & Osterlund, K. (1998). Tunnel memory for traumatic events. *Applied Cognitive Psychology, 12,* 99–117.

Sales, J. M., Fivush, R., Parker, J., & Bahrick, L. (2002). Stressing memory: Long-term relations among children's stress, recall, and psychological outcome following Hurricane Andrew. *Journal of Cognition and Development, 6,* 529–545.

Salmon, K., Price, M., & Pereira, J. K. (2002). Factors associated with young children's long-term recall of an invasive medical procedure: A preliminary investigation. *Journal of Developmental and Behavioral Pediatrics, 23,* 347–352.

Scherer, K. R. (1998). The role of culture in emotion-antecedent appraisal. *Journal of Personality and Social Psychology, 73,* 902–922.

Shah, J. Y., Friedman, R., & Kruglanski, A. W. (2002). Forgetting all else: On the antecedents and consequences of goal shielding. *Journal of Personality and Social Psychology, 83,* 1261–1280.

Shaver, P., Schwartz, J., Kirson, D., & O'Connor, C. (1987). Emotion knowledge: Further exploration of a prototype approach. *Journal of Personality and Social Psychology, 52,* 1061–1086.

Skinner, E. A., & Wellborn, J. G. (1994). Coping during childhood and adolescence: A motivational perspective. In R. Lerner (Ed.), *Life-span development and behavior* (pp. 91–133). Hillsdale, NJ: Erlbaum.

Smith, M. A., & Houston, B. K. (1987). Hostility, anger expression, cardiovascular responsivity, and social support. *Biological Psychology, 24,* 39–48.

Smith, C. A., & Lazarus, R. S. (1993). Appraisal components, core relational themes, and the emotions. *Cognition & Emotion, 7,* 233–269.

Sroufe, L. A., & Waters, E. (1977). Attachment as an organizational construct. *Child Development, 48,* 1184–1199.

Steblay, N. M. (1992). A meta-analytic review of the weapon focus effect. *Law and Human Behavior, 16,* 413–424.

Stein, N. L., & Levine, L. J. (1987). Thinking about feelings: The development and organization of emotional knowledge. In R. E. Snow & M. Farr (Eds.), *Aptitude, learning, and instruction: Vol. 3. Cognition, conation and affect* (pp. 165–197). Hillsdale, NJ: Erlbaum.

Stein, N. L., & Levine, L. J. (1989). The causal organization of emotional knowledge: A developmental study. *Cognition & Emotion, 3,* 343–378.

Stein, N. L., & Levine, L. J. (1999). The early emergence of emotional understanding and appraisal: Implications for theories of development. In T. Dalgleish & M. J. Power (Eds.), *Handbook of cognition and emotion* (pp. 383–408). New York: Wiley & Sons Ltd.

Stein, N. L., Trabasso, T., & Liwag, M. D. (2000). A goal appraisal theory of emotional understanding: Implications for development and learning. In M. Lewis &

J. M. Haviland-Jones (Eds.), *Handbook of emotions* (2nd ed., pp. 436–457). New York, NY: Guilford Press.

Stenberg, C. R., Campos, J. J., & Emde, R. N. (1983). The facial expression of anger in seven-month-old infants. *Child Development, 54,* 178–184.

Vaandermaas, M. O., Hess, T. M., & Baker-Ward, L. (1993). Does anxiety affect children's reports of memory for a stressful event? *Applied Cognitive Psychology, 7,* 109–127.

Valiente, C., Fabes, R., Eisenberg, N., & Spinrad, T. (2004). The relations of parental expressivity and support to children's coping with daily stress. *Journal of Family Psychology, 18,* 97–106.

von Baeyer, C. L., Marche, T. A., Rocha, E. M., & Salmon, K. (2004). Children's memory for pain: Overview and implications for practice. *Journal of Pain, 5,* 241–249.

Watkins, E., & Teasdale, J. D. (2001). Rumination and overgeneral memory in depression. *Journal of Abnormal Psychology, 110,* 353–357.

Weiner, B. (1985). An attributional theory of achievement motivation and emotion. *Psychological Review, 92,* 548–573.

Wessel, I., & Merckelbach, H. (1998). Memory for threat-relevant and threat-irrelevant cues in spider phobics. *Cognition & Emotion, 12,* 93–104.

Witherington, D. C., Campos, J. J., & Hertenstein, M. J. (2001). Principles of emotion and its development in infancy. In G. Bremner & A. Fogel (Eds.), *Blackwell handbook of infant development* (pp. 427–464). Oxford, England: Blackwell.

Part III
Clinical and Legal Perspectives

8

Pursuing "the Truth, the Whole Truth, and Nothing but the Truth"

Forensic Interviews with Child Victims or Witnesses of Abuse

DEIRDRE BROWN, MICHAEL E. LAMB,
MARGARET-ELLEN PIPE, AND YAEL ORBACH

Maltreatment is widely recognized as one of the more serious forms of trauma that children experience, and there is now a substantial literature documenting its adverse effects on children's behavior and adjustment. Yet often in cases of maltreatment such as sexual, emotional, or physical abuse, the child victim is the only available source of information about what has happened. How well, then, do children remember and report such stressful, painful, and/or distressing experiences when they are victims of, or indeed even witnesses to, traumatizing experiences (for example, the homicide of a parent or sibling)? Because of the importance of children's accounts of such experiences for intervention (both legal and clinical), many researchers, especially in the last decade, have examined children's memories of abusive incidents. Our goal in this chapter is to review our current understanding of children's abilities to recall and recount instances of abusive experiences, particularly in the course of an investigation where "the truth, the whole truth, and nothing but the truth" is of paramount importance.

In pursuing "the truth" about an alleged instance of child abuse, the ability of the alleged victim to give a clear and comprehensive account of his or her experience is crucial, because corroborating or alternative sources of information are frequently unavailable. Eliciting "the whole truth" while at the same time ensuring that it is "nothing but the truth" is especially challenging for forensic interviewers because children's spontaneous accounts of their experiences are typically too brief to be useful in forensic interviews, and yet the pursuit of more detailed information may lead to errors in recall and reporting. These issues speak to both the completeness and the accuracy of the elicited testimony. Over the past 25 years it has become abundantly clear that both the amount and the reliability of information reported by children may be enhanced or reduced by several factors, including those pertaining to the developmental level of the child, characteristics of the event in question, and techniques used by interviewers to elicit testimony. In this review, we discuss how the amount and quality of information elicited in forensic interviews with children reflects the behavior and capacities of not only the child witness but also the adult interviewers.

Eliciting "the Truth" from Child Witnesses

Numerous studies have shown a developmental progression in the amount of information children recall, with younger children typically recalling less than older children (e.g., Gee & Pipe, 1995; Goodman, Aman, & Hirschman, 1987; Goodman & Reed, 1986; Marin, Holmes, Guth, & Kovac, 1979; Oates & Shrimpton, 1991; Saywitz, 1987). Age in itself is not sufficient to account for the variability in children's recall, however, since variability in recall among children of similar ages is common (Leichtman, Ceci, & Morse, 1997; Pipe & Salmon, 2002; Quas, Goodman, Ghetti, & Redlich, 2000; Quas, Qin, Schaaf, & Goodman, 1997). Furthermore, when task demands are manipulated by using recognition rather than free-recall tasks, for example, age effects are attenuated or even disappear (Ceci, Ross, & Toglia, 1987b; Cole & Loftus, 1987; Jones, Swift, & Johnston, 1988; Saywitz, 1987), indicating that variables other than what the children actually know or remember about their experience contribute to age-related differences in memory. Thus, age per se does not provide an accurate index of children's ability to recount personal experiences (Goodman & Schwartz-Kenney, 1992) but rather serves to summarize the influence of a number of variables relating to children's abilities, the effects of which may differ across interview/recall contexts.

Studies of the development of autobiographical memory show that younger children's impoverished recall, relative to older children and adults, may be due in part to limited retrieval skills, metalinguistic deficits, and immature narrative skills (for reviews see Gordon, Baker-Ward, & Ornstein, 2001; Nelson & Fivush, 2004; Ornstein, Haden, & Hedrick, 2004). Developmental differences in the selection and use of cognitive strategies, both for encoding and retrieval (see Schneider & Bjorklund, 1998 for review), affect children's ability to talk about past events, and therefore the amount of support they may need to help them describe the event completely. Encoding and retrieval strategies develop with age and experience, and the use of effective retrieval strategies is usually associated with increases in recall and reporting of information (Flavell, 1970; Ornstein et al., 2004). Young children may use strategic behaviors when explicitly instructed to do so but still not benefit as much as older children (Flavell, Miller, & Miller, 1993). In other words, younger and older children may use the same strategies but recall different amounts, possibly because the cognitive effort required to implement the strategy decreases the recall capacity of younger children (Miller, 1990). Older children do not need to invest as much cognitive effort because strategy use becomes more automatic with age, thereby enabling more effort and attention to be allocated to retrieval (Schneider & Bjorklund, 1998). As children become older, they also become better at generating internal retrieval cues, which makes them less reliant on support provided during the interview (Quas et al., 2000).

Deficiencies in the retrieval of *accurate* event-related information may arise from errors in children's source-monitoring—that is, the ability to identify the source of one's knowledge or memory, particularly if interviewers pose leading or misleading questions that refer to details observed, experienced, or heard about in other contexts (Roberts & Blades, in press; Roberts & Powell, 2001). Inaccurate source-monitoring during the retrieval process may lead children to incorporate and report information that they have heard from others, seen (e.g., on television), or imagined. Children may use or remember information without remembering where they learned it, or they may attribute their knowledge to the wrong source (Roberts & Blades, 2000).

The clarity and completeness of children's testimony is also affected by their developing communicative abilities. The vocabularies of young children are much more limited and less descriptive than those of adults (Brown, 1973; Dale, 1976), and their statements are likely to lack adjectival and adverbial modifiers (de Villiers & de Villiers, 1999). Misunderstandings between children and interviewers may occur because children's rapid vocabulary growth often leads adults to overestimate their linguistic capacities and thus use words, sentence structures, or concepts that exceed the children's competencies (Saywitz & Camparo, 1998; Saywitz, Nathanson, & Snyder, 1993; Walker, 1994). Despite their apparent maturity, young children—especially preschoolers—frequently use words before they know their conventional adult meaning, may use words that they do not understand at all, and may understand poorly some apparently simple concepts, such as "any," "some," "touch," "yesterday," and "before" (Harner, 1975; Walker, 1994). Furthermore, children frequently use very concrete and restricted interpretations of words (e.g., a child may refute a question about something that happened at "home" if the child lives in an apartment) and idiosyncratic vocabulary, as well as comparisons or references that fall outside of the listener's knowledge base (e.g., "he looked like my English teacher"), making their accounts ambiguous.

Increases in the amounts of information reported by children as they grow older may also reflect their increasingly sophisticated skills as narrators. Young children are still developing their metalinguistic abilities—coming to know what listeners want to know and how to report information coherently, monitor the success of their communication, and modify strategies as necessary to ensure that the listener has understood (Lamb & Brown, 2006; Saywitz & Snyder, 1996). For this reason, young children may not understand that their intended audience (e.g., the interviewer or jury member) is naïve with respect to what they have experienced and thus may fail to provide sufficient detail to ensure complete and accurate reports. Typically, in interactions between children and adults, children are questioned by adults who are already knowledgeable about the topic of conversation (Lamb, Orbach, Warren, Esplin, & Hershkowitz, in press). By contrast, alleged victims of abuse are often the sole sources of information about the suspected events. If children fail to appreciate that the interviewer has little, if any, knowledge of the alleged events or if they attribute superior knowledge to the adult interviewers (e.g., Ceci, Ross, & Toglia, 1987a; Ceci et al., 1987b), they may refrain from reporting all they know. In addition, if children infer that interviewers would prefer particular responses, in attempting to be cooperative conversational partners they may compromise their accounts rather than communicate their actual experiences (Ceci & Bruck, 1993, 1995). In the forensic context, therefore, interviewers must be sensitive to children's perceptions of their knowledge and status. To facilitate comprehensive and accurate reporting by children, for example, interviewers should emphasize that they do not know what the children experienced and that it is thus important for the children to tell as much as they know (e.g., Sternberg, Lamb, Esplin, Orbach, & Hershkowitz, 2002).

"The Whole Truth": When Do Children Provide the Most Complete Accounts of Their Experiences?

As researchers have come to understand the difficulties child victims may have recalling and reporting their experiences, they have focused attention on techniques that may minimize their impact. Before discussing techniques that may be useful for eliciting detailed information from children, however, we must first acknowledge that the nature of the to-be-remembered events may affect children's ability to recall and report them (see Chapter 5 for review; also Cordón, Pipe, Sayfan, Melinder, & Goodman, 2004). This raises, in turn, the question of whether findings from analogue studies using staged stimulus events (varying from short videos to interactive personally experienced events) be generalized to the real-world context to which they are meant to apply. Early analogue studies produced inconsistent findings with respect to the influence of stress on memory, with some studies showing a positive effect and others showing a negative effect or no effect at all (Chapter 5; Christianson, 1992; Cordón et al., 2004; Howe, 1997). The inconsistencies may arise in part from the degree of stress (or distress) experienced, methodological differences in the definition and measurement of stress across studies, differing delay intervals, and differences in the assessment of memory (e.g., central versus peripheral information, reliability versus suggestibility). Studies of children's memories for more salient or stressful events such as naturally occurring disasters (Parker, Bahrick, Lundy, Fivush, & Levitt, 1998), painful medical procedures (e.g., Goodman, Quas, Batterman-Faunce,

Riddlesberger, & Kuhn, 1994, 1997; Steward, O'Connor, Acredolo, & Steward, 1996), and injuries resulting in emergency room visits (Howe, Courage, & Peterson, 1994; Peterson & Bell, 1996; Peterson & Whalen, 2001) suggest that, in general, stress may be associated with increased memory and decreased forgetting over time, particularly with respect to central or core information. Nonetheless, studies involving less stressful experiences still make a valid contribution to forensic psychology, because abuse victims may not always perceive their experiences as painful or traumatic, and children's ignorance or misunderstanding of events may decrease their salience (Pipe et al., in press). Moreover, analogue studies provide a basis for the development of safe and effective forensic interview techniques.

Such techniques include different questioning styles; the use of ancillary aids such as prop items, dolls, and drawings; and the reinstatement of context and pre-interview training. An exhaustive review of the empirical support for these techniques is beyond the scope of this chapter (see reviews by Lamb & Brown, 2006; Pipe, Lamb, Orbach, & Esplin, 2004; Salmon, 2001); rather, we briefly summarize the rationale and evidence for each of these approaches and their effects on children's recall and reporting.

Interviewer Question Type

The methods used by interviewers to elicit children's accounts of their experiences affect both the quantity and quality of information elicited from children. Children's responses to open invitations tapping recall memory (e.g., "Tell me about that") are typically more accurate than responses to more focused questions ("Was his hat red?"), which tap recognition memory (e.g., Dent, 1982, 1986; Dent & Stephenson, 1979; Hutcheson, Baxter, Telfer, & Warden, 1995; Lamb & Fauchier, 2001; Oates & Shrimpton, 1991; Orbach & Lamb, 2001). The completeness of these initially brief accounts can be increased when interviewers use the information provided by children in their first spontaneous utterance as prompts for further elaboration (e.g., "You said the man touched you; tell me more about that touching") (Lamb et al., 2003). Unfortunately, however, forensic interviewers frequently ask very specific questions ("Did he touch you?"). Young children (those under 6) have special difficulty answering specific questions and may exhibit a response bias (e.g.,

Fivush, Peterson, & Schwarzmeuller, 2002; Peterson, Dowdin, & Tobin, 1999) or a reluctance to give "don't know" responses in the absence of knowledge (Davies, Tarrant, & Flin, 1989; Saywitz & Snyder, 1993). In addition, Waterman, Blades, and Spencer (2000, 2001, 2004) showed that children (5 to 9 years) often attempt to answer impossible (nonsensical) or unanswerable (where the information has not been provided) questions, especially if they are phrased as yes/no rather than "wh-" questions. The type of questions asked and the context in which they are introduced thus determine whether they enhance or degrade the reliability of children's reports (Poole & Lamb, 1998; Saywitz & Lyon, 2002).

Prop Items

Several researchers have explored alternative techniques aimed at facilitating more complete recall. The use of prop items relevant to the event in question (e.g., real items, scale models, toys, photographs) may increase the similarity between the event and the retrieval condition (interview), thereby enhancing recall by providing reminders of the event (Tulving & Thomson, 1973), or providing opportunities for children to overcome linguistic deficits by demonstrating rather than, or as well as, telling what they remember (Pipe, Gee, & Wilson, 1993). Although the use of props in interviews with young children (especially those 5 years or younger) may increase the amount of information reported, the amount of erroneous information reported may also increase, particularly when toys are involved (see Salmon, 2001, for a review). In forensic contexts, it is also unlikely that interviewers can exactly match the conditions of the event with those at the time of recall. The risk of contaminating children's reports by inadvertently including items that were not part of the target events and therefore misleading the children is thus likely to outweigh the possible benefits of eliciting additional information.

Anatomically Detailed Dolls

The use of anatomical dolls as interview aids has been highly controversial. Everson and Boat (2002) have argued that blanket condemnation or endorsement of anatomical dolls is inappropriate without considering the specific function for which the doll is used within the interview (e.g., as a demonstration aid, as an icebreaker). They noted that analogue studies using anatomical dolls do not mimic the conditions under which the dolls are likely to be used in forensic practice and therefore cannot elucidate the effects of doll use on the reliability and completeness of children's reports. Field studies have produced inconsistent findings regarding their efficacy (Lamb, Hershkowitz, Sternberg, Boat, & Everson, 1996; Leventhal, Hamilton, Rededal, Tebano-Micci, & Eyster, 1989).

Critics have argued that anatomical dolls may stimulate sexual play that could be misinterpreted, but Everson and Boat's review (2002) identified no studies showing that dolls stimulate sexual play in sexually naïve children. Critics have also argued that anatomical dolls may lead to an increase in children's suggestibility or false reports of the occurrence of genital touch when coupled with suggestive questions (e.g., Bruck, Ceci, Francoeur, & Renick, 1995; Steward, Steward, et al., 1996). A recent field study showed that suggestive play and inconsistent information were indeed more likely when anatomical dolls were used in interviews with very young children (3- to 6-year-olds) (Thierry, Lamb, Orbach, & Pipe, 2005). Findings regarding the accuracy of children's reports when interviewed with anatomically detailed dolls are inconsistent, however, and other studies have shown increases in the amounts of information reported with little or no effects on accuracy (e.g., Goodman et al., 1997; Saywitz, Goodman, Nicholas, & Moan, 1991; Steward, Steward, et al., 1996). Explanation of these different effects is likely to lie in the way in which the dolls are used, when and how they are introduced, and the general interview context, although there has been little research isolating the important variables.

A third concern about the use of dolls, especially with very young children, derives from the fact that children may have difficulty with their symbolic nature or representational use (e.g., DeLoache & Marzolf, 1995). Young children may have difficulty in understanding that, in the interview context, dolls are intended to act as representations of the children, but they also, simultaneously, have their identity as dolls. Children may thus treat a doll as a plaything instead of understanding that the interviewer expects their interaction with the doll to reflect and represent personal experiences. When used cautiously and not in conjunction with suggestive questions, there is some evidence that dolls used as anatomical models or to allow the demonstration of touches that may not otherwise be reported because the information is painful, embarrassing, or sensitive may be helpful, at least for children above 5 years of age (Everson & Boat,

2002; Saywitz et al., 1991). Again, however, there is a paucity of research to guide safe and effective use in the forensic context.

Drawings

Drawings can also be used in forensic interviews as a means of enhancing children's accounts. Drawings have been used in two different ways: as direct communicative aids whereby, during the interview, children draw and talk about what they have experienced (Butler, Gross, & Hayne, 1995; Gross & Hayne, 1998, 1999; Salmon, Roncolato, & Gleitzman, 2003; Wesson & Salmon, 2001), and as representational aids whereby children are provided with drawings (e.g., of objects or people) and are asked about events connected with the drawings (e.g., presence or absence of the items, or the location of possible touches; Aldridge et al., 2004; Brown, Pipe, Lewis, Lamb, & Orbach, 2007; Willcock, Morgan, & Hayne, 2006).

Asking children to draw while talking during the interview may potentially facilitate children's reporting in several different ways. Drawing may help children generate retrieval cues for further recall (Butler et al., 1995). Drawing may also reduce the social-demand characteristics of the interview by increasing rapport, increasing the child's comfort level, and prolonging the interview so that children have more opportunity to retrieve and report information (Gross & Hayne, 1998; Salmon et al., 2003). Providing representational drawings may help children to report aspects of an event that they do not have the language for, would not spontaneously report because the information is embarrassing or painful, or would not normally report because conversational conventions restrict the level of detail spontaneously incorporated into descriptions of past experiences (Butler et al., 1995). To date, the mechanisms by which providing drawings in interviews facilitates children's ability to recount experiences have not been conclusively established. Indeed, any or all of these explanations may come into play.

Studies examining the use of drawings to enhance children's reports of personally experienced events have shown that, under ideal circumstances (i.e., when asking children about true events using nonsuggestive questioning), drawing while talking yields an increase in the amount of information recalled, without compromising accuracy (e.g., Butler et al., 1995; Gross & Hayne, 1998, 1999; Salmon et al., 2003; Wesson & Salmon, 2001), although drawing may also be associated with decreased accuracy, especially after a delay (Salmon & Pipe, 2000). Several studies have also demonstrated, however, that in addition to encouraging more complete recall of true events, drawing may also encourage children to report information about events that never occurred (e.g., Bruck, Melnyk, & Ceci, 2000; Gross, Hayne, & Poole, in press; Strange, Garry, & Sutherland, 2003). Taken together, these studies suggest that drawing and talking may generally increase children's responsiveness, about both true and false events.

With respect to interviewer-provided drawings, many clinical and forensic psychologists use human-figure drawings to aid the reporting of specific information (e.g., the location of touch experienced as part of an abusive act) during interviews (Aldridge et al., 2004; Brown et al., 2007; Willcock et al., 2006). It is unclear, however, to what extent young children in particular are able to use these drawings as "maps" of their own body to accurately communicate their experiences. Steward, Steward, and colleagues (1996) explored young children's recall of a pediatric exam that included body touch and found that although anatomically detailed drawings were associated with a marginal increase in the completeness of information reported, false reports of forensically relevant information also increased.

In a recent field study, children between the ages of 4 and 13 years were shown a human-figure drawing following an exhaustive verbal interview conducted using the National Institute of Child Health and Human Development (NICHD) investigative interview protocol and were asked to show on the drawing where touching had occurred (Aldridge et al., 2004). Children were then asked to elaborate on any reported touches. A large amount of new information (86 new forensically relevant details on average) was reported during this phase of the interview, even though it occurred after an exhaustive verbal interview. The drawings appeared to be particularly helpful for the youngest (4- to 7-year-old) children, who reported 27% of their total information in response to the drawing, but because specific questions, which are typically associated with lower accuracy, predominated, the authors cautioned that much of the information elicited may have been unreliable. Consistent with this, Willcock et al. (2006) demonstrated that children's reports of touches that had occurred as part of a staged event were poor: almost 67% of the touches were not reported, and the accuracy of reported information was 48%. Of particular concern, a significant number of children falsely reported touches of the genital (11.3%) and breast regions (25.5%). Brown et al.

(2007) explored the amount and accuracy of information reported about touches during a staged event using either a human-figure drawing or verbal questions about touch. As in the Aldridge et al. (2004) study, children were interviewed exhaustively using the NICHD protocol and then shown a human-figure drawing and asked about touches that may have occurred. Like the children in Aldridge et al.'s (2004) study, the majority of children reported unique information during the "touch" phase of the interview, but the accuracy of this information was low (overall accuracy for information reported to open questions was 33%). More than half of the information reported in response to open questions about touch was inaccurate, although it tended to be plausible in the context of the event. Forensically relevant errors were infrequent and were rarely elaborated on. Taken together, the results of these studies suggest that although human figure drawings may increase the amount of information reported by children, the information elicited may be highly unreliable. This conclusion must, however, be qualified by the limited number of studies conducted to date and the way in which the drawings have been used—for example, at the end of an exhaustive interview, rather than for purposes of clarification during the interview following children's spontaneous recall of touch having occurred. Whether and at what age children can use human-figure drawings to elucidate their accounts under such conditions has yet to be examined empirically.

Mental Context Reinstatement

Studies of cognitive techniques such as mental context reinstatement (MCR: guiding children to mentally reconstruct the settings in which the events occurred) indicate that this can be a useful technique for helping children retrieve as much information as possible (Bekerian, Dennet, Hill, & Hitchcock, 1990; Hershkowitz, Orbach, Lamb, Sternberg, & Horowitz, 2001; McCauley & Fisher, 1995, 1996). Using MCR, children are instructed to think about different sensory features of the event (e.g., what they could hear, see, smell) and different aspects of the event (e.g., what the place looked like) before beginning to verbally recount what they remember. Consistent with the expectation that mental reinstatement of context will help witnesses to mentally travel back in time and "relive" the experience, MCR increases the similarity between the conditions at recall and those at the time of the experience, thereby making the information associated with the event more accessible. Mental rein-statement of context is one of the main components of the Cognitive Interview (Fisher, Geiselman, Raymond, Jurkevich, & Warhaftig, 1987), which is used widely by police officers interviewing adult witnesses. The Cognitive Interview progresses through five stages, beginning with an introduction to the purpose of the interview and going on to a request for open-ended recall, probed recall, review, and closure. During the probed recall stage of the interview, four techniques are used to encourage complete recall and reporting. First, witnesses are encouraged to report everything they can remember, even small details that they may consider unimportant. Second, they are asked to mentally reinstate the context of the incident and report any details that they can recall, including de-scriptions of the environment, the people, smells, feelings, and reactions to events. Third, witnesses are asked to recall the event in different tem-poral sequences (e.g., reverse order, starting from the most salient aspect and moving forward and then backward in time from that aspect), and fourth, they are asked to recall the event from different perspectives (e.g., from the perspective of others who were present). The Cognitive Inter-view has also been used successfully with children (e.g., Köhnken, Milne, Memon, & Bull, 1999), although some of the component techniques (e.g., changing perspectives, changing the temporal ordering) may make de-mands that exceed the cognitive competencies of children under 8 years of age (Geiselman, 1999; Hayes & Delamothe, 1997; Saywitz, Geiselman, & Bornstein, 1992).

   Interventions designed to ameliorate the difficulties children have pro-viding satisfactory narratives without adult support include the use of a practice interview (e.g., Sternberg et al., 1997; Sternberg, Lamb, Orbach, Esplin, & Mitchell, 2001), explicit training in the essential components of informative narratives before recalling the target events (e.g., Brown & Pipe, 2003b; Saywitz & Snyder, 1996; Saywitz, Snyder, & Lamphear, 1996), and prompting by interviewers for forensically relevant categories of in-formation (Bowen & Howie, 2002; Brown & Pipe, 2003a; Elischberger & Roebers, 2001). In a field study of investigative interviews with children, Sternberg et al. (1997) showed that open-ended questions and prompts for elaborative responses in a practice interview about a neutral event (e.g., a recent holiday) increased the amounts of information reported in response to the first prompt regarding the alleged abuse. These find-ings suggested that even in authentic forensic interviews, it is possible to entrain response styles that enhance the richness of information provided by children by having them practice providing detailed narrative accounts of experienced events before turning attention to substantive issues. A practice interview is recommended in best practice guidelines for forensic interviewers (e.g., Home Office, 2002) because it (a) provides opportunities to enhance rapport between children and interviewers and (b) prepares children for the task at hand by demonstrating what level of detail is expected in their responses and illustrating the style of questioning interviewers may use to help them achieve it.

Saywitz and her colleagues developed an innovative interviewing technique, Narrative Elaboration Training (NET), to explore the effectiveness of pre-interview training and practice in talking about the past on children's subsequent reports of a target event (Saywitz & Snyder, 1993, 1996). The NET addresses metalinguistic deficits by teaching children what information is necessary to provide a complete and coherent narrative about a past experience, and it addresses retrieval deficits by providing pictorial cue cards to prompt retrieval of forensically relevant categories of information (people, setting, actions, conversation, and affect). Children are first trained to talk about one experienced event using the cards and are then asked about the to-be-remembered event. In the laboratory, the NET helps children, including preschoolers and children with mental retardation, to report events more completely, without compromising accuracy (Brown & Pipe, 2003a, 2003b; Dorado & Saywitz, 2001; Nathanson, Crank, & Saywitz, in press; Saywitz & Snyder, 1996; Saywitz et al., 1996), and it does not elicit reports of false events (Camparo, Wagner, & Saywitz, 2001). However, verbal prompting for categories of information, without training, can be just as effective as NET (Bowen & Howie, 2002; Brown & Pipe, 2003a; Elischberger & Roebers, 2001).

"Nothing But the Truth": Suggestibility of Child Witnesses

The credibility of children's accounts is often challenged on the grounds that they are especially vulnerable to suggestion (Ceci & Bruck, 1993, 1995). Initial laboratory-based research appeared to produce inconsistent findings regarding the suggestibility of young children, however. Goodman and her colleagues have shown that children as young as 3 to 4 years of age can successfully resist misleading questions suggesting actions that are very different from those that have occurred or been witnessed

(Goodman & Aman, 1990; Goodman et al., 1987; Goodman, Bottoms, Schwartz-Kenney, & Rudy, 1991; Goodman, Hirschman, Hepps, & Rudy, 1991; Goodman, Rudy, Bottoms, & Aman, 1990; Goodman, Wilson, Hazan, & Reed, 1989). In other laboratory settings, however, preschoolers have appeared especially susceptible to suggestion (e.g., Ceci et al., 1987a, 1987b; King & Yuille, 1987; Toglia, Ceci, & Ross, 1989; see McAuliff, Kovera, & Viswesvaran, 1998, for a review). Indeed, children may, under certain conditions, come to provide elaborate accounts of entire events that have never been experienced (e.g., Ceci, Huffman, Smith, & Loftus, 1994; Ceci, Loftus, Leichtman, & Bruck, 1994; Strange et al., 2003). Such findings are not limited to children, however, with several studies demonstrating that adults too may come to produce detailed "memories" of entirely false events (e.g., Garry, Manning, Loftus, & Sherman, 1996; Hyman, Husband, & Billings, 1995; Loftus & Pickrell, 1995).

The apparently contradictory findings regarding children's suggestibility may be resolved by examining methodological differences in both the manipulation and measurement of suggestibility and reliability. Suggestibility is multiply determined by cognitive, social, motivational, and individual difference variables. Suggestive techniques may include instructions from the interviewer to pretend, draw, or imagine what might have happened, introduction of information by the interviewer that has not been reported by the child, and pressure to provide a response or comply with propositions made by the interviewer (e.g., telling children they will feel better if they tell, alluding to statements made by other children, introduction of stereotypes about the alleged perpetrator or descriptions of him/her as "bad" and "needing to be punished"), and repetitive questioning over a series of interviews with encouragement to speculate about what might have happened. Laboratory-based research has demonstrated that there are valid reasons for skepticism regarding the reliability of children's responses in these circumstances (e.g., Garven, Wood, Malpass & Shaw, 1998; Leichtman & Ceci, 1995).

As discussed earlier, source-monitoring errors may also lead children to inaccurately describe their experiences. Children's sensitivity to the status and knowledge of the interviewer may also foster compliance with suggestive techniques, because they misunderstand the purpose of the interviewer's statements, assume that the interviewer has superior knowledge, or simply want to be cooperative. When interviewers adequately prepare children for their role as experts, empower them to correct interviewers, and admit that they "don't know" some answers, and when interviewers avoid asking children to pretend or imagine, avoid being coercive, do not repeat misleading questions within the interview, and keep children focused on central details of personally experienced events, children are able to resist misleading questions and provide meaningful and accurate accounts of their experiences (Pipe et al., 2004).

Promoting Reliable Evidence

As research on factors affecting the reliability of children's eyewitness testimony has accumulated, a consensus has emerged about the safest and most effective ways of helping maltreated children to recall and report their experiences without compromising the reliability of their reports (e.g., American Professional Society on the Abuse of Children [APSAC], 1990, 1997; Fisher & Geiselman, 1992; Jones, 1992; Lamb, Sternberg, & Esplin, 1994, 1995, 1998;Home Office, 1992, 2002; Orbach et al., 2000; Poole & Lamb, 1998; Raskin & Esplin, 1991; Sattler, 1998). Forensic interviewers are advised to establish rapport before discussing the alleged incident, and to use open-ended invitations while avoiding suggestive techniques. Specific or closed questions should be used only at the end of the interview to clarify inconsistencies or elicit information crucial to the investigation that may not have been spontaneously disclosed. Unfortunately, several studies have demonstrated discrepancies between recommended best practice and the conduct of forensic interviews with children (Cederborg, Orbach, Sternberg, & Lamb, 2000; Sternberg, Lamb, Davies, & Westcott, 2001; Sternberg, Lamb, & Hershkowitz, 1996; Sternberg et al., 1997). Training programs for forensic interviewers produce initial improvements in interviewers' knowledge of developmentally appropriate interviewing but do not reliably affect behavior, with interviewers reverting to practices they know may compromise the reliability of the children's evidence (e.g., closed or focused questions, option-posing prompts, suggestive questions, anatomical dolls) (Aldridge & Cameron, 1999; Cederborg & Lamb, 2006; Craig, Scheibe, Kircher, Raskin, & Dodd, 1999; Lamb, Orbach, Sternberg, Esplin, & Hershkowitz, 2002; Stevenson, Leung, & Cheung, 1992; Warren et al., 1999). To help interviewers to conduct developmentally appropriate interviews, researchers at NICHD thus created an interview protocol that operationalized the recommendations from research (Orbach et al., 2000; Sternberg, Lamb, Orbach, et al., 2001).

The NICHD Interview Protocol

The NICHD protocol begins with an introductory phase that promotes rapport; includes a "truth and lie ceremony" to communicate to children the importance of truth telling; and establishes the ground rules for the interview, such as the acceptability of saying "I don't know" and correcting the interviewer. Children are then asked for information about themselves, their families, and their schools, using open-ended questions. Following this, children are asked to describe two recent experiences (e.g., Christmas, Passover, or a recent birthday) and are prompted for further elaboration using open-ended prompts, followed by more focused prompts such as time segmentation (e.g., "Tell me everything that happened from the time you went home until you went to the store"; Sternberg et al., 2002, p. 420). The substantive portion of the interview is then introduced, with a series of open-ended prompts used, to encourage the child to discuss the alleged abuse (e.g., "Tell me why you came here today"). None of these prompts refer to the actions, perpetrator, or location of the alleged abuse. The NICHD protocol includes specific questions to be used if a child has not disclosed the abuse in response to more open-ended prompts. The questions were formulated to be minimally leading, should they be required to prompt the child to report the alleged abuse. The NICHD protocol recommends following any direct questions with open-ended prompts for further information ("pairing"), such as "Tell me everything about that," to minimize the risk of subsequent information being contaminated by leading or suggestive questioning. When children indicate that there were multiple instances of abuse, the NICHD protocol recommends eliciting a description of the most recent incident first, followed by the first incident, and then any other specific, well-remembered incidents (e.g., "the time in the bathroom," "the time when you were camping"). Again, prompting for further information involves open-ended prompts, followed by more focused questions if necessary. The interview then finishes with a discussion of a neutral event. One of the distinctive features of the protocol is that it uses children's responses as cues for further information, resulting in a child-directed rather than an interviewer-directed approach throughout all phases of the interview.

Field studies have compared interviews conducted by investigators before and after they have been trained to use the protocol. Interviewers using the protocol adhere better to recommended practices. In a study of 50 interviews conducted by Israeli youth investigators using the protocol, Orbach et al. (2000) found that interviewers offered more than five times as many open-ended invitations as they did in comparable interviews conducted before the structured protocol was introduced. The number of option-posing questions dropped by almost 50% as well, and much more of the information was obtained using free recall rather than investigator-directed recognition probes in the protocol-guided interviews.

Similar results were obtained with investigative interviews conducted by police officers in the western United States (Sternberg et al., 2002; Sternberg, Lamb, Orbach, et al., 2001). The proportion of invitations increased from 10% to approximately one-third, while option-posing and suggestive prompts decreased from 41% to 24%. The total amount of information elicited from free-recall memory also increased dramatically; whereas only 16% of the information was elicited using free-recall prompts in the pre-protocol interviews, about half of the information was obtained using free recall in the protocol interviews. Furthermore, this pattern of results was similar regardless of the children's age. Although younger children provided shorter and less detailed responses than did older children, analyses of interviews with 4- to 6-year-old children revealed that the interviewers relied heavily on invitations (34% of their questions) and succeeded in eliciting a substantial amount of information (49% of the total) using free-recall prompts. Recent research using a British English version of the protocol in England (Lamb et al., 2006) and a French version in Quebec (Cyr, Lamb, Pelletier, Leduc, & Perron, 2006) has confirmed that the protocol leads to comparably dramatic increases in the use and productiveness of open-ended prompts.

In interviews using the protocol, children thus provided substantially more details in response to open-ended invitations. Because these studies involved criminal events, the accuracy of the children's responses could not be established, but research has consistently demonstrated that responses to open-ended questions are more likely to be accurate (Lamb, Sternberg, Orbach, Hershkowitz, & Esplin, 1999). Orbach et al. (2000) showed that almost all of the children who made a disclosure provided a narrative account of the alleged abuse in response to the first invitation. Likewise, Sternberg, Lamb, Orbach, et al. (2001); Lamb et al. (2006); and

Cyr et al. (2006) showed major increases in the amounts of information elicited using invitations. In each case, the total amount of information elicited from free-recall memory increased from about one-seventh of the information in the pre-protocol interviews to about half in the protocol interviews.

There are conflicting views as to whether very young children require more direct interviewing strategies to provide the required level of support and scaffolding for recall and reporting or whether open-ended strategies are sufficient, just as with older children (e.g., Lamb, 1994; Lamb et al., in press; Perry & Wrightsman, 1991). To further clarify the ability of preschoolers to address open-ended questions, Lamb et al. (2003) studied protocol interviews of 130 4- to 8-year-olds and showed that children as young as 4 years were able to report substantial numbers of details about the alleged abuse in response to open-ended invitations. On average, one-half of the information provided by the children came in response to open-ended prompts.

More recently, research using the NICHD protocol has been focused on understanding special groups of witnesses—those who are reluctant or unwilling to disclose, and those who have learning disabilities. Although much attention has been given to the dangers of eliciting false reports of abuse from children, little has been directed toward an equally serious issue—children who have experienced abuse but do not disclose. In Israel, for example, approximately one-third of the suspected child victims interviewed do not disclose abuse during forensic interviews, despite suspicion that abuse might have occurred (Hershkowitz, Horowitz, & Lamb, in press). In a smaller-scale study of interviews conducted using the NICHD protocol, Pipe et al. (in press) reported that 23% of the 294 children interviewed did not make a disclosure, despite sound reasons to suspect that abuse had occurred (e.g., suspect confession). The likelihood of disclosure increased with age and decreased if the suspected perpetrator was a close family member, especially for the younger children in the sample.

Children may be reluctant to disclose abuse for many reasons, including the desire to protect familiar perpetrators, especially family members (Paine & Hansen, 2002; Yuille, Tymofievich, & Marxsen, 1995), or because they have been coerced into secrecy (DeYoung, 1988; Goodman-Brown, 1995; Goodman-Brown, Edelstein, Goodman, Jones, & Gordon, 2003), assume some responsibility or blame (Lyon, 2002; Sjöberg & Lindblad,

2002), feel ashamed or embarrassed (Lyon, 1995; Saywitz et al., 1991), or fear threatened or imagined negative outcomes (Berliner & Conte, 1995; DeYoung, 1988; Paine & Hansen, 2002; Palmer, Brown, Rae-Grant, & Loughlin, 1999). In addition, young victims may not understand that they have been abused and may have failed to encode or remember experiences that did not appear salient to them (Cederborg, Lamb, & Laurel, in press).

Three new studies (Hershkowitz et al., in press; Hershkowitz, Horowitz, & Lamb, in preparation; Orbach, Shiloach, & Lamb, in press) show that children who are reluctant to disclose or who do not disclose at all, despite substantial evidence that abuse occurred, differ from children who are willing to disclose abuse even in the early presubstantive phases of the interview. Hershkowitz et al. (in press; in preparation) examined the transcripts of forensic interviews conducted with 70 children (4 to 13 years old) about whom there was compelling evidence that abuse had indeed occurred. Half of the children disclosed abuse and half did not, with children who did not disclose any abuse being more uncooperative and providing fewer details and more uninformative responses to the interviewers' prompts during the presubstantive rapport-building and episodic-memory practice segments of the interview. During the substantive phase, interviewers posed fewer free-recall prompts and made fewer supportive comments when interviewing children who did not disclose. Hershkowitz et al. concluded that the presubstantive portion of the interview may be important for identifying reluctant witnesses, and that a premature focus on getting an allegation may result in nondisclosure from these children. Similar conclusions were reached by Orbach et al. (in press), who explored the relation between the type of prompt needed to elicit allegations of abuse and the amount of information subsequently disclosed by the alleged victims. The 70 4- to 12-year-old children studied were classified as either nonreluctant disclosers (those who made allegations in response to open free-recall prompts) or reluctant disclosers (those children who did not make an allegation until focused prompts were used). Nonreluctant disclosers reported more forensically relevant information in response to free-recall prompts throughout the interview. Furthermore, the amount of information reported during the presubstantive segment of the interview was positively correlated with the amount reported during the substantive segment, indicating that reluctant witnesses are less communicative even during the nonsubstantive segments of the interview and continue to report less information following disclosure. Both studies thus highlight the importance of understanding the motivations and factors that may increase or decrease the likelihood that children will make genuine disclosures of abuse, particularly against the backdrop of statistics suggesting high rates of nonreporting (e.g., Hershkowitz et al., in press; London, Bruck, Ceci, & Shuman, 2005; Pipe et al., in press). The identification of such variables may pave the way for the development of strategies to support reluctant or nondisclosing witnesses, and thus enhance our ability to protect these children from continued exposure to abusive situations.

On another front, lawyers, forensic interviewers, child psychiatrists, and psychologists are increasingly calling for research exploring the abilities and vulnerabilities of witnesses with mental retardation and other learning disabilities (e.g., Jones, 2003; Kebbell & Davies, 2003; O'Kelly, Kebbell, Hatton, & Johnson, 2003; Stobbs & Kebbell, 2003). Children with mental retardation are much more likely than their typically developing counterparts to either witness or experience abuse, but they are less likely to have their complaints investigated and/or prosecuted because their capacity to provide reliable evidence is often doubted (Hershkowitz et al., in preparation; Westcott & Jones, 1999). Hershkowitz et al. (in preparation) examined the extent to which children with mental retardation were vulnerable to different types of abuse, characteristics that may be associated with abuse of these children, and reluctance to disclose as measured by denials of abuse and delayed disclosure by analyzing records of forensic interviews conducted in Israel between 1998 and 2004 ($n =$ 40,430) with children between 3 and 14 years of age who had been classified as slightly disabled (11%), severely disabled (1.2%), or not disabled (87.8%). Children with disabilities (both slight and severe) were more likely than those without disabilities to experience sexual, but not physical, abuse. They were also less likely to disclose, and disclosure was more likely to occur after a delay; they were more likely to experience serious offenses, and the perpetrators were more likely to be family members. Thus, these children were at particular risk of serious abuse within the family but were less likely to make disclosures that would have allowed their complaints to be investigated.

The limited research on eyewitness memory in children with mental retardation suggests that these children are as capable of providing reliable information about their experiences as children matched for developmental level (mental age) when interviewed with optimal techniques (free recall using open questions), although they may perform worse than children of the same chronological ages (Agnew & Powell, 2004; Dent, 1986; Henry & Gudjonsson, 2003; Michel, Gordon, Ornstein, & Simpson, 2000), with suggestive and/or specific questions being especially problematic (e.g., Agnew & Powell, 2004; Henry & Gudjonsson, 2003). In an ongoing program of research, we are exploring the ability of children with mental retardation (CWMR) to provide meaningful accounts of a personally experienced event when interviewed with the NICHD interview protocol compared to typically developing children matched for both mental age (MA) and chronological age (CA). In addition to examining the memorial and narrative abilities of CWMR and the effectiveness of different levels of interviewer prompting within the NICHD protocol, we are exploring the impact of the severity of mental retardation (mild versus moderate), the effects of delay between the experience and the interview, the effect of repeated interviews, and children's ability to answer suggestive questions that vary in structure (open versus closed) and content (central versus peripheral detail). Preliminary analyses from a subset of the sample (CWMR, $n = 17$; MA, $n = 15$; CA, $n = 12$) interviewed after a short delay (1 week) revealed no significant differences in the completeness of the accounts provided by the three groups of children or in the total amount of correct, incorrect, or ambiguous information reported. CWMR and their MA matches were, however, less accurate than the CA matches. In terms of the amount of support required from the interviewer to elicit the information, some interesting patterns emerged. CWMR required more prompts to orient them to the event of interest than CA matches. When the proportion of all information reported was considered, CWMR and MA children reported significantly less information to free-recall and open prompts and more information in response to focused prompts than CA children. There were no significant differences in the accuracy of children's responses to the suggestive questions, and no differences in the numbers of correct, incorrect or "don't know" answers between the CWMR, CA, and MA groups (Brown, Lewis, Stephens, Lunn, & Lamb, 2006).

In a small study of forensic interviews conducted in Sweden with alleged victims of abuse (6 to 22 years old) who had a learning disability ($n = 11$), Cederborg and Lamb (in preparation) showed that interviewers relied heavily on focused questions, although children were able to answer open questions when given the opportunity to do so and provided many forensically relevant details. The interviewers spoke more than the children, used questions that were developmentally inappropriate, and did not demonstrate an awareness of the needs and capacities of the children they were interviewing. Such findings are consistent with two recent studies demonstrating that the manner in which lawyers and judges interact with witnesses who have learning disabilities may also limit their participation in court and compromise the likelihood of just verdicts. Cederborg and Lamb (2006) examined court transcripts of Swedish cases where the alleged victims had learning disabilities and found that little or no information was provided to the court regarding the children's disabilities or their possible impact on the children's ability to give testimony. Judges expected them to provide reports much the same as those provided by typically developing children. Similarly, O'Kelly et al. (2003) examined court transcripts involving adults with learning disabilities and found that lawyers asked the same types of questions of them as of nondisabled adults and that judges did not differentially intervene. It is thus clear that research-based guidelines are needed to inform professionals (e.g., social workers, forensic investigators, police, lawyers, judges, and jurors) about the capacities of children with learning disabilities to recall and communicate their experiences and strategies that may enhance or detract from their capabilities.

Conclusion

Several decades of research on the frailties and competencies of young witnesses have demonstrated the advantages of a developmentally sensitive approach to interviewing in terms of both how much information children provide and, importantly, the accuracy of that information. Although the quality of children's testimony is influenced by a number of factors pertaining to the children themselves and the events they have experienced, the ways in which interviewers attempt to elicit information are critical. Valid reasons for caution about the accuracy of children's responses to suggestive questioning techniques or following exposure to coercive or highly suggestive prior interviews notwithstanding, even quite young children *are* able to provide reliable testimony about abusive experiences when questioned appropriately. However, we must also recognize that children may need help retrieving, structuring, and reporting their experiences in an elaborative manner, and there are a number of constructive approaches to interviewing that provide the appropriate support without degrading the quality of children's accounts. For example, when children understand their role as informants, the naivety of the interviewer, the importance of only reporting what they know and not guessing, and the permissibility of "don't know" responses and of correcting an interviewer's mistakes; when they feel comfortable with the interviewer and have had an opportunity to practice talking about the past in a detailed manner; and when interviewers avoid relying on closed, leading, or misleading questions, even very young children are able to provide meaningful and accurate accounts of their experiences. The onus is therefore on interviewers to ensure that they provide the optimal conditions for children to provide accurate and detailed accounts of even very distressing and traumatic experiences. In this way, we can, in turn, ensure that children are protected from their abusers and that innocent adults are not falsely accused.

References

Agnew, S., & Powell, M. B. (2004). The effect of intellectual disability on children's recall of an event across different question types. *Law and Human Behavior, 28,* 273–294.

Aldridge, J., & Cameron, S. (1999). Interviewing child witnesses: Questioning techniques and the role of training. *Applied Developmental Science, 3,* 136–147.

Aldridge, J., Lamb, M. E., Sternberg, K. J., Orbach, Y., Esplin, P. W., & Bowler, L. (2004). Using a human figure drawing to elicit information from alleged victims of child sexual abuse. *Journal of Consulting and Clinical Psychology, 72,* 304–316.

American Professional Society on the Abuse of Children. (1990). *Guidelines for psychosocial evaluation of suspected sexual abuse in young children.* Chicago, IL: Author.

American Professional Society on the Abuse of Children. (1997). *Guidelines for psychosocial evaluation of suspected sexual abuse in young children* (Rev. ed.). Chicago, IL: Author.

Baker-Ward, L., Gordon, B. N., Ornstein, P. A., Larus, D., & Clubb, P. (1993). Young children's long-term retention of a pediatric examination. *Child Development, 56,* 1103–1119.

Bekerian, D. A., Dennet, J. L., Hill, K., & Hitchcock, R. (1990). *Effects of detailed imagery on simulated witness recall.* Paper presented at the Second European Conference on Law and Psychology, Nuremberg, Germany.

Berliner, L., & Conte, J. R. (1995). The effects of disclosure and intervention on sexually abused children. *Child Abuse & Neglect, 19,* 371–384.

Bowen, C. J., & Howie, P. M. (2002). Context and cue cards in young children's testimony: A comparison of brief narrative elaboration and context reinstatement. *Journal of Applied Psychology, 87,* 1077–1085.

Brown, D. A., Pipe, M.-E., Lewis, C., Lamb, M. E., & Orbach, Y. (2007). Supportive or suggestive: Do human figure drawings help 5–7 year old children to report touch? *Journal of Consulting and Clinical Psychology, 75,* 33–42.

Brown, D. A., Lewis, C., Stephens, E., Lunn, J., & Lamb, M. E. (2006, March). *Facilitating eyewitness testimony in children with learning disabilities.* Paper presented at the Annual Meeting of the American Psychology and Law Society, Florida..

Brown, D. A., & Pipe, M.-E. (2003a). Individual differences in children's event memory reports and the narrative elaboration technique. *Journal of Applied Psychology, 88,* 195–206.

Brown, D. A. & Pipe, M.-E. (2003b). Variations on a technique: Enhancing children's recall using narrative elaboration training. *Applied Cognitive Psychology, 17,* 377–399.

Brown, D. A., Salmon, K., Pipe, M.-E., Rutter, M., Craw, S., & Taylor, B. (1999). Children's recall of medical experiences: The impact of stress. *Child Abuse and Neglect, 23,* 209–216.

Brown, R. (1973). *A first language.* Cambridge, MA: Harvard University Press.

Bruck, M., Ceci, S. J., Francoeur, E., & Renick, A. (1995). Anatomically detailed dolls do not facilitate preschoolers' reports of a pediatric examination involving genital touching. *Journal of Experimental Psychology: Applied, 1,* 95–109.

Bruck, M., Melnyk, L., & Ceci, S. J. (2000). Draw it again Sam: The effect of drawing on children's suggestibility and source monitoring ability. *Journal of Experimental Child Psychology, 77,* 169–196.

Butler, S., Gross, J., & Hayne, H. (1995). The effect of drawing on memory performance in young children. *Developmental Psychology, 31,* 597–608.

Camparo, L. B., Wagner, J. T., & Saywitz, K. J. (2001). Interviewing children about real and fictitious events: Revisiting the narrative elaboration procedure. *Law and Human Behavior, 25,* 63–80.

Ceci, S. J., & Bruck, M. (1993). Suggestibility of the child witness: A historical review and synthesis. *Psychological Bulletin, 113,* 403–439.

Ceci, S. J., & Bruck, M. (1995). *Jeopardy in the courtroom: A scientific analysis of children's testimony.* Washington, DC: American Psychological Association.

Ceci, S. J., Huffman, M. L. C., Smith, E., & Loftus, E. F. (1994). Repeatedly thinking about a non-event: Source misattributions among preschoolers. *Consciousness and Cognition, 3,* 388–407.

Ceci, S. J., Loftus, E. F., Leichtman, M. D., & Bruck, M. (1994). The possible role of source misattributions in the creation of false beliefs among preschoolers. *International Journal of Clinical and Experimental Hypnosis, 42,* 304–320.

Ceci, S. J., Ross, D. F., & Toglia, M. P. (1987a). Suggestibility of children's memory: Psychological issues. *Journal of Experimental Psychology: General, 116,* 38–49.

Ceci, S. J., Ross, D. F., & Toglia, M. P. (1987b). Age differences in suggestibility: Narrowing the uncertainties. In S. J. Ceci, M. P. Toglia, & D. F. Ross (Eds.), *Children's eyewitness memory* (pp. 79–91). New York: Springer-Verlag.

Cederborg, A.-C., & Lamb, M. E. (2006). How does the legal system respond when disabled children are victimized? *Child Abuse and Neglect, 30,* 537–547.

Cederborg, A.-C., & Lamb, M. E. (in preparation). *Interviewing alleged victims with mental disabilities.*

Cederborg, A.-C., Lamb, M. E., & Laurel, O. (in press). Delay of disclosure, minimization, and denial when the evidence is unambiguous: A multivictim case. In M.-E. Pipe, M. E. Lamb, Y. Orbach, & A.-C. Cederborg (Eds.), *Child sexual abuse: Disclosure, delay, and denial.* Mahwah, NJ: Lawrence Erlbaum.

Cederborg, A., Orbach, Y., Sternberg, K. L., & Lamb, M. E. (2000). Investigative interviews of child witnesses in Sweden. *Child Abuse and Neglect, 24,* 1355–1361.

Christianson, S. (1992). Emotional stress and eyewitness memory: A critical review. *Psychological Bulletin, 112,* 284–309.

Cole, C. B., & Loftus, E. F. (1987). The memory of children. In S. J. Ceci, M. P. Toglia, & D. F. Ross (Eds.), *Children's Eyewitness Testimony* (pp. 178–208). New York: Springer-Verlag.

Cordón, I. M., Pipe, M.-E., Sayfan, L., Melinder, A., & Goodman, G. S. (2004). Memory for traumatic experiences in early childhood. *Developmental Review, 24,* 101–132.

Craig, R. A., Scheibe, R., Kircher, J., Raskin, D. C., & Dodd, D. (1999). The influence of the form of the question on the eyewitness testimony of preschool children. *Applied Developmental Science, 3,* 77–85.

Cyr, M., Lamb, M. E., Pelletier, J., Leduc, P., & Perron, A. (2006, July). *Assessing the effectiveness of the NICHD Investigative Interview protocol in Francophone Quebec.* Paper presented at the Second International Investigative Interviewing Conference, University of Portsmouth, UK.

Dale, P. S. (1976). *Language development: Structure and function.* New York: Holt, Rinehart, & Winston.

Davies, G., Tarrant, A., & Flin, R. (1989). Close encounters of the witness kind: Children's memory for a simulated health inspection. *British Journal of Psychology, 80,* 415–429.

DeLoache, J., & Marzolf, D. P. (1995). The use of dolls to interview young children: Issues of symbolic representation. *Journal of Experimental Child Psychology, 60,* 155–173.

Dent, H. R. (1982). The effects of interviewing strategies on the results of interviews with child witnesses. In A. Trankell (Ed.), *Reconstructing the past: The role of psychologists in criminal trials* (pp. 279–297). Stockholm: Norstedt.

Dent, H. R. (1986). Experimental study of the effectiveness of different techniques of questioning child witnesses. *British Journal of Social and Clinical Psychology, 18,* 41–51.

Dent, H. R., & Stephenson, G. M. (1979). An experimental study of the effectiveness of different techniques of questioning child witnesses. *British Journal of Social and Clinical Psychology, 18,* 41–51.

de Villiers, J., & de Villiers, P. (1999). Language development. In M. H. Bornstein & M. E. Lamb (Eds.), *Developmental psychology: An advanced textbook* (4th ed., pp. 313–373). Mahwah, NJ: Erlbaum.

DeYoung, M. (1988). Issues in determining the veracity of sexual abuse allegations. *Children's Health Care, 17,* 50–57.

Dorado, J. S., & Saywitz, K. J. (2001). Interviewing preschoolers from low- and middle-SES communities: A test of the Narrative Elaboration recall improvement technique. *Journal of Clinical Child Psychology, 30,* 566–578.

Elischberger, H. B., & Roebers, C. M. (2001). Improving young children's free narratives about an observed event: The effects of nonspecific verbal prompts. *International Journal of Behavioral Development, 25,* 160–166.

Everson, M. D., & Boat, B. W. (2002). The utility of anatomical dolls and drawings in child forensic interviews. In M. L. Eisen, J. A. Quas, & G. S. Goodman (Eds.), *Memory and suggestibility in the forensic interview* (pp. 383–408). Mahwah, NJ: Erlbaum.

Fisher, R. P., & Geiselman, R. E. (1992). *Memory-enhancing techniques for investigating interviewing: The cognitive interview.* Springfield, IL: Charles C. Thomas.

Fisher, R. P., Geiselman, R. E., Raymond, D. S., Jurkevich, L. M., & Warhaftig, M. L. (1987). Enhancing enhanced eyewitness memory: Refining the cognitive interview. *Journal of Police Science and Administration, 15,* 291–297.

Fivush, R., Peterson, C., & Schwarzmueller, A. (2002). Questions and answers: The credibility of child witnesses in the context of specific questioning techniques. In M. L. Eisen, J. A. Quas, & G. S. Goodman (Eds.), *Memory and suggestibility in the forensic interview* (pp. 331–354). Mahwah, NJ: Erlbaum.

Fivush, R., Sales, J. M., Goldberg, A., Bahrick, L., & Parker, J. (2004). Weathering the storm: Children's long-term recall of Hurricane Andrew. *Memory, 12,* 104–118.

Flavell, J. (1970). Developmental studies of mediated memory. In H. Reese & L. Lipsitt (Eds.), *Advances in child development and behavior* (pp. 181–211). New York: Academic Press.

Flavell, J. H., Miller, P. H., & Miller, S. A. (1993). *Cognitive Development* (3rd ed.). New Jersey: Prentice-Hall Inc.

Garry, M., Manning, C. G., & Loftus, E. F., & Sherman, S. J. (1996). Imagination inflation: Imagining a childhood event inflates confidence that it occurred. *Psychonomic Bulletin and Review, 3,* 208–214.

Garven, S., Wood, J. M., Malpass, R. S., & Shaw, J. S. (1998). More than suggestion: The effect of interviewing techniques from the McMartin Preschool case. *Journal of Applied Psychology, 83,* 347–359.

Gee, S., & Pipe, M.-E. (1995). Helping children to remember: The influence of object cues on children's accounts of a real event. *Developmental Psychology, 31,* 746–758.

Geiselman, R. E. (1999). Commentary on recent research with the cognitive interview. *Psychology, Crime, and Law, 5,* 197–202.

Geiselman, R. E., & Padilla, J. (1988). Cognitive interviewing with child witnesses. *Journal of Police Science and Administration, 16,* 236–242.

Goodman, G. S., & Aman, C. (1990). Children's use of anatomically detailed dolls to recount an event. *Child Development, 61,* 1859–1871.

Goodman, G. S., Aman, C., & Hirschman, J. (1987). Child sexual and physical abuse: Children's testimony. In S. J. Ceci, M. P. Toglia & D. F. Ross (Eds.), *Children's eyewitness testimony,* (pp. 1–23). New York: Springer-Verlag.

Goodman, G. S., Bottoms, B. L., Schwartz-Kenney, B. M., & Rudy, L. (1991). Children's testimony about a stressful event: Improving children's reports. *Journal of Narrative Life History, 1,* 69–99.

Goodman, G. S., Hirschman, J. E., Hepps, D., & Rudy, L. (1991). Children's memory for stressful events. *Merrill-Palmer Quarterly, 37,* 109–158.

Goodman, G. S., Quas, J. A., Batterman-Faunce, J. M., Riddlesberger, M. M., & Kuhn, J. (1994). Predictors of accurate and inaccurate memories of traumatic events experienced in childhood. *Consciousness and Cognition, 3,* 263–294.

Goodman, G. S., Quas, J. A., Batterman-Faunce, J. M., Riddlesberger, M. M., & Kuhn, J. (1997). Children's reactions to and memory for a stressful event: Influences of age, anatomical dolls, knowledge, and parental attachment. *Applied Developmental Sciences, 1,* 54–75.

Goodman, G. S., & Reed, R. S. (1986). Age differences in eyewitness testimony. *Law and Human Behavior, 10,* 317–332.

Goodman, G. S., Rudy, L., Bottoms, B., & Aman, C. (1990). Children's concerns and memory: Issues of ecological validity in the study of children's eyewitness testimony. In R. Fivush & J. A. Hudson (Eds.), *Knowing and remembering in young children. Emory symposia in cognition* (Vol. 3, pp. 249–284). New York: Cambridge University Press.

Goodman, G. S, & Schwartz-Kenney, B. M. (1992). Why knowing a child's age is not enough: Influences of cognitive, social, and emotional factors on children's testimony. In H. Dent & R. Flin. (Eds.), *Children as witnesses* (pp. 15–32). Chichester, UK: John Wiley & Sons.

Goodman, G. S., Wilson, M. E., Hazan, C., & Reed, R. S. (1989, April). *Children's testimony nearly four years after an event.* Paper presented to the Eastern Psychological Association, Boston, MA.

Goodman-Brown, T. B. (1995). Why children tell: A model of children's disclosure of sexual abuse. *Dissertation Abstracts International, 56,* 2325.

Goodman-Brown, T. B., Edelstein, R. S., Goodman, G. S., Jones, D. P. H., & Gordon, D. S. (2003). Why children tell: A model of children's disclosure of sexual abuse. *Child Abuse and Neglect, 27,* 525–540.

Gordon, B. N., Baker-Ward, L., & Ornstein, P. A. (2001). Children's testimony: A review of research on memory for past experiences. *Clinical Child and Family Psychological Review, 4,* 157–181.

Gross, J., & Hayne, H. (1998). Drawing facilitates children's verbal reports of emotionally laden events. *Journal of Experimental Psychology: Applied, 14,* 163–179.

Gross, J., & Hayne, H. (1999). Drawing facilitates children's verbal reports after long delays. *Journal of Experimental Psychology: Applied, 5,* 265–283.

Gross, J., Hayne, H., & Poole, A. (2006). The use of drawing in interviews with children: A potential pitfall. In J. R. Marrow (Ed.), *Focus on child psychology research* (pp. 119–144). New York: Nova Publishers.

Harner, L. (1975). Yesterday and tomorrow: Development of early understanding of the terms. *Developmental Psychology, 11,* 864–865.

Hayes, B. K., & Delamothe, K. (1997). Cognitive interviewing procedures and suggestibility in children's recall. *Journal of Applied Psychology, 82,* 562–577.

Henry, L. A., & Gudjonsson, G. H. (2003). Eyewitness memory, suggestibility, and repeated recall sessions in children with mild and moderate intellectual disabilities. *Law and Human Behavior, 27,* 481–505.

Hershkowitz, I., Horowitz, D., & Lamb, M. E. (in press). Trends in children's disclosure of abuse in Israel: A national study. *Child Abuse and Neglect.*

Hershkowitz, I., Horowitz, D., & Lamb, M. E. (in preparation). *Victimization of children with learning, mental and communicative difficulties.*

Hershkowitz, I., Orbach, Y., Lamb, M. E., Sternberg, K. J., & Horowitz, D. (2001). The effects of mental context reinstatement on children's accounts of sexual abuse. *Applied Cognitive Psychology, 15,* 235–248.

Home Office. (1992). *Memorandum of good practice on video recorded interviews with child witnesses for criminal proceedings.* London: Author, with Department of Health.

Home Office. (2002). *Achieving the best evidence in criminal proceedings: Guidance for vulnerable and intimidated witnesses, including children.* London: Author.

Howe, M. L. (1997). Children's memory for traumatic experiences. *Learning and Individual Differences, 9,* 153–174.

Howe, M. L., Courage, M. L., & Peterson, C. (1994). How can I remember when "I" wasn't there: Long-term retention of traumatic experiences and emergence of the cognitive self. *Consciousness and Cognition, 3,* 327–355.

Hutcheson, G. D., Baxter, J. S., Telfer, K., & Warden, D. (1995). Child witness statement quality: Question type and errors of omission. *Law and Human Behavior, 19,* 631–648.

Hyman, I. E., Husband, T. H., & Billings, J. F. (1995). False memories of childhood experiences. *Applied Cognitive Psychology, 9,* 181–197.

Jones, D. P. H. (1992). *Interviewing the sexually abused child.* Oxford: Gaskell.

Jones, D. P. H. (2003). *Communicating with vulnerable children.* London: Gaskell and Royal College of Psychiatrists.

Jones, D. C., Swift, D. J., & Johnson, M. A. (1988). Nondeliberate memory for a novel event among preschoolers. *Developmental Psychology, 24,* 641–645.

Kebbell, M., & Davies, G. (2003). People with intellectual disabilities in the investigation and prosecution of crime. *Legal and Criminological Psychology, 8,* 219–222.

King, M. A., & Yuille, J. C. (1987). Suggestibility and the child witness. In S. J. Ceci, D. F. Ross, & M. P. Toglia (Eds.), *Children's eyewitness memory* (pp. 24–35). New York: Springer-Verlag.

Köhnken, G., Milne, R., Memon, A., & Bull, R. (1999). The cognitive interview: A meta-analysis. *Psychology, Crime, and Law, 5,* 3–27.

Lamb, M. E. (1994). The investigation of child sexual abuse: An interdisciplinary consensus statement. *Child Abuse and Neglect, 18,* 1021–1028.

Lamb, M. E., & Brown, D. A. (2006). Conversational apprentices: Helping children become competent informants about their own experiences. *British Journal of Developmental Psychology, 24,* 215–234.

Lamb, M. E., & Fauchier, A. (2001). The effects of question type on self-contradictions by children in the course of forensic interviews. *Applied Cognitive Psychology, 15,* 483–491.

Lamb, M. E., Hershkowitz, I., Sternberg, K. J., Boat, B., & Everson, M. D. (1996). Investigative interviews of alleged sexual abuse victims with and without anatomical dolls. *Child Abuse and Neglect, 20,* 1239–1247.

Lamb, M. E., Hershkowitz, I., Sternberg, K. J., Esplin, P. W., Hovav, M., Manor, T., & Yudilevitch, L. (1996). Effects of investigative utterance types on Israeli children's responses. *International Journal of Behavioral Development, 19,* 627–637.

Lamb, M. E., Orbach, Y., Sternberg, K. J., Esplin, P. W., & Hershkowitz, I. (2002). The effects of forensic interview practices on the quality of information provided by alleged victims of child abuse. In H. L. Westcott, G. M. Davies, & R. Bull (Eds.), *Children's testimony: Psychological research and forensic practice* (pp. 131–146). Chichester, England: Wiley.

Lamb, M. E., Orbach, Y., Warren, A. R., Esplin, P. W., & Hershkowitz, I. (in press). Getting the most out of children: Factors affecting the informativeness of young witnesses. In M. P. Toglia, J. D. Read, D. F. Ross, & R. C. L. Lindsay (Eds.), *Handbook of eyewitness psychology: Vol 1. Memory for events.* Mahwah, NJ: Erlbaum.

Lamb, M. E., Sternberg, K. J., & Esplin, P. W. (1994). Factors influencing the reliability and validity of the statements made by young victims of sexual maltreatment. *Journal of Applied Developmental Psychology, 15,* 255–280.

Lamb, M. E., Sternberg, K. J., & Esplin, P. W. (1995). Making children into competent witnesses: Reactions to the amicus brief In re Michaels. *Psychology, Public Policy, and the Law, 1,* 438–449.

Lamb, M. E., Sternberg, K. J., & Esplin, P. W. (1998). Conducting investigative interviews of alleged sexual abuse victims. *Child Abuse and Neglect, 22,* 813–823.

Lamb, M. E., Sternberg, K. J., Orbach, Y., Aldridge, J., Bowler, L., Pearson, S., & Esplin, P. W. (2006, July). *Enhancing the quality of investigative interviews by British police officers.* Paper presented at the Second International Investigative Interviewing Conference, University of Portsmouth, UK.

Lamb, M. E., Sternberg, K. J., Orbach, Y., Esplin, P. W., Stewart, H., & Mitchell, S. (2003). Age differences in young children's responses to open-ended invitations in the course of forensic interviews. *Journal of Consulting and Clinical Psychology, 71,* 926–934.

Lamb, M. E., Sternberg, K. J., Orbach, Y., Hershkowitz, I., & Esplin, P. W. (1999). Forensic interviews of children. In A. Memon & R. Bull (Eds.), *Handbook of the psychology of interviewing* (pp. 253–277). New York: Wiley.

Leichtman, M. D., & Ceci, S. J. (1995). The effects of stereotypes and suggestions on preschoolers' reports. *Developmental Psychology, 31,* 568–578.

Leichtman, M. D., Ceci, S. J., & Morse, M. B. (1997). The nature and development of children's event memory. In P. S. Applebaum & L. A. Uyehara (Eds.), *Trauma and memory: Clinical and legal controversies* (pp. 158–187). New York: Oxford University Press.

Leventhal, J. M., Hamilton, J., Rededal, S., Tebano-Micci, A., & Eyster, C. (1989). Anatomically correct dolls used in interviews of young children suspected of having been sexually abused. *Pediatrics, 84,* 900–906.

Loftus, E. F., & Pickrell, J. E. (1995). The formation of false memories. *Psychiatric Annals, 25,* 720–725.

London, K., Bruck, M., Ceci, S. J., & Shuman, D. W. (2005). Disclosure of child sexual abuse: What does the research tell us about the ways that children tell? *Psychology, Public Policy, and the Law, 11,* 194–226.

Lyon, T. D. (1995). False allegations and false denials in child sexual abuse. *Psychology, Public Policy, and the Law, 1,* 429–437.

Lyon, T. D. (2002). Scientific support for expert testimony on child sexual abuse accommodation. In J. R. Conte (Ed.), *Critical issues in child sexual abuse* (pp.107–138). Newbury Park, CA: SAGE.

Marin, B. V., Holmes, D. L., Guth, M., & Kovac, P. (1979). The potential of children as eyewitnesses: A comparison of children and adults on eyewitness tasks. *Law and Human Behavior, 3,* 295–306.

McCauley, M. R., & Fisher, R. P. (1995). Facilitating children's eyewitness recall with the revised cognitive interview. *Journal of Applied Psychology, 80,* 510–516.

McCauley, M. R., & Fisher, R. P. (1996). Enhancing children's eyewitness testimony with the Cognitive Interview. In G. Davies, S. Lloyd-Bostock, M. McMurran, & C. Wilson (Eds.), *Psychology, law, and criminal justice: International developments in research and practice* (pp. 127–134). Berlin, Germany: Walter de Gruyter.

McAuliff, B. D., Kovera, M. B., & Viswesvaran, C. (1998, March). *Methodological issues in child suggestibility research: A meta-analysis.* Paper presented to the American Psychology-Law Society Convention, Redondo Beach, CA.

Memon, A., Cronin, O., Eaves, R., & Bull, R. (1993). The cognitive interview and child witnesses. In N. Clark & G. M. Stephenson (Eds.), *Children, evidence, and procedure* (pp. 3–9). Leicester, England: British Psychological Society.

Memon, A., Cronin, O., Eaves, R., & Bull, R. (1995). An empirical test of the mnemonic components of the cognitive interview. In G. Davies, S. Lloyd-Bostock, M. McMurran, & C. Wilson (Eds.), *Psychology, law, and criminal justice: International developments in research and practice* (pp. 135–145). Berlin: Walter de Gruyter & Co.

Memon, A., Wark, L., Bull, R., & Köhnken, G. (1997). Isolating the effects of the cognitive interview techniques. *British Journal of Psychology, 88,* 179–197.

Michel, M. K., Gordon, B. N., Ornstein, P. A., & Simpson, M. A. (2000). The abilities of children with mental retardation to remember personal experiences: Implications for testimony. *Journal of Clinical Child Psychology, 29,* 453–463.

Miller, P. H. (1990). The development of strategies of selective attention. In D. F. Bjorklund (Ed.), *Children's strategies: Contemporary views of cognitive development* (pp. 157–184). Hillsdale, NJ: Lawrence Erlbaum Associates.

Nathanson, R., Crank, J. N., & Saywitz, K. J. (in press). Enhancing the oral narratives of children with learning disabilities. *Reading and Writing Quarterly.*

Nelson, K., & Fivush, R. (2004). The emergence of autobiographical memory: A social cultural developmental theory. *Psychological Review, 111,* 486–514.

Oates, K., & Shrimpton, S. (1991). Children's memories for stressful and non-stressful events. *Medicine, Science, and the Law, 31,* 4–10.

O'Kelly, C. M. E., Kebbell, M. R., Hatton, C., & Johnson, S. D. (2003). Judicial intervention in court cases involving witnesses with and without learning disabilities. *Legal and Criminological Psychology, 8,* 229–240.

Orbach, Y., Hershkowitz, I., Lamb, M. E., Sternberg, K. J., Esplin, P. W., & Horowitz, D. (2000). Assessing the value of structured protocols for forensic interviews of alleged abuse victims. *Child Abuse and Neglect, 24,* 733–752.

Orbach, Y., & Lamb, M. E. (2001). The relationship between within-interview contradictions and eliciting interviewer utterances. *Child Abuse and Neglect, 25,* 323–333.

Orbach, Y., Shiloach, H., & Lamb, M. E. (in press). Reluctant disclosers of child sexual abuse. In M.-E. Pipe, M. E. Lamb, Y. Orbach, & A.-C. Cederborg (Eds.), *Child sexual abuse: Disclosure, delay, and denial.* Mahwah, NJ: Erlbaum.

Ornstein, P. A. (1995). Children's long-term retention of salient personal experiences. *Journal of Traumatic Stress, 8,* 581–605.

Ornstein, P. A., Gordon, B. N., & Larus, D. M. (1992). Children's memory for a personally experienced event: Implications for testimony. *Applied Cognitive Psychology, 6,* 49–60.

Ornstein, P. A., Haden, C. A., & Hedrick, A. M. (2004). Learning to remember: Social-communicative exchanges and the development of children's memory skills. *Developmental Review, 24,* 374–395.

Paine, M. L., & Hansen, D. J. (2002) Factors influencing children to self-disclose sexual abuse. *Clinical Psychology Review, 22,* 271–295.

Palmer, S. E., Brown, R. A., Rae-Grant, N. I., & Loughlin, M. J. (1999). Responding to children's disclosure of familial abuse: What survivors tell us. *Child Welfare, 78,* 259–282.

Parker, J. F., Bahrick, L., Lundy, B., Fivush, R., & Levitt, M. (1998). Effects of stress on children's memory for a natural disaster. In C. P. Thompson, D. G. Payne, M. P. Toglia, J. D. Read, & D. Bruce (Eds.), *Eyewitness memory: Theoretical and applied perspectives* (pp. 31–54). Mahwah, NJ: Erlbaum.

Perry, N. W., & Wrightsman, L. S. (1991). *The child witness: Legal issues and dilemmas.* Newbery Park, CA: SAGE.

Peters, D. P. (1987). The impact of naturally occurring stress on children's memory. In S. J. Ceci, M. P. Toglia, & D. F. Ross (Eds.), *Children's eyewitness testimony* (pp. 122–142). New York: Springer-Verlag.

Peters, D. P. (1991). The influence of stress and arousal on the child witness. In J. Doris (Ed.), *The suggestibility of children's recollections* (pp. 60–76). Washington, DC: American Psychological Association.

Peterson, C. (1999). Children's memory for medical emergencies: 2 years later. *Developmental Psychology, 35,* 1493–1506.

Peterson, C., & Bell, M. (1996). Children's memory for traumatic injury. *Child Development, 67,* 3045–3070.

Peterson, C., Dowden, C., & Tobin, J. (1999). Interviewing preschoolers: Comparison of yes/no and wh- questions. *Law and Human Behavior, 23,* 539–555.

Peterson, C., & Whalen, N. (2001). Five years later: Children's memory for medical emergencies. *Applied Cognitive Psychology, 15 ,* S7–S24.

Pipe, M.-E., Gee, S., & Wilson, J. C. (1993). Cues, props and context: Do they facilitate children's event reports? In G. S. Goodman & B. L. Bottoms (Eds.), *Child victims, child witnesses: Understanding and improving testimony* (pp. 25–46). New York: Guilford Press.

Pipe, M.-E., Lamb, M. E., Orbach, Y., & Esplin, P. W. (2004). Recent research on children's testimony about experienced and witnessed events. *Developmental Review, 24,* 440–468.

Pipe, M.-E., Lamb, M. E., Orbach, O., Stewart, H. L., Sternberg, K. J., & Esplin, P. W. (in press). Factors associated with non-disclosure of suspected abuse during forensic interviews. In M.-E. Pipe, M. E. Lamb, Y. Orbach, & A.-C. Cederborg (Eds.), *Child sexual abuse: Disclosure, delay, and denial.* Mahwah, NJ: Erlbaum.

Pipe, M.-E., & Salmon, K. (2002). What children bring to the interview context: Individual differences in children's event reports. In M. L. Eisen, J. A. Quas, & G. S. Goodman (Eds.), *Memory and suggestibility in the forensic interview* (pp. 235–261). Mahwah, NJ: Erlbaum.

Poole, D. A., & Lamb, M. E. (1998). *Investigative interviews of children: A guide for helping professionals.* Washington, DC: American Psychological Association.

Quas, J. A., Goodman, G. S., Bidrose, S., Pipe, M.-E., Craw, S., & Ablin, D. S. (1999). Emotion and memory: Children's long-term remembering, forgetting, and suggestibility. *Journal of Experimental Child Psychology, 72,* 235–290.

Quas, J. A., Goodman, G. S., Ghetti, S., & Redlich, A. D. (2000). Questioning the child witness: What can we conclude from the research thus far? *Trauma, Violence & Abuse, 1,* 223–249.

Quas, J. A., Qin, J. J., Schaaf, J. M., & Goodman, G. S. (1997). Individual differences in children's and adults' suggestibility and false event memory. *Learning and Individual Differences, 9,* 359–390.

Raskin, D. C., & Esplin, P. W. (1991). Statement validity assessments: Interview procedures and content analyses of children's statements of sexual abuse. *Behavioral Assessment, 13,* 265–291.

Roberts, K. P., & Blades, M. (2000). *Children's source monitoring.* Mahwah, NJ: Erlbaum.

Roberts, K. P., & Blades, M. (in press). The effects of interacting with events on children's eyewitness memory and source monitoring. *Applied Cognitive Psychology.*

Roberts, K. P., & Powell, M. B. (2001). Describing individual incidents of sexual abuse: A review of research on the effects of multiple sources of information on children's reports. *Child Abuse and Neglect, 25,* 1643–1659.

Salmon, K. (2001). Remembering and reporting by children: The influence of cues and props. *Clinical Psychology Review, 21,* 267–300.

Salmon, K., & Pipe, M.-E. (2000). Recalling an event one year later: The impact of props, drawing and a prior interview. *Applied Cognitive Psychology, 14,* 261–292.

Salmon, K., Roncolato, W., & Gleitzman, M. (2003). Children's report of emotionally laden events: Adapting the interview to the child. *Applied Cognitive Psychology, 17,* 65–80.

Sattler, J. M. (1998). *Assessment of children* (3rd ed.). San Diego, CA: Jerome M. Sattler.

Saywitz, K. (1987). Children's testimony: Age-related patterns of memory errors. In S. J. Ceci, M. P. Toglia, & D. F. Ross (Eds.), *Children's eyewitness testimony* (pp. 36–52). New York: Springer-Verlag.

Saywitz, K. J., & Camparo, L. (1998). Interviewing child witnesses: A developmental perspective. *International Journal of Child Abuse and Neglect, 22,* 825–843.

Saywitz, K. J., Geiselman, R. E., & Bornstein, G. K. (1992). Effects of cognitive interviewing and practice on children's recall performance. *Journal of Applied Psychology, 77,* 744–756.

Saywitz, K. J., Goodman, G. S., Nicholas, E., & Moan, S. F. (1991). Children's memories of a physical examination involving genital touch: Implications for reports of child sexual abuse. *Journal of Consulting and Clinical Psychology, 59,* 682–691.

Saywitz, K. J., & Lyon, T. D. (2002). Coming to grips with children's suggestibility. In M. L. Eisen, J. A. Quas, & G. S. Goodman (Eds.), *Memory and suggestibility in the forensic interview* (pp. 85–113). Mahwah, NJ: Erlbaum.

Saywitz, K. J., Nathanson, R., & Snyder, L. S. (1993). Credibility of child witnesses: The role of communicative competence. *Topics of Language Disorders, 13,* 59–78.

Saywitz, K. J., & Snyder, L. (1993). Improving children's testimony with preparation. In G. S. Goodman & B. L. Bottoms (Eds.), *Child victims, child witnesses: Understanding and improving testimony* (pp. 117–146). New York: Guilford.

Saywitz, K. J., & Snyder, L. (1996). Narrative elaboration: Test of a new procedure for interviewing children. *Journal of Consulting and Clinical Psychology, 64,* 1347–1357.

Saywitz, K. J., & Snyder, L., & Lamphear, V. (1996). Helping children tell what happened: A follow-up study of the narrative elaboration procedure. *Child Maltreatment, 1,* 200–212.

Schneider, W., & Bjorklund, D. F. (1998). Memory. In W. Damon (Series Ed.), D. Kuhn, & R. S. Siegler (Vol. Eds.), *Handbook of child psychology: Vol 2. Cognition, perception and language* (pp. 467–521). New York: Wiley.

Sjöberg, R. L., & Lindblad, F. (2002). Delayed disclosure and disrupted communication during forensic investigation of child sexual abuse: A study of 47 corroborated cases. *Acta Paediatrica, 91,* 1391–1396.

Sternberg, K. J., Lamb, M. E., Davies, G. M., Westcott, H. L. (2001). The memorandum of good practice: Theory versus application. *Child Abuse and Neglect, 25,* 669–681.

Sternberg, K. J., Lamb, M. E., Esplin, P. W., Orbach, Y., & Hershkowitz, I. (2002). Using a structured protocol to improve the quality of investigative interviews. In M. Eisen, G. Goodman, & J. Quas (Eds.), *Memory and suggestibility in the forensic interview* (pp. 409–436). Mahwah, NJ: Erlbaum.

Sternberg, K. J., Lamb, M. E., & Hershkowitz, I. (1996). Child sexual abuse investigations in Israel. *Criminal Justice and Behavior, 23,* 322–337.

Sternberg, K. J., Lamb, M. E., Hershkowitz, I., Yudilevitch, L., Orbach, Y., Esplin, P. W., et al. (1997). Effects of introductory style on children's abilities to describe experiences of sexual abuse. *Child Abuse and Neglect, 21,* 1133–1146.

Sternberg, K. J., Lamb, M. E., Orbach, Y., Esplin, P. W., & Mitchell, S. (2001). Use of a structured investigative protocol enhances young children's responses to free-recall prompts in the course of forensic interviews. *Journal of Applied Psychology, 86,* 997–1005.

Stevenson, K. M., Leung, P., & Cheung, K. M. (1992). Competency-based evaluation of interviewing skills in child sexual abuse cases. *Social Work Research and Abstracts, 28,* 11–16.

Steward, M. S. (1993). Understanding children's memories of medical procedures: "He didn't touch me and it didn't hurt!" In C. A. Nelson (Ed.), *Memory and affect in development* (pp. 171–225). Hillsdale, NJ: Erlbaum.

Steward, M. S., O'Connor, J., Acredolo, C., & Steward, D. S. (1996). The trauma and memory of cancer treatment in children. Crosscurrents in contemporary psychology. In M. H. Bornstein & J. L. Genevro (Eds.), *Child development and behavioral pediatrics* (pp. 105–127). Mahwah, NJ: Erlbaum.

Steward, M. S., Steward, D. S., Farquar, L., Myers, J. E. B., Reinhart, M., Welker, J., et al. (1996). Interviewing young children about body touch and handling. *Monographs of the Society for Research in Child Development, 61*(4–5, Serial No. 248).

Stobbs, G., & Kebbell, M. R. (2003). Jurors' perception of witnesses with intellectual disabilities and the influence of expert evidence. *Journal of Applied Research in Intellectual Disabilities, 16,* 107–114.

Strange, D., Garry, M., & Sutherland, R. (2003). Drawing out children's false memories. *Applied Cognitive Psychology, 17,* 607–619.

Thierry, K. L., Lamb, M. E., Orbach, Y., & Pipe, M.-E. (2005). Developmental differences in the function and use of anatomical dolls during interviews with alleged sexual abuse victims. *Journal of Consulting and Clinical Psychology, 73,* 1135–1134.

Toglia, M. P., Ceci, S. J., & Ross, D. F. (1989, April). *Prestige vs. source monitoring in children's suggestibility.* Paper presented to the Biennial Meeting of the Society for Research in Child Development, Kansas City, MO.

Tulving, E., & Thomson, D. M. (1973). Encoding specificity and retrieval processes in episodic memory. *Psychological Review, 80,* 359–380.

Walker, A. G. (1994). *Handbook on questioning children: A linguistic perspective.* Washington, DC: American Bar Association Center on Children and the Law.

Warren, A. R., Woodall, C. E., Thomas, M., Nunno, M., Keeney, J. M., Larson, S. M., et al. (1999). Assessing the effectiveness of a training program for interviewing child witnesses. *Applied Developmental Science, 3,* 128–135.

Waterman, A. H., Blades, M., & Spencer, C. P. (2000). Do children try to answer nonsensical questions? *British Journal of Developmental Psychology, 18,* 211–226.

Waterman, A. H., Blades, M., & Spencer, C. P. (2001). Interviewing children and adults: The effect of question format on the tendency to speculate. *Applied Cognitive Psychology, 15,* 1–11.

Waterman, A. H., Blades, M., & Spencer, C. P. (2004). Indicating when you do not know the answer: The effect of question format and interviewer knowledge on children's "don't know" responses. *British Journal of Developmental Psychology, 22,* 335–348.

Wesson, M., & Salmon, K. (2001). Drawing and showing: Helping children to report emotionally laden events. *Applied Cognitive Psychology, 15,* 301–320.

Westcott, H. L., & Jones, D. P. H. (1999). Annotation: The abuse of disabled children. *Journal of Child Psychology and Psychiatry, 40,* 497–506.

Willcock, E., Morgan, K., & Hayne, H. (2006). Body maps do not facilitate children's reports of touch. *Applied Cognitive Psychology, 20,* 607–615.

Yuille, J. C., Tymofievich, M., & Marxsen, D. (1995). The nature of allegations of child sexual abuse. In T. Ney (Ed.), *True and false allegations of child sexual abuse: Assessment and case management* (pp. 21–46). New York: Brunner/Mazel.

9

Developmental Trends in Spontaneous False Memory, with Implications for the Law

CHARLES J. BRAINERD AND VALERIE F. REYNA

The present chapter focuses on the scientific study of children's false memories and how susceptibility to false memories changes with age. These topics are instructive examples of how applied issues in child development—in this instance, a form of child maltreatment—can stimulate research literatures that are not only vigorous but also rigorous and theory driven. The form of maltreatment in question is child sexual abuse (CSA). Although it is always important, as a matter of principle, to assess the reliability of children's memory reports of any form of maltreatment, it is of overwhelming significance in the case of CSA. There are two general reasons: when witnesses are seen as unreliable, the guilty are free to re-offend, and innocent defendants pay exceptionally high prices, including conviction, for false accusations.

Strict penalties are applied in CSA cases. CSA is not only a major (class 1) felony throughout the United States, it is a crime for which the law metes out harsh punishments. Readers will be aware, of course, that allegations of CSA produce instant public calumny, and convictions on first-time CSA charges lead to lifetime public branding of adult defendants as child sex offenders. However, readers may be unaware of the following additional facts:

1. In some states (e.g., Illinois), an elementary school child or adolescent who is found guilty in juvenile court of a first-time count of CSA must register for life as a child sex offender.
2. The minimum term of imprisonment for conviction on any count of CSA is usually 15 to 25 years, and the maximum term is life. In many states, the law requires that the sentences that are imposed for convictions on separate counts of CSA must run consecutively, so that adult defendants who receive even the minimum term for two counts are effectively imprisoned for life. For purposes of comparison, in most states a defendant who is convicted of capital murder might expect to receive a sentence of 10 to 15 years and to serve roughly 8 years.

Moreover, if a child has been sexually abused and the wrong person is accused, charged, and/or tried, then by definition the guilty person is at large and can continue to prey upon children. While investigation and prosecution are following the wrong path, the guilty person is free to create a succession of new victims or to pile trauma upon trauma by revictimizing the same child. Thus, convicting innocent defendants in CSA cases has extremely undesirable consequences—regardless, as lawyers like to say, of whether you are pro-defense or pro-prosecution—and that brings us back to the study of children's false memories.

CSA is a very private crime that typically leaves little physical evidence, is rarely observed by third parties, and frequently involves only a single child victim and a single perpetrator. Consequently, children's memory reports are practically the whole of the evidence when it comes to implicating a specific person in such a crime (Ceci & Bruck, 1995; Ceci & Friedman, 2000). The memory reports that provide such evidence range from informal statements made to adults and other children to somewhat more formal statements that are made during initial police investigations, to very formal statements that are made during forensic interviews and sworn testimony. A forensic assessment of the probable reliability of such reports in specific cases must rely on the research literature on children's memories, and the science of false memory is the pertinent segment of that literature (Brainerd & Reyna, 2005).

Consequently, the study of children's false memories, in contrast to the parallel literature on adult false memory, is a field that has been embroiled in controversy since its inception—specifically controversy about its implications for the investigation and prosecution of CSA. Interestingly, although such research has provoked contention, there is little or no dispute among researchers about the basic results of the experiments. The bone of contention is forensic application. It is advisable, therefore, to begin this review with a sketch of some historical facts about the law's treatment of CSA and about how research findings have figured in CSA prosecutions. Those topics form the substance of the first section below. The remainder of the chapter is then devoted to the scientific literature, summarizing what has been discovered about children's false memories and the theoretical ideas that are used to explain those findings. An important feature of this summary is that it is heavily theory driven; it is as much about the theoretical hypotheses that are confirmed and disconfirmed by particular results as it is about the results themselves. The predictions that are made about children's false memory by theories such as constructivism (Bransford & Franks, 1971), the source-monitoring framework (Johnson, Hashtroudi, & Lindsay, 1993), and fuzzy-trace theory (Reyna & Brainerd, 1995) figure centrally. A key reason for this emphasis, as we have pointed out elsewhere (Brainerd, Reyna, & Poole, 2000), is that when it comes to legal applications of research on children's false memory, there is nothing so practical as a good theory. The details of legal cases differ from one another, as well as from the features of experimental procedures (Reyna, Holliday, & Marche, 2002). If the evidence that is presented by scientific experts is to be maximally useful, it must provide triers of fact with valid principles of memory that cut across the details of specific situations. It is theoretical principles, not data points from individual studies, that triers of fact most need to help them understand the facts of a case, reconcile inconsistencies, and fulfill their constitutional obligation to determine the credibility of testimony.

CSA and the Law: A Précis of Some Recent History

Although this was not true a century ago (see Binet, 1900; Stern, 1910), in recent decades the study of children's false memories has been intimately connected to the investigation and prosecution of CSA (for reviews, see Brainerd & Reyna, 2005; Ceci & Friedman, 2000). For instance, the literature is replete with studies that focus squarely on phenomena that often figure in CSA cases but that might not otherwise have been studied in the context of children's false memories, such as whether rumors create false memories (e.g., Principe, Kanaya, Ceci, & Singh, 2006), whether false memories are more or less common for traumatic than for nontraumatic experiences (e.g., Howe, 1997; Howe, Courage, & Peterson, 1995), whether forensic interviews that use anatomically detailed dolls falsify children's memories (e.g., Goodman & Aman, 1990), whether children have false memories of genital touches (e.g., Saywitz, Nicholas, Goodman, & Moan, 1991), and whether secrecy instructions falsify children's memories (e.g., Bottoms, Goodman, Schwartz-Kenney, & Thomas, 2002; Pipe & Goodman, 1991). In short, the topography of research has been shaped by forensic considerations.

In modern societies, sexual contacts with children are heavily punished because they are viewed as particularly heinous crimes that are deeply repugnant to our moral conceptions. The historical record documents little concern with issues of child welfare in the United States or Western Europe until the seventeenth century; indeed, infanticide of babies who were thought to be unhealthy was common practice until that era. Subsequently, public concern with child welfare grew in direct proportion to the changes in sanitation and medical practice that steadily reduced the death rate for infants and young children. The child labor laws of the nineteenth century are well-known examples of this evolving concern. Still, the recognition of CSA, in particular, by the law is a surprisingly recent phenomenon.

In 1962, a seminal paper in the history of child welfare was published by Kempe, Silver, Silverman, Droegemueller, and Silver (1962). Kempe et al., who were pediatric researchers, identified the battered child syndrome, which soon received wide publicity and stimulated a flood of state statutes that were aimed at protecting children against physical abuse. Eventually, in 1974, the U.S. Congress passed a federal statute, the Child Abuse Prevention and Treatment Act. A very important feature of this law is that it encompassed sexual and emotional abuse of children as well as the physical abuse that Kempe et al. had focused on. The National Center on Child Abuse and Neglect was also established by Congress and was charged with gathering national statistics on abuse and making periodic reports of their findings to the nation. Data that were presented in early reports by the Center seemed to show that reports of CSA were rising steeply (Poole & Lamb, 1998). Although some scientists argued that these data were seriously flawed (for a review, see Ceci & Bruck, 1995), the result was that investigations and prosecutions of CSA also rose sharply, with over 1 million adults having been charged with CSA by the early 1990s. False-memory research became imperative as an adjunct to these prosecutions.

In CSA cases, the burden of proof is primarily on children's memory: CSA typically does not leave physical evidence that can be used to prosecute suspects, and when it does, that evidence (e.g., trauma to vaginal or rectal tissue) is not usually a reliable indicator that one person rather than another is guilty. Further, many of the acts that the law defines as CSA are not the sorts of behaviors that would leave physical traces on children's bodies or on their clothing. Examples are adults who make statements to children that contain explicit sexual content and suggest specific sexual acts; adults who show sexually explicit films or pictures to children; adults who read stories containing sexually explicit content to children; adults who instruct children to observe them while they masturbate or engage in sexual activity with other adults; and adults who touch the surface of a child's vagina, rectum, or breast. If penetration of a child's rectum or vagina by an adult does leave detectable tissue damage, the damage may no longer be detectable by the time a medical examination is conducted. Finally, even when such tissue damage is present and is verified in a medical examination, it is not the sort of evidence that points to the guilt of a *specific* person. The latter determination requires that additional physical evidence be present—such as hair, tissue, or bodily fluids—that can be linked to a specific person. Statistically speaking, such evidence is rare in CSA cases (Brainerd & Reyna, 2005).

In the modal CSA case, then, the only reliable information about specific acts of abuse and about specific perpetrators is stored in children's memories. Consequently, children's memory reports supply the key evidence. In the United States, some major changes were made in the investigation and prosecution of CSA that were designed to ensure that such memory evidence finds its way into the courtroom. One change involved modifications to the legal procedures that were used with child witnesses, and another change involved modifications in the investigative procedures that were used to secure memory reports from children. Once those procedures were in place and several defendants had been convicted, reviews of a few of the more high-profile cases by scientists and by attorneys raised doubts about the reliability of the evidence upon which the convictions were based (e.g., Bruck & Ceci, 1995). This, in turn, stimulated research on the conditions that foment false-memory reports in children. Before considering such research, we briefly summarize two changes in legal procedures that prompted doubts about evidentiary reliability in CSA cases.

Memory Reports During Forensic CSA Interviews

As we have said, children's memory reports are often the key evidence of guilt in CSA cases, but gathering reports that are sufficiently detailed to support prosecutions is problematical owing to the age of the typical victim. When looking at cases based on memory reports, the victims are primarily preschool children and children in the first few elementary grades (pertinent statistics can be found in Poole & Lamb, 1998). Memory development is far from complete in this age range. When it comes to CSA, a particular problem with children of this age range is that when they are asked to provide a narrative of a recent, salient life experience ("What happened when you went to the mall yesterday?"), the result is often either no report ("I don't know") or a report that is highly truncated ("We ate lunch"). (See Howe [1991] for experimental evidence of the limited narrative recall of young children.) Obviously, these are not the sorts of reports on which prosecutions of child sexual predators can be based. The good news is that even very young children will report many details of their experiences when they are interviewed with more pointed questions. For instance, although "What did you do when you went to the mall yesterday?" may produce only an "I don't know" answer, questions such as "Did you see a clown?," "You ate some pizza for lunch, didn't you?," "You shopped for birthday presents, didn't you?," and "Did your mom buy some groceries?" may provoke rapid, confident answers of "no," "yes," "yes," and "no," all of which prove to be accurate when the facts are checked with the child's mother. The parallel circumstance in CSA investigations is that young children who disclose sexual abuse may provide no usable information when asked to give a narrative of what happened, but they will typically provide usable information when questions refer to specific abuse details. Because perpetrators cannot be convicted and are hence free to re-offend without memory reports from victims, some legal experts (e.g., Lyon, 1995;

Myers, 1995) have argued for the inclusion of questions about specific abuse details in CSA interviews.

The inclusion of such questions would certainly reduce false negatives (when guilty suspects are not identified as perpetrators), but it may also increase false positives (when innocent suspects are identified as perpetrators). The latter concern was prompted by a long tradition of research on the effects of suggestive questioning in both the adult memory literature and the adult social psychological literature (for a review, see Brainerd & Reyna, 2005). The general finding that prompts this concern is that suggestive questioning of adults, *even questioning about crimes of which they are victims or to which they are witnesses*, stimulates false-memory reports of events that did not happen (e.g., Kassin & Kiechel, 1996; Loftus, 1997; Wells et al., 1998). Common sense says that young children's memories are far more fragile than adults'; thus, if suggestive questioning falsifies adults' memory reports, should it not do likewise, and to an even greater degree, with children's memory reports? Surprisingly, some legal experts proposed that although the answer is yes in general, the answer is no for CSA. More explicitly, while not denying the well-established susceptibility of adults' memory reports to suggestive questioning, and while not denying the equal or greater susceptibility of children's memory reports to such questioning, it was proposed that children's memories of CSA belong to a special category of stored information—namely memories of trauma to children's bodies—that is not affected by the normal distorting influences of suggestion (Ceci & Friedman, 2000).

Was this claim merely wishful thinking? No; this argument had a scientific basis, although not one that was as firm as legal experts thought, that seemed to confirm the argument. Some prior studies had been published that focused on children's memory for experiences that were sexualized in nature. For example, two studies that are frequently mentioned in this connection are those by Saywitz et al. (1991) and by Rudy and Goodman (1991). Saywitz et al. questioned girls who had received a pediatric examination. The researchers included direct questions of the type that, in forensic CSA interviews, yield detailed allegations of abuse in children who would not provide such details in narratives. They interviewed 35 girls, and they found that only 1 of them provided a false report of being touched on the genitalia and only 2 provided a false report of being touched on the anus. Rudy and Goodman went one step further and studied the effects of suggestive questioning about sexualized experiences. They studied a group of children who played with a strange adult in a controlled experimental situation in which the adult–child interactions followed a predetermined script. Some days later, the children were questioned about these interactions, and some of the questions were suggestive ones that resembled questions in CSA interviews (e.g., "How many times did he spank you?" "Did he put anything in your mouth?"). The adult did not do any of these things, of course. The participating children were 4- and 7-year-olds. Less than 10% of the 4-year-olds and *none* of the 7-year-olds gave false answers to these suggestive questions.

Although this seems to settle the issue, the results are not as unambiguous as they look. The most important problem is a technical one that is well known to researchers but is not well understood by people who are not steeped in the scientific method (e.g., legal experts). This is the problem of null effects: the logic of statistical inference from samples to populations enjoins that one can never draw a *positive conclusion* from a failure to reject the null hypothesis; if researchers failed to detect that children's memories were falsified by suggestive questioning, it does not follow that no such falsification can happen. A null effect is not positive evidence of anything because it can always be the result of any number of unknown factors that could not be controlled in the experimental design or the result of known factors that were not controlled. Here, it has been pointed out that the level of suggestion sometimes consisted of only a single question about a single false event. In actual CSA interviews of child victims that are conducted by police investigators, suggestive questioning is sometimes stronger and more extensive. Relevant data on this point have been reported by Bruck and Ceci (1999) and by Ceci and Bruck (1995), who reviewed records of many court cases. Their review showed that actual field interviews of children in CSA cases involved problematic tactics such as demonizing suspects who are under investigation, telling children that other children have already made allegations against suspects, asking children to visualize being abused by suspects, and repeatedly asking questions that do not initially produce abuse allegations. However, their review involved selected cases, not a random sample of cases nationwide, and hence it failed to provide normative evidence about average levels of investigative practices in CSA cases.

Another important point about the Saywitz et al. (1991) and Rudy and Goodman (1991) studies is that although they did not produce statistically reliable evidence that direct or suggestive questions stimulated false memory reports about events associated with children's bodies, as noted, some children did make false reports in response to such questions. Although the percentages were low, considering the thousands of sexual abuse cases that are reported each year in the United States, those percentages would translate into a large absolute number of false reports.

More than any other single event, the need for such research was made apparent by the longest and perhaps the most controversial CSA prosecution in U.S. legal history: the McMartin preschool case (*State of California v. Buckey*, 1990). To many people, this case epitomizes the levels of suggestion and potential tainting of victims' and witnesses' memories that can occur during CSA investigations. In the summer of 1983, the mother of a 2-year-old child who attended a preschool in the Los Angeles area reported to her local police department that her child had been sexually abused by Mr. Raymond Buckey, the son of the owner of the preschool. The mother told the police that she had taken her child for a medical examination after she had noticed a spot of blood on the child's anus. Approximately 2 weeks following her report, her child was interviewed by police investigators, and the child's statements appeared to the investigators to confirm the alleged CSA. The local chief of police, Mr. Harry Kuhlmeyer, then drafted a highly suggestive letter and sent it to the parents of children who were currently attending or had formerly attended the McMartin preschool. The letter informed parents that a CSA investigation of Mr. Buckey was being conducted, and it asked parents to question their children about whether the children had been witnesses to or victims of sexual crimes involving any of the following acts: genital fondling, oral sex, bust or buttocks fondling, sodomy, rectal penetration with a thermometer, or the taking of nude photographs of children. Because the letter was sent to a large number of people, a local child advocacy center (Children's Institute International [CII]) was employed by the police department to conduct sexual abuse interviews of the children of any families who came forward. Hundreds eventually came forward and were interviewed, and the interviews were preserved on videotape. Approximately 6 months after the initial CSA report to the police, CII staff diagnosed over 350 children as having been sexually abused at the McMartin preschool. This resulted in the filing of over 100 counts of CSA against Mr. Buckey, his mother, and other teachers at the preschool.

The case continued to progress slowly and had still not gone to trial by the beginning of 1986, when all charges against defendants other than Mr. Buckey and his mother were dropped. Finally, 4 years after the original police report, in July of 1987, Mr. Buckey and his mother went to trial on 65 counts of CSA. The trial continued until January of 1990, when the jury returned with a verdict. Mr. Buckey's mother was acquitted on all counts, Mr. Buckey was acquitted on 52 counts, and the jury was hung on the remaining 13 counts. Most interesting from the perspective of false-memory research, the jurors' statements in post-trial interviews made it clear that they had grave reservations about whether the allegations of abuse that had been obtained in child interviews were false-memory reports. They stated that, on the one hand, they were convinced that some of the children had been victims of CSA. The jurors also stated, though, that they could not return convictions against either defendant on any of the counts because the videotapes of the child interviews revealed that they were fraught with leading and highly suggestive questions. Later in 1990, Mr. Buckey was retried on 8 of the 13 counts on which he had not been acquitted, but the result was the same: a hung jury. Prosecutors then decided that further retrials would be fruitless.

The Law's Treatment of Child Witnesses

In the wake of the McMartin case, an important series of changes in the law's approach to CSA consists of certain procedures whose objective is to ensure that child victims and witnesses can provide their testimony in atmospheres that are as supportive as possible. Those changes fall into three categories, the first two of which are uncontroversial: (1) to take testimony in rooms that are pleasant and child friendly, rather than in the usual formal and austere courtroom; and (2) to simplify the children's participation in the pretrial investigative phase, especially by limiting the number of times that they can be interviewed and reinterviewed by police and attorneys. The third and more controversial change was to reduce the criminal law's normal barriers to presenting evidence against defendants in forms other than testimony. This change has been controversial because it permits evidence such as sworn testimony by people *other than child victims* about acts of CSA that have been reported to them by alleged victims, as well as records of statements that have been made by alleged child victims prior to trial in informal, unsworn circumstances.

The controversy stems from the fact that, to many observers, although this change is intended to ensure that reliable memory reports that children have made at some prior time are not excluded from evidence (a false-negative error), they also ensure that tainted reports that children have made are admitted in evidence (a false-positive error). For instance, the third change permits hearsay testimony. Although hearsay is generally prohibited in criminal trials, the prohibition is not absolute. To illustrate, deathbed statements that are made to third parties by witnesses are often admissible when they go directly to guilt or innocence, as are statements that have been made to third parties by witnesses who are unavailable by reason of incapacity or whose whereabouts are unknown. The third change in CSA extends the hearsay waiver. However, the third parties to whom children have made allegations of abuse are not trained interviewers who are knowledgeable with respect to scientific findings on the effects of how children are questioned. They may unknowingly taint children's reports. Moreover, research has shown that adults who question children in suggestive and otherwise inappropriate ways are not very good at remembering just how suggestive they were when they are subsequently asked about it (Warren & Woodall, 1999; Brainerd & Reyna, 2005). Hence, one cannot trust cross-examination to reveal that reports may have been tainted by inappropriate questioning procedures, and cross-examination can itself create further inaccuracies in children's reports (Zajac & Hayne, 2003, 2006; Zajac, Gross, & Hayne, 2003).

A similar problem arises in connection with the other consequence of this change. A fundamental principle of criminal procedure is that defendants are able, through their attorneys, to confront and challenge the testimony of the witnesses against them. This is done through cross-examination. That is, through cross-examination, attorneys attempt to provide evidence to the jury in the *witnesses' own words* that their prior testimony is flawed. Video or audio recordings cannot be cross-examined. The best one can hope to do is to present other evidence, in the form of expert scientific testimony or closing arguments, that there is reasonable doubt as to the reliability of the information in those recordings, which is a much weaker and less-convincing tactic than using witnesses' own words to impeach their testimony.

How Shall We Study Children's False Memories?

Although the conditions surrounding the prosecution of CSA have motivated research on children's false memories, it does not follow that the research should be restricted to designs that emulate those conditions (Reyna, 2004). That would greatly narrow the range of application of experimental findings and would not lead to the general explanatory principles that are the most important objectives of such research. Here, it is important to remind ourselves that the law's reliance on children's memory reports is not confined to CSA. Such reports supply evidence in many types of legal cases (e.g., arson, assault, domestic disputes, murder, production and sale of drugs, robbery), and CSA cases are only a small fraction of the total. For instance, defendants in capital murder cases have been convicted on the basis of children's recollections of events. One type of case, however, outnumbers all others combined: divorce and custody proceedings (McGough, 1993). The question of whether and under what conditions children are at heightened risk of making false-memory reports is pertinent to any legal proceeding in which children are witnesses, victims, or even defendants. In connection with cases in which children are defendants, which are normally juvenile court proceedings, it is well established that adult defendants are susceptible to false confessions that are stimulated by the highly suggestive questioning tactics that are used in police interrogations (Kassin, 1997). Child defendants are often subjected to the same types of interviewing tactics, especially when they are charged with serious crimes such as arson or murder (Armstrong, Milles, & Possley, 2001). If children's memories are more susceptible to the distorting influence of those tactics than adults', then reports that are obtained from child defendants are even more apt to be infected with false self-incrimination.

Because the legal ramifications of research on children's false memories extend far beyond CSA, research that is restricted to CSA-like conditions is of only limited use in the law. To illustrate, the question of whether children can have false memories of traumatic experiences involving their own bodies, which was the touchstone of early studies of children's false memories, is simply irrelevant in the vast preponderance of cases in which children are witnesses, victims, or defendants. What the law is most in need of is general principles and findings that are not bound by the specific situations in which children's memories are stored and which therefore can be applied in a broad range of legal cases. We now turn to those topics.

Children's Spontaneous False Memories: Theory and Data

As we pointed out in an earlier review (Brainerd & Reyna, 1998), the study of children's false memories can be segmented into research on two classes of phenomena: spontaneous false memories and implanted false memories. The former arise from normal, uncontrolled distortion processes that all memory is heir to, whereas the latter are due to misinformation ("Remember when you drank that Pepsi at the game last week?"), whether accidental or deliberate, that is imposed between the time that an event occurred (e.g., drinking a Coke at the game) and the time that memory for the event is tested ("Did you have anything to drink at the game last week?"). This segmentation is somewhat arbitrary because, as Reyna and Lloyd (1997) showed, there is a gradation of misinformation in studies of children's false memories, and even an old–new recognition probe ("Did you drink a Pepsi at the game last week?") is somewhat suggestive (Lamb & Fauchier, 2001), more so when it is repeated (Ceci & Bruck, 1995). Nevertheless, the segmentation is highly serviceable because there are important differences between the methodologies and findings of studies that focus on spontaneous versus implanted false memories.

Our own research program has centered on spontaneous rather than implanted false memories, for both theoretical and forensic reasons. Theoretically, the paradigms that are used to study spontaneous false memories are more attractive because they are simpler than those that are used to study implanted false memories. Greater simplicity means that it is easier to test theoretical hypotheses because there is only one source of memory falsification to deal with—spontaneous distortion processes— and one need not control for possible interactions between spontaneous distortion processes and other distortion processes that are pursuant to misinformation. Most importantly, one need not worry about controlling for *developmental* interactions between spontaneous distortion processes and susceptibility to misinformation, interactions that are both ubiquitous and powerful (Brainerd & Reyna, 2005), because misinformation is not present. Forensically, the question of children's implanted false memories is already settled law. The law has already recognized, in a number of legal opinions, that children are at heightened risk of making false memory reports when they receive misinformation (e.g., in the form of suggestive questioning about their experiences; Ceci & Friedman, 2000). Therefore, the law concedes that it is particularly important not to subject child witnesses and victims to misinformation as part of investigative procedures. This does not mean that this prescription is followed in most cases in which children are involved, and indeed, the data indicate that it is not followed (e.g., Warren & McGough, 1996; Warren & Woodall, 1999). Because the prescription is settled law, however, when it is not followed, children's memory reports can be legally challenged on scientific grounds as being unreliable, both at trial and in pretrial procedures (see Rosenthal, 2002). Unlike implanted false memories, the question of spontaneous false memories is not settled law. For these reasons, the review that follows focuses on spontaneous rather than implanted false memories in children. Insofar as children's implanted false memories are concerned, multiple reviews of the relevant literature are already extant (e.g., Bruck & Ceci, 1997, 1999; Ceci & Bruck, 1993, 1995), and interested readers are directed to those documents.

The modern scientific literature on spontaneous false memories may properly be said to have begun with two articles, one by Underwood (1965) that focused on false memory for words and one by Bransford and Franks (1971) that focused on false memory for sentences from narratives. Bransford and Franks' article caused an immediate sensation, stimulated an extensive literature on false memory for narratives, and soon became a staple of undergraduate psychology textbooks. Underwood's article, on the other hand, was less well known initially, but it has become prominent in recent years as research on false memory for word lists has exploded, with the advent of the Deese/Roediger-McDermott (DRM) paradigm (Deese, 1959; Roediger & McDermott, 1995). In the review that follows, we focus first on developmental studies of false memories for information from narratives and then take up developmental studies of false memory for words. Our review concentrates on research that is conducted under controlled laboratory conditions, rather than on naturalistic studies, for the same reasons that motivate concentrating on spontaneous false memory: theoretical probity and forensic application. In the former connection, tests of theoretical hypotheses demand research designs in which causal factors are carefully separated, rather than confounded. As is well known, controlled laboratory research is unparalleled in its ability to achieve such separation and thereby to provide clear answers to alternative theoretical hypotheses. It is less well understood that forensic application demands comparable clarity and rigor. Naturalistic studies of false memory that confound multiple factors are of limited use in the courtroom (see Reyna, Mills, Estrada, & Brainerd, 2007). The law recognizes this fact and has enshrined it in the standards that courts have adopted for the introduction of scientific evidence. The most notable of these is the Daubert standard, which governs scientific evidence in all federal courts and many state courts. It is designed to ensure that such evidence approximates the ideal of controlled laboratory experimentation to the greatest extent possible.

Owing to this emphasis, readers of this volume may be disposed to wonder about the generality of the findings on children's false memory to real-life situations. Although we will return to this topic at the close, we offer two preliminary observations. First, developmental scientists are inclined to treat the notion of naturalism and ecological validity in research as though it were a self-evident truth, not because there is vast empirical support for it but because it resonates so well with some deeply Rousseauian presuppositions (White, 1970). In fact, however, the empirical evidence, which ought to be the ultimate arbiter of our beliefs, is almost entirely on the other side of the issue. As Banaji and Crowder (1989), Ceci and Bronfenbrenner (1991), and other respected authorities have commented, there appears to be no extant example of a major laboratory principle of memory that does not hold or that holds in the opposite way in everyday remembering. To take just few examples, laws such as serial position, encoding variability, the forgetting curve, and massed practice operate in memory for birthday parties and classroom lectures as well as in memory for controlled laboratory tasks. Although quantitative results for these laws may be somewhat different for some everyday experiences versus some laboratory tasks, there is also quantitative variability among laboratory tasks. The evidence that laboratory memory laws operate in the same general ways in everyday remembering is so extensive that it is clear what our baseline assumption should be. That assumption should not be that well-replicated laboratory patterns are somehow suspicious because they are not based on real-life situations but, rather, that they apply to such situations *unless there are positive data to the contrary.*

The other observation, as Reyna, Holliday, and Marche (2002) have discussed, is that, ironically, the findings that are generated in laboratory experimentation are usually more applicable to legal cases than naturalistic memory research. The reason is simple: Carefully controlled laboratory work has as its hallmark the ability to identify causes of children's false memories and to rule out other possible explanations by disentangling various factors. Those same factors are mixed and confounded in everyday life, so that no clear conclusions about what causes what are possible. Moreover, it should be obvious that no single naturalistic study or collection of studies can hope to match the specific details of legal cases. What the law requires of science, as we have said, are well-supported general principles that cut across different remembering situations. That is the stock in trade of laboratory experimentation.

False Memory for Narrative Statements

A good novel encourages readers to make inferences about events that are happening behind the scenes. However, that leads to a common mistake: as readers proceed through the novel, they may mistake inferences that they have made based on the plot for events that were specifically discussed at some point in the story. In a classic paper, Bransford and Franks (1971) studied a laboratory analogue of this situation and showed that participants' recollections of narratives are thoroughly infected with false memories, and that false memories seem to be as strong as true ones (later research showed the latter result to be qualified by faulty instructions; Reyna & Kiernan, 1994). Perhaps most importantly, they found that those false memories are by-products of making sense of narratives, of integrating sentences into more general ideas—a process known as gist memory in fuzzy-trace theory (Reyna & Brainerd, 1995). The adult participants in Bransford and Franks' research listened to a series of sentences that had been constructed so as to contain different numbers of meaning units (propositions), and after they had studied the sentences they were given an old–new recognition test on which some of the probes were old (i.e., sentences that they had just read) and others were new sentences that contained the same meaning units. To take a concrete example that has often been recounted in textbooks, the participants studied 12 sentences that contained the following four propositions:

The ants are in the kitchen.
The jelly is sweet.

The jelly is on the table.
The ants ate the jelly.

Examples of the sentences that were studied are shown in Table 9.1. Note that the sentences varied in complexity, with complexity being determined by the number of propositions in each sentence—one, two, or three. All of these sentences were presented on the old–new recognition test, along with new sentences such as, "The ants ate the jelly that was on the table," "The ants in the kitchen ate the sweet jelly," and "The ants in the kitchen ate the sweet jelly that was on the table." Although none of the latter sentences was studied, it is obvious that each is consistent with the gist of the ant story.

Bransford and Franks' (1971) participants listened to a total of four narratives (six sentences apiece) before they responded to the recognition test. There were three types of probes on the test: presented and unpresented sentences of the sort just described, plus further unpresented sentences that violated the gist of that narrative. After each probe was presented, participants were required to make two responses: to indicate whether the sentence was old or new and to rate how confident they were in this old–new judgment on a scale of 1 to 5. There are two key results that are very surprising. First, although the participants were very good at identifying new sentences as new *when they violated the gist of the narratives*, they made poor choices when new sentences preserved the gist of the narratives. Second, the participants' confidence in their memories for presented sentences and in their false memories for unpresented gist-preserving sentences were similar. This second pattern is shown in Figure 9.1. Participants' confidence ratings for a sentence were given a positive sign when the recognition judgment was old and a negative sign

TABLE 9.1. Sentences from Bransford and Franks (1971) Narrative False Memory Study

Complexity Levels	Sentences
1	The ants were in the kitchen.
	The jelly was on the table.
2	The ants in the kitchen ate the jelly.
	The ants ate the sweet jelly.
3	The ants ate the sweet jelly which was on the table.

when it was new, regardless of whether the sentence was actually old or new. Common sense (and memory theories of that era) would say that presented sentences would be recognized as old with high positive ratings, while unpresented sentences would be recognized as new with high negative ratings. Instead, unpresented sentences were recognized as *old* at very high levels. What is more, it can be seen in Figure 9.1 that participants' confidence in their erroneous recognition of unpresented sentences was indistinguishable from their confidence in their correct recognition of presented sentences. In fact, as can also be seen, confidence ratings *were not predicted at all by whether a sentence was actually old or new*. Instead, confidence was predicted by how many narrative propositions from the story a test sentence contained (one, two, three, or four). In other words, the more completely a test sentence recapitulated the gist of a narrative, the more confident participants were in their memory judgments about it, regardless of whether the judgment was correct or incorrect.

In the years that followed the publication of this research, a number of developmental investigators studied the question of whether children also display these extremely high levels of spontaneous memory distortion for narratives. The earliest publication was an article by Paris and Carter (1973). These investigators presented children with shorter narratives than Bransford and Franks (1971) had used. The narratives consisted

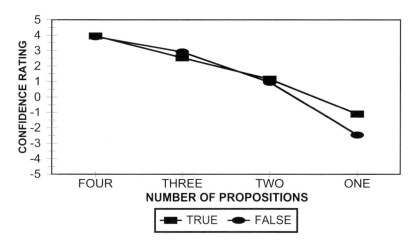

FIGURE 9.1. Relations between number of meaning propositions contained in sentence-recognition probes, true memory (hits), and false memory (false alarms) in Bransford and Franks's (1971) research.

of two sentences that specified a spatial relation between some common objects (e.g., "The bird is in the cage. The cage is under the table") and a filler sentence (e.g., "The bird has yellow feathers"). It was found that, like Bransford and Franks's adults, children were very likely to state that new sentences were old when those sentences preserved the gist of the short narrative (e.g., "The bird is under the table"). Other studies of children's false memory for narrative states were soon reported by investigators such as Johnson and Scholnick (1979), Liben and Posnansky (1977), Paris and Mahoney (1974), Prawatt and Cancelli (1976), and Small and Butterworth (1981). Paris and Carter's original finding continued to hold. Children falsely recognized new sentences that preserved the gist of narratives, and they did so at much higher levels than they falsely recognized new sentences that violated the gist of narratives. Other investigators found that it was not only sentences for which children displayed this effect. They also falsely recognized numbers and pictures that preserved the gist of narratives (Brainerd & Reyna, 1993; Brainerd & Gordon, 1994; Paris & Mahoney, 1974).

As interesting as these results are, the question of what causes them—their theoretical interpretation, in other words—is of far greater significance (see Reyna, 1996; Reyna & Kiernan, 1994, 1995). For the most part, the aforementioned investigators relied on an interpretation known as constructivism, which Bransford and Franks (1971) had used to explain their data and that had originally been proposed by Bartlett (1932). According to constructivism, people do not retain memories of the individual sentences in a narrative but instead store the meaning content of sentences and develop memories that Bransford and Franks called *holistic semantic structures* or *schemas*. The crux of this hypothesis is that information about the exact details of sentences is not preserved in memory, at least not beyond a few minutes, and instead an overall, integrated semantic representation is preserved that is then used to make judgments about memory probes. Considering the extensive developmental literature on limitations in young children's meaning-making (e.g., Bjorklund & Hock, 1982; Bjorklund & Jacobs, 1985) and in making meaning-driven inferences (e.g., Piaget & Inhelder, 1973), a straightforward developmental prediction of constructivism is that false memory for narratives should be less pronounced in young children than in older children and less pronounced in older children than in adolescents or adults.

Although Bransford and Franks's (1971) data certainly seem to suggest that the formation of overall meaning structures controls memory judgments, from which the prediction of developmental increases in narrative false memory falls out, developmental studies failed to generate consistent findings confirming that prediction. Actually, the findings were rather confusing. On the one hand, investigators such as Liben and Posnansky (1977) and Paris and Carter (1973) reported studies in which no definite pattern of development was detected. Regardless of whether development was measured by chronological age or tests of conceptual understanding, children from both more and less advanced developmental levels exhibited comparable levels of false memory for meaning-preserving statements. On the other hand, as constructivism predicts, investigators such Johnson and Scholnick (1979) and Prawatt and Cancelli (1976) reported that false memory for meaning-preserving statements increased with age in all conditions. If that were not sufficiently confusing, still other studies were reported by Ackerman (1992, 1994) and by Poole and White (1991) in which developmental decreases in false memory were obtained in all conditions. Finally, there were published studies whose developmental patterns were internally inconsistent. Here, Brown, Smiley, Day, Townsend, and Lawton (1977) and Paris and Mahoney (1974) reported studies in which in narrative false memories displayed *different age trends in different conditions.*

To muddy the waters further, some investigators pointed to a potential methodological problem in these studies, a problem in which the familiarity of the *meaning* of test probes is confounded with the familiarity of their *surface form.* In the sorts of test materials that were used to measure true and false memory for narratives, true test sentences contained only words that were presented to the children earlier (in a prior example: "The bird is under the table"), and false sentences always contained new words (in a prior example: "The bird is out of the cage") Thus, when true sentences are correctly recognized or when false sentences are correctly rejected, contrary to constructivism, this may simply be because the words are familiar, not because the meanings of narrative sentences have been understood and remembered. This problem of confounding the meaning familiarity of narratives with the familiarity of the words that are used in the sentences of which narratives are composed was eventually solved by Paris and Mahoney (1974) and Liben and Posnansky (1977; see also Reyna & Kiernan, 1994, 1995, who further unconfounded paraphrases from inferences, separating comprehension from reasoning). These authors developed a narrative procedure in which meaning familiarity and word familiarity were factorially manipulated. However, when this design was applied in a series of developmental studies, the data ran decidedly against constructivism. Contrary to that hypothesis, false memory for statements that preserved the meaning of narratives declined with age in all conditions.

That this disconfirmation of constructivism is a correct finding is suggested by disconfirmation of another key prediction of constructivism that is concerned with dissociations between true and false memory. The prediction in question follows from the fact that constructivism is what memory theorists call a one-process theory; that is, it posits that a single memory representation of a narrative, a schema, underlies participants' responses to all test probes—true statements, false-but-gist-consistent statements, and false-and-gist-violating statements. Because the same schema is used for all responses, children's performance on the different types of probes should be related as follows: the stronger and more accessible a schema is, the *more* likely children should be to recognize both true statements and unpresented-but-gist-consistent statements as old, because both fit the schema, and the *less* likely they should be to recognize unpresented-and-gist-violating statements as old. In the earliest article using Bransford and Franks's (1971) procedures with children, Paris and Carter (1973) focused attention on the first half of this prediction, noting that false recognition of unpresented-but-gist-consistent statements should increase as correct recognition of presented statements increased. This half of the prediction is the more interesting one because it seems counterintuitive. It says, paradoxically, that the more accurate children's memories are (as indexed by the hit rate for *actual* statements), the less accurate children's memories are (as indexed by the false-alarm rate for unpresented-but-gist-consistent statements).

Of the various papers that were published prior to the appearance of Reyna and Kiernan's (1994, 1995) articles, we know of none that reported credible evidence that confirmed the putative association between hit and false-alarm rates that constructivism expects. The prediction was examined in detail in these latter articles. Reyna and Kiernan's studies, with children in the elementary grades, disconfirmed the prediction in all conditions and at all age levels. Rather than being positively associated, children's hit and false-alarm rates were dissociated on recognition tests: hits and false alarms were uncorrelated within experimental conditions, and they were driven in opposite directions by certain experimental manipulations. In the latter connection, it was found that when narratives were changed from statements about spatial relations (e.g., the bird narrative, above) to statements about magnitude relations (e.g., "The coffee is hotter than the tea. The tea is hotter than the cocoa. The cocoa is sweet"), the hit rate went *up* and the false alarm rate went *down*. Although Reyna and Kiernan's dissociation findings disconfirmed a core prediction of constructivism, their findings were replicated in other contexts. For instance, in a doctoral dissertation that grew out their work, Lim (2003) found that adults exhibited the same patterns of dissociation. Similarly, Brainerd and Gordon (1994) and Brainerd and Reyna (1995) found analogous dissociations between hit and false-alarm rates in children's memory for numbers that had been presented in narratives, and Brainerd and Reyna (1993) found dissociations when pictures were used to measure children's memory for true narrative statements and unpresented-but-gist-consistent statements.

Summing up the story so far, constructivism was developed to explain the powerful false-memory effects that are present in narrative tasks, but the developmental data ran heavily against its most central predictions, which leads one to ask, what other theory can handle the data? Two possibilities are spreading-activation theories, which are in the classical associationist tradition of verbal learning research, and by the source-monitoring framework (e.g., Johnson et al., 1993). Although spreading-activation theories have most commonly been applied to memory for individual items, rather than memory for connected statements, Anderson and his associates have developed models of this sort for sentences (e.g., Anderson, Budiu, & Reder, 2001). In such models, recognition of unpresented-but-gist-consistent sentences is explained on the ground that (a) presented sentences and unpresented sentences activate certain areas (nodes) of underlying associative (or semantic) networks, and (b) the areas that are activated by presented sentences overlap considerably with the areas that are activated by unpresented-but-gist-consistent sentences (making it difficult to discriminate between them). Readers will probably have noticed that there is already an empirical problem with spreading-activation models. They, too, are one-process theories (the same network is activated by presented and unpresented-but-gist-consistent sentences), and hence, unless they are enriched with ad hoc assumptions, they predict the same patterns of association between hits and false alarms that constructivism predicts (Reyna et al., 2007). It is easy to see that spreading activation has a difficult time with the finding that some manipulations drive hit and false-alarm rates in opposite directions. When two sentences activate the same area of a network (because they have the same meaning), how can activation simultaneously go up for one sentence and down for the other? Activation theories also have difficulty accounting for the fact that in certain types of experimental conditions, participants recognize unpresented-but-gist-consistent sentences at *higher* rates than true sentences (Reyna & Lloyd, 1997).

What about the source-monitoring framework? Although, historically, this has been one of the most influential theories in false-memory research (for reviews, see Reyna, 2000a; Reyna & Lloyd, 1997), it makes the same predictions of association between hit and false-alarm rates as constructivism, which is perhaps not surprising considering that it evolved from constructivism. This account focuses on participants' ability to judge the points of origin of familiar information. (Was it actually presented to me in the experiment? Is it just similar to something that was presented in the experiment? Did I dream it? Did I hear it on the radio this morning? Did I read it in the newspaper last night?) The core claim is that these judgments rely on the content of the memories that were stored in connection with experienced events. As Reyna and Lloyd (1997) and Reyna (2000a) showed, constructivism's prediction of positive association between hit and false-alarm rates then falls out because the same memory content is used to make judgments about experienced events (which controls the hit rate) and about closely related events that were not actually experienced (which controls the false-alarm rate). More specifically, contrary to many findings of dissociation in the literature, the source-monitoring framework forecasts association between presented and related (but unpresented) items in memory because rememberers are said to decide that unpresented-but-gist-consistent sentences were actually presented (rather than inferred) because they share a great deal of the memory content of actual experience and because rememberers do not necessarily access the few features of memory content that they do not share. With respect to developmental trends in false memory, the source-monitoring framework is more successful in accounting for the developmental declines in false memory that have been observed in experiments that eliminated the aforementioned confound between meaning familiarity and word familiarity. Several developmental source-monitoring studies have been reported, and the consistent prediction in those studies has been that children's ability to make accurate judgments of the points of origin of their memories will improve steadily with age. The prediction has been repeatedly confirmed using designs in which children make source judgments about probes (Was this sentence presented in red or green letters? Was this sentence presented in large or small letters?), rather than old/new memory judgments (Roberts, 2002). If erroneous source judgments are responsible for false memories, narrative false memories should decline with age, as they do in unconfounded experimental designs. However, as we saw, contrary developmental trends were obtained in experiments that used other designs. The source-monitoring framework has nothing definite to say in that connection.

However, fuzzy-trace theory (FTT; see Brainerd & Reyna, 2001; Reyna & Brainerd, 1995) is able handle those conflicting developmental patterns. FTT is an attempt to avoid the mistake of throwing out the theoretical baby with the theoretical bath water by preserving and integrating the successful parts of two important traditions, verbal learning and psycholinguistics, and then applying them to relations between memory and reasoning (Reyna & Brainerd, 1995). False memory is a prime area of application because it is not quite memory and not quite reasoning. FTT posits that children store dissociated verbatim and gist representations of their experience, that they do so in parallel (rather than the gist of experience being distilled from memory for its verbatim form), that verbatim and gist representations also exhibit retrieval dissociation because they are accessed by different types of cues, and that verbatim and gist representations become inaccessible (i.e., are "forgotten") at different rates as time passes. Developmentally, FTT posits that both verbatim and gist memory improve with age: older children are better able to store, retrieve, and preserve traces of the exact surface form of their experience; older children understand and are able to extract a broader range of meanings from experience (e.g., robin is a bird but is also a mascot); and when different experiences exemplify related meanings, older children are better able to connect that meaning across the different experiences (e.g., "There were several animals—birds, cows, and cats—on that list that was just read to me") Reyna and Kiernan's (1994, 1995) experiments were designed not only to eliminate the meaning/word familiarity confound but also to test explicit predictions that FTT makes about children's true and false memories. According to Reyna and Kiernan, the predictions that one makes about different experimental manipulations turn on a simple question, namely, how would those manipulations be expected to affect the relative accessibility of verbatim and gist traces of experience? Examples of forensically significant manipulations for which the answer is straightforward include delay (verbatim traces become inaccessible more rapidly than gists), age (verbatim and gist memory both improve with age), materials (some types of memory materials, such as pictures and or metaphorical statements, enhance verbatim traces more than gist traces, while other materials have the opposite effect), and memory test instructions (some instructions encourage verbatim processing and others encourage gist processing). But how does this translate into concrete predictions about children's true and false memories? The answer is that predictions follow from the fact that FTT is an opponent-processes model with specific representational assumptions: gist processing is assumed to support true memories of actual events ("I drank a Coke at the baseball game") and false memories that preserve the meaning of those events ("I drank a Pepsi at the baseball game"), whereas verbatim processing is assumed to support true memories and to suppress false ones ("No, I didn't drink a Pepsi because I clearly remember Mom telling me to buy Cokes for us"). At this point, it is easy to see that FTT expects the sorts of dissociations that have been observed between true and false memories (because they are controlled by opposing processes). Further, predictions about the preceding manipulations are now obvious: false memory will tend to increase with delay (because the traces that suppress false memories become inaccessible more rapidly than the traces that support false memories); materials that strengthen verbatim traces will reduce false memories, but materials that strengthen gist traces will increase false memories; test instructions that stress verbatim processing will reduce false memories, but test instructions that stress gist processing will increase false memories. All of these predictions were studied by Reyna and Kiernan (1994, 1995) and also by Brainerd and Gordon (1994), and all were confirmed.

What does FTT say about age or developmental variability in false memory? As will be readily apparent to most readers, all possible developmental trends (increase, decrease, no change) can occur *under specific experimental conditions* because (a) verbatim and gist processing both improve with age and (b) they are opponent processes with respect to false memory. Thus, as we have discussed elsewhere (Brainerd & Reyna, 1998), developmental trends in false memory are not monolithic across experimental conditions but rather are variable as a function of experimental conditions. To put it another way, the age trend that is observed in a particular condition will depend in the first instance on the mix of verbatim and gist processing that occurs in that condition, and in the second on the respective amounts of verbatim and gist development that occur during the target age range.

An important feature of this analysis is that it has no difficulty handling the basic finding of inconsistent age trends in studies of children's narrative false memories. A far more important feature, however, is that different age trends are not actually inconsistent, but they are expected to occur on theoretical grounds and, even more important, their direction can be predicted. Assuming that we are dealing with some age range in which there are substantial age improvements in both verbatim and gist processing, it is obvious that age declines are predicted for tasks in which performance variability is primarily under the control of verbatim processing, age increases are predicted for tasks in which performance variability is primarily under the control of gist processing, and age invariance is predicted when verbatim and gist processing make reasonably equivalent contributions to performance variability. Are such predictions confirmed? One way to answer this question is to conduct a retrospective analysis of the aforementioned studies of children's false memories of narratives in order to determine whether there are salient methodological differences that divide along verbatim-gist lines and are therefore probably responsible for the contrasting results. A more satisfactory approach is to study the development of false memory using other paradigms that allow the mix of verbatim and gist processing to be brought under experimental control. We take up that issue in the next section, where developmental studies of false memory for words are considered.

Before we move to that topic, however, it should be mentioned that FTT makes predictions about false memory phenomena in children that are of considerable forensic interest. Four examples are the mere-testing effect (Brainerd & Reyna, 1996), the false-persistence effect (Brainerd, Reyna, & Brandse, 1995), the false-recognition reversal effect (Brainerd, Reyna, Kneer, 1995), and the repeated gist cuing effect (Reyna, 2000b; Reyna & Lloyd, 1997). The mere-testing effect is the tendency for there to be elevated errors on follow-up memory tests (as opposed to initial memory tests), the false-persistence effect is the tendency of false memories to be stable over time, the false-recognition reversal effect is the fact that participants can sometimes be highly accurate at rejecting false memories, and the repeated gist cuing effect is the tendency of false memories to increase as memories of the meaning of experience become stronger. The first effect, which bears on the aforementioned issue of repeated questioning of children in legal cases, is based on the theoretical idea that the mere administration of a false-but-gist-consistent information on a memory test ("Did you drink Pepsi at the baseball game?") stimulates memory-falsifying gist processing. If this principle is correct, false memory for that information should be elevated on later tests—and it is. The second effect, which bears on the types of retrieval environments that are provided when children are questioned in legal cases, such as returning to the scene of the crime, is based on the principle that providing exact surface cues from the target experience will stimulate memory-defalsifying verbatim processing. If this principle is correct, testing participants in the presence of such cues should reduce false memory when questions are asked about false-but-gist-consistent information; it does. The third effect, which bears on whether children who are questioned in legal cases should be interviewed in a timely fashion, is based on the principle that verbatim traces become inaccessible more rapidly than gist. If this principle is correct, false memory for gist-consistent information should be higher a few days after events, than, say, shortly after; it is. The last effect, which is relevant to legal cases in which children have been repeatedly exposed to the same crime, such as CSA, is based on the principle what when people are repeatedly exposed to situations in which the gist remains the same but the details vary, memory-falsifying gist processing is strengthened. If this principle is correct, false memory for gist-consistent information should increase as repetition increases, and it does. This last effect can have especially pernicious consequences for convicting CSA perpetrators when their victims have been repeatedly abused, however. The same repetition of superficially different, but related, events that reinforces memory for gist interferes with accurate memory for verbatim details. Thus, repeated abuse, in which separate events resemble one another but differ in details, should lead to poor memory for details. Thus, the theory says, with repeated abuse, it will be easier for defense investigators and cross-examining attorneys to impeach children's allegations of abuse by showing that their testimony is inaccurate with respect to key details. That is especially tragic because the gist memories of repeated victims of CSA (i.e., that they were in fact abused) are more likely to be accurate than the gist memories of children who have suffered a single incident of abuse. However, the law bases convictions on verbatim details, such as whether the perpetrator had a tattoo on his left or right arm. Also, as we saw earlier, whether or not a crime has occurred may depend on precise differences in behavior (e.g., exactly where a touch occurred), and if a crime has occurred, differences in its judged severity likewise depend on precise differences in behavior (e.g., whether a touch occurred over or under a child's clothing).

False Memory for Words

The developmental literature contains early examples of papers on false memory for words, with articles by Felzen and Anisfeld (1970) and Cramer (1972) being classics in the area. For most of the past 3 decades, however, the study of children's false memories has been dominated by memory for heavily schematized information, such as that which is presented in narrative tasks. Recently, this situation has begun to change, with an increasing number of studies appearing in which children recall or recognize items from word lists. In the past 4 to 5 years, the flow of studies that rely on these more traditional Ebbinghaus-like designs has exceeded those that focus on false memory for schematized information. There are at least two reasons for the move toward such designs. First, developmental investigators have become increasingly concerned with formulating and testing theoretical hypotheses about the causes of false memories. Traditional word-list methodologies make it possible to achieve the high levels of experimental control that are necessary to precisely discriminate among contrasting hypotheses (similarly, for sentence paradigms; Brainerd, Reyna, & Estrada, 2006; Reyna & Kiernan, 1994). Also, existing mathematical models of false memory are defined over such methodologies, for both word lists and sentences, so that they provide the opportunity to secure uncontaminated estimates of key theoretical processes (Brainerd & Reyna, 2005). The second reason (see Reyna et al., 2007) is the advent of a particular word-list methodology that is simple and easy to use, that does not make excessive demands on the abilities of young children (as some schematic memory tasks do), and that is able to produce very high levels of false memory in adults. That task is the DRM paradigm, which we briefly mentioned earlier. We focus on research in which this paradigm was used to study children's false memory, both because those studies are more numerous than those with any other word-list methodology and, more important, because those studies have produced a rich yield of theoretically incisive findings. Below, we begin with a synopsis of the DRM procedure and key findings with adults. Then, we move on to a consideration of developmental studies.

THE DRM PARADIGM

Although intense scientific interest in false memory is a recent phenomenon, this methodology for inducing such errors was devised much earlier—nearly a half-century ago, in fact. In this task, participants study short word lists and perform free recall ("Tell me all the words you can remember, in any order") immediately after the last one is presented. Such word lists can vary in the extent to which the words are related to each other in meaning. The words might be chosen so that they share no meaning at all, or each word might share meaning with a few others (e.g., the list might be composed of 15 words, with 3 words apiece from each of 5 taxonomic categories, such as animals, cities, colors, furniture, and foods). As the degree of shared meaning increases, so does false memory: participants tend to recall unpresented words, called intrusions, that have meanings that are similar to the meanings that have been repeatedly cued by list words. Intrusion rates are not normally very high, and are almost always lower than 5% in young adults (e.g., Bjorklund & Muir, 1988).

Deese (1959) found that intrusion rates can be much higher, however. He devised an extreme version of semantically related lists in which all the list words shared meaning by virtue of their association with a single common word, which was not presented as part of the list. To take a concrete example, suppose that participants study the following word list: *song, note, sound, piano, sing, noise, band, horn, art, instrument, symphony*. This list strikes one as having a coherent meaning inasmuch as the words seem to revolve around music. Indeed, word association norms from the 1950s (Russell & Jenkins, 1954) show that when college students were given the word *music* and asked to write the first word that comes to mind, these 12 words were the most frequently written ones. Deese used these same norms to construct a total of 36 different lists, each of which consisted of the 12 most frequently given associates of a different common word (e.g., *chair, foot, rough, window*). His participants listened to each list, and, immediately after the 12th word was heard, they were told to recall as many words from the list as they could remember. The remarkable finding was that, even though the entire list took only about 20 seconds to present, semantic intrusions occurred at very high rates. Nearly all of the 36 stimulus words (usually called "critical distractors") were recalled at much higher levels than the nominal 5% intrusion rate for unpresented exemplars of categorized lists. Far more strikingly, two-thirds of them were falsely recalled 20% or more of the time. To appreciate just how powerful this illusion is, remember that the list is very short (only 12 words) and that participants have just finished listening to it.

Many years later, Roediger and McDermott (1995) rediscovered Deese's task, which is why it is now called the DRM paradigm. They extended the procedure to old/new recognition. Explicitly, participants listened to a series of Deese's (1959) lists, recalling each list immediately after the last word was heard. After the lists had been recalled, the subject responded to a comprehensive recognition test that covered all of the lists. The test probes consisted of some words from each list (e.g., *song, note, sound, piano*), the unpresented critical distractor for each list (e.g., *music*), and some unpresented words that were unrelated to any of the lists (e.g., *computer, soccer*). They found that the level of false memory was even higher for recognition than for recall. The overall false-alarm rates for the critical distractors were in the range of 70% to 80%. This rather astonishing level of memory falsification has been replicated many times by other researchers (e.g., Payne, Elie, Blackwell, & Neuschatz, 1996).

Developmental Studies

In the years that immediately preceded the recent surge of developmental DRM studies, we reported several experiments on children's false memory for words using other paradigms (Brainerd & Reyna, 1996, 1998; Brainerd, Reyna, & Brandse, 1995; Brainerd, Reyna, & Kneer, 1995; Brainerd, Stein, & Reyna, 1998). In all of these studies, the measure of children's false memory was the false-alarm rate to unpresented words (which are usually called distractors or lures) that were related, usually *semantically* related, to words that had been presented on the list (which are usually called targets). Actually, the measure of false memory was the *difference* between the false-alarm rate for distractor words that were related to target words and distractor words that were unrelated to targets. This controls for the fact that there is always some baseline tendency to misrecognize distractors as old on the basis of guessing or other irrelevant strategies, a tendency that is normally higher in younger children than in older ones (e.g., Brainerd, Reyna, & Kneer, 1995) and is usually called response bias. Thus false memory, in the sense of erroneously remembering information that is related to information that was experienced, can only be said to be present if the false-alarm rate for related distractors exceeds the level of response bias. It is this difference, called the *false-recognition effect*, that is the standard index of false memory in recognition.

Although age levels and procedural details varied from study to study, all of the aforementioned experiments used a core design that emulates the standard technique that Underwood (1965) introduced for investigating false memory in adults. First, children were exposed to a fairly long list of familiar words, typically at least 30 words (e.g., *couch, tree, snake, cat, happy, shirt, car, sky*). To control for age differences in reading ability, the list was always presented orally. It was also presented at a rather leisurely pace (no faster than 2 seconds per word). Finally, the list had no obvious structure—each successive word seemed to be pretty much unrelated to its predecessors, unlike the categorized lists and DRM lists that were described above. Next, children responded to an orally presented old/new recognition test, typically under instructions to say "yes" whenever the experimenter said a word that they had just heard on the list and to say "no" otherwise. Further, children were cautioned not to fall prey to new words that were similar to old words in some way. The test list itself consisted of the same three types of probes that were administered in studies of children's narrative false memories (i.e., targets, related distractors, and unrelated distractors). Across our experiments, the type of false memory that was measured was varied by varying the relations between related distractors and targets. False memories based on all of the following semantic relations were studied: antonymy (e.g., *sad* is an antonym of *happy*), synonymy (e.g., *sofa* is a synonym of *couch*), within-category (e.g., *pants* is an exemplar of the same taxonomic category as *shirt*), superordinate category (e.g., *furniture* is the name of the category to which *couch* belongs), subordinate category (e.g., *oak* is an exemplar of the *tree* category), and association (e.g., *blue* is a strong associate of *sky*). Considering that study and test lists were orally presented, we also investigated false memory for distractors that were phonologically related to targets in some experiments (e.g., *sat* rhymes with *cat*).

The overall patterns that emerged from these experiments, which serve as background for recent studies of the DRM paradigm, ran as follows. First, children of all ages displayed false memory for all of the aforementioned target-distractor relations; false-alarm rates were always higher for related than for unrelated distractors. Second, the pattern of age change was usually the intuitive "memory gets better" trend: the tendency for children to recognize related distractors as old declined with age. (The overall age span in our experiments was 5 years to early 20s.) Generally speaking, although the amount of age change depended on the specific target-distractor relation, of course, the initial decline in false memory, across the elementary grades, was more marked than the subsequent decline. According to the distinctions that were discussed earlier, this developmental pattern has a straightforward interpretation: children's performance in the generic paradigm that we described is chiefly controlled by age improvements in the verbatim-processing abilities that suppress false alarms to related distractors. That this paradigm would not, instead, be highly sensitive to age improvements in the gist-processing abilities that foment such false alarms is apparent from two considerations. As mentioned, the lists that children heard were composed only of familiar words whose meanings were well understood by even the youngest children, leaving little latitude for age improvements in sheer meaning comprehension to increase false memory. Second, also as mentioned, the lists were constructed in such a way that there were no salient semantic relations between successive targets, leaving no way for age improvements in children's ability to connect meaning across different words to increase false memory. Thus, the developmental data argue that variations in false memory on the standard Underwood-type task are dominated by variations in verbatim processing rather than gist processing.

This brings us back to the main topic of this section: developmental DRM studies. We summarize the results of those studies in two waves. First, we consider initial baseline work, so called because it established and replicated the core developmental trends and ruled out possible artifactual explanations of those trends, which was published between 2002 and 2004. Next, we consider studies that have been subsequently published. These studies are concerned with more refined questions that are connected to theoretical explanations of false memory.

INITIAL STUDIES

A few years before developmental DRM studies began to appear, Brainerd and Reyna (1998) and Ceci and Bruck (1998) noted that FTT made the counterintuitive prediction that false memory would increase with age in tasks that met certain theoretically specified conditions. Brainerd, Reyna, and Forrest (2002) reported the first experiments that evaluated this prediction in connection with the DRM paradigm. They noted that this paradigm differs from Underwood-type tasks in two key respects, both of which have ramifications for how false memory should be found to change with age. One of the differences is obvious: although the words that compose DRM lists are mostly familiar ones whose meanings will be understood even by young children, all of the words share meaning, so that listening to a DRM list repeatedly cues certain meanings. Owing to the way that the lists are constructed, the word that shares more of these repeatedly cued meanings than any other is a critical distractor, of course. So, in the terminology of FTT, a hallmark of DRM lists is that they cause very strong gist traces to be stored by adults ("I heard a list with lots of medical words"; "I heard a list with lots of furniture words") because adults are adept at connecting meaning across distinct exemplars (e.g., Seamon et al., 2002). The other difference between the DRM paradigm and Underwood-type tasks is more subtle. The high level of meaning connection among targets makes the use of verbatim processes to suppress false memories far more problematical than on Underwood-type tasks. Returning to the illustrative *music* list, suppose that a subject who is responding to a recall or recognition test is able to retrieve clear verbatim memories of having heard the words *song, piano, band, horn,* and *symphony* but cannot retrieve a clear verbatim memory of having heard *music.* This does not constitute compelling evidence that *music* was not presented and therefore should not be recalled or recognized for adults because adults, by virtue of their excellent meaning-connection abilities, are well aware that they heard several music-related words other than these five, which they also cannot clearly recollect (Brainerd, Reyna, Wright, & Mojardin, 2003).

Brainerd et al. pointed out that, taken together, these two features of the DRM paradigm, coupled with FTT's distinctions, lead to a clean prediction of the counterintuitive developmental trend that, as we saw earlier, constructivism made for narrative false memory: false memory for critical distractors ought to increase with age. Why? One reason is that DRM lists encourage a form of gist processing—specifically, the spontaneous connection of meaning across several words—that is far more difficult for young children than it is for older children or adults. Note particularly that we did not say that meaning connection was impossible for young children or utterly absent in young children, which would conflict with certain types of evidence. We merely said that it is far more difficult, which is demonstrated by the fact that they usually fail to exhibit the standard adult signs of connecting meaning across different words, such as semantic clustering in free recall (e.g., Bjorklund & Jacobs, 1985) and semantic proactive inference (e.g., Bjorklund & Hock, 1982). Thus, young children will be less likely than older children or adults to engage in this particular form of gist processing, which means that the strong gist memories that result from such processing will be less likely to be available to support intrusions and false alarms to critical distractors. The other reason for the age-increase prediction is that although verbatim memory for DRM targets will be improving with age, it will not have much effect on performance. More concretely, the fact that, say, 10-year-old children can remember more of the targets from the *music* list than 5-year-old children can does not necessarily put the 10-year-olds in a better position to suppress *music*, because they are also more likely to know that there are still remaining words that cannot be clearly remembered. In short, according to FTT, the DRM paradigm is an example of a procedure in which performance variations are primarily controlled by gist processing, both because a form of gist processing (connecting meaning across words) is encouraged that leads to particularly strong gist memories and because verbatim processing is not very helpful in suppressing false memories. Hence, the DRM paradigm is also a procedure that should reveal age increases in false memory, because the focal form of gist processing is known to increase with age (Reyna et al., 2007).

In three experiments, Brainerd et al. (2002) confirmed the predicted age increases with both recall and recognition tests, and the increases for recall, in particular, were dramatic. The initial experiment was an exceedingly simply one. They administered a series of DRM lists to a sample of 5-year-olds, using standard free-recall procedures from the adult literature (e.g., Deese, 1959; Roediger & McDermott, 1995). Children studied and recalled a total of 10 lists, each of which consisted of 12 words. The task was not difficult; 5-year-olds were able to recall a quarter of the list words after hearing them only once. False recall of the critical distractors was virtually nonexistent, however. Critical distractors are falsely recalled 35%

to 45% of the time when adults study these lists, but children recalled them only 6% of the time. Children falsely recalled other words, however, and when Brainerd et al. examined those words, they noted qualitative differences between what young children and adults remembered about DRM lists. The adult data show, not surprisingly, that adults "get the gist" of a DRM list. When they recall an unpresented word, over 80% of the time it is the critical word (e.g., *music*), and when they falsely recall other unpresented words, these intrusions are consistent with the meaning of that same list (e.g., *drums, guitar*). In sharp contrast, although 5-year-olds recalled words that were not on the list, their intrusions seemed to show that they did not get the gist of the lists. As noted, critical words did not usually intrude, and neither did other words that preserved the meaning of the list. Instead, children's intrusions consisted primarily of novel words that were unrelated to the meaning of list words (e.g., *pirate* following the *music* list) or were targets that had been presented on a previous list (e.g., *nurse* or *sick* if the *doctor* list was presented before the *music* list). (*Nurse* or *sick* are not gist errors, because if children get the gist of the *music* list, they will know that only music-related words should be recalled.) Naturally, all of this is congruent with the larger literature on memory development that, as we said, points to young children's limitations in connecting shared meaning across different words.

The other two experiments replicated and extended the finding of age increases in false memory. In Experiment 2, Brainerd et al. (2002) simply replicated the first experiment with an age manipulation. Children from two age levels, 5- and 7-year-olds, studied and recalled DRM lists. This particular age change was chosen both because the advent of formal school might affect false memory and because many developmental changes occur during these 2 years that are known to affect how children learn (e.g., White, 1970). In addition, a list manipulation was included. Deese (1959) found that although he constructed all of his lists in the manner described earlier, some of them produced much higher false recall than others, a result that was replicated many years later by Stadler, Roediger, and McDermott (1999). Half of the lists that were presented to the children were ones that produce the very highest levels of false recall, and half were lists that produce much lower levels of false recall. This was done to test the hypothesis that young children might show adult-like false memory on the "high" lists. They did not: levels of false recall of critical distractors continued to be quite low, averaging 5% for younger children and 7% for older children, and there was no difference in false recall for "high" versus "low" lists. Thus, for recall at least, the development of DRM false memory seemed to be very slow indeed.

The final experiment centered on false memory in old/new recognition, rather than recall. Three age levels were included in the design: 5-, 11-, and 20-year-olds (undergraduates). At all three age levels, the participants first studied and recalled a series of "high" and "low" DRM lists. After that, however, they responded to a single old/new recognition test for all the lists, which contained three types of probes: some of the targets from each list, the critical distractor for each list, and some distractors that were not related to any of these lists. The overall patterns can be seen in Figure 9.2, where the plotted data involve the familiar signal detection statistic A' rather than raw hit and false-alarm probabilities (to control for the fact that response bias was higher at younger age levels). Contrary to the commonsense "memory gets better" thesis about development, it is starkly apparent that memory simultaneously gets better and worse: this tendency to judge targets to be old increases steadily between early childhood and young adulthood, but so does the tendency to judge critical distractors to be old. Moreover, one could not say that there is any overall improvement in memory accuracy because false alarms to critical distractors and hits to targets increased by about the same amount. With respect to false memory per se, note that false alarms to critical distractors

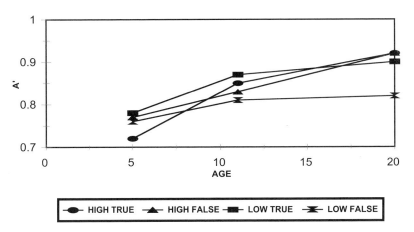

FIGURE 9.2. Relation between age and a corrected measure (A') of false recognition of the critical distractors of high and low Deese/Roediger-McDermott paradigm lists in Experiment 3 of Brainerd, Reyna, and Forrest (2002).

increased during childhood, but they continued to increase between age 11 and young adulthood, continuing to reinforce the theme of very gradual emergence of false memory in the DRM paradigm. Another finding that reinforces the same theme concerns false memories on "high" versus "low" lists. Specifically, a glance at the A' values for false memory reveals that the high–low list difference, which is so prominent in adults, did not emerge until after age 11.

We followed up these experiments with further experiments on children and adolescents, the novel feature of which was that an experimental paradigm and mathematical model were used that allowed investigators to tease apart and quantify the different retrieval processes that support and suppress false memory (Brainerd, Holliday, & Reyna, 2004). The objective was to determine whether the developmental increases were confined to a specific process or processes and, more particularly, to determine whether they would be confined to gist processing (as the earlier analysis implies). The paradigm that was used is called *conjoint recognition*, and it is an instructional variant on a standard old/new recognition design. Participants study a word list and then respond to a recognition test on which there are target probes, related distractors, and unrelated distractors, with the difference between the false-alarm rates for the two types of distractors being the false-memory index. However, participants respond to these probes under three types of instructions: *verbatim* (V: accept targets and reject all distractors); *gist* (G: accept related distractors while rejecting targets and unrelated distractors); and *verbatim + gist* (VG: accept targets and related distractors and reject unrelated distractors). When data from these conditions are analyzed with a mathematical model that was developed by Brainerd, Reyna, and Mojardin (1999), three distinct retrieval processes can be measured for false alarms to related distractors: (1) recollection rejection (suppresses recognition of related distractors by retrieving verbatim traces of targets, which neutralizes the familiarity of distractors' meanings); (2) similarity judgment (supports recognition of related distractors by retrieving gist traces of targets, which make distractors' meanings seem familiar); and (3) phantom recollection (supports recognition of related distractors by retrieving gist traces that are so strong that participants have illusory vivid mental experiences of distractors' prior "presentations"). An intriguing feature of false memory in the DRM paradigm, which was first detected by Roediger and McDermott (1995) with Tulving's (1985) remember/know procedure, is that critical distractors tend to provoke phantom recollective experiences (their prior "presentations" echo in the mind's ear or flash in the mind's eye). In contrast, false memories in other tasks are dominated by the weaker and less illusory experience of meaning familiarity (i.e., similarity judgment rather than phantom recollection). The fact that the DRM task provokes high levels of phantom recollection squares nicely, of course, with the high levels of false memory that this paradigm produces, but, more important for our purposes, it suggests that age increases in false memory may be primarily due to age increases in phantom recollection.

In the research that Brainerd et al. (2004) reported, participants from three age levels studied a total of nine DRM lists. Following the first three lists, the participants responded to a recognition test containing four types of probes: some targets from each of the lists, the critical distractor for each list (e.g., *music*), some other related distractors (e.g., *drums*, *guitar*), and some unrelated distractors. One-third of the participants at each age level responded under each of the three types of instructions (V, G, VG). The age increases in false memory that had been reported by Brainerd et al. (2002) were replicated in that the tendency to judge critical distractors as old under V instructions was much higher at older age levels than among the 7-year-olds. The more instructive findings, which are displayed in Figure 9.3, are for the underlying retrieval process. There are three results, in particular, that are of considerable theoretical interest. First, age increases in phantom recollection were driving the age increases in false memory. Of the two retrieval processes that support old responses to critical distractors, one, phantom recollection, increased steadily between the ages of 5 and 14, while the other, similarity judgment, remained invariant. Thus, the fact that the potency of the DRM illusion waxes with age is somehow tied to its ability to induce illusory vivid mental phenomenology. The second finding of theoretical interest is that the age increases in illusion potency occur despite the fact that the retrieval process that suppresses old responses to critical distractors also increases. Here, although recollection rejection remained relatively constant between the ages of 5 and 11, it jumped dramatically between the ages of 11 and 15. Taken together, the first two findings illustrate one of the most illuminating benefits of using mathematical models to separate and quantify underlying memory mechanisms: developmental variation in important types of memory performance (false memories in this instance) can be the net result of developmental variation in processes that work against each other—that is, of processes that produce age increases (phantom recollection in this instance) and processes that produce age decreases (recollection rejection in this case). The third finding of theoretical interest is that the patterns of developmental variation in underlying retrieval processes explained the detailed age trends in false memory performance. Concerning the latter trends, the false-alarm rate for critical distractors increased dramatically between the ages of 5 and 11, but it increased only slightly between the ages of 11 and 14. A glance at Figure 9.3 reveals the explanation. Phantom recollection increased substantially between the ages of 5 and 11—doubled, in fact—whereas recollection rejection did not increase; hence, age increases false memory. Phantom recollection increased again between the ages of 11 and 14, but recollection rejection also increased, allowing no net age change in false memory. Thus, the process-level analyses revealed that major developmental changes in underlying mechanisms can be underway during age ranges in which false memory would not appear to be changing if only raw memory performance were considered. This is yet another example of one of the fundamental lessons that has been learned from the application of mathematical models in the study of development (e.g., see Howe, Brainerd, & Kingma, 1985): that an absence of developmental variability

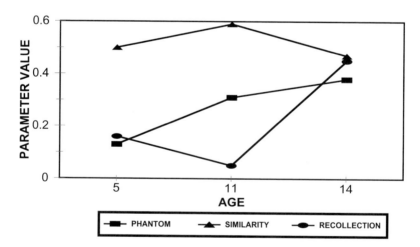

FIGURE 9.3. Relationship between age and three retrieval processes that control false memory in Experiment 1 of Brainerd, Holliday, and Reyna (2004). Phantom = phantom recollection, similarity = similarity judgment, and recollection = recollection rejection.

in surface level performance can occur in the presence of variability, even massive variability, at the more important level of the processes that control surface performance.

So far, we have seen that, contrary to the commonsense view of memory development, the DRM illusion increases dramatically between early childhood and young adulthood, when it is measured by both intrusions during recall and false alarms during recognition. Because this outcome is so counterintuitive, before proceeding any further we ought to consider a possible artifactual explanation—specifically, age differences in association norms. Deese (1959) constructed his lists by selecting associates of critical distractors from the Russell and Jenkins (1954) word-association norms. Those norms were gathered from University of Minnesota students. Suppose that young children's associations to these same critical distractors are markedly different. If so, one would not expect them to have false memories for *music*, *rough*, and so on, the way older children and adults do, because they are not being exposed to the correct DRM lists—correct for them, that is. Metzger et al. (2004) investigated this potential artifact and ruled it out. They reported a study in which new association norms for some of Deese's critical distractors were obtained from a sample of children. In agreement with prior developmental research on word association (e.g., Bjorklund & Jacobs, 1985), Metzger et al. found a strong correlation ($r = 0.75$) between the associates that were given by children and the corresponding data in the Russell and Jenkins norms. They also reported a developmental study in which these child-generated lists were administered to children of various ages and to adults, using a recall-followed-by-recognition design as in the third experiment of Brainerd et al. (2002). They found that these "child appropriate" DRM lists also yielded age increases in false recall and false recognition of critical distractors. Another crucial finding was that child appropriateness made no difference at all in the performance of the young children. They showed the same low levels of false memory, regardless of whether they were exposed to standard DRM lists or child-appropriate lists.

Next, Howe, Cicchetti, Toth, and Cerrito (2004) reported a developmental DRM study that is highly relevant to the aims of this volume, as it was concerned with true and false memories in maltreated children. Howe et al. were particularly interested in whether the effects of the chronic stress that is associated with maltreatment might influence the basic processes that control false memory. The authors used a 3 (age level: 5 to 7, 8 to 9, or 10 to 12 years old) × 3 (middle socioeconomic status (SES), low SES nonmaltreated, low SES maltreated) × 2 ("high" or "low" DRM list) design in which the effects of each of these factors on children's false memory were separately assessed. Children were exposed to 12 DRM lists in a recall-followed-by-recognition design. A key aspect of the design is that related distractors *other than the critical distractor* were included on the recognition test. The developmental increases in false memory that had been observed in prior studies were again detected. Both recognition and recall of critical distractors increased with age, the age increases were greater for recall than for recognition (a finding that Brainerd et al. [2004] also obtained), and there were age increases in false recognition of related distractors as well as false recognition of critical distractors. The most informative new finding is that developmental increases in false memory were observed, although in varying degrees, for all three types of child populations—middle SES, low-SES nonmaltreated, and low-SES maltreated. This is informative because although middle-SES children would be comparable to the children in prior developmental studies, low-SES nonmaltreated and low-SES maltreated would not. As mentioned, age trends in false memory did vary somewhat as a function of which population children were drawn from, but the central hypothesis under investigation—that levels of false memory might be different for maltreated children owing to their history of chronic stress—was not borne out.

VERY RECENT STUDIES

Since the above research appeared, the developmental literature on the DRM paradigm has been growing apace, which is surely connected to fact that an age trend has been identified that, though surprising, has proven to be easily replicable and highly robust (but see Ghetti, Qin, & Goodman, 2002). Surprising data stimulate investigators to formulate and test possible theoretical accounts, though this is one of those rare instances in which the data were predicted on theoretical grounds long before they were obtained. Most of the recent work on the DRM illusion is in this vein in the sense that it includes new manipulations or new measures that are intended to generate data on a specific theoretical hypothesis or to pit different hypotheses against each other. Considering that theoretical understanding is the surest way to make progress, this is a welcome development. In the remainder of this section, we consider six articles that are representative of this hypothesis-testing orientation: Dewhurst and Robinson (2004); Howe (2005); Holliday and Weekes (in press); Howe (2006); Brainerd, Forrest, Karibian, and Reyna (2006); and Brainerd and Reyna (2007).

Dewhurst and Robinson (2004)

These authors conducted a simple developmental recall study of DRM lists in which they added a measurement wrinkle that bears on FTT's hypothesis that young children's limitations in connecting the gist across words is a major factor in developmental increases in intrusions. Children from three age levels (5-, 8-, and 11-year-olds) studied and recalled a total of five DRM lists. Remember in this connection that Brainerd et al. (2002) found that young children's intrusions were qualitatively different than that of older children and adults in that they were not dominated by unpresented words that were semantically related to lists. Dewhurst and Robinson hypothesized that there is a developmental shift in the informational basis of false memory and, specifically, that young children's false memories may be dominated by a reliance on perceptual similarity (e.g., auditory or visual resemblance) that is later supplanted by a reliance on semantic similarity. To test this hypothesis, they classified the intrusions that children made into three categories: phonologically related (unpresented words that *sounded* like one of the list words when spoken), semantically related, and unrelated. When the mean numbers of the different types of errors were plotted for the different age levels, a dramatic Age × Type of Relatedness crossover was detected. On the one hand, as predicted by FTT, the number of semantically related intrusions increased from 0.7 to 1.4 to 2.7. On the other hand, the number of phonologically related intrusions decreased from 1.2 at the two youngest age levels to 0.2 at the oldest age level. Thus these data provide preliminary evidence of a perceptual-to-semantic shift in the basis for false memory, a theme that is echoed in two other recent studies (Brainerd & Reyna, 2007; Holliday & Weekes, in press).

Howe (2005)

Howe employed a directed-forgetting design that had been introduced in some adult DRM studies by Kimball and Bjork (2002). The directed-forgetting procedure consists of simply telling participants to forget (or remember) previously studied information, with "forget" or "remember" cues being given either immediately after each item is presented (the item method) or after a series of items has been presented (the list method). Kimball and Bjork used the list method to test a prediction from FTT: directed forgetting should suppress true memory for DRM list words more than it should suppress false memory for critical distractors, because the verbatim traces that support true recall/recognition are more sensitive to post-presentation interference than the gist traces that support false recall/recognition. Their results were as predicted in that directed forgetting had no effect on false recall, though it suppressed true recall. Howe used this basic design in a DRM experiment with 5-, 7-, and 11-year-old children. Some children simply studied and recalled individual DRM lists in the usual way. Other children studied DRM lists in pairs, receiving a "forget" instruction following one of the lists and a "remember" instruction following the other. Like adults, the true memories of children of all age levels were suppressed by directed-forgetting instructions. Unlike adults, however, children's false memories were also suppressed by directed-forgetting instructions. Howe concluded that adults' DRM false memories are so automatic that they are not amenable to conscious control via instructions, but that children's are effortful and deliberate, which leaves them open to conscious control. Considering that adults are known to be better than children at virtually all forms of conscious control of memory, this is a counterintuitive hypothesis, but then the developmental pattern that needs to be explained is equally counterintuitive.

Holliday and Weekes (in press)

These investigators followed up Dewhurst and Robinson's perceptual → semantic shift hypothesis and provided more differentiated data on this shift, as a test of FTT's analysis of false memory. Holliday and Weekes proposed that FTT would expect such a shift on the ground that although children's ability to connect the gist across multiple words increases with age, they are able to detect and transfer phonological resemblance at a very early age. To evaluate this proposal, they studied false recognition of related distractors in 8-, 11-, and 13-year-old children with two types of lists. First, DRM lists, as we know, consist of semantic associates of critical distractors. Half the children at each age level studied such lists, followed by the usual recognition test with targets, semantically related distractors, and unrelated distractors. The other half of the children studied lists that were phonologically related to each other. Lists of this sort were

developed by Sommers and Lewis (1999) using procedures that are remi-
niscent of Deese's (1959) method of list generation. First, Sommers and
Lewis selected 24 stimulus items, each of which was a familiar three-letter
word (e.g., *cat*, *hit*). Next, English lexical databases were used to select the
15 words that were most phonologically related to each stimulus word. To
take a concrete example, the first 15 phonological associates of *cat* are *fat*,
that, *cab*, *caught*, *cot*, *sat*, *cut*, *hat*, *kit*, *vat*, *cap*, *mat*, *bat*, *cad*, and *chat*.

The key feature of Holliday and Weekes's (in press) data is that, in line
with the perceptual → semantic shift hypothesis, developmental trends
for semantic associates of lists and phonological associates of lists were
mirror images. This can be seen in Figure 9.4, where false-alarm rates
for DRM critical distractors and unpresented phonological associates are
plotted by age level. The two developmental trends are virtually mirror
images of each other. The tendency to recognize unpresented semantic
associates as old increased from a little over 60% to a little over 80%,
whereas the tendency to recognize unpresented phonological associates as
old decreased by almost exactly the same amount, from a little below 40%
to a little below 20%. Also, it can be seen that perceptual and semantic
illusions were equally seductive to 8-year-olds, whereas semantic illusions
were more seductive to 11- and 13-year-olds. A prediction that would
follow from the shape of the trends in Figure 9.3 is that if this design

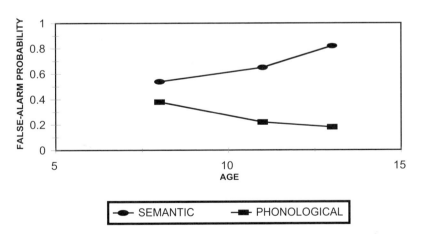

FIGURE 9.4. Developmental trends in false memory for distractors that are
semantically related to list targets and developmental trends in false memory for
distractors that are phonologically related to list targets, as reported by Holliday
and Weekes (in press).

were extended downward to include children as young as Dewhurst and Robinson's (2004) youngest participants, perceptual illusions would be more seductive than semantic illusions.

Howe (2006)

This article answers an important question: are age increases in false memory for semantically related words observed for procedures other than the DRM paradigm? Of course, FTT's analysis of false memory would expect age increases in other tasks for which the ability to connect meaning across different words supports false recall/recognition and for which it is difficult to use recollection rejection to suppress false memories. In the research that Howe reports, children's recall of DRM lists was compared to their recall of another familiar type of list: categorized lists. Whereas DRM lists are generated by selecting the first few associates of critical distractors, categorized lists are constructed by selecting the most common exemplars from production norms for familiar taxonomic categories (e.g., animals, flowers, furniture; see, e.g., Battig & Montague, 1969). In Experiment 1, a total of 180 children were tested from each of three age levels (5-, 7-, and 11-year-olds). Half the children at each age level recalled eight DRM lists, and the other half recalled eight categorized lists. The important new finding, as would be expected on theoretical grounds, was that false recall increased with age (from 0.16 to 0.27 to 0.32) for *both* categorized lists and DRM lists. Further, false recall for the two types of lists did not differ in reliability, and their age trends were the same. Thus, age increases in false recall did not seem to depend on whether false-memory items are associatively related or taxonomically related to targets.

Howe's (2006) second experiment incorporated an additional novel design feature, gist cuing. A further sample of 180 children, evenly divided with respect to the same three age levels, studied and recalled *only categorized lists*. However, they did so under one of two conditions: category cuing or no cuing. In the former condition, children were told the name of the category just before each list was read (e.g., "the words that you are about to hear are all names of animals"), whereas children in the latter condition were told nothing. FTT predicts that if limitations in younger children's meaning-connection abilities contribute to age increases in false memory, false memory should be higher in the cuing condition. It was not, which does not support the prediction. However, this is a null effect, and such null results are always difficult to interpret, as we mentioned earlier in connection with studies of the suggestibility of children's memories of traumatic experiences involving their bodies. In this particular instance, other data suggest that the null effect may be a Type 2 error (i.e., a failure to reject a false null hypothesis). Evidence for this possibility may be found in Experiment 2 of Brainerd et al. (2004). The same cuing procedure was used in connection with false memory for categorized lists, and in line with FTT's prediction, children displayed more false memory following category cues than following no cues. There was also an important procedural difference: false memory was measured with recognition rather than recall tests. Further evidence that, as expected on theoretical grounds, gist cuing increases children's false memories and that this effect is not confined to recognition can be found in DRM experiments by Brainerd et al. (2004) and by Holliday, Reyna, and Brainerd (2006). In both studies, the authors cued the meanings of DRM lists just before each list was presented for half the children and provided no pre-presentation meaning cues for the other half of the children. Brainerd et al.'s children (6-, 11-, and 14-year-olds) showed elevated levels of false recall of critical words in the gist-cuing condition relative to the no-cues condition. Likewise, Holliday et al.'s children (9-, 11-, 13-, and 15-year-olds) displayed higher levels of false recall and false recognition of critical distractors in the gist-cuing condition relative to the no-cues condition.

Howe's (2006) final experiment incorporated the further design modification of pictorial presentation. As Schacter, Israel, and Racine (1999) noted, FTT predicts that, other things being equal, false memory should be reduced by any manipulation that enhances verbatim memory for individual targets, while leaving gist memory unaffected. Howe pointed out that pictorial presentation of lists is often considered to be just such a manipulation. Moreover, considering that the false-memory responses that are made for lists that repeatedly cue the same meanings, whether categorized or DRM, have been consistently found to be more fragile in children, verbatim-strengthening manipulations would be expected to have especially marked effects in children. To evaluate these ideas, categorized lists were again studied and recalled by 5-, 7-, and 11-year-old children. The lists were again read aloud to children, but now each word was illustrated by a picture of the named object as it was read. As expected on theoretical grounds, this presentation method suppressed false recall of unpresented exemplars to very low levels (below 20% at all age levels), and it completely eliminated the age increases that have been so consistently obtained with oral presentation (see also Ghetti et al., 2002).

Brainerd et al. (2006)

These investigators asked whether developmental increases in the DRM illusion were more than quantitative by studying possible qualitative differences between the false memories of children and adults. They also measured these increases in a new way by implementing an ability-based definition of "development." With respect to qualitative change, Brainerd et al. studied whether children exhibit any or all of five effects that have been obtained in adult DRM studies: (1) list strength (some DRM lists produce high rates of false recall and false recognition, whereas other lists produce low rates); (2) recall inflation (on an immediate memory test, false memory for critical distractors is higher if participants have responded to a prior recall test than if they have not) and delayed inflation (on a delayed memory test, false memory for critical distractors is higher if participants have responded to an immediate recall test than if they have not); (3) delayed stability (when memory tests are postponed for a few days, true memory levels decline, but false memory levels for critical distractors remain relatively stable); (4) thematic intrusion (false recall is dominated by intrusions that are consistent with list themes); and (5) true–false dissociation (true recall and true recognition of DRM targets correlate negatively with false recall and false recognition of critical distractors). To the extent that children display all of these effects, Brainerd et al. proposed, the indicated conclusion is that children's reduced levels of false memory are not due to qualitative changes in the nature of the DRM illusion, whereas the conclusion that qualitative change is involved is forced to the extent that children do not display these effects. Two experiments were reported, in which the children were between the ages of 7 and 11 and in which both recognition and recall tests were used to measure false memory for critical distractors. None of the six effects was observed in the youngest children, and five of them were found to emerge with age, all of which is consistent with the qualitative-change view.

In the second of their two experiments, Brainerd et al. (2006) compared developmental trends in false memory for two different definitions of development: the usual chronological-age definition and an ability-based definition that was based on children's school performance. Participants came from two age levels, 7- and 11-year-olds. Within each age level, children of two ability levels were included: children whose school performance was within the normal range and children who had been classified as learning disabled (but whose measured IQs were in the normal range). Learning-disabled children provide a further test of FTT's hypothesis that younger children's meaning-connection limitations contribute to age increases in false memory because learning-disabled children's limitations in this area are even greater (e.g., Swanson, 1991). The children studied and recalled DRM lists in the usual way. Nondisabled children displayed the usual developmental increases in false memory, with intrusions of critical distractors increasing from 0.16 in younger children to 0.30 in older children. The ability measure produced the same picture of developmental increases *within* chronological age levels. The intrusion levels were 0.16 and 0.06, respectively, for nondisabled and disabled 7-year-olds, and the corresponding intrusion levels for nondisabled and disabled 11-year-olds were 0.30 and 0.19, respectively. Although false memory increased with chronological age in both nondisabled and disabled children, the contribution of ability to false memory is dramatically illustrated by the fact that the intrusion rate for disabled 11-year-olds (0.19) was not reliably higher than the intrusion rate for nondisabled 7-year-olds.

Brainerd and Reyna (2007)

This research was aimed at securing stronger tests of the theoretical ideas that have dominated our discussion of false memory in the narrative and word tasks. According to those ideas, predicting the direction of developmental trends in false memory turns on three considerations: (1) that participants store and retrieve dissociated verbatim and gist traces of target materials; (2) that verbatim and gist retrieval are opponent processes in false memory (i.e., verbatim retrieval suppresses false memories while gist retrieval supports it); and (3) that developmental lags exist in extracting the semantic information from target materials, especially semantic relations among events that share familiar meanings. As we have seen, this leads one to expect age increases in false memory in situations in which false-memory items tap meaning relations that are repeatedly cued by target materials (as in the sentences that compose narratives, DRM lists, or categorized lists). Although this expectation has been consistently confirmed, an even stronger prediction follows: the *same* unpresented items should exhibit *opposite* age trends, depending on whether the target material allows semantic relations to be formed for those words. Imagine that children study a single long list of words whose meanings are all familiar. For instance, suppose that the words are exemplars of everyday categories, such as colors, flowers, foods, and the like. Further, imagine that the list exemplifies some category *once* to half the children (e.g., the color category is exemplified by *red*), but the list exemplifies that same category *multiple times* to other children (e.g., color is exemplified by *black*, *blue*, *brown*, *green*, *pink*, *purple*, *red*, and *white*). Finally, suppose that a recognition test is presented on which the related distractors *color* and *yellow* appear. The theoretical analysis makes the surprising prediction that these distractors will display opposite age trends for the two groups of children: (a) the false-alarm rate should decrease with age if the list contained only a single color exemplar because developmental variability in false alarms to unpresented exemplars will be chiefly controlled by improvements in verbatim suppression, and (b) the false-alarm rate should increase with age if the list contained a large number of color exemplars because developmental variability in false alarms to unpresented exemplars will be chiefly controlled by improvements in the ability to connect the gist across target words.

We tested these predictions in experiments with 6-, 10-, and 14-year-olds. Children listened to two different lists and responded to a recognition test following each list. Each list contained exemplars of taxonomic categories that are very familiar to children. For three of the categories (e.g., animals, colors, men's names), the list contained eight exemplars, and for the other three categories (e.g., clothing, flowers, furniture), the list contained a single exemplar. On the test list, there were two false-memory items for each category: the category label and an unpresented exemplar (e.g., *color* and *yellow*). The prediction was that these distractors' false-alarm rates should increase with age if eight color exemplars had been presented but decrease with age if only a single color exemplar had been presented. The results are plotted in Figure 9.5, where it can be seen that, indeed, false-alarm rates increased with age when categories had been cued eight times but decreased when they had been cued once.

We also tested a control sample of children from the same age range to determine whether it was *semantic relatedness* in particular that was responsible for the contrasting developmental trends in Figure 9.5. These children participated in an experiment that used the same design, except that phonological relatedness rather than semantic relatedness was the

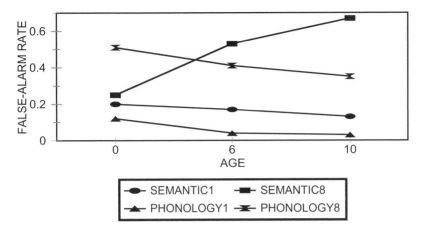

FIGURE 9.5. Developmental trends in false memory for distractors that are semantically or phonologically related to list targets as a function of the number of times (1 vs. 8) that semantic or phonological relations were cued by target materials. *Source:* Brainerd & Reyna, 2007.

basis of false memory. Specifically, as in Holliday and Weekes's research, the Sommers and Lewis (1999) phonological lists were used to create target lists in which some phonological relations (e.g., for the word *cat*) were exemplified once and other phonological relations (e.g., for the word *hit*) were exemplified eight times. The unpresented critical distractor for each relation was the false-memory item on the recognition test. The false-alarm rates for those items are shown in Figure 9.5. There, it can be seen that phonological false memory, unlike semantic false memory, did not display opposite developmental trends as a function of whether phonological relations had been repeatedly cued by the target materials. Instead, repeated cuing produced higher levels of false memory at all age levels, and phonological false memory decreased with age regardless of the level of phonological cuing.

Conclusions

By now, it should be evident that a great deal has been learned about the precise variables that control children's false memories and about how the mix of those variables leads to different patterns of developmental change in false memory. A key feature of the memory illusions that have been explored—narrative tasks in the constructivist tradition and word tasks in the verbal learning tradition—is that they are illusions of meaning: that false recall and false recognition are apt to occur when rememberers rely on meaning information that was instantiated by target materials. However, current theoretical analyses of this situation propose that more is involved. Those analyses are dominated by an opponent-processes principle, which is simply the idea that rememberers store and retrieve two basic forms of information, such as verbatim traces of the surface form of target materials and gist traces of materials' meaning content, with one type of processing supporting false memories ("Yes, I ate a hot dog, because that's what people usually eat at baseball games") and the other suppressing false memories ("No, I didn't eat a hot dog, because I clearly remember eating that cold, soggy slice of pizza") We have seen that the opponent-processes conception has been able to explain and, far more important, to predict a broad range of developmental findings. With narrative false memory, for example, we have seen that this conception was able to account for the conflicting age trends that have accumulated over the years in developmental studies of Bransford-Franks-type tasks. With false memory for words, we have seen that the same conception explains why Underwood-type tasks have usually produced age declines in false memory. The most important accomplishment, however, has been the prediction, some years before confirmation was obtained, of developmental increases in false memory for words. Such increases were predicted for tasks in which false-memory items access meanings that are repeatedly cued by target materials—most notably the DRM paradigm, but also tasks that involve repeated cuing of familiar taxonomic categories. Although this prediction is counterintuitive under the commonsense "memory gets better" view of development, it has been confirmed in so many recent studies that its validity is no longer in doubt. Crucially, the most recent studies in this literature have begun the process of drilling down to more precise hypotheses about the mechanisms that control age variability in false memory. In the end, it is findings from these tests of more precise hypotheses that will have the greatest yield in forensic work, as well as in theory development.

If some types of false memories can increase with age, this has important implications for a baseline assumption that the law currently makes about age variability in false memory. The classical finding, mentioned earlier in this chapter, that the incidence of false-memory declines between early childhood and young adulthood has figured prominently in many trials, but especially CSA cases, in which evidence was provided by child victims or witnesses (e.g., Ceci & Friedman, 2000). That finding has been used to challenge children's competence to testify in pretrial motions and pretrial hearings and to challenge children's courtroom testimony as being unreliable, all on the specific ground that research shows that their statements are far more likely than adults' to be tainted with false memories (Brainerd & Reyna, 2005). For example, a common occurrence in CSA cases is that there are two versions of events that bear on a defendant's guilt. One version is exculpatory and one is incriminating, and one version is provided by adults and the other by children. In such circumstances, the law requires juries to render a verdict by assessing the relative credibility of the contrasting stories. If research shows that children's memories are invariably more likely to be tainted with false information than adults', then, other factors being equal, the adult version should be assigned a higher credibility rating.

This is precisely the thrust of much expert testimony in CSA cases. In fact, such expert testimony has become so commonplace and the research that supports it has been so widely disseminated in the popular media that judges sometimes rule against allowing it to be presented in court, on the grounds that the heightened susceptibility of children to false memories is well understood by jurors and, therefore, expert testimony is not needed to educate them on it (McAuliff, Nicholson, & Ravenshenas, 2007). However, a key implication of the more recent research that we reviewed earlier is that the law errs when it makes such a baseline assumption about the fallibility of children's memories. More recent research demonstrates that the direction of age variability in false memory depends on specific storage and retrieval factors. Therefore, in particular court cases, the scientifically appropriate course for expert witnesses is to analyze the circumstances of each case to determine which factors are present that are known to affect age variability in false memory and to educate juries (a) on the results of their analysis and (b) on the research literature that substantiates the factors that have been identified.

However, some readers may be disposed to be uneasy about the applicability of findings from research on laboratory tasks that involve narrative false memory to legal cases and, still more, about the applicability of findings from research on false memory for words. We can do no better than refer them to contemporary discussions of this question by Howe et al. (2004) and by Reyna et al. (2007), both of whom explore the question in connection with the more extreme of the two situations, false memory for word lists. This gist of their discussion runs as follows.

Superficially, to those who are steeped in the study of everyday memory it might seem that false memories for words have little or nothing to do with the real-life events that are the stuff of forensic work. Perception is not necessarily reality, however. It is often the case in science that differences that seem to be fundamental at first blush fade out upon deeper consideration, and indeed, tasks such as the DRM paradigm and the categorized-list paradigm share some of the most basic features of forensically relevant memories. For that reason, these paradigms may be quite relevant to such memories. In familiar real-life crimes, such as robberies or assaults, there are certain events that are characteristic of those crimes (e.g., fear, threatening statements, weapons), so much so that they are formulaic elements of crime novels and the scripts that writers produce for movies and television programs. Thus, when children are witnesses or victims of familiar crimes, they are exposed to collections of target events that are interconnected in meaning by virtue of the fact that, like hot dogs and home runs at baseball games, the events are prototypical of those situations. In the DRM and categorized-list paradigms, too (and in narratives, by the way), children are also exposed to multiple targets that are related in meaning. As we have seen, children falsely recall and falsely recognize unpresented exemplars of these shared meanings, these errors are affected by theoretically specified variables, and these errors display age trends that can be predicted on theoretical grounds. Considering the extensive data base on these paradigms, therefore, it is not surprising that children would have false memories of events that cohere with the gist of crimes, or that those false memories could vary with age.

Further, in CSA and other crimes of abuse and neglect, the phenomenon of encountering multiple exemplars of a meaning (the gist of the crime) can occur across multiple exposures to that crime (Powell, Roberts, Ceci, & Hembrooke, 1999; Reyna et al.,2007). A hallmark of such crimes is that they may occur in children's homes, with the perpetrators being children's caretakers or even other children. When they do, children may be victims or witnesses of multiple instances of a crime. Each instance of the crime exposes children to events that share meaning with prior instances but that are not exactly the same in key details as prior events. Moreover, each subsequent exposure is apt to cue memories for earlier events from prior exposures, particularly if children access stable gist memories and realize that the different experiences are connected. If children are aware that later events are not exact repetitions of earlier events but are related to earlier events, the fact that those different events were part of different episodes may become blurred, interfering with accurate verbatim memories of the details of the individual events.

This problem of interference with verbatim memory is exacerbated by the fact that when children have been victims or witnesses of multiple instances of index crimes, spaced over extended time intervals, investigative interviews and sworn testimony often will not occur until months or years after the initial instances. In such circumstances, their memory reports of *what* happened may be highly accurate (especially the gist of what happened) but their memory reports of *when* it happened will undoubtedly be highly inaccurate. Powell et al. have reported data showing that this extrapolation from word-memory studies is indeed borne out in experimentation on children's memory for everyday events that are of forensic significance, and other examples of forensically relevant data have been reviewed by Reyna et al. (2002).

Howe et al. (2004) raised the following important consideration: Because the types of paradigms that have been the foci of this chapter rely on target materials that have nothing to do with crimes or with physical or psychological trauma, it might be thought that children would be less likely to develop false memories for such crimes than for word lists or sentences. However, these crimes involve gists, strong gists in fact, as surely as the list *"black, blue, brown, green, pink, purple, red,* and *white"* does. Hence it is not clear what the experimentally verified, *as opposed to speculative,* basis for such an argument would be. Perhaps the most obvious basis that might be invoked is that the events of crimes are usually experienced in conjunction with high levels of anxiety and stress, which may inoculate memory against falsification. Indeed, some research has shown that stress and anxiety lead to greater memory accuracy (Christianson, 1992). As Reyna et al. (2007) pointed out, though, experimental findings on how anxiety and stress affect children's false memories are equivocal. Further, there is a good deal of evidence in the adult forensic memory literature that the anxiety and stress of crimes foment false memories, rather than suppress them (e.g., Kassin, 1997, 2001), and there is also a good deal of evidence that adults can develop false memories of complex life experiences, including crimes, that are fraught with anxiety and stress (for a review, see Brainerd & Reyna, 2005). Thus, the fact that crimes normally involve stress and anxiety apparently does not inoculate people against developing false memories.

References

Ackerman, B. P. (1992). The sources of children's source errors in judging causal inferences. *Journal of Experimental Child Psychology, 54,* 90–119.

Ackerman, B. P. (1994). Children's source errors in referential communication. *Journal of Experimental Child Psychology, 58,* 432–464.

Anderson, J. R., Budiu, R., & Reder, L. M. (2001). A theory of sentence memory as a general theory of memory. *Journal of Memory and Language, 45,* 337–367.

Armstrong, K., Milles, S., & Possley, M. (2001, December 16). Coercive and illegal tactics torpedo scores of Cook County murder cases. *Chicago Tribune.*

Banaji, M. R., & Crowder, R. G. (1989). Bankruptcy of everyday memory. *American Psychologist, 44,* 1185–1193.

Bartlett, F. C. (1932). *Remembering: A study in experimental and social psychology.* Cambridge, UK: Cambridge University Press.

Battig, W. F., & Montague, W. E. (1969). Category norms for verbal items in 56 categories: A replication and extension of the Connecticut category norms. *Journal of Experimental Psychology Monograph, 80* (3, Pt. 2)

Binet, A. (1900). *La suggestibilite.* Paris: Schleicher Feres.

Bjorklund, D. F., & Hock, H. H. (1982). Age differences in the temporal locus of memory organization in children's recall. *Journal of Experimental Child Psychology, 33,* 347–362.

Bjorklund, D. F., & Jacobs, J. W. (1985). Associative and categorical processes in children's memory: The role of automaticity in the development of free recall. *Journal of Experimental Child Psychology, 39,* 599–617.

Bjorklund, D. F., & Muir, J. E. (1988). Children's development of free recall memory: Remembering on their own. *Annals of Child Development, 5,* 79–123.

Bottoms, B. L., Goodman, G. S., Schwartz-Kenney, B. M., & Thomas, S. N. (2002). Understanding children's use of secrecy in the context of eyewitness reports. *Law and Human Behavior, 26,* 285–313.

Brainerd, C. J., Forrest, T. J., Karibian, D., & Reyna, V. F. (2006). Development of the False Memory Illusion. *Developmental Psychology, 42,* 662–679.

Brainerd, C. J., & Gordon, L. L. (1994). Development of verbatim and gist memory for numbers. *Developmental Psychology, 30,* 163–177.

Brainerd, C. J., Holliday, R. E., & Reyna, V. F. (2004). Behavioral measurement of remembering phenomenologies: So simple a child can do it. *Child Development, 75,* 505–522.

Brainerd, C. J., & Reyna, V. F. (1993). Memory independence and memory interference in cognitive development. *Psychological Review, 100,* 42–67.

Brainerd, C. J., & Reyna, V. F. (1995). Autosuggestibility in memory development. *Cognitive Psychology, 28,* 65–101.

Brainerd, C. J., & Reyna, V. F. (1996). Mere memory testing creates false memories in children. *Developmental Psychology, 32,* 467–476.

Brainerd, C. J., & Reyna, V. F. (1998). Fuzzy-trace theory and children's false memories. *Journal of Experimental Child Psychology, 71,* 81–129.

Brainerd, C. J., & Reyna, V. F. (2001). Fuzzy-trace theory: Dual-processes in reasoning, memory, and cognitive neuroscience. *Advances in Child Development and Behavior, 28,* 49–100.

Brainerd, C. J., & Reyna, V. F. (2005). *The science of false memory.* New York: Oxford University Press.

Brainerd, C. J., & Reyna, V. F. (2007). Explaining developmental reversals in false memory. *Psychological Science, 18,* 442–448.

Brainerd, C. J., Reyna, V. F., & Brandse, E. (1995). Are children's false memories more persistent than their true memories? *Psychological Science, 6,* 359–364.

Brainerd, C. J., Reyna, V. F., & Estrada, S. (2006). Recollection rejection of false narrative statements. *Memory, 14,* 672–691.

Brained, C. J., Reyna, V. F., & Forrest, T. J. (2002). Are young children susceptible to the false-memory illusion? *Child Development, 73,* 1363–1377.

Brainerd, C. J., Reyna, V. F., & Kneer, R. (1995). False-recognition reversal: When similarity is distinctive. *Journal of Memory and Language, 34,* 157–185.

Brainerd, C. J., Reyna, V. F., & Mojardin, A. H. (1999). Conjoint recognition. *Psychological Review, 106,* 160–179.

Brainerd, C. J., Reyna, V. F., & Poole, D. A. (2000). Fuzzy-trace theory and false memory: Memory theory in the courtroom. In D. F. Bjorklund (Ed.), *False memory creation in children and adults* (pp. 93–128). Mahwah, NJ: Erlbaum.

Brainerd, C. J., Reyna, V. F., Wright, R., & Mojardin, A. H. (2003). Recollection rejection: False-memory editing in children and adults. *Psychological Review, 110,* 762–784.

Brainerd, C. J., Stein, L., & Reyna, V. F. (1998). On the development of conscious and unconscious memory. *Developmental Psychology, 34,* 342–357.

Bransford, J. D., & Franks, J. J. (1971). The abstraction of linguistic ideas. *Cognitive Psychology, 2,* 331–380.

Brown, A. L., Smiley, S. S., Day, J. D., Townsend, M. A. R., & Lawton, S. C. (1977). Intrusion of a thematic idea in children's comprehension and retention of stories. *Child Development, 48,* 1454–1466.

Bruck, M., & Ceci, S. J. (1995). Amicus brief for the case of *State of New Jersey v. Michaels* presented by committee of concerned social-scientists. *Psychology, Public Policy, and Law, 1,* 272–322.

Bruck, M., & Ceci, S. J. (1997). The nature of applied and basic research on children's suggestibility. In N. Stein, P. A. Ornstein, B. Tversky, & C. J. Brainerd (Eds.), *Memory for everyday and emotional events* (pp. 371–400). Hillsdale, NJ: Erlbaum.

Bruck, M., & Ceci, S. J. (1999). The suggestibility of children's memory. *Annual Review of Psychology, 50,* 419–439.

Ceci, S. J., & Bronfenbrenner, U. (1991). On the demise of everyday memory: The rumors of my death are much exaggerated. *American Psychologist, 46,* 27–31.

Ceci, S. J., & Bruck, M. (1993). The suggestibility of the child witness: A historical review and synthesis. *Psychological Bulletin, 113,* 403–439.

Ceci, S. J., & Bruck, M. (1995). *Jeopardy in the courtroom.* Washington, DC: American Psychological Association.

Ceci, S. J, & Bruck M. (1998). The ontogeny and durability of true and false memories: A fuzzy trace account. *Journal of Experimental Child Psychology, 71,* 165–169.

Ceci, S. J., & Friedman, R. D. (2000). The suggestibility of children: Scientific research and legal implications. *Cornell Law Review, 86,* 33–108.

Christianson, S. A. (1992). Emotional stress and eyewitness memory. *Psychological Bulletin, 112,* 284–309.

Cramer, P. (1972). Developmental study of errors in memory. *Developmental Psychology, 7,* 204–209.

Deese, J. (1959). On the prediction of occurrence of certain verbal intrusions in free recall. *Journal of Experimental Psychology, 58,* 17–22.

Dewhurst, S. A., & Robinson, C. A. (2004). False memories in children: Evidence for a shift from phonological to semantic associations. *Psychological Science, 15,* 782–786.

Felzen, E., & Anisfeld, M. (1970). Semantic and phonetic relations in false recognition of words by third-grade and sixth-grade children. *Developmental Psychology, 3,* 163–168.

Ghetti, S., Qin, J., & Goodman, G. S. (2002). False memories in children and adults: Age, distinctiveness, and subjective experience. *Developmental Psychology, 38,* 705–718.

Goodman, G. S., & Aman, C. (1990). Children's use of anatomically detailed dolls to recount an event. *Child Development, 61,* 1859–1871.

Holliday, R. E., Reyna, V. F., & Brainerd, C. J. (2006). *Memory illusions in children and adolescents: Gist cues and verbatim repetition.* Manuscript submitted for publication.

Holliday, R. E., & Weekes, B. S. (in press). Dissociated developmental trajectories for semantic and phonological false memories. *Memory.*

Howe, M. L. (1991). Misleading children's story recall: Forgetting and reminiscence of the facts. *Developmental Psychology, 27,* 746–762.

Howe, M. L. (1997). Children's memory for traumatic experiences. *Learning and Individual Differences, 2,* 153–174.

Howe, M. L. (2005). Children (but not adults) can inhibit false memories. *Psychological Science, 16,* 927–931.

Howe, M. L. (2006). Developmentally invariant dissociations in children's true and false memories: Not all relatedness is created equal. *Child Development, 77,* 1112–1123.

Howe, M. L., Brainerd, C. J., & Kingma, J. (1985). Development of organization in recall: A stages-of-learning analysis. *Journal of Experimental Child Psychology, 39,* 230–251.

Howe, M. L., Cicchetti, D., Toth, S. L., & Cerrito, B. M. (2004). True and false memories in maltreated children. *Child Development, 75,* 1402–1417.

Howe, M. L., Courage, M. L., & Peterson, C. (1995). Intrusions in preschoolers' recall of traumatic childhood events. *Psychonomic Bulletin & Review, 2,* 130–134.

Johnson, J. W., & Scholnick, E. K. (1979). Does cognitive development predict semantic integration? *Child Development, 50,* 73–78.

Johnson, M. K., Hashtroudi, S., & Lindsay, D. S. (1993). Source monitoring. *Psychological Bulletin, 114,* 3–28.

Kassin, S. M. (1997). The psychology of confession evidence. *American Psychologist, 52,* 221–233.

Kassin, S. M. (2001). On the "general acceptance" of eyewitness testimony research: A new survey of experts. *American Psychologist, 56,* 405–416.

Kassin, S. M., & Kiechel, K. L. (1996). The social psychology of false confessions: Compliance, internalization, and confabulation. *Psychological Science, 7,* 125–128.

Kempe, C. H., Silver, H. K., Silverman, F. N., Droegemueller, W., & Silver, H. (1962). Battered-child syndrome. *Journal of the American Medical Association, 181,* 17–24.

Kimball, D. R., & Bjork, R. A. (2002). Influences of intentional and unintentional forgetting on false memories. *Journal of Experimental Psychology: General, 131,* 116–130.

Lamb, M. E., & Fauchier, A. (2001). The effects of question type on self-contradictions by children in the course of forensic interviews. *Applied Cognitive Psychology, 15,* 483–491.

Liben, L. S., & Posnansky, C. J. (1977). Inferences on inference: Effects of age, transitive ability, memory load, and lexical factors. *Child Development, 48,* 1490–1497.

Lim, P. L. (1993). *Meaning versus verbatim memory in language processing: Deriving inferential, morphological, and metaphorical gist.* Unpublished doctoral dissertation. University of Arizona, Tucson, AZ.

Loftus, E. F. (1997). Creating false memories. *Scientific American, 277*(3), 70–75.

Lyon, T. D. (1995). False allegations and false denials in child sexual abuse. *Psychology, Public Policy, and Law, 1,* 429–437.

McAuliff, B. D., Nicholson, E., & Ravenshanes, D. (2007, March). *Hypothetically speaking: Can expert testimony improve jurors' understanding of developmental differences in suggestibility?* Paper presented at the Biennial Meeting of the Society for Research in Child Development, Boston, MA.

McGough, L. S. (1993). *Child witnesses: Fragile voices in the American legal system.* New Haven, CT: Yale University Press.

Metzger, R. L., Warren, A. R., Price, J. D., Reed, A. W., Shelton, J., & Williams, D. (2004, June). *Do children "D/R-M" like adults? False memory production in children.* Paper presented at American Psychological Society, New York, NY.

Myers, J. E. B. (1995). New era of skepticism regarding children's credibility. *Psychology, Public Policy, and Law, 1,* 387–398.

Paris, S. G., & Carter, A. Y. (1973). Semantic and constructive aspects of sentence memory in children. *Developmental Psychology, 9,* 109–113.

Paris, S. G., & Mahoney, G. J. (1974). Cognitive integration in children's memory for sentences and pictures. *Child Development, 45,* 633–643.

Payne, D. G., Elie, C. J., Blackwell, J. M., & Neuschatz, J. S. (1996). Memory illusions: Recalling, recognizing, and recollecting events that never occurred. *Journal of Memory and Language, 35,* 261–285.

Piaget, J., & Inhelder, B. (1973). *Memory and intelligence.* New York: Basic Books.

Pipe, M.-E., & Goodman, G. S. (1991). Elements of secrecy: Implications for children's testimony. *Behavioral Sciences and the Law, 9,* 33–41.

Poole, D. A., & Lamb, M. E. (1998). *Investigative interviews of children.* Washington, DC: American Psychological Association.

Poole, D. A., & White, L. T. (1991). Effects of question repetition on the eyewitness testimony of children and adults. *Developmental Psychology, 27,* 975–986.

Powell, M. B., Roberts, K. P., Ceci, S. J., & Hembrooke, H. (1999). The effects of repeated exposure on children's suggestibility. *Developmental Psychology, 35,* 1462–1477.

Prawatt, R. S., & Cancelli, A. (1976). Constructive memory in conserving and non-conserving first graders. *Developmental Psychology, 12,* 47–50.

Principe, G. F., Kanaya, T., Ceci, S. J., & Singh, M. (2006). Believing is seeing: How rumors can engender false memories in preschoolers. *Psychological Science, 17,* 243–248.

Reyna, V. F. (1996). Meaning, memory and the interpretation of metaphors. In J. Mio & A. Katz (Eds.), *Metaphor: Implications and applications* (pp. 39–57). Hillsdale, NJ: Erlbaum.

Reyna, V. F. (2000a). Fuzzy-trace theory and source monitoring: An evaluation of theory and false-memory data. *Learning and Individual Differences, 12,* 163–175.

Reyna, V. F. (2000b, November). *Phantom recollection of narratives.* Paper presented at the Psychonomic Society meeting, New Orleans, LA.

Reyna, V. F. (2004). Why scientific research? The importance of evidence in changing educational practice. In P. McCardle & V. Chlabra (Eds.), *The voice of evidence in reading research,* (pp. 47–58). Baltimore, MD: Brookes Publishing.

Reyna, V. F., & Brainerd, C. J. (1995). Fuzzy-trace theory: An interim synthesis. *Learning and Individual Differences, 7,* 1–75.

Reyna, V. F., Holliday, R., & Marche, T. (2002). Explaining the development of false memories. *Developmental Review, 22,* 436–489.

Reyna, V. F., & Kiernan, B. (1994). The development of gist versus verbatim memory in sentence recognition: Effects of lexical familiarity, semantic content, encoding instructions, and retention interval. *Developmental Psychology, 30,* 178–191.

Reyna, V. F., & Kiernan, B. (1995). Children's memory and interpretation of psychological metaphors. *Metaphor and Symbolic Activity, 10,* 309–331.

Reyna, V. F., & Lloyd, F. (1997). Theories of false memory in children and adults. *Learning and Individual Differences, 9,* 95–123.

Reyna, V. F., Mills, B., Estrada, S., & Brainerd, C. J. (2007). False memory in children: Data, theory, and legal Implications. In M. P. Toglia, J. D. Read, D. F. Ross, & R. C. L. Lindsay (Eds.), *Handbook of eyewitness psychology.* Mahwah, NJ: Erlbaum.

Roberts, K. P. (2002). Children's ability to distinguish between memories from multiple sources: Implications for the quality and accuracy of eyewitness statements. *Developmental Review, 22,* 403–435.

Roediger, H. L. III, & McDermott, K. B. (1995). Creating false memories: Remembering words not presented on lists. *Journal of Experimental Psychology: Learning, Memory, and Cognition, 21,* 803–814.

Rosenthal, R. (2002). Suggestibility, reliability, and the legal process. *Developmental Review, 22,* 334–369.

Rudy, L., & Goodman, G. S. (1991). Effects of participation on children's reports: Implications for children's testimony. *Developmental Psychology, 27,* 527–538.

Russell, W. A., & Jenkins, J. J. (1954). *Minnesota norms for responses to 100 words from the Kent-Rosanoff association test.* Technical Report No. 11, Department of Psychology, University of Minnesota.

Saywitz, K. J., Nicholas, E., Goodman, G. S., & Moan, S. F. (1991). Children's memories of a physical examination involving genital touch: Implications for reports of child sexual abuse. *Journal of Consulting and Clinical Psychology, 59,* 682–691.

Schacter, D. L., Israel, L., & Racine, C. (1999). Suppressing false recognition in younger and older adults: The distinctiveness heuristic. *Journal of Memory and Language, 40,* 1–24.

Seamon, J. G., Luo, C. R., Schwartz, M. A., Jones, K. J., Lee, D. M., & Jones, S. J. (2002). Repetition can have similar or different effects on accurate and false recognition. *Journal of Memory and Language, 46,* 323–340.

Small, M. Y., & Butterworth, J. (1981). Semantic integration and the development of memory for logical inferences. *Child Development, 52,* 732–735.

Sommers, M. S., & Lewis, B. P. (1999). Who really lives next door: Creating false memories with phonological neighbors. *Journal of Memory and Language, 40,* 83–108.

Stadler, M. A., Roediger, H. L., & McDermott, K. B. (1999). Norms for words that create false memories. *Memory & Cognition, 27,* 494–500.

State of California v. Buckey. (1990). Superior Court, Los Angeles County, California.

Stern, W. (1910). Abstracts of lectures on the psychology of testimony and on the study of individuality. *American Journal of Psychology, 21,* 270–282.

Swanson, H. L. (1991). Learning disabilities, distinctive encoding, and hemispheric resources: An information-processing perspective. In J. E. Obrzut & G. W. Hynd (Eds.), *Neuropsychological foundations of learning disabilities* (pp. 241–280). San Diego, CA: Academic Press.

Tulving, E. (1985). Memory and consciousness. *Canadian Psychologist, 26,* 1–12.

Underwood, B. J. (1965). False recognition produced by implicit verbal responses. *Journal of Experimental Psychology, 70,* 122–129.

Warren, A. R., & McGough, L. S. (1996). Research on children's suggestibility: Implications for the investigative interview. *Criminal Justice and Behavior, 23,* 269–303.

Warren, A. R., & Woodall, C. E. (1999). The reliability of hearsay testimony: How well do interviewers recall their interviews with children? *Psychology, Public Policy, and Law, 5,* 355–371.

Wells, G. L., Small, M., Penrod, S., Malpass, R. S., Fulero, S. M., & Brimacombe, C. A. E. (1998). Eyewitness identification procedures: Recommendations for lineups and photospreads. *Law and Human Behavior, 23,* 603–648.

White, S. H. (1970). Learning theory. In P. H. Mussen (Ed.), *Carmichaels' manual of child psychology* (Vol. 1). New York: Wiley.

Zajac, R., Gross, J., & Hayne, H. (2003). Asked and answered: Questioning children in the courtroom. *Psychiatry, Psychology and Law, 10,* 199–209.

Zajac, R., & Hayne, H. (2003). I don't think that's what really happened: The effect of cross-examination on the accuracy of children's reports. *Journal of Experimental Psychology: Applied, 9,* 187–195.

Zajac, R., & Hayne, H. (2006). The negative effect of cross-examination on children's accuracy: Older children are not immune. *Applied Cognitive Psychology, 20,* 3–16.

10

Translating Research on Children's Memory and Trauma into Practice

Clinical and Forensic Implications

SHEREE L. TOTH AND KRISTIN VALENTINO

Debate continues in the current literature regarding how, or whether, traumatic experiences affect memory (Howe, Cicchetti, Toth, & Cerrito, 2004; Howe, Toth, & Cicchetti, 2006). Although the resolution of whether or not trauma has a unique impact on memory is important from a theoretical and scientific perspective, it also possesses significant clinical and social policy implications. Issues such as the age at which trauma occurs and the relation between trauma and emotional and behavioral difficulties have major consequences for determining when, or if, one should intervene with children who have been traumatized. In addition, the accuracy of eyewitness memory and the suggestibility of young children's memories affect decisions regarding whether officials are confident about relying on child reports to substantiate abuse and neglect, as well as the viability of child testimony in the courtroom.

In this chapter, we briefly highlight the extant literature on trauma and memory, with a particular focus on child maltreatment and memory. This précis serves as the foundation for examining the clinical and social-policy

implications of this body of research for children who have been victimized by abuse and neglect.

Trauma and Memory

Although some contend that traumatic experiences, as distinctive and
emotionally salient events, *enhance* memory for the trauma (e.g., Howe,
Courage, & Peterson, 1994, 1995), others argue that trauma *hampers* recall
due to alterations in brain structure that accompany exposure to prolonged
stress (Bremner & Narayan, 1998; DeBellis et al., 1999; Sapolsky, 1992).
A particularly active area of inquiry concerning memory for trauma has
centered on whether or not children's susceptibility to false memories and
their suggestibility is affected by trauma. Despite a rather extensive data-
base, research findings in this area have been inconsistent. Although there
is some evidence among nontraumatized children that stress may increase
the likelihood of memory inaccuracy through suggestion (e.g., Bugental, Blue, Cortez, Fleck, & Rodriguez, 1992), research with maltreated
children thus far generally has not supported a link between trauma and
suggestibility (e.g., Goodman, Bottoms, Rudy, Davis, & Schwartz-Kenny,
2001) or semantic-associate false memory (Howe et al., 2004).

In efforts to clarify the relation between trauma and memory, researchers have approached the examination of trauma and stress in various ways.
Typically, investigators have assessed memory for traumatic/stressful experiences among individuals with or without trauma histories or have
evaluated memory for nontraumatic stimuli among individuals with or
without trauma histories. As a result, it has been difficult to synthesize
the findings of the extant research into a coherent picture given that
both the type of memory (autobiographical versus semantic) and the history of study participants (trauma history versus no trauma history) have
varied across studies. Moreover, it is important to consider that research
on memory for stressful experiences among nontraumatized populations
has burgeoned, whereas research focusing on basic memory processes of
encoding, storage, and retrieval among samples of traumatized individuals remains in its infancy. Therefore, we must be cautious regarding the
generalizability of the conclusions that can be drawn regarding the effects
of trauma on memory.

Investigations that approach the assessment of memory for stressful
experiences via the utilization of analogue paradigms support the notion

that increased levels of stress lead to enhanced memory for the event (for review, see Howe, 1998, 2000). This facilitation of memory may arise as a function of studies that have shown that attention may become hyperfocused on the main stressor when an event is occurring, to the detriment of memory retention for information that is more peripheral to the stressor (Christianson, 1992; Goodman, Hirschman, Hepps, & Rudy, 1991). In fact, to date the main deficiencies revealed in memory for trauma have been in relation to recall of the peripheral aspects of the event (Bugental et al., 1992).

Although analogue studies have provided a useful first step in shedding light on the effect of high levels of emotionality and stress on children's memories (Howe et al., 1994, 1995; Goodman & Quas, 1997), it is unclear whether the intensity of the emotions invoked by analogue traumas is at all comparable to the reactions that accompany actual maltreatment. Therefore, before clinical and policy decisions affecting maltreated children can be based on solid research knowledge, much more extensive investigations of memory functioning among populations of children traumatized by maltreatment are necessary.

Unfortunately, the literature on maltreatment and memory, particularly among children, is in its infancy (Eisen, Qin, Goodman, & Davis, 2002). One challenge for advancing research in this area has emanated from difficulty in verifying the accuracy of trauma reports among maltreated children. In response to this problem, recent studies have followed children who recalled traumatic experiences over time to assess for the reliability of the initial memory of the trauma at a later period (Alexander et al., 2005; Greenhoot, McCloskey, & Glisky, 2005). For example, long-term follow-up of children who had experienced childhood sexual abuse (CSA) revealed that post-traumatic stress disorder (PTSD) severity was positively associated with memory for the abuse. Furthermore, irrespective of PTSD, individuals who indicated that the CSA was their most traumatic life event exhibited relatively accurate memory for the trauma, even when the abuse had occurred over a decade ago (Alexander et al., 2005). Thus, research does not support the presence of memory for trauma recall deficits in maltreated children, and in fact provides some support for memory enhancement among those with PTSD, particularly in adolescents and adults.

Despite the overall weak association between maltreatment and memory deficits described thus far, we must highlight the fact that this conclusion is based exclusively on studies examining memory for traumatic events (either analogue traumas or abuse experiences). Although certainly an important line of inquiry, it is possible that maltreatment might exert an impact on memory in situations not directly related to traumatic memories. For example, evidence of core deficits in cognitive processing and impairment in memory for autobiographical events exists among adult women who experienced maltreatment as children (Henderson, Hargreaves, Gregory, & Williams, 2002). Moreover, child maltreatment and/ or the development of PTSD symptomatology may impact memory as a function of physiological changes in neural mechanisms related to memory processes (e.g., Bremner, Krystal, Southwick, & Charney, 1995; Cicchetti & Rogosch, 2001a, 2001b; Pollak, Cicchetti, Klorman, & Brumaghim, 1997). Furthermore, in the absence of PTSD, evidence of a tendency among maltreated children to shift their attentional focus away from threatening stimuli suggests that the initial encoding of information may be compromised (Rieder & Cicchetti, 1989).

Until recently, investigations of basic memory processes (i.e., encoding, storage, and retrieval of neutral, nontraumatic stimuli) among populations of maltreated children were virtually nonexistent. In order to begin to address this gap in the literature, Howe and colleagues (2004) assessed true and false recall for neutral stimuli on the Deese/Roediger-McDermott (DRM) paradigm among maltreated and nonmaltreated school-age children. Results of this investigation did not reveal differences in memory as a function of maltreatment. Similarly, a recent examination of the neurobehavioral sequelae of CSA did not find significant differences in memory function between abused and nonabused children (Porter, Lawson, & Bigler, 2005), despite elevations in psychopathology and diminished performance on tests of attention and executive function in the abused group. Research conducted with maltreated children who had PTSD corroborates such findings, with maltreated children who have PTSD performing more poorly on measures of attention and abstract reasoning/executive function, but not on memory tasks (Beers & De-Bellis, 2002, but see Moradi, Taghavi, Doost, Yule, & Dalgleish, 1999).

As is evident in our review, the literature coheres to suggest that maltreatment does not exert a direct effect on children's memory. However, it remains possible that the sequelae of maltreatment, such as psychopathology, may be related to alterations in memory processes (Goodman, 2005). For example, some contend that maltreatment may eventuate in impaired memory as a result of stress and dissociation (e.g., Putnam, 1997). Because maltreated children are at risk for the development of dissociative symptomatology (Macfie, Cicchetti, & Toth, 2001a, 2001b; Ogawa, Sroufe, Weinfield, Carlson, & Egeland, 1997; Putnam, 2000), it is possible that their memories may be adversely affected as a result of these symptoms.

Despite research among adults that has demonstrated links between a number of memory impairments and dissociation (including episodes of time loss, recall delays for abuse-related information, total memory loss for the traumatic event, and gaps in autobiographical memory [Goodman et al., 2001; Henderson et al., 2002; Putnam, 1997, 2000]), research with children has largely failed to detect an association between dissociation and impaired memory for the trauma. For example, studies of maltreated children have shown that increased dissociative symptomatology is related to more detailed memories of abuse (Eisen et al., 2002), as well as to the expression of more negative emotion when asked about the abuse (Sayfan et al., 2002). More recently, however, cortisol level and trauma symptoms in maltreated children who reported more dissociative tendencies were found to be related to increased memory error for stressful medical procedures (Eisen, Goodman, Qin, Davis, & Crayton, in press). There may be important differences between the manner in which maltreated children remember trauma-related and non-trauma-related information (Foa & Riggs, 1994), particularly as these memories relate to the self. Thus, it will be important for future research to address the role of dissociation in maltreated children's autobiographical memory for non-trauma-related information.

Dissociation also has been linked to the presence of false memory (for review see Kihlstrom, 2005). Among adults, dissociation has been correlated with false positives in recognition memory tests (Merckelbach, Muris, Horselenberg, & Stougie, 2000), interrogative suggestibility (Merckelbach, Muris, Rassin, & Horselenberg, 2000), and the creation of pseudomemories (Hyman & Billings, 1998). Although associations between false memory and dissociation have been found with adults, such relationships have not been detected in children (Eisen et al., 2002). Therefore, further research is needed to determine whether or not dissociative symptomatology is related to other aspects of maltreated children's memory functioning (cf. Eisen et al., in press).

In addition, because child maltreatment is associated with an increased risk for depressive symptomatology (e.g., Cicchetti & Toth, 1995;

Cicchetti & Valentino, 2006; Toth, Manly, & Cicchetti, 1992), and because depression is linked with memory deficits, investigations of memory in maltreated children with depressive symptoms may reveal difficulties in memory. Williams and colleagues have shown an adverse impact of depression on memory, such that there is a tendency toward general rather than specific memories (e.g., Williams & Broadbent, 1986; Williams & Scott, 1988). Similar results have been obtained in depressed adults who were abused as children (e.g., Kuyken & Brewin, 1995), as well as in depressed children who were exposed to family violence (Greenhoot et al., 2005; Orbach, Lamb, Sternberg, Williams, & Dawud-Noursi, 2001). However, with respect to memory functioning, the majority of these studies have been unable to disentangle the effects of depression from those of maltreatment.

Another major sequela of maltreatment that may affect memory performance involves insecure attachment. In fact, insecure attachment has been related to memory performance in both children and adults (Alexander, Quas, & Goodman, 2002; Goodman, 2005, for review). Several empirical investigations have examined associations between children's attachment and their memory for positive and negative emotional information (Alexander & Edelstein, 2001; Belsky, Spritz, & Crnic, 1996; Kirsh & Cassidy, 1997). Although few in number, these studies cohere to support implications of attachment for memory. In two of the investigations, children with secure attachment relationships were able to recall attachment-related information better than were children with insecure attachments (Alexander & Edelstein, 2001; Kirsh & Cassidy, 1997). In the one study that found that boys with secure attachment histories remembered positive events better than negative events, the to-be-remembered events were not directly related to attachment (Belsky et al., 1996). Although these investigations are useful in suggesting relations between attachment and memory, they do little to shed light on how attachment might mediate the pathway from maltreatment to memory. In an examination of trauma, mental representation, and memory for mother-referent material, Lynch and Cicchetti (1998) found that maltreated children with insecure models of relationships encode and retrieve words in ways that are congruent with negative maternal schemas, such that they recalled the highest proportion of negative maternal-referent stimuli. More recently, Valentino, Cicchetti, Rogosch, and Toth (2007) utilized a depth-of-processing incidental recall task for maternal-referent stimuli to assess basic memory processes and the affective valence of maternal representations among abused, neglected, and nonmaltreated children. Results revealed that abused children demonstrated deficits in recall performance in comparison to neglected and nonmaltreated children. Interestingly, memory differences were not detected as a function of maltreatment on a similar depth-of-processing task for self-referent stimuli (Valentino, Cicchetti, Rogosch, & Toth, in press). Therefore, these two investigations cohere to suggest that abused children have deficits in memory processes under conditions that activate maternal representations.

In summary, research on the relation between trauma and memory has not consistently supported deficiencies in memory performance or increased susceptibility to false recall or suggestibility among maltreated children, despite contrary evidence among adults. Rather, maltreated children have shown diminished performance in other domains of neuropsychological functioning, such as tests of attention and executive function. Moreover, although maltreated children are at heightened risk for psychopathology, such as depression and dissociation, to date definitive studies regarding psychopathology and memory in maltreated children have not been conducted. A particularly promising area of inquiry, and one with significant implications for clinical contexts, pertains to the role of attachment relationships as mediators of memory in children who have experienced maltreatment.

Is the Glass Half Full or Half Empty?

As our review indicates, advances have been made in the availability of research on child maltreatment and its relation to memory. However, within the field we remain in the early stages of conducting the seminal work that can guide clinical and policy decisions for children who have experienced maltreatment. Although there are limitations inherent in the work conducted to date, not the least of which being that the majority of investigations were not designed with the goal of informing real-world decision making for this victimized population, decisions are being made daily based on assumptions regarding the memory of children who have experienced maltreatment. Therefore, we next direct our attention to an examination of implications of the research on maltreatment and memory for clinical and policy arenas. We acknowledge that, given the currently available data, much of our discussion is necessarily speculative. However, we believe that critically examining the current data and noting their possible implications, as well as limitations, will not only assist those professionals who must make decisions in the best interest of maltreated children but also will serve to advance a research agenda that ultimately will contribute to a solid framework on which to base such decisions. We first discuss the clinical implications of this work and then examine policy and forensic considerations.

Clinical Implications

Memory is particularly relevant to clinical treatment, as the recollection and sharing of past experiences are integral to many forms of psycho-therapy (Berliner & Briere, 1999). Moreover, although the accuracy of recalled memories may not be particularly salient for therapeutic work to occur, it is critical that clinicians recognize the impact of trauma on memory and that they be aware of the possibility of inadvertently influencing their clients' recall of events. Such suggestibility becomes particularly problematic when forensic issues are being decided.

In a 1998 editorial for a special issue of *Development and Psychopathology* devoted to risk, trauma, and memory, Toth & Cicchetti (1998) concluded that significant gaps existed in the research literature pertaining to trauma and memory. In particular, the fact that a paucity of investigations had been conducted with traumatized populations of children was noted. Although progress has occurred over the last decade, significant work remains to be done before research on maltreatment and memory can confidently be applied to intervention and policy decisions.

Based on our review of the extant literature to date, it is fair to conclude that memory in children with histories of maltreatment generally is no worse than memory in nonvictimized age-mates. As with memory more generally, memories of trauma are just as durable and are subject to the same factors that affect retention and deterioration in normative populations (Howe, Cicchetti, & Toth, 2006). However, potential influences on memory, such as the role of psychopathology, as well as other indirect factors, such as attachment, need to be considered. In addition, a number of issues warrant examination when providing clinical treatments for maltreated children. These include developmental considerations, timing of the provision of intervention, degree of caregiver involvement, and therapist role.

Developmental Considerations

When considering the impact of trauma on memory, one is immediately confronted with questions about the earliest age at which a traumatic experience may exert a negative impact on development. More specifically, the question of whether a trauma that occurs during the preverbal period can be remembered, affects development, and therefore needs to be a target of intervention assumes central importance. Historically, there has been a paucity of research addressing the question of whether or not infants can internally register a traumatic experience (Gaensbauer, 2002). The absence of administration of pain medication during medical procedures provides a compelling illustration of the belief that infants cannot experience or recall pain. Interestingly, the increased administration of pain medication during infant circumcisions suggests that awareness is growing among the medical community regarding the likelihood that pain can be experienced very early in life (American Academy of Pediatrics, 1999). In fact, available data does support physiologic responses to pain (Anand & Hickey, 1987; Marshall, 1989), as well as instrumental and classical conditioning responses in infants (Blass, Ganchrow, & Steiner, 1984; DeCasper & Fifer, 1980; Little, Lipsitt, & Rovee-Collier, 1984).

Drawing upon investigations of early development as well as clinical observation, Gaensbauer (2002) concludes that "possibly in the first weeks of life and certainly by two to three months of age infants are able to recognize stimulus cues associated with a traumatic experience and show expectable distress reactions and behavioral responses" (p. 267). Although the body of research in support of this assertion is limited and clinical case material is subject to being influenced by suggestibility imposed by the clinician or caregiver, we cannot rule out the possibility that trauma occurring early in life does exert an impact on development and memory. Of course, it also is likely that early occurring traumas will fade and, if they are encoded, that they will be subject to the same process of deterioration that affects all memories. Therefore, it becomes particularly challenging as to whether intervention should be directed toward helping a child "recall" a traumatic event that occurred in the early years of life and that may have dissipated over time. If symptoms associated with the trauma are absent, then this question becomes more philosophical than practical, as it is unlikely that the child will be referred for treatment. However, if socioemotional or behavioral problems are present, then the form of intervention to be provided assumes importance.

Some theoreticians and clinicians argue that it is important to help the child gain mastery over the trauma through the use of play and gradual modification of the trauma scenario/narrative (Gaensbauer, 2002). Reenactment of the trauma may make it possible for children to process their experiences and also may provide parents and therapists a venue through which to intervene. Although a compelling clinical argument for such approaches can be made, work on suggestibility proffers a more cautious stance. For example, rather than enlisting a caregiver in helping a child to reenact a traumatic event, it may be sufficient to direct intervention toward symptom alleviation, such as reduction of anxiety. Based on the albeit limited literature to date, we believe that an initial approach to treatment, particularly when dealing with trauma occurring during the early years of life, might best focus on symptom reduction. If such directed and time-limited treatment is ineffective, then more trauma-focused intervention may be appropriate.

It is important to note, however, that although clinicians need to be cautious about fostering false recall through suggestibility, the goal of clinical intervention for children who have experienced trauma is quite different from the demands imposed by forensic contexts. From a clinical perspective, the accuracy of the memory report is not nearly as important as is the processing of the emotions that accompany the traumatic experience.

For children who are maltreated during the preschool years or beyond, whether or not to deal with the trauma directly is seemingly more straightforward. For example, extrapolating from the adult literature, proven effective treatments for adults with PTSD frequently involve repeated exposure to memories of the trauma (Foa, Rothbaum, Riggs, & Murdock, 1991; Keane, Fairbank, Caddell, & Zimering, 1989). Similarly effective memory-specific treatments have been shown to reduce PTSD symptoms in children exposed to naturally occurring disasters, such as earthquakes (Goenjian et al., 1996). One would assume that when a child is currently experiencing a traumatic event, addressing it directly would be appropriate and relatively easy to do. Unfortunately, this is not necessarily the case. In our work with maltreated preschoolers we often find that children are quite reluctant to engage in any direct dialogue either about the occurrence of abuse or about their affective reactions to the event. In such cases, more supportive techniques, often utilizing play that may gradually incorporate components of the trauma, are indicated.

It is important to note that support for the utilization of abuse-specific treatment with victims of CSA has been obtained (Cohen & Mannarino, 1996; Deblinger, Lippmann, & Steer, 1996). However, significantly more work is needed to develop and evaluate the efficacy of treatments for children who are victims of physical abuse, neglect, and emotional maltreatment (Toth & Cicchetti, 2006). Because trauma may alter neuronal connections in the brain (Cicchetti, 2002; DeBellis, 2001), therapies that require victims to repeatedly recall traumatic events may inadvertently result in the consolidation of maladaptive neuronal pathways that are associated with the experience of the trauma (Howe, Toth, et al., 2006). In fact, in work with depressed adults, neurological "kindling" has been discussed as cautioning against the utilization of insight-oriented psychotherapeutic approaches (Post, Weiss, & Leverich, 1994; for exception see Monroe & Harkness, 2005).

Timing of the Intervention

Toth and Cicchetti (1998) previously urged that investigations on the efficacy of intervention for trauma be conducted to ascertain the relation between the proximity of the trauma to the implementation of clinical intervention. Because memory for trauma would be expected to be most accurate soon after the occurrence of a traumatic event, timing the initiation of a therapeutic intervention contiguous with the actual trauma does have intuitive appeal. Moreover, it is possible that the initiation of intervention as soon as possible after the trauma could more effectively impact neural organization, thereby preventing alterations in brain structure and function that might be less malleable over time (Cicchetti & Curtis, 2006). This position does have some empirical support, as we next detail.

In a recent investigation of the effect of maltreatment occurring during the first year of life on the neural correlates of the processing of facial emotion recognition, Cicchetti and Curtis (2005) found that maltreated infants exhibited increased event-related potential (ERP) amplitude in response to angry facial stimuli. Cicchetti and Curtis interpret this finding as suggesting that, based on maltreated infants' early experiences, they allocate more attention to the angry faces. In concert with other investigations (Pollak et al., 1997; Pollak, Klorman, Thatcher, & Cicchetti, 2001), these psychophysiological findings provide corroborative evidence for the existence of schemas, or working models, that assist in the integration of relevant information with extant knowledge structures (Bowlby, 1969/1982; Bretherton, 1990).

These results further suggest that children who have experienced maltreatment during the first year of life exhibit brain-based abnormalities when processing facial affect at 30 months of age and, as such, that early interventions are needed to prevent the possible cascade of effects on brain development and functioning over time (Cicchetti & Curtis, 2005). Such interventions might be as basic as working with maltreated youngsters to identify affect accurately. However, taken in tandem with our discussion on attachment and memory, it might be necessary to implement more intensive interventions specifically designed to modify representations of cognitive and emotion processes. Toth and her colleagues previously demonstrated that maltreated children's negative mental and emotional representations of self and of caregivers can be altered through the provision of intervention (Toth, Maughan, Manly, Spagnola, & Cicchetti, 2002). Specifically, an attachment-theory informed intervention was found to result in decreases in children's negative maternal and self-representations, as well as increases in positive mother–child relationship expectations. To our knowledge, psychophysiological measures that may accompany these positive changes have not yet been attained.

The effect of maltreatment on the overall organization of development also must be considered when providing clinical intervention (Toth & Cicchetti, 1993). This is particularly important when determining how to approach memory of abuse. For example, the provision of developmentally sequenced treatment has been recommended, as past traumatic events may assume different meanings as new developmental competencies emerge (James, 1989). In fact, the delayed symptomatic sequelae often noted in victims of CSA can be explained as a function of developmental progression (Berliner, 1991). For example, a young child who has not yet attained social comparison skills may not experience shame in response to sexual abuse. However, as the child matures and learns that her experience is atypical when compared with peers, shame and low self-esteem may arise. Thus, even when memory for trauma is present at an earlier developmental period, the effect of the memory and the way in which the memory is reorganized may change over time and also may contribute to varied symptom manifestation, as well as to different intervention strategies.

Caregiver Involvement

Several clinicians who treat young children with histories of trauma advocate for the importance of parental involvement in the intervention (Cohen & Mannarino, 1996; Gaensbauer, 2002). These recommendations stem from a number of considerations. First, parents may provide important background information that could be useful in assisting the therapist in interpreting the meaning of the child's play. Second, the therapist may educate parents and model therapeutic approaches that can be implemented in the home environment. Addressing parental reactions to the child's trauma symptoms and providing support also are critical in helping parents to provide their child with a sense of safety. If parents are uncomfortable with child behavioral or verbal expression, then they are unlikely to be able to help their child process the potentially overwhelming affects. Finally, involving parents in the therapeutic process may help the child to recognize the parent as being capable of providing comfort to the child in ways not possible when the actual trauma occurred.

The utility of parental involvement in treatment is supported by research on the role of parents in influencing how, and whether, children discuss emotions and emotional events (Eisenberg, 1999; Harris, 1994). The prevalence of such parent–child discourse, in turn, most likely affects children's memory for events. In fact, several studies have found relations between a mother's attachment with her romantic partner and her child's memory for stressful events (Alexander, Goodman, et al., 2002; Goodman, Quas, Batterman-Faunce, Riddlesberger, & Kuhn, 1997; Quas, Goodman, Bidrose, Pipe, Craw, & Ablin, 1999). Such relations may be a function of parental reactions during a stressful event (Edelstein et al., 2002; Goodman et al., 1997) and the amount of verbal discourse between parent and child about past emotional events (Quas et al., 1999). Although some parents are able to openly discuss and process traumatic events with their children, others either avoid talking about the event or provide the child with misinformation (Alexander, Quas, et al., 2002). Distortion of the occurrence is quite likely to occur in maltreating families, where a caregiver may directly or indirectly try to modify child recall of an abusive event. Although not definitive, there is evidence that links such divergent strategies with adult attachment style (Fraley & Shaver, 1999). Research has found that children of mothers who have high structure and who are supportive of their children's autonomy in their reminiscing styles have better autobiographical memory (Cleveland & Reese, 2005). Findings such as these strongly suggest that the manner in which a caregiver responds to the trauma and discusses it with her child may exert a significant impact on what the child later remembers.

Unfortunately, despite the merit of involving caregivers of traumatized children in the therapeutic process, in cases of child maltreatment such participation often is not possible, and at times is counterindicated. In the majority of cases, child maltreatment involves a family member, most commonly a parent, as the perpetrator (USDHHS, 2004). Whether the child remains in the care of the perpetrator or is subsequently removed to alternate housing, it is unlikely that the child will benefit from parental involvement around the trauma. Moreover, maltreated children may have been threatened against disclosing the event or, as suggested earlier, provided with inaccurate information regarding the traumatic occurrence. In such situations, it becomes much more important to assist children in coping with their fears and emotions than to involve caregivers in the therapeutic process.

Although not directly related to intervention with maltreated children, another interesting avenue to consider with respect to parents involves the possible provision of intervention to parents who were maltreated as children. Research has demonstrated that parents with histories of maltreatment are at heightened risk for perpetrating abuse and neglect on their offspring (Egeland, Bosquet, & Chung, 2002; Kaufman & Zigler, 1987). Although the intergenerational transmission of maltreatment is not inevitable, research has demonstrated that mothers who continue the commission of maltreatment are more likely to lack an understanding of how their past experiences have influenced their current maternal behavior (Egeland, 1988; Egeland, Jacobvitz, & Sroufe, 1988). Thus, the failure to process and integrate prior maltreatment experiences into conscious awareness emerges as a significant risk factor for perpetuating the intergenerational transmission of maltreatment. Conversely, mothers who have the capacity to regulate and organize their thoughts and feelings about their caregiving histories are better able to regulate, organize, and respond sensitively to their children (Carlson & Sroufe, 1995; Main, 1995, 2000; van IJzendoorn, 1995). In this regard, reflective function (RF) assumes importance.

RF is defined as the overt manifestation in narrative form of an individual's mentalizing capacity, and it relates to parents' ability to coherently access the emotions and memories of their early experiences and to provide a secure base for their children (Fonagy et al., 1995). In a recent examination of RF in mothers with histories of major depressive disorder (MDD), women who reported more adverse early experiences also evidenced less RF on an interview assessing their attachment relationships (Toth, Rogosch, & Cicchetti, in press). Moreover, RF increased in mothers who participated in an intervention designed to foster a secure mother–child attachment relationship. Interestingly, maternal recollections of their early experiences did not vary as a function of intervention, suggesting that mothers' memories and depictions of their early experiences are stable and not readily changed. This finding is important as, at least in this instance, it allays concerns about the role of therapists in contributing to false memories.

Extrapolating from this research, we believe that it is possible that interventions developed to assist parents with histories of maltreatment in recollecting and organizing their experiences may help to prevent the perpetration of future maltreatment on their children. Although interventions designed to help adult victims recall and process trauma are available, the proactive provision of such treatments to parents in order to decrease the likelihood of continued intergenerational transmission of maltreatment emerges as an important and heretofore untapped strategy.

Therapist Role

Theoreticians, researchers, and clinicians have written extensively about recovered memories of trauma and have debated the possible role that therapists play in "planting" such memories in their clients (see Destun & Kuiper, 1996; Loftus, 2003). Much of this discussion has been guided as much by affect as it has by empirical data. An in-depth examination of this area is not within the scope of this chapter, largely because we do not believe that there is a sufficient body of methodologically rigorous research to adequately resolve this issue. However, as stated earlier, it is increasingly clear that children who have experienced maltreatment are no more likely to be influenced by exposure to inaccurate information than are nontraumatized children of comparable age (e.g., Eisen et al., 2002; Goodman et al., 2001). In fact, when considering the possible implantation of distorted memories, maltreating caregivers are much more likely to be invested in, and capable of, contributing to false recall in their children than are therapists.

With that said, a number of issues that emanate from the empirical literature are relevant to clinical practice and, specifically, to how clinicians choose to intervene with children who have been maltreated. First, it is critical that clinicians recognize that a reaction to a trauma is influenced not only by the traumatic stressor but also by the capacity of the post-traumatic environment to respond to the stressor (deVries, 1996). In families where maltreatment is ongoing, caregivers may actively discourage awareness of the trauma, and subsequently emotional recovery from the trauma may be extremely difficult (Goldsmith, Barlow, & Freyd, 2004). It is critical that such denial of trauma not be perpetuated by therapists. Because children most typically are referred for treatment based on the manifestation of symptoms, unless therapists specifically assess the possible presence of maltreatment, they may appear to be avoiding the topic or inadvertently supporting the appropriateness of caregiver denial of the experiences. If this occurs, then the child may be reluctant to share their abusive experiences. Interestingly, research has shown that mental health service providers often fail to detect childhood trauma histories (Briere & Zaidi, 1989; Wurr & Patridge, 1996), largely because therapists frequently do not inquire about past trauma (Read & Fraser, 1998; Young, Read, Barker-Collo, & Harrison, 2001). Thus, although therapists do need to recognize the power that they hold and exert care when helping children to process traumatic experiences, total avoidance of trauma experiences might be countertherapeutic, as an implicit message may be conveyed that it is unacceptable to discuss the abuse or neglect. This may contribute to the child's sense of responsibility and shame and, ultimately, delay recovery from trauma.

Because the therapeutic arena, in effect, alters the post-traumatic environment, therapy may itself contribute to a child's ability to share traumatic experiences. In fact, if therapists function appropriately, then they become a support that might not otherwise be present, particularly when a child remains in a maltreating environment. As previously discussed, a variety of therapeutic modalities are available for treating individuals who have experienced trauma. While the majority of approaches address trauma-related affect in some way, strategies differ in the extent to which they actively promote awareness of the past traumatic experience as it relates to current psychosocial functioning (Goldsmith et al., 2004). We suggest that the extent to which child maltreatment is addressed actively in therapy depends on a number of factors, including the current context in which the child resides and their resulting felt safety, and the child's developmental level and capacity to process affectively arousing content without becoming overwhelmed and disorganized. In essence, this recommendation is tied closely to our prior discussion about developmental capacities and the timing of intervention.

We strongly urge clinicians to be aware of the literature on suggestibility when devising intervention strategies for child victims of maltreatment. This is particularly salient when an act of abuse or neglect has been recently disclosed. If the therapist is the initial point of disclosure, then particular care must be exercised to in no way influence the child's narrative. Practice guidelines for interviewing child victims so as to minimize repeated questioning that might alter the child's narrative are particularly relevant when maltreatment is disclosed to the therapist (Pence, Everson, & Wilson, 2002). Even if the therapist is not the first professional to learn of abuse, care must be exercised when the maltreatment is being actively investigated. We recommend that in such cases the early course of treatment focus on listening empathically and providing children with a safe forum in which to express their stories and their resulting anxiety. These issues have significant implications for forensic settings, and it is to this area that we next direct our attention.

Forensic Implications

Over the past several decades, research regarding the nature of children's memory and suggestibility has flourished, partly in response to a number of highly publicized sexual abuse allegation cases involving young children. Whereas previous research on suggestibility had mainly focused on misinformation effects in adult memory (e.g., Loftus, 1975), the field shifted toward the examination of memory processes in children to determine the extent to which child testimony could be upheld as valid evidence in the forensic arena. Findings from the extensive body of literature that has emerged have informed the field in two main areas: (1) the interviewing factors and contexts that influence children's suggestibility and (2) factors that might account for individual differences in children's suggestibility.

Interviewing Factors and Contexts

There is a substantial amount of support for specific interview factors that are related to children's memory and resistance to misleading information. These include the type of information recounted, the use of repeated questioning, and the type of questions employed during interviews, among others (for more detailed review see Eisen, Goodman, Qin, & Davis, 1998; and Koss, Tromp, & Tharan, 1995).

TYPE OF INFORMATION RECOUNTED

One of the more robust findings in the memory literature is that information that is central or salient to an event tends to be better remembered than information that is peripheral or nonsalient information (e.g., Goodman & Reed, 1986; Loftus, 1979). Regarding memory for emotional or stressful events, there is an extensive body of literature on the role of emotion in memory that coheres to demonstrate that information about central details is better remembered for emotional compared to nonemotional events, even over long time intervals (Christianson, 1984, 1992).

It is important to acknowledge that studies that assess children's memory and suggestibility for mundane events may have little applicability to our understanding of children's reporting of significant, often traumatic, events in their lives. Moreover, from a forensic perspective, it is important to underscore the relative accuracy and persistence of traumatic memories compared to nonemotional ones. For example, a prospective investigation of children who experienced sexual abuse reveals that children who had the most severe PTSD symptoms following sexual abuse had the best memory for the event 12 to 21 years later (Alexander et al., 2005). Thus evidence supports that greater emotional impact is associated with better memory for the central details of the event. Because forensic interviews are primarily interested in the recall of central details regarding salient emotional experiences, empirical evidence supports the veracity of traumatized children's memory reports.

REPEATED VERSUS SINGLE INTERVIEWS

It has long been assumed that *multiple* suggestive interviews may be necessary to taint a memory report and, minimally, will increase the potential for memory contamination (Bruck & Ceci, 2004). However, empirical evidence does not unequivocally support such a contention. Research informing this topic can be categorized into two main approaches: (1) to repeatedly interview children about an actual experienced event or (2) to interview them about something that never occurred (see Poole & White, 1991, for review). Findings from many studies indicate that repeatedly interviewing children in *a nonmisleading* fashion has no negative influence on memory; rather, it may actually improve recall through rehearsal (Brainerd & Ornstein, 1991; Howe, 1991) or through memory reinstatement (Howe, Courage, & Bryant-Brown, 1993; Rovee-Collier & Shyi, 1992). In contrast, repeated interviewing with the use of misleading suggestions can lead to significant alterations in memory reports (e.g., Bruck, Ceci, Francoeur, & Barr, 1995). However, Eisen and colleagues (1998) note that the majority of the variance in errors produced by misleading questions occurs after the first round of questioning in these studies. Additionally, several investigations exist in which children's memory reports became significantly tainted after just one suggestive interview (e.g. Garven, Wood, & Malpass, 2000; see Bruck & Ceci, 2004, for a review). Therefore it seems that the type of questioning and language used during the interview is much more relevant to suggestibility than is the frequency of interview occurrence.

It also should be noted, however, that repetition of specific questions during a single interview is associated with increases in errors in children's reporting (Poole & White, 1991), and it appears that these errors might be attributable to social-context demands during the interview. In particular, children often assume that because they were asked the same question previously that their former answer must be incorrect; thus they change their answer or say "I don't know" when asked the same question again (e.g., Siegal, Waters, & Dinwiddie, 1988). Importantly, Saywitz and Moan-Hardie (1994) found that informing children before the interview that they might be asked the same question repeatedly and that this would not mean that their first response was incorrect helped children maintain their initial response. Such a finding is extremely relevant for the interrogation of children who are victims of abuse, where repeated questioning is common practice.

TYPE OF QUESTIONING

Regarding the forensic interview, a clear and consistent finding in the literature is that open-ended questions lead to the most accurate memory reports (e.g., Dent & Stephenson, 1979; see Reed, 1996, for review). Unfortunately, open-ended questions also tend to produce short and nondescript responses, especially among young children, who are able to provide more detailed responses when asked specific questions (Hutcheson, Baxter, Telfer, & Warden, 1995). Despite the rather circumscribed nature of responses generated by open-ended questions, this type of questioning is generally recommended for initial queries because it does provide the least inaccurate information.

Following children's initial response, some contend that it may then be appropriate to encourage children to elaborate through more specific or direct questioning. Although empirical evidence demonstrates that the amount of information elicited increases in response to direct questions, the amount of recall errors also increases (e.g., Hutchenson et al., 1995). Therefore, research regarding the differences in impact on suggestibility for particular types of direct questioning is informative for determining how one might proceed in a forensic interview. For example, Peterson and Biggs (1997) examined two kinds of specific questions—"wh-" questions (which request particular information) and "yes/no" questions (which require only confirmation or disconfirmation)—in relation to children's memory about a prior traumatic injury. Findings revealed that yes/no questions were particularly problematic for preschool children (Peterson & Biggs, 1997).

In addition to direct or forced-choice questioning, other interviewing techniques that have been observed to negatively impact the accuracy of memory reports include delaying questioning for long periods of time (Melnyk & Bruck, 2004), emphasizing the interviewer's authoritative status (e.g., Tobey & Goodman, 1992), using misleading cues or props (Gee & Pipe, 1995; Salmon & Pipe, 1997), intimidation (Carter, Bottoms, & Levine, 1996), selective reinforcement (Garven et al., 2000), and the misleading use of anatomically detailed dolls (e.g., Bruck, Ceci, & Francoeur,

2000). Clearly, the implication of this research urges caution when going beyond open-ended questioning in a forensic interview.

More recent work (Lamb, Sternberg, Orbach, Hershkowitz, & Horowitz, 2003) challenges the use of direct questioning and suggests optimism regarding the potential of open-ended questions to elicit sufficient information. Lamb and his colleagues trained experienced investigators to interview children (aged 4 to 8 years) who had made allegations of sexual abuse by encouraging them to provide a detailed narrative through the guidance of open-ended questions. Only following the use of open-ended questioning could interviewers utilize direct questions to obtain information. Findings revealed that 83% of all allegations were elicited through free-recall questions, and 66% of all children identified the suspect through open-ended questions. Therefore, interviewers need not utilize suggestive techniques to elicit details of trauma; rather, open-ended prompts can be used effectively and with a reduced risk of influencing child report.

INDIVIDUAL DIFFERENCES

Beyond the evaluation of specific interviewing factors that influence children's memory, researchers have more recently turned their attention toward the identification of factors that might account for individual differences in children's and adults' suggestibility. Exemplified by a 2004 special issue of *Applied Cognitive Psychology* devoted to this topic, many researchers now stress the importance of both developmental and individual differences when attempting to understand suggestibility.

Developmental Considerations

The individual difference factor that has been most consistently related to memory and suggestibility is age (Bruck & Ceci, 1999; Goodman, Quas, Batterman-Faunce, Riddlesberger, & Kuhn, 1994). For example, age emerged as the strongest predictor of suggestibility in a study of 3- to 7-year-olds during an interview about their experiences 2 weeks after receiving an inoculation (Alexander et al., 2002). Empirical evidence coheres to suggest that preschool children are more susceptible to misleading questions than are older children and adults (Ceci & Bruck, 1993, 1995). From a neuropsychological perspective, evidence that frontal lobe function, which is associated with source memory ability, confabulation, false recognition, and temporal memory, does not reach full maturity until mid-adolescence (e.g., Lee, 2004), is consistent with findings regarding preschool-aged children's increased susceptibility to suggestion. Similarly, recall errors among young children may reflect incomplete or immature brain development (Schacter, Kagan, & Leichtman, 1995).

However, Bruck and Ceci (2004) caution that this focus on younger children's susceptibility to suggestion reflects the disproportionate number of studies that have been conducted with preschool-aged children in comparison to older school-aged children or adolescents in the past several decades. Nonetheless, there is evidence that susceptibility to suggestion is common in middle childhood, and that developmental differences in suggestibility are not always significant (e.g., Bruck & London, 2003; Finnila, Mahlberg, Santtila, Sandnabba, & Niemi, 2003; Loftus, 2003). Moreover, it is clear that age is not the only predictor of an individuals' susceptibility to suggestion (e.g., Geddie, Fradin, & Beer, 2000). In particular, evidence of pronounced individual differences in suggestibility within a given age group has precipitated research to evaluate the likelihood of suggestion on an individual basis (Crossman, Scullin, & Melnyk, 2004).

Language Abilities

Language ability has emerged as another individual difference factor that is related to children's susceptibility to suggestions. The detection of language ability as an important predictor of children's memory performance arose as a result of attempts to link children's intelligence to suggestibility. When children's cognitive functioning was assessed through nonverbal intelligence tests, associations were not uncovered between IQ and suggestibility (e.g., Eisen et al., 2002; Roebers & Schneider, 2001). However, when full-scale intelligence batteries or verbal subtests were selected, a significant association between suggestibility and lower IQ was identified (Geddie et al., 2000; McFarlane, Powell, & Dudgeon, 2002; Young, Powell, & Dudgeon, 2003).

To address the role of language directly, Clarke-Stewart, Malloy, and Allhusen (2004) focused on children's verbal performance among other predictors and demonstrated that children who were more advanced in verbal abilities were better able to resist interviewers' suggestions. Moreover, in a comprehensive review of cognitive and memory factors that might predict suggestibility in children across 69 studies, Bruck & Melnyk (2004) reported that language emerged as one of the two strongest predictors of children's suggestibility. More in-depth analysis of specific aspects of language abilities demonstrates that children are less suggestible when the language used in the forensic interview is more easily understood (Imhoff & Baker-Ward, 1999). However, no link between children's mean length of utterance (Imhoff & Baker-Ward, 1999) or verbal fluency (Payment, 2002) and suggestibility has been detected. Therefore, it seems that receptive language skills are more relevant to suggestibility than are expressive language abilities.

Impulsivity or Inhibitory Control

Another individual difference factor that may be related to children's susceptibility to suggestion involves impulsivity or impulse control. Theoretically, it was hypothesized that children with poor inhibition would be less able to resist interviewers' misleading suggestions and would impulsively report false information (Bruck, Melnyk, & Ceci, 1997; Quas & Schaaf, 2002). Thus far, evidence of such an association has been inconsistent. However, because this is a relatively new area of research, continued empirical work is warranted to clarify the pattern of results. An initial investigation found no association between impulsivity on a cognitive matching task and suggestibility among children (Quas & Schaaf, 2002). Similarly, Payment (2002) did not detect an association between suggestibility and inhibitory control using the Stroop task. In contrast, other studies have found significant associations between children's inhibitory control and their resistance to suggestion. For example, Alexander, Goodman, and colleagues (2002) found that cognitive inhibition on the Stroop task and effortful control on the Child Behavior Questionnaire were related to more correct responses to misleading questions, even with age statistically controlled. Similarly, inhibitory control assessed through a test of retroactive inhibition (Roberts & Powell, 2001) and through a continuous performance task (Clarke-Stewart et al., 2004) was found to be related to resistance to suggestions. Given these inconsistent findings, it is important to consider whether other factors, such as those that are socially motivated, might be contributing to children's eagerness to agree or comply with an interviewer's suggestions.

Attachment

Quas and colleagues (1997) suggested that if children do not have secure relationships with their parents, then they may be more susceptible to demand characteristics of the interview because they are trying to please an interviewer rather than relying on their memory of the event (Quas, Qin, Schaaf, & Goodman, 1997). Although several studies have examined the link between parental attachment styles and children's memory performance and suggestibility (e.g., Goodman et al., 1997; Quas et al., 1999), research on child attachment and suggestibility is just beginning. There is some empirical support for a link between children's attachment and recognition memory (Belsky et al., 1996); however, there is a paucity of literature on the relationship between child attachment and suggestibility. To date, the only extant empirical study found that secure attachment with healthy, supportive parents served as a protective factor against children's suggestibility (Clarke-Stewart et al., 2004).

Other studies of relational influences on memory have focused more generally on maternal support, rather than on specific attachment organizations. For example, in an investigation of 3- to 10-year-old children interviewed after a stressful medical procedure, parental communication and emotional support predicted memory accuracy (Goodman et al., 1994). Specifically, mothers who did not sympathetically talk to or physically comfort their children following the stressful event had children who provided more incorrect recall during the subsequent interview. Not discussing and explaining the procedure to children was associated with more omission errors to the misleading questions, indicating greater suggestibility and a greater proportion of errors in response to misleading questions. These findings are consistent with other studies that have acknowledged the importance of maternal conversation for young children's retention of events (Tessler & Nelson, 1994) and possess significant implications, particularly in maltreating families where emotional support for memories of abuse is highly unlikely.

It is important to note that studies have not considered the role of parental communication among children who have experienced trauma, nor have they included the evaluation of disorganized attachment patterns in relation to suggestibility. Because there is a preponderance of disorganized attachment organization among children who have been maltreated (Barnett, Ganiban, & Cicchetti, 1999), such research needs to be conducted before results of these studies can be generalized to the understanding of memory and suggestibility among traumatized children.

To summarize, in contrast to the conclusive evidence of specific interviewing factors that influence children's memory, studies that have examined the role of individual differences in children's memory are far less decisive. Therefore, the forensic implications of this research are that the empirical evidence cannot identify children who are most at risk for heightened suggestibility. As Bruck & Melnyk (2004) note in their evaluation and review of empirical work on children's suggestibility, even when individual difference effects are found, they are not large and therefore cannot reliably identify or suggest to the court that a specific child's profile indicates high or low suggestibility. However, it is clear that children's susceptibility to suggestion is multidetermined. Although the complex interaction of individual difference factors does not lend itself to the identification of suggestibility risk, research does pinpoint particular interviewing techniques that have a high likelihood of tainting children's reported recall of trauma. Therefore, although we cannot advise the courts regarding who is likely to be at heightened risk for being misled during forensic interviewing; we can caution against the utilization of misleading interview techniques.

Conclusions

Considerable progress has occurred with respect to our knowledge regarding the effects of trauma, specifically child maltreatment, on memory functioning. Based on research reviewed herein, there is increasing evidence that the experience of maltreatment does not appear to adversely affect, nor does it enhance, memory for nontraumatic or for traumatic material (Howe, Toth, et al., 2006). However, findings regarding possible mediators of maltreatment and memory have begun to emerge. In particular, some research suggests that attachment may be an important factor that influences recall, particularly with respect to material that is relationship relevant. The presence of dissociative symptoms in maltreated children also has been linked with impaired memory, and this area requires further investigation. Although much of the research reported in this chapter was not designed with the goal of informing social policies, we have highlighted implications of this work for clinical and forensic contexts. Attention to a number of recommendations will ultimately enhance the utility of research on trauma and memory for informing social policies on behalf of victims of child maltreatment.

A significant area that requires further investigation pertains to the age at which traumatic experiences can be recalled accurately. Although there is a general consensus that children can talk about traumatic experiences by 2 years of age (Hamond & Fivush, 1991; Peterson & Parsons, 2005), it is less clear whether these experiences are remembered over longer periods of time (Quas et al., 1999). Resolution of this issue possesses significant implications for the provision of therapeutic interventions to young victims of maltreatment.

In a related vein, much more work is needed to determine the efficacy of trauma-specific versus more symptom-focused interventions for children who have been maltreated. Although work with adults suggests that attention to trauma increases the effectiveness of the intervention, there is considerably less research to inform these decisions with maltreated children. In particular, investigations designed to address these questions will require careful attention to the age at which the trauma occurred, the time that has elapsed between the trauma and the provision of treatment, and the developmental period during which the intervention is initiated. When evaluating intervention efficacy, measurement strategies also should incorporate assessments of both psychological and biological functioning.

Importantly, more work needs to be directed toward designing and evaluating interventions for parents who were maltreated as children. Although attachment-theory-informed interventions have shown promising results in promoting attachment security in offspring (Cicchetti, Rogosch, & Toth, 2006; Toth, Rogosch, Manly, & Cicchetti, 2006), further thought on how best to address parental memories of trauma and to foster reflective function are needed.

In the forensic arena, it is fairly clear that aspects of the interviewing process can foster or impede the accuracy of children's memories of traumatic events. However, more research is needed to inform how individual differences may enter into the accuracy of recall, independent of variables associated with the interview itself.

In summary, our extant research knowledge on trauma and memory can be used to facilitate factually based decision making for maltreated children. However, much work remains if policies in the best interest of the child are to be developed consistently, widely disseminated, and routinely utilized.

Acknowledgments

The preparation of this chapter was supported by funding from the National Institute of Mental Health (R01 MH68413). We appreciate Maureen Carroll's assistance with the preparation of this manuscript. We also thank the children and families we have worked with over the years, who have helped to formulate our thinking on the provision of intervention.

References

Alexander, K. W., & Edelstein, R. S. (2001, April). *Children's attachment and memory for an experienced event.* Poster presented at the Biennial Meeting of the Society for Research in Child Development, Minneapolis, MN.

Alexander, K. W., Goodman, G. S., Quas, J. A., Ghetti, S., Edelstein, R., Redlich, A. D., et al. (2005). Traumatic impact predicts long-term memory for documented child sexual abuse. *Psychological Science, 16,* 33–40.

Alexander, K. W., Goodman, G. S., Schaaf, J. M., Edelstein, R. S., Quas, J. A., & Shaver, P. R. (2002). The role of attachment and cognitive inhibition in predicting children's memory for a stressful event. *Journal of Experimental Child Psychology, 83,* 262–290.

Alexander, K. W., Quas, J. A., & Goodman, G. S. (2002). Theoretical advances in understanding children's memory for distressing events: The role of attachment. *Developmental Review, 22,* 490–519.

American Academy of Pediatrics. (1999). Circumcision policy statement. *Pediatrics, 103*(3), 686–693.

Anand, K. J., & Hickey, P. R. (1987). Pain and its effects in the human neonate and fetus. *New England Journal of Medicine, 317*(21), 1321–1329.

Barnett, D., Ganiban, J., & Cicchetti, D. (1999). Maltreatment, negative expressivity, and the development of Type D attachments from 12- to 24-months of age. *Society for Research in Child Development Monograph, 64,* 97–118.

Beers, S. R., & DeBellis, M. D. (2002). Neuropsychological function in children with maltreatment-related stress disorder. *American Journal of Psychiatry, 159,* 483–486.

Belsky, J., Spritz, B., & Crnic, K. (1996). Infant attachment security and affective–cognitive information processing at age 3. *Psychological Science, 7,* 111–114.

Berliner, D. C. (1991). Educational Psychology and pedagogical expertise: New findings and new opportunities for thinking about training. *Educational Psychologist, 26,* 145–155.

Berliner, L., & Briere, J. (1999). Trauma, memory, and clinical practice. In L. M. Williams & V. L. Banyard (Eds.), *Trauma & Memory.* London: SAGE.

Blass, E. M., Ganchrow, J. R., & Steiner, J. E. (1984). Classical conditioning in newborn humans 2–48 hours of age. *Infant Behavior and Development, 7,* 223–235.

Bowlby, J. (1969/1982). *Attachment and loss* (Vol. 1). New York: Basic Books.

Brainerd, C. J., & Ornstein, P. A. (1991). Children's memory for witnessed events: The developmental backdrop. In J. Doris (Ed.), *The suggestibility of children's recollections.* Washington, DC: American Psychological Association.

Bremner, J. D., Krystal, J. H., Southwick, S. M., & Charney, D. S. (1995). Functional neuroanatomical correlates of the effects of stress on memory. *Journal of Traumatic Stress, 8,* 527–553.

Bremner, J. D., & Narayan, M. (1998). The effects of stress on memory and the hippocampus throughout the life cycle: Implications for childhood development and aging. *Development and Psychopathology, 10,* 871–885.

Bretherton, I. (1990). Open communication and internal working models: Their role in the development of attachment relationships. In R. Thompson (Ed.), *Nebraska Symposium on Motivation: Vol. 36. Socioeconomic development* (pp. 57–113). Lincoln, NE: University of Nebraska Press.

Briere, J., & Zaidi, L. Y. (1989). Sexual abuse histories and sequelae in female psychiatric emergency room patients. *American Journal of Psychiatry, 146,* 1602–1606.

Bruck, M., & Ceci, S. J. (1999). The suggestibility of children's memory. *Annual Review of Psychology, 50,* 419–439.

Bruck, M., & Ceci, S. J. (2004). Forensic Developmental Psychology: Unveiling Four Scientific Misconceptions. *Current Directions in Psychology, 13,* 229–232.

Bruck, M., Ceci, S. J., & Francoeur, E. (2000). A comparison of three and four year old children's use of anatomically detailed dolls to report genital touching in a medical examination. *Journal of Experimental Psychology: Applied, 6,* 74–83.

Bruck, M., Ceci, S. J., Francoeur, E., & Barr, R. (1995). "I hardly cried when I got my shot!": Influencing children's reports about a visit to a pediatrician. *Child Development, 66,* 193–208.

Bruck, M., & London, K. (2003, April). *Memory and suggestibility during middle childhood.* Paper presented at the biennial meeting of the Society for Research in Child Development, Tampa, FL.

Bruck, M., & Melnyk, L. (2004). Individual differences in children's suggestibility: A review and synthesis. *Applied Cognitive Psychology, 18,* 947–996.

Bruck, M., Melnyk, L., & Ceci, S. (1997). External and internal sources of variation in the creation of false reports in children. *Learning and Individual Differences, 9,* 289–316.

Bugental, D., Blue, J., Cortez, V., Fleck, K., & Rodriguez, A. (1992). Influences of witnessed affect on information processing in children. *Child Development, 63,* 774–786.

Carlson, E. A., & Sroufe, L. A. (1995). Contribution of attachment theory to developmental psychopathology. In D. Cicchetti & D. J. Cohen (Eds.), *Developmental Psychopathology: Theory and Methods* (Vol. 1, pp. 581–617). New York: Wiley.

Carter, C. A., Bottoms, B. L., & Levine, M. (1996). Linguistic and socioemotional influences on the accuracy of children's reports. *Law and Human Behavior, 20,* 335–359.

Ceci, S. J., & Bruck, M. (1993). Suggestibility of the child witness: A historical review and synthesis. *Psychological Bulletin, 113,* 403–439.

Ceci, S. J., & Bruck, M. (Eds.). (1995). *Jeopardy in the courtroom: A scientific analysis of children's testimony.* Washington, DC: American Psychological Association.

Christianson, S. A. (1984). The relationship between induced emotional arousal and amnesia. *Scandinavian Journal of Psychology, 25,* 147–160.

Christianson, S. A. (1992). Emotional stress and eyewitness memory: A critical review. *Psychological Bulletin, 112,* 284–309.

Cicchetti, D. (2002). How a child builds a brain: Insights from normality and psychopathology. In W. W. Hartup & R. A. Weinberg (Eds.), *The Minnesota symposia on child psychology: Child psychology in retrospect and prospect* (Vol. 32, pp. 23–71). Mahwah, NJ: Lawrence Erlbaum Associates.

Cicchetti, D., & Curtis, W. J. (2005). An event-related potential study of the processing of affective facial expressions in young children who experienced maltreatment during the first year of life. *Development and Psychopathology, 17*(3), 641–677.

Cicchetti, D., & Curtis, W. J. (2006). The developing brain and neural plasticity: Implications for normality, psychopathology, and resilience. In D. Cicchetti & D. Cohen (Eds.), *Developmental Psychopathology: Vol. 2. Developmental Neuroscience* (2nd ed., pp. 1–64). New York: Wiley.

Cicchetti, D., & Rogosch, F. A. (2001a). Diverse patterns of neuroendocrine activity in maltreated children. *Development and Psychopathology, 13,* 677–694.

Cicchetti, D., & Rogosch, F. A. (2001b). The impact of child maltreatment and psychopathology upon neuroendocrine functioning. *Development and Psychopathology, 13,* 783–804.

Cicchetti, D., Rogosch, F. A., & Toth, S. L. (2006). Fostering secure attachment in infants in maltreating families through preventive interventions. *Development and Psychopathology, 18*(3), 623–650.

Cicchetti, D., & Toth, S. L. (1995). Developmental psychopathology and disorders of affect. In D. Cicchetti & D. J. Cohen (Eds.), *Developmental psychopathology: Risk, disorder, and adaptation* (Vol. 2, pp. 369–420). New York: Wiley.

Cicchetti, D., & Valentino, K. (2006). An ecological transactional perspective on child maltreatment: Failure of the average expectable environment and its influence upon child development. In D. Cicchetti & D. J. Cohen (Eds.), *Developmental psychopathology: Vol. 3. Risk, disorder, and adaptation* (2nd ed., pp. 129–201). New York: Wiley.

Clarke-Stewart, K. A., Malloy, L. C., & Allhusen, V. D. (2004). Verbal ability, self-control, and close relationships with parents protect children against misleading suggestions. *Applied Cognitive Psychology, 18,* 1037–1058.

Cleveland, E. S., & Reese, E. (2005). Maternal structure and autonomy support in conversations about the past: Contributions to children's autobiographical memory. *Developmental Psychology, 41*(2), 376–388.

Cohen, J. A., & Mannarino, A. P. (1996). Factors that mediate treatment outcome of sexually abused preschool children. *Journal of the American Academy of Child and Adolescent Psychiatry, 35,* 1402–1410.

Crossman, A. M., Scullin, M. H., & Melnyk, L. (2004). Individual and developmental differences in suggestibility. *Applied Cognitive Psychology, 18,* 941–945.

DeBellis, M. D. (2001). Developmental traumatology: The psychobiological development of maltreated children and its implications for research, treatment, and policy. *Development and Psychopathology, 13,* 539–564.

DeBellis, M. D., Keshavan, M. S., Casey, B. J., Clark, D. B., Giedd, J., Boring, A. M., et al. (1999). Developmental traumatology: Biological stress systems and brain development in maltreated children with PTSD part II: The relationship between characteristics of trauma and psychiatric symptoms and adverse brain development in maltreated children and adolescents with PTSD. *Biological Psychiatry, 45,* 1271–1284.

Deblinger, E., Lippmann, J., & Steer, R. (1996). Sexually abused children suffering posttraumatic stress symptoms: Initial treatment outcome findings. *Child Maltreatment, 1,* 310–321.

DeCasper, A., & Fifer, W. (1980). Of human bonding: Newborns prefer their mothers' voices. *Science, 208,* 1174–1176.

Dent, H. R., & Stephenson, G. M. (1979). An experimental study of the effectiveness of different techniques of questioning child witnesses. *British Journal of Social and Clinical Psychology, 18,* 41–51.

Destun, L. M., & Kuiper, N. A. (1996). Autobiographical memory and recovered memory therapy: Integrating cognitive, clinical, and individual difference perspectives. *Clinical Psychology Review, 16*(5), 421–450.

deVries, M. W. (1996). Trauma in cultural perspective. In B. A. van der Kolk, A. C. McFarlane, & L. Weisaeth (Eds.), *Traumatic stress: The effects of overwhelming experience on mind, body and society* (pp. 3–23). New York: Guilford Press.

Edelstein, R. S., Alexander, K. W., Shaver, P. R., Schaaf, J. M., Quas, J. A., & Goodman, G. S. (2002). *Parental attachment style and children's reactions to a stressful event.* Unpublished manuscript.

Egeland, B. (1988). Breaking the cycles of abuse: Implications for prediction and intervention. In K. Browne, C. Davies, & P. Stratton (Eds.), *Early prediction and prevention of child abuse* (pp. 87–99). New York: Wiley.

Egeland, B., Bosquet, M., & Chung, A. L. (2002). Continuities and discontinuities in the intergenerational transmission of child maltreatment: Implications for breaking the cycle of abuse. In K. D. Browne, H. Hanks, P. Stratton, & C. E. Hamilton (Eds.), *Early prediction and prevention of child abuse: A handbook* (pp. 217–232). New York: Wiley.

Egeland, B., Jacobvitz, D., & Sroufe, L. A. (1988). Breaking the cycle of abuse. *Child Development, 59,* 1080–1088.

Eisen, M. L., Goodman, G. S., Qin, J., & Davis, S. L. (1998). Memory and suggestibility in evaluating allegations of abuse in children. In S. J. Lynn & K. M. McConkey (Eds.), *Truth in memory* (pp. 163–189). New York: Guilford.

Eisen, M. L., Goodman, G. S., Qin, J., Davis, S. L., & Crayton, J. (in press). Maltreated children's memory: Accuracy, suggestibility, and psychopathology. *Developmental Psychology.*

Eisen, M. L., Qin, J., Goodman, G. S., & Davis, S. L. (2002). Memory and suggestibility in maltreated children: Age, stress arousal, dissociation and psychopathology. *Journal of Experimental Child Psychology, 83,* 167–212.

Eisenberg, A. R. (1999). Emotion talk among Mexican American and Anglo American mothers and children from two social classes. *Merrill-Palmer Quarterly, 45,* 267–284.

Finnila, K., Mahlberg, N., Santtila, P., Sandnabba, K., & Niemi, P. (2003). Validity of a test of children's suggestibility for predicting responses to two interview situations differing in their degree of suggestiveness. *Journal of Experimental Child Psychology, 85*(1), 32–49.

Foa, E. B., & Riggs, D. S. (1994). Post-traumatic stress disorder and rape. In R. S. Pynoos (Ed.), *Post-traumatic stress disorder: A clinical review* (pp. 207–224). Baltimore, MD: Plenum Press.

Foa, E. B., Rothbaum, E. O., Riggs, D., & Murdock, T. (1991). Treatment of PTSD in rape victims: A comparison between cognitive-behavioral procedures and counseling. *Journal of Consulting and Clinical Psychology, 59,* 715–723.

Fonagy, P., Steele, M., Steele, H., Leigh, T., Kennedy, R., Mattoon, G., et al. (1995). Attachment, the reflective self, and borderline states: The predictive specificity of the Adult Attachment Interview and pathological emotional development. In S. Goldberg, R. Muir, & J. Kerr (Eds.), *Attachment theory: Social, developmental and clinical perspectives.* Hillside, NJ: Analytic Press.

Fraley, R. C., & Shaver, P. R. (1999). Loss and bereavement: Attachment theory and recent controversies concerning grief work and the nature of detachment. In J. Cassidy & P. R. Shaver (Eds.), *Handbook of attachment: Theory, research, and clinical applications.* New York: Guilford Press.

Gaensbauer, T. J. (2002). Representations of trauma in infancy: Clincial and theoretical implications for the understanding of early memory. *Infant Mental Health Journal, 23*(3), 229–277.

Garven, S., Wood, J. M., & Malpass, R. S. (2000). Allegations of wrongdoing: The effects of reinforcement on children's mundane and fantastic claims. *Journal of Applied Psychology, 85,* 38–49.

Geddie, L., Fradin, S., & Beer, J. (2000). Child characteristics which impact accuracy of recall and suggestibility in preschoolers: Is age the best predictor? *Child Abuse & Neglect, 24*(2), 223–235.

Gee, S., & Pipe, M.-E. (1995). Helping children to remember: The influence of object cues on children's accounts of a real event. *Developmental Psychology, 31*(5), 746–758.

Goenjian, A. K., Yehuda, R., Pynoos, R. S., Steinberg, A. M., Tashjian, M., Yang, R. K., et al. (1996). Basal cortisol, dexamethasone suppression of cortisol, and MHPG in adolescents after the 1988 earthquake in Armenia. *American Journal of Psychiatry, 153,* 929–934.

Goldsmith, R. E., Barlow, M. R., & Freyd, J. J. (2004). Knowing and not knowing about trauma: Implications for therapy. *Psychotherapy: Theory, Research, Practice, Training, 41*(4), 448–463.

Goodman, G. S. (2005, May). Discussant: *Effects of childhood trauma on memory.* American Psychological Society Convention, Los Angeles, CA.

Goodman, G. S., Bottoms, B. L., Rudy, L., Davis, S. L., & Schwartz-Kenney, B. M. (2001). Effects of past abuse experiences on children's eyewitness memory. *Law and Human Behavior, 25*(3), 269–298.

Goodman, G. S., Hirschman, J., Hepps, D., & Rudy, L. (1991). Children's memory for stressful events. *Merrill-Palmer Quarterly, 37,* 109–158. (Reprinted in R. Baker

[Ed.]. [1998]. *Child sexual abuse and false memory syndrome.* Buffalo, NY: Prometheus Books.)

Goodman, G. S., Quas, J. A., Batterman-Faunce, J. M., Riddlesberger, M., & Kuhn, J. (1994). Predictors of accurate and inaccurate memories of traumatic events experienced in childhood. *Consciousness and Cognition, 3,* 269–294.

Goodman, G. S., Quas, J. A., Batterman-Faunce, J. M., Riddlesberger, M., & Kuhn, J. (1997). Children's reactions to and memory for a stressful experience: Influences of ages, knowledge, anatomical dolls, and parental attachment. *Applied Developmental Sciences, 1,* 54–75.

Goodman, G. S., & Quas, J. A. (1997). Trauma and memory: Individual differences in children's recounting of a stressful experience. In N. L. Stein, P. A. Ornstein, B. Tversky, & C. Brainerd (Eds.), *Memory for everyday and emotional events* (pp. 267–294). Mahwah, NJ: Lawrence Erlbaum.

Goodman, G. S., & Reed, R. (1986). Age differences in eyewitness testimony. *Law and Human Behavior, 10,* 317–332.

Greenhoot, A. F., McCloskey, L. A., & Glisky, E. (2005). A longitudinal study of adolescents' recollections of family violence. *Applied Cognitive Psychology, 19,* 719–743.

Hamond, N. R., & Fivush, R. (1991). Memories of Mickey Mouse: Young children recount their trip to Disneyworld. *Cognitive Development, 6,* 433–448.

Harris, P. L. (1994). The child's understanding of emotion: Developmental changes and family environment. *Journal of Child Psychology and Psychiatry, 35,* 3–28.

Henderson, D., Hargreaves, I., Gregory, S., & Williams, J. M. G. (2002). Autobiographical memory and emotion in a nonclinical sample of women with and without a reported history of childhood sexual abuse. *British Journal of Clinical Psychology, 41,* 129–141.

Howe, M. L. (1991). Misleading children's story recall: Forgetting and reminiscence of the facts. *Developmental Psychology, 27,* 746–762.

Howe, M. L. (1998). Language is never enough: Memories are more than words reveal. *Applied Cognitive Psychology, 12,* 475–481.

Howe, M. L. (2000). *The fate of early memories: Developmental science and the retention of childhood experiences.* Washington, DC: American Psychological Association.

Howe, M. L., Cicchetti, D., & Toth, S. L. (2006). Children's basic memory processes, stress, and maltreatment. *Development and Psychopathology, 18*(3), 759–769.

Howe, M. L., Cicchetti, D., Toth, S. L., & Cerrito, B. M. (2004). True and false memories in maltreated children. *Child Development, 75*(5), 1402–1417.

Howe, M. L., Courage, M. L., & Bryant-Brown, L. (1993). Reinstating preschoolers' memories. *Developmental Psychology, 29,* 854–869.

Howe, M. L., Courage, M. L., & Peterson, C. (1994). How can I remember when "I" wasn't there: Long-term retention of traumatic memories and emergence of the cognitive self. *Consciousness and Cognition, 3,* 327–355.

Howe, M. L., Courage, M. L., & Peterson, C. (1995). Intrusions in preschoolers' recall of traumatic childhood events. *Psychonomic Bulletin & Review, 2*(1), 130–134.

Howe, M. L., Toth, S. L., & Cicchetti, D. (2006). Memory and developmental psychopathology. In D. Cicchetti & D. Cohen (Eds.), *Developmental psychopathology: Vol. 2. Developmental neuroscience* (2nd ed., pp. 629–656). New York: Wiley.

Hutcheson, G., Baxter, J., Telfer, K., & Warden, D. (1995). Child witness statement quality: Question type and errors of omission. *Law and Human Behavior, 19,* 631–648.

Hyman, I. E. Jr., & Billings, F. J. (1998). Individual differences and the creation of false childhood memories. *Memory, 6,* 1–20.

Imhoff, M. C., & Baker-Ward, L. (1999). Preschoolers' suggestibility: Effects of developmentally appropriate language and interviewer supportiveness. *Journal of Applied Developmental Psychology, 20*(3), 407–429.

James, B. (1989). *Treating traumatized children: New insights and creative interventions.* Lexington, MA: Lexington Books.

Kaufman, J., & Zigler, E. (1987). Do abused children become abusive parents? *American Journal of Orthopsychiatry, 57,* 186–192.

Keane, T. M., Fairbank, J. A., Caddell, J. M., & Zimering, R. T. (1989). Implosive (flooding) therapy reduces symptoms of PTSD in Vietnam combat veterans. *Behavior Therapy, 20,* 245–260.

Kihlstrom, J. F. (2005). Dissociative Disorders. In S. Nolen-Hoeksema, T. Cannon, & T. Widiger (Eds.), *Annual Review of Clinical Psychology* (Vol. 1, pp. 227–253). Palo Alto, CA: Annual Reviews.

Kirsh, S. J., & Cassidy, J. (1997). Preschoolers' attention to and memory for attachment relevant information. *Child Development, 68,* 1143–1153.

Koss, M. P., Tromp, S., & Tharan, M. (1995). Traumatic memories: Empirical foundations, forensic and clinical implications. *Clinical Psychology: Science and Practice, 2*(2), 111–132.

Kuyken, W., & Brewin, C. (1995). Autobiographical memory functioning in depression and reports of early abuse. *Journal of Abnormal Psychology, 104,* 585–591.

Lamb, M. E., Sternberg, K. J., Orbach, Y., Hershkowitz, I., & Horowitz, D. (2003). Differences between accounts provided by witnesses and alleged victims of child sexual abuse. *Child Abuse & Neglect, 27,* 1019–1031.

Lee, K. (2004). Age, neuropsychological, and social cognitive measures as predictors of individual differences in susceptibility to the misinformation effect. *Journal of Applied Cognitive Psychology, 18,* 997–1019.

Little, A. H., Lipsitt, L. P., & Rovee-Collier, C. K. (1984). Classical conditioning and retention of the infant's eyelid response: Effects of age and interstimulus interval. *Journal of Experimental Child Psychology, 37,* 512–524.

Loftus, E. F. (1975). Leading questions and the eyewitness report. *Cognitive Psychology, 7,* 560–572.

Loftus, E. F. (1979). *Eyewitness testimony.* Cambridge, MA: Harvard University Press.

Loftus, E. F. (2003). Make-believe memories. *American Psychologist, 58*(11), 864–873.

Lynch, M., & Cicchetti, D. (1998). An ecological-transactional analysis of children and contexts: The longitudinal interplay among child maltreatment, community violence, and children's symptomatology. *Development and Psychopathology, 10,* 235–257.

Macfie, J., Cicchetti, D., & Toth, S. L. (2001a). Dissociation in maltreated versus non-maltreated preschool-aged children. *Child Abuse and Neglect, 25,* 1253–1267.

Macfie, J., Cicchetti, D., & Toth, S. L. (2001b). The development of dissociation in maltreated preschool-aged children. *Development and Psychopathology, 13,* 233–254.

Main, M. (1995). Recent studies in attachment: Overview, with selected implications for clinical work. In S. Goldberg, R. Muir, & J. Kerr (Eds.), *Attachment theory: Social, developmental, and clinical perspectives* (pp. 407–474). Hillsdale, NJ: Analytic Press.

Main, M. (2000). The organized categories of infant, child, and adult attachment: Flexible vs. inflexible attention under attachment-related stress. *Journal of the American Psychological Association, 48,* 1055–1096.

Marshall, R. E. (1989). Neonatal pain associated with caregiving procedures. *Pediatric Clinics of North America, 36,* 885–903.

McFarlane, F., Powell, M. B., & Dudgeon, P. (2002). An examination of the degree to which IQ, memory performance, socio-economic status and gender predict young children's suggestibility. *Legal and Criminological Psychology, 7,* 227–239.

Melnyk, L., & Bruck, M. (2004). Timing moderates the effects of repeated suggestive interviewing on children's eyewitness memory. *Applied Cognitive Psychology, 18,* 613–631.

Merckelbach, H., Muris, P., Horselenberg, R., & Stougie, S. (2000). Dissociation, reality monitoring, and response bias. *Journal of Personality and Individual Differences, 28,* 49–58.

Merckelbach, H., Muris, P., Rassin, E., & Horselenberg, R. (2000). Dissociative experiences and interrogative suggestibility in college students. *Journal of Personality and Individual Differences, 29,* 1133–1140.

Monroe, S. M., & Harkness, K. L. (2005). Life stress, the "kindling" hypothesis, and the recurrence of depression: Considerations from a life stress perspective. *Psychological Review, 112*(2), 417–445.

Moradi, A. R., Taghavi, M. R., Doost, H. T. N., Yule, W., & Dalgleish, T. (1999). Performance of children and adolescents with PTSD on the Stroop colour-naming task. *Psychological Medicine, 29,* 415–419.

Ogawa, J. R., Sroufe, L. A., Weinfield, N. S., Carlson, E. A., & Egeland, B. (1997). Development and the fragmented self: A longitudinal study of dissociative symptomatology in a normative sample. *Development and Psychopathology, 9,* 855–879.

Orbach, Y., Lamb, M. E., Sternberg, K. J., Williams, J. M. G., & Dawud-Noursi, S. (2001). The effect of being a victim or witness of family violence on the retrieval of autobiographical memories. *Child Abuse and Neglect, 25,* 1427–1437.

Payment, K. E. (2002). The relationship between childrens' metacognitive and executive functioning skills and source-monitoring accuracy in an eyewitness suggestibility paradigm. *Dissertation Abstracts International: Section B: The Sciences and Engineering, 63*(1-B), 568.

Pence, D., Everson, M. D., & Wilson, C. (2002). *Investigative interviewing in cases of alleged child abuse.* Charleston, SC: American Professional Society on the Abuse of Children.

Peterson, C., & Biggs, M. (1997). Interviewing children about trauma: Problems with "specific" questions. *Journal of Traumatic Stress, 10,* 279–290.

Peterson, C., & Parsons, B. (2005). Interviewing former 1- and 2-year-olds about medical emergencies five years later. *Law and Human Behavior, 29,* 743–754.

Pollak, S. D., Cicchetti, D., Klorman, R., & Brumaghim, J. (1997). Cognitive brain event-related potentials and emotion processing in maltreated children. *Child Development, 68,* 773–787.

Pollak, S. D., Klorman, R., Thatcher, J. E., & Cicchetti, D. (2001). P3b reflects maltreated children's reactions to facial displays of emotion. *Psychophysiology, 38,* 267–274.

Poole, D. A., & White, L. T. (1991). Effects of question repetition on the eyewitness testimony of children and adults. *Developmental Psychology, 27,* 975–986.

Porter, C., Lawson, J. S., & Bigler, E. D. (2005). Neurobehavioural sequelae of child sexual abuse. *Child Neuropsychology, 11,* 203–220.

Post, R., Weiss, S. R. B., & Leverich, G. S. (1994). Recurrent affective disorder: Roots in developmental neurobiology and illness progression based on changes in gene expression. *Development and Psychopathology, 6,* 781–814.

Putnam, F. W. (1997). *Dissociation in children and adolescents.* New York: Guilford Press.

Putnam, F. W. (2000). Dissociative disorders. In A. Sameroff, M. Lewis, & S. Miller (Eds.), *Handbook of developmental psychopathology* (Vol. 771, pp. 708–715). New York: Kluwer Academic/Plenum Publishers.

Quas, J. A., Goodman, G. S., Bidrose, S., Pipe, M.-E., Craw, S., & Ablin, D. S. (1999). Emotion and memory: Children's long-term remembering, forgetting, and suggestibility. *Journal of Experimental Child Psychology, 72,* 235–270.

Quas, J. A., Qin, J., Schaaf, J. M., & Goodman, G. S. (1997). Individual differences in children's and adults' suggestibility and false event memory. *Learning and Individual Differences, 9,* 359–390.

Quas, J. A., & Schaaf, J. M. (2002). Children's memories of experienced and nonexperienced events across repeated interviews. *Journal of Experimental Child Psychology, 83,* 304–338.

Read, J., & Fraser, A. (1998). Abuse histories of psychiatric inpatients: To ask or not to ask? *Psychiatric Services, 49,* 355–359.

Reed, L. D. (1996). Findings from research on children's suggestibility and implications for conducting child interviews. *Child Maltreatment, 1*(2), 105–120.

Rieder, C., & Cicchetti, D. (1989). Organizational perspective on cognitive control functioning and cognitive-affective balance in maltreated children. *Developmental Psychology, 25,* 382–393.

Roberts, K., and Powell, M. (2001). Describing individual incidents of sexual abuse: A review of research on the effects of multiple sources of information on children's reports. *Child Abuse and Neglect, 25*(12),1643–1659.

Roebers, C. M., & Schneider, W. (2001). Memory for an observed event in the presence of prior misinformation: Developmental patterns in free recall and identification accuracy. *British Journal of Developmental Psychology, 19,* 507–524.

Rovee-Collier, C., & Shyi, C. W. G. (1992). A functional and cognitive analysis of infant long-term retention. In M. L. Howe, C. J. Brainerd, & V. F. Reyna (Eds.), *Development of long-term retention* (pp. 3–55). New York: Springer-Verlag.

Salmon, K., & Pipe, M.-E. (1997). Providing props to facilitate young children's event recall: The impact of a one-year delay. *Journal of Experimental Child Psychology, 65,* 261–292.

Sapolsky, R. M. (1992). *Stress, the aging brain, and the mechanisms of neuron death*. Cambridge, MA: MIT Press.

Sayfan, L., Mitchell, E., Goodman, G. S., Eisen, M. L., Qin, J., & Davis, S. L. (2002). Children's emotional reaction when they disclose abuse. Unpublished manuscript.

Saywitz, K. J., & Moan-Hardie, S. (1994). Reducing the potential for distortion of childhood memories. *Consciousness and Cognition, 3,* 408–425.

Schacter, D. S., Kagan, J., & Leichtman, M. D. (1995). True and false memories in children and adults: A cognitive neuroscience perspective. *Psychology, Public Policy, & Law, 1,* 411–428.

Siegal, M., Waters, L., & Dinwiddie, L. (1998). Misleading children: Causal attributions for inconsistency under repeated questioning. *Journal of Experimental Child Psychology, 45,* 438–456.

Tessler, M., & Nelson, K. (1994). Making memories: The influence of joint encoding on later recall by young children. *Consciousness and Cognition, 3,* 307–326.

Tobey, A., & Goodman, G. (1992). Children's eyewitness memory: Effect of participation and forensic context. *Child Abuse and Neglect, 16,* 807–821.

Toth, S. L., & Cicchetti, D. (1993). Child maltreatment: Where do we go from here in our treatment of victims? In D. Cicchetti & S. L. Toth (Eds.), *Child abuse, child development, and social policy* (pp. 399–438). Norwood, NJ: Ablex.

Toth, S. L., & Cicchetti, D. (1998). Remembering, forgetting, and the effects of trauma on memory: A developmental psychopathology perspective. *Development and Psychopathology, 10,* 589–605.

Toth, S. L. & Cicchetti, D. (2006). Promises and possibilities: The application of research in the area of child maltreatment to policies and practices. *Journal of Social Issues, 62*(4), 863–880.

Toth, S. L., Manly, J. T., & Cicchetti, D. (1992). Child maltreatment and vulnerability to depression. *Development and Psychopathology, 4,* 97–112.

Toth, S. L., Maughan, A., Manly, J. T., Spagnola, M., & Cicchetti, D. (2002). The relative efficacy of two interventions in altering maltreated preschool children's representational models: Implications for attachment theory. *Development and Psychopathology, 14,* 777–808.

Toth, S. L., Rogosch, F. A., & Cicchetti, D. (in press). Attachment-theory informed intervention and reflective functioning in depressed mothers. In B. Steele (Ed.), *The adult attachment interview in clinical context.* Guilford Press.

Toth, S. L., Rogosch, F. A., Manly, J. T., & Cicchetti, D. (2006). The efficacy of Toddler-Parent Psychotherapy to reorganize attachment in the young offspring of mothers with major depressive disorder: A randomized preventive trial. *Journal of Consulting and Clinical Psychology, 74*(6), 1006–1016.

USDHHS; Administration for Children and Families; Administration on Children, Youth and Families; Children's Bureau. (2004). *The AFCARS Report.* Retrieved April 8, 2007, from www.acf.hhs.gov/programs/cb.

Valentino, K., Cicchetti, D., Rogosch, F. A., & Toth, S. L. (2007). Memory, maternal representations and internalizing symptomatology among abused, neglected and nonmaltreated children. Manuscript in preparation.

Valentino, K., Cicchetti, D., Rogosch, F. A., & Toth, S. L. (in press). True and false memory and dissociation among maltreated children: The role of self-schema. *Development and Psychopathology.*

van IJzendoorn, M. H. (1995). Adult attachment representations, parental responsiveness, and infant attachment: A meta-analysis on the predictive validity of the Adult Attachment Interview. *Psychological Bulletin, 117,* 387–403.

Williams, J. M. G., & Broadbent, K. (1986). Autobiographical memory in attempted suicide patients. *Journal of Abnormal Psychology, 95,* 144–149.

Williams, J. M. G., & Scott, J. (1988). Autobiographical memory in depression. *Psychological Medicine, 18,* 689–695.

Wurr, C., & Partridge, I. (1996). The prevalence of a history of childhood sexual abuse in an acute adult inpatient population. *Child Abuse & Neglect, 20,* 867–871.

Young, K., Powell, M. B., & Dudgeon, P. (2003). Individual differences in children's suggestibility: A comparison between intellectually disabled and mainstream samples. *Personality and Individual Differences, 35,* 31–49.

Young, M., Read, J., Barker-Collo, S., & Harrison, R. (2001). Evaluating and overcoming barriers to taking abuse histories. *Professional Psychology: Research and Practice, 32,* 407–414.

Author Index

401

Subject Index

Abuse, and accessibility of childhood
    memories. *See also* child abuse terms;
    child sexual abuse (CSA) terms
  emotional language study
    explanations, 159–160
    methods/participants, 156–157
    results, 157–159, 162
  trauma-related memory problem
    study
    explanations, 161
    general linear model predictions,
      153–154
    methods/participants, 152–153
    results, 155–156
Adrenocorticotropic hormone (ACTH)
  in neurobiology of PTSD, 21*f*, 22
  response to CRF challenge, 24–25
AMI (autobiographical memory interview),
    193–195
Amnesia
  and abuse reminders, 35
  in declarative memory, 59
  dissociative, 20, 32
  and false memory, 18
  infantile, 7, 174
  and "spin-doctoring," 18, 20
AMT (autobiographical memory test), 141,
    178–179, 192–193
Autobiographical memory, development
    theories
  functional avoidance, 176

impaired executive control, 178
infantile amnesia, 174
overgeneral memory, 176, 177–179
personalization theory, 174–175
social interactionist theory, 175
Autobiographical memory, in child sexual
    abuse victims
  AMI, 193–195
  DRM paradigm, 195
  SAMT, 193–194
  study findings, 195
  study methods/participants, 193
Autobiographical memory, in traumatized
    populations
  accuracy
    documented events, 188–189
    memory deficits/advantages, 188
    prospective memory studies, 189
    PTSD studies, 172, 190
    retention, 189–190
  in child sexual abuse victims, 172–173
  future research needs, 195–196
  intrusive thoughts, 173
  specificity
    family violence, 192
    negative cues, 191
    overgeneral memory, 190–191
    retrieval style, 191
    study/methodological limitations,
      192–193
    trama exposure, 192

417